the Wine Pocket List

A GUIDE TO TOP-RATED WINES
$30 A BOTTLE AND UNDER

2004
WINE BUYING GUIDE

Featuring
OVER 1700 WINES

Compiled from
MAJOR WINE PERIODICALS

Sorted by
COUNTRY, TYPE & WINERY

MICHAEL HINSHAW

THE WINE POCKETLIST
2004 WINE BUYING GUIDE

Published by The Innes Group, Inc.

The Wine PocketList
Post Office Box 2867
San Rafael, California 94912
www.winepocketlist.com
getinfo@winepocketlist.com

First Edition Published 1994
(As the Quarterly PocketList of Wine)
The Quarterly PocketList of Wine was published quarterly through 2001
Revised and updated Wine PocketList 2004 Buying Guide published in 2003
All quotations which appear on the front and back cover refer to the Quarterly
PocketList of Wine.

The author and publishers welcome any information which will assist them in
keeping future editions of this book up to date. Although great care has been
taken in the production of this book, neither the author nor the publisher will
accept any liability from the use of, or any information in, this book.

EDITOR Denise della Santina
RESEARCH Cameron Hinshaw
ART DIRECTION & DESIGN Richard Miller
PRODUCTION Keith Granger

Printed and Bound by BookSurge

DEDICATIONS

———— ✍ ————

I dedicate this book to my wife, Cameron, without whose unfailing support it would never have been published.

"I LOVE YOUR LIPS WHEN
THEY'RE WET WITH WINE AND
RED WITH A WICKED DESIRE."
Ella Wheeler Wilcox

I also dedicate this book to the wine lover in each of you. While there are those who would shroud the enjoyment of wine with mystique, the true wine lover is swayed by one opinion only – their own.

"THERE ARE NO STANDARDS OF
TASTE IN WINE... EACH MAN'S OWN
TASTE IS THE STANDARD, AND A
MAJORITY VOTE CANNOT DECIDE
FOR HIM OR IN ANY SLIGHTEST
DEGREE AFFECT THE SUPREMACY
OF HIS OWN STANDARD."
Mark Twain

"WINE COMES IN AT THE MOUTH
AND LOVE COMES IN AT THE EYE;
THAT'S ALL WE SHALL KNOW FOR TRUTH
BEFORE WE GROW OLD AND DIE.
I LIFT THE GLASS TO MY MOUTH,
I LOOK AT YOU, AND SIGH."

William Butler Yeats

"GREEN HELMET" AND OTHER POEMS

TABLE OF CONTENTS

WELCOME TO THE WINE POCKETLIST

*S*ince 1994, the Wine PocketList (formerly the *Quarterly PocketList of Top-Rated Wines*) has been the only source of its kind for highly rated, reasonably priced wines. Until now, the Wine PocketList had appeared in print only as a quarterly publication, mailed to subscribers throughout the United States and Canada. This book represents a big change for us.

Now, we've moved new ratings online (www.winepocketlist.com), where we can deliver more wines—much more quickly—than we ever could in print. While new wines are added to the online PocketList regularly, this book recaps those rated over the last 12 months.

Before I Became Publisher, I Was a Loyal Subscriber

I started using the Wine PocketList in late 1996. My wife, Cameron, purchased subscriptions for Uncle Alan (a much loved drinking companion whose red wine exploits are legendary in our home) and me as a Christmas present. She'd heard Wine PocketList founder John Vankat on KGO Radio in San Francisco, and thought it would make a great gift for us. It did.

I've enjoyed wine for as long as I can remember (only after the age of 21 of course…), and this gift proved to be a turning point in my appreciation for good wine. Starting in 1996, I purchased hundreds of new wines using the Wine PocketList as a buying guide. And while I enjoyed some more than others, every wine I tried had merit.

Prior to the Wine PocketList I'd gotten in the habit of walking into a store, chatting with the proprietor, maybe reading a shelf talker or two, and grabbing three or four bottles. These included a couple I knew well (BV Rutherford was—and still is—a personal "house" favorite) as well as a few new wines, and chances were good that the contents of at least one previously unknown bottle would end up down the drain.

With my method of wine buying, it's no surprise that I tended towards less expensive bottles of wine, considering $30 a splurge.

I knew it would be more cost efficient to do some research, read the wine magazines, maybe even take them into the store to make sure I got the right ones. But I'm always in a hurry, want to get in and out, and would rather dump a bottle (or two) down the drain than spend an hour wandering the aisles with a couple of wine journals tucked precariously under my arm

That waste—of money and grape—stopped in 1996. With a subscription to the Wine PocketList in hand, I tried new wines with confidence and gusto, enjoying almost everything I tried as a result of the Wine PocketList's rating system and buying guides. The Wine PocketList didn't rely on one taster's preference, or one school of thought, and its focus on affordable, available wines was just the kind of democratic reference I'd been lacking.

The Winds of Change

In December of 2001, however, Wine PocketList founder John Vankat sent a letter to his loyal subscribers. It was, like John, gracious, to the point, and intelligent. "Dear Subscribers," he wrote, "With mixed emotions, I announce that this is the last issue of the Quarterly PocketList." A college professor for over 20 years, John had decided to retire and move from his longtime home in Ohio to Flagstaff, Arizona.

When John sent that letter out, nothing could have prepared him for the deluge of mail and emotion that resulted.

> *"I can't live without it..."*
> *"You'll be sorely missed."*
> *"John, you never steered me wrong."*

Letters and entreaties in a similar vein poured in from subscribers all over the United States and Canada. Like them, I was very disappointed. But quickly the germ of an idea took hold. And after dozens of emails, phone conversations and three solid days of wine tasting and good food with John and his delightful wife Betty, that idea led to my current enviable position as publisher of the new incarnation of the Wine PocketList.

For the thousands of subscribers who, over the years, have relied on the Wine PocketList as a source for finding great wines at a reasonable price; for everyone who's used its pages as a confidence builder for trying something new and different; I say this book's for you. And welcome back.

And of course, for all those who have yet to enjoy the ease and simplicity of finding wine the Wine PocketList way I say welcome, and enjoy.

Cheers!

Michael Hinshaw
Publisher, The Wine PocketList

ABOUT THE WINE POCKETLIST

*T*oday, wine buyers have more choices than ever. Yet finding the right wines to buy can be a daunting task. That's why the unique approach of the Wine PocketList has been so well received by subscribers and wine lovers alike.

Founded in 1994, the Wine PocketList was the brainchild of John L. Vankat, PhD, college professor and avid wine enthusiast. After years of poring over wine publications for favorably reviewed wines and compiling wine prices along with lists of anything well reviewed by multiple publications (especially at a good price), John had so many friends asking for copies that he decided to launch a business. John published the Wine PocketList quarterly until his retirement in late 2001. After years of refinement, the Wine PocketList went from print to digital in late 2002.

Solid, Believable Ratings in a Format You Can Use

The Wine PocketList provides you with solid, believable ratings in a usable format. We help you find reasonably priced, highly rated wines that you'll usually have a chance of finding at a local store. Our goal is to help you explore new wines and varietals with confidence, without spending a fortune.

Why? Because we love wine and think that everyone has a right to enjoy it, no matter what his or her budget or experience.

Every month, our staff records hundreds of wines recently reviewed by wine critics around the world. Then we compile scores using our analytical process, blending wine quality, price, and scoring information from the top wine periodicals with historical, regional and qualitative data, in much the same way a master vintner blends a fine wine.

Our system compiles all available data, and delivers an easy-to-understand score—letter grades. Then we publish only those wines that merit grades of A+, A, A– or B+. As a point of reference, a wine rated 87 in any major wine periodical won't make the cut. Keep this in mind when you see the "shelf talkers" in the wine section at your local BevMo touting the "85" this wine or that received in a recent review.

WHY NOT "DESCRIBE" THE WINES WE RATE?

You'll find extravagant prose describing the aromas and flavors of wines in almost every wine magazine or periodical. For example, here's a description we came across for an $8 Cabernet Sauvignon:

> *"A bouquet of vanillin oak, cedar and mocha with wisps of cinnamon. Full-bodied tobacco, tea and dark cedar flavors with tart acids in the background. Persistent, coffee-spiked finish."*

That's nine different aromas and flavors—all in one $8 wine.

Does that mean that these aromas and flavors aren't legitimate? No. There's little doubt that the descriptions are real...to the people who wrote them. This simply underscores the fact that people can't expect to consistently find the same aromas and flavors in wines. After all, we each have different tastebuds, different tasting experiences, and different taste.

One head-to-head tasting for the *Wine Spectator* featured two authorities—one from California, the other from Bordeaux—comparing 40 Cabernet Sauvignons from California and France. The results? Vastly different experiences and opinions on both quality and taste.

In fact, the two experts disagreed on nearly 90 percent of the 40 wines. Their tasting notes had no descriptive words in common for 60 percent of the wines, and only one word in common for 25 percent. For example, one found "bell pepper, green olive, ripe, lush currant and black cherry" in a Cabernet by Stag's Leap. But the other found "berry, earth, chocolate and coconut" in the same wine.

So, while describing wine can help each of us articulate the experience that we have with a given wine, that experience simply isn't consistent from palate to palate.

This natural lack of a consistent measure led us to the decision that descriptions don't belong in our buying guide. But we encourage you to find those wines that you enjoy, go ahead and describe them, and carry on a spirited discussion with your friends and family!

A Note About Wine Rating Systems

"At last" you say, "an objective method to purchase wine." Well...maybe. Is the practice of wine rating primarily good or bad for the wine industry? Does it provide real tools for wine lovers? Is a single taster's opinion most reliable, or is it only valid to rely on the results of composite tasting panels? Is the enjoyment of wine such a personal experience that only you can tell what you do and don't enjoy? Or do the "experts" have the answers?

The fact is, wine tasting is, has always been, and always will be, an intensely personal experience. And for many, there is still a mystique surrounding fine wine (a mystique that some in the wine industry are heavily invested in perpetuating, as they put as much time and energy into creating "brands" as they do increasing the quality of their wines). But absent your close relationship with a respected sommelier, a local bottle shop owner interested in catering to your tastes—not just moving the 48 cases of Château X they have sitting in the back room—or the time to read and truly acquaint yourself with the palates of well-respected wine reviewers, wine ratings can help you negotiate the maze of thousands of available wines.

We recognize that wine rating systems are an imperfect method of judging wine, no matter whose (or which) system you subscribe to. We've seen experts and everyday wine lovers prove that any single system can't assure consistent results. But ratings and scoring systems do help to take some of that mystery away, and if used in sensible context, can serve as a good guide.

Why Rate Wines at All?

People are bound to have differences of opinion on something as deliciously subjective as wine. The different wine rating systems and the vocal dialogue surrounding their efficacy is proof alone of this point.

Enjoying wine should be simple. You taste it, and either you like it or you don't. But like it or not, the point system gives many consumers a frame of reference. And due to its proliferation and its increasing importance to the wine trade, ratings are unlikely to change anytime soon.

There is plenty of spirited debate surrounding the prevalence and influence of wine ratings on the way wine lovers buy—and try—wine in the United States. No matter which side of the discussion you come down on, we believe that in proper context, scoring systems do have the ability to help educate and inform wine lovers, allowing them to try new wines with confidence. For the average wine buyer, scoring is a subjective measurement, but it *is* a measurement. Certainly, it's more reliable than the shape of a bottle or the design of the label. Or, heaven forbid, the assumption that price always equals quality.

The 100 Point System

Though the UC Davis 20 point system is widely used in competitions, the wine rating system most commonly known by consumers in the United States is the 100 point system. Setting aside the fact that it is really only a 50 point system (all a wine has to do to earn 50 points is show up), the level of implied precision behind the numbers on the 100 point scale is virtually meaningless to the average consumer.

Would you really be able to tell the objective quality difference between a wine that's rated 89 and a wine rated 90? Or between a 94 and a 95? That's analogous to the Academy Awards® rating films on a similar scale. Would you find a meaningful difference if Chicago was given a 94 and The Hours a 93?

In fact, when we've blind tasted against this scale, we found that wine "X" might earn a 91 one day, and an 89 on another. Still a good wine, but for most of us (including the majority of professional wine tasters) it's simply too subjective to consistently discern the differences that would affect a score by a few points.

Add to this the fact that each individual, publication or group that rates by a 100 point system applies it slightly differently, and it further muddles the implied value of a given score. For instance, you're not likely to find that the *Wine Spectator* and *Wine Advocate* award points using the same set of criteria. *Wine Enthusiast* rates differently still.

THE WINE POCKETLIST: A GUIDE EVERYONE CAN USE

Originally devised by Wine PocketList founder John Vankat, our system is pretty straightforward.

You'll Find Only Highly Rated Wines for $30 or Less

While there are many exceptional wines with price tags of $50, $60, $80 and up, we focus on wines that score well *and* are good values. For that reason, the Wine PocketList includes only wines that cost $30 or less. That way, you won't waste energy reviewing a wine that only scored an 87 and is priced at $50. The score is too low, the price is too high, and there are better wines on which to spend your time and money.

Ratings are Compiled from Top Wine Periodicals

The Wine PocketList compiles its scores from wines reviewed, rated and published in the following publications, as well as exclusive tastings and recommendations from our advisory board.

1) *Connoisseurs Guide to California Wine*

2) *International Wine Cellar*

3) *Wine Access*

4) *Wine Advocate*

5) *Wine and Spirits*

6) *Wine Enthusiast*

7) *Wine News*

8) *Wine Spectator*

Every day, every month, every quarter, we scour these publications and update our database with every wine—$30 and under—that's been reviewed. Then we weight, grade and store the information, until any given wine achieves a score high enough to become part of the Wine PocketList. We strive to collect multiple scorings for individual wines whenever possible, in order to bring more than one opinion to bear on a final grade.

Letter Grades

The Wine PocketList utilizes a grading system that people intuitively grasp. Letter grades. After all, which of us doesn't understand that an A+ is the best you can get? Or that a C is mediocre? At the same time, a letter grade is not absolute. An A+ doesn't have to be 100 percent. In school, you can get an A+ with 98, 99 or 100 percent. 94 percent to 97 percent earns you an A. And so on.

An equally important part of our process is to appropriately "weight" the scores. Our weighting criteria are designed to balance price, publication bias and other factors, and help ensure consistent ratings validity across all varietals and vineyards. For example, an 89 in *Wine Spectator* will not have the same weight as an 89 by Robert Parker, and a $30 wine with an 89 point rating will likely be dropped, while an $8 wine with the same score is probably worth a try, and will remain.

Once each individual rating has been documented and weighted, we average the final scores together to arrive at the Wine PocketList grade. If a composite score falls below our cutoff point due to a low scoring review, the wine hides in our database until a high score nudges it onto the public list. If it makes the list, then we show you not only the Wine PocketList grade, but the individual grades upon which the composite score is based.

Here's a breakdown of what you can expect from wines that have earned different grades in the Wine PocketList system:

A+: TRULY OUTSTANDING As good as gets. Flawless, nearly perfect in every way; a wine that brings you to your knees. Around five percent of the wines in our complete online database boast an A+ rating. But because reviewers have such trouble agreeing on what constitutes a dazzling wine, very few of the A+ wines are made up of multiple scores.

A: EXCEPTIONAL An "A" rated wine should knock your socks off, and is highly recommended. Fabulous taste, finish and body. On average, you'll find around 20 percent of the wines in our complete online database feature a composite A rating.

A–: EXCELLENT These wines are well worth seeking out, especially if they can retain an A– rating with more than one review. About 35 percent of the wines in our database sport an A–.

B+: VERY GOOD These wines are typically very well made with some obvious appeal. We'd certainly give them a try if the price is right and they've received multiple reviews. Around 40 percent of Wine PocketList wines are rated B+.

WHAT'S YOUR WINE BUYING TYPE?

*B*uying a bottle of wine isn't usually a momentous event. While the pleasure is transitory, for many the search, acquisition and holding of a particular bottle or vintage are as much a part of the enjoyment as the drinking. That said, there's nothing quite like a good bottle of wine to accompany a meal, a celebration, or a gathering of friends. Whether you're having a night out or people over, we all go about finding the right wine for the right occasion in slightly different ways.

By its very nature, wine is shrouded in a bit of mystery. You can't always rely on a label, a price, or the quality of a prior year's vintage to assure the purchase of an enjoyable wine today. So how do people buy wine? What decisions, characteristics, tools and methods do people employ to find the "right" bottle?

The fact is, it's different for us all. The way we go about buying wine is a uniquely individual process. Like any group of individuals, wine drinkers (and buyers) fall into several different categories. While you may use a combination of the methods described below, one style is typically the most dominant for each of us.

DOMINANT WINE BUYING TYPE: BIG RED

Defining Statement: "I want the '98 XYZ. Now, please."
There are those who approach wine buying quickly and decisively. For the sake of identification, let's call these buyers *Big Reds*. These folks want it **now**, whether it be wine or anything else in their lives. Often their quick decisions are good ones, based on multiple criteria sensed, sorted and decided in seconds. But they take big risks as well.

If you're a *Big Red*, you'll occasionally end up with mediocre bottles of high-priced wine. Or a case of something you decide you hate. But that's okay. If a bottle doesn't measure up, this group will toss it in a heartbeat, or send it back in a restaurant, and move on to the next one without thinking twice.

Best way to use this guide if you're a *Big Red*? Go straight to the Winery Listings, look for those with the most wines listed in this year's guide, and grab whatever they make that suits your style.

DOMINANT WINE BUYING TYPE: CULT CAB

Defining Statement: "Isn't this label cool?"

Let's face it. Some people just have to have the newest, flashiest, and most popular of everything. Why should it be any different when they buy wine? Fast moving and quick like the *Big Reds*, these wine lovers are impetuous, and often figure a good looking label plus a high price equals a great wine purchase.

In a restaurant, these are the people you'll hear cry out, "Bring me a bottle of your best bubbly!" Unfortunately, as much as the *Cult Cabs* want these high-priced bottles to inspire and impress their friends or business associates, price and beautiful labels often don't add up to a truly enjoyable bottle. And no one ever said *Cult Cabs* didn't have a highly refined sense of taste.

Best way to use this guide if you're a *Cult Cab*? Go straight to our Splurge Quick Buying Guide. Or go to the Wines Sorted by Type section, and pick out those wines with the highest scores and highest price.

DOMINANT WINE BUYING TYPE: BOUTIQUE VIN

Defining Statement: "The winemaker is so nice, and he told me…"

Wine clubs were made for these buyers. Typically warm and friendly, they can also be cautious. *Boutique Vins* need information to make a decision they feel good about. But this information is less data driven and more feeling based. If they've visited a winery and like the winemaker, they're loyal lifelong customers (providing the quality keeps up).

If a friend says "Hey, I just had this awesome wine, you've got to try it!" that carries more weight than a score in a wine journal or review in the local paper's food and wine section. And while the *Boutique Vins* may tend to end up with (on average) "better" bottles of wine than *Big Reds* or *Cult Cabs*, their reliance on personal recommendations and relationships means they're slower to build a cellar, and have a harder time branching out into new wines and new varietals.

Best way to use this guide if you're a *Boutique Vin*: Start with the "Wines Sorted by Type" section, and look for those wines with multiple individual evaluations…and the lowest prices. Once you've established your trust in certain wineries or regions, you'll feel comfortable increasing your price range and branching out.

DOMINANT WINE BUYING TYPE: THE VITICULTURALIST

Defining Statement: "The '99 scored an A, and the '01 an A–. However, if you cross reference this against…"

You know them. Maybe you are one. Life is organized and structured, defined by to-do lists and guides and newsletters, scores and tasting notes. *Viticulturalists* are analysts, and they ask questions. Logical and detail oriented, they're cautious to commit without all the data. They'll know which vintages were good, where and why.

If your wine drinking experience is defined by tasting notes—written by you or another "expert"—or you track your cellar with a computer program, chances are you fall into this category. In general, Viticulturalists make great wine buyers. There are so many choices out there that a process is almost required to get consistently good wine. But the one stumbling block that affects *Viticulturalists* is that there are only so many hours in a day.

Best way to use this guide if you're a *Viticulturalist*? Dig straight into the Wines Sorted by Type or Region sections, and highlight the wines with the highest scores and multiple individual evaluations. Of course, you really need a subscription to the online Wine PocketList, so you can slice, dice and search the database to your heart's content, sort the list to your specifications, name it however you like, and save it in your Virtual Cellar for future reference or refinement.

Whatever your wine buying type, you'll find that the ratings and lists in the Wine PocketList have been organized in several different ways to accommodate your uniquely individual approach to finding a great bottle of wine.

"THE ONLY GOOD WINE IS THE ONE YOU LIKE."

Lois Stansberry

ST. SUPERY VINEYARDS

THE TOP WINE PRODUCING COUNTRIES REPRESENTED IN THE WINE POCKETLIST

———— ✍ ————

*W*hile we have 14 countries represented in the online Wine PocketList database, the majority of wines in our lists are typically those produced in the United States, France, Australia, Italy and Spain.

NUMBER ONE: UNITED STATES

California: The Home of American Wines

Though nearly every state in the U.S. produces wine (ranging from one winery each in Utah, Hawaii and Nevada, 33 in Texas, to over 100 in Washington), the 800-plus wineries in California produce 70 percent of America's wines. In California, winemakers are free to try just about anything—and do. Planting different varieties in different regions, experimenting with blends, California wines are widely recognized as among the best new wines produced today. In addition, California is where the grape became the star of the wine; Cabernet, Merlot, Pinot Noir and Chardonnay used to be in the background, but no longer. California wines put these names on the tongues (literally) of wine lovers worldwide.

Due in part to the amount of wine produced here that stays in the United States, and in part to the wide selection of highly rated wines made here (California is also home to the Wine PocketList—we're 30 minutes each from downtown Napa and Sonoma), California wines are widely represented in the Wine PocketList's ratings guide. If you're looking for a comprehensive wine guide to red or white California wine, you'll find hundreds of recent ratings, though the number of highly rated wines in the "Bargain" (under $10) and "Moderate" ($11–$15) categories is fewer than those wines priced at $16 and up.

Not Just Napa Anymore

Napa Valley. One of the smallest, most expensive and best-known wine producing regions in the world. Even though less than five percent of California's wine grapes are grown here, close to three hundred wineries call it home. Almost every winery based here produces a Cabernet Sauvignon, Chardonnay and Merlot.

While Napa is the king of California wines, and arguably the birthplace of the food and wine revolution in America, Sonoma (the next county to the west of Napa) boasts wines whose reviews often match up to those of its better known neighbor. Also well known for Cabernet Sauvignon, Merlot and Chardonnay, Sonoma's more varied climate (cooler towards the coast) also allows Pinot Noir, Zinfandel and Sauvignon Blanc to thrive.

While the Wine PocketList shows several red and white Bargain and Moderately priced wines from Napa, the story told by the Price/Rating ratio in a typical Wine PocketList search shows that many great California bargains can be found in the central coast regions (north and south, from Santa Cruz and Monterey down through San Luis Obispo to Santa Barbara) with many of the same varieties found in Sonoma.

NUMBER TWO: FRANCE

The Most Famous Wine Region Since the Dark Ages

Why is France the most famous place in the world for wine? In a word, history. French wines have their roots in the Roman Empire, whose legions planted vineyards as they spread across the continent. The religious orders in France took care to protect the grape vines during the Dark Ages, and the records they kept have helped the French continue to make wine perfected over centuries.

Where the Name of the Wine is Where it's From

Most French wines are named after the regions from which they originate. This works primarily because each region specializes in the production of different types of wines and flavors. There are ten wine producing regions in France, including: Burgundy (Pinot Noir, Gamay, Chardonnay), Bordeaux (Cabernet Sauvignon, Cabernet Franc, Merlot) the Loire Valley and Alsace (Sauvignon Blanc, Pinot Noir, Pinot Gris), the Rhône Valley (Syrah, Cabernet Sauvignon, Muscat), and Champagne (Pinot Noir, Pinot Meunier, Chardonnay).

Why Knowing French Wine Law is Key to Understanding a French Label

In France, there are four legal ranks of wine that are good indicators of how relatively cheap or expensive the wine is, as well as the relative quality of one wine versus another. The rank usually appears on the label, and indicates (from highest to lowest) the general status of the wine: "Appellation Contrôlée" (AOC or AC) ratings are the highest grade. "Vins Délimités de Qualité Supérieure (VDQA) ratings translate to "demarcated wine of superior quality." A "Vins de Pays" rating essentially means "country wine," and is usually followed with the name of the area from which the grapes are grown. And lastly, "Vins de Table,"

French table wines that have no region, vintage or grape variety indicated on the label.

A recent Wine PocketList search showed that—in general, and perhaps not surprisingly—the French wines with higher ratings tended also to be those with higher prices. But beyond the correlation of cheap or expensive French wines, we found more than one A– wine (white and red) represented in the "bargain" category of $10 and under. And while not many of these highly rated wines are widely available (over 20,000 cases imported), when you do find them they are worth the effort and the purchase.

NUMBER THREE: AUSTRALIA

Some of the Best Ratings—and Great Prices

In the last decade, Australian red and white wines have gained recognition as some of the best priced, most highly rated wines in the world. Most importantly, the price/quality ratio you'll find is quite remarkable. As befitting the success and popularity of Australian wines, there are many high ratings coming from wines "down under" in the Wine PocketList. A recent search for Australian wines yielded several hundred recent reviews, with an emphasis on Shiraz and Chardonnay, along with a healthy mix of Semillon and Muscat. The vast majority of the wines in our Australian results were under $20, with several A+ wines. That's well over a 94 rating on the *Wine Spectator* scale.

Shiraz and Chardonnay

Though Australia's 850 or so wineries produce about a third as much wine as California, the well priced, well made wines have earned admirers the world over. Shiraz (the uniquely Australian adaptation of the French syrah grape from the northern Rhône Valley) is a big, flavorful red that has helped put Australian wine on the map with its stellar reviews, and Chardonnay is now their third most produced wine (behind Shiraz and Cabernet).

One uniquely Australian trend is to blend two grapes, and include both in the wine's name. One of the most successful pairings—in our opinion—is the Cabernet Sauvignon/Shiraz (or vice versa, depending on which grape is dominant) blend.

A Consistent Climate

Typically pleasant to drink early in its life, Australian wines benefit from the country's generally warm, dry climate. Though there are many wine growing regions (the Barossa Valley, Coonawarra, and Clare Valley in South Australia, Yarra Valley and Rutherglen in Victoria, and the Upper and Lower Hunter Valleys in New South

Wales to name just a few), the majority of Australian wines are simply labeled "South Eastern Australia."

NUMBER FOUR: ITALY

Enjoying Its Own Wine

If the Romans are to be noted for spreading vineyards across France, the Greeks or Etruscans should be credited for bringing wine to the land now known as Italy.

Primarily considered a red wine producer, the main Italian wine growing regions are Piedmont in the northwest (Barolo, Barbaresco), Tuscany in north-central Italy (Chianti and Brunello di Montalcino), and Veneto in northeastern Italy, the third largest wine producing region (Soave, Bardolino, Amarone and Valpolicella). Despite being one of the world's biggest producers of wine (along with France, they produce two-thirds of the world's wine), Italy only exports about a quarter of its wine.

Uniquely Italian Wines

Many Italian wines are produced with native grape varieties that aren't as familiar to the international wine market. Varietals such as Nebbiolo, Vernaccia and Trebbiano are little seen outside Italy (though many of these imported gems can be found on the Wine PocketList). Other traditional Italian varieties such as Barbera and Sangiovese are now gaining broader awareness and recognition in other countries.

Ranging from the coast to the foothills, the cool north to the hot, dry south, the variety of soils and climates in Italy's wine producing regions ensure an incredible range of wines. From Chianti, dry red wines that are usually best five to eight years after the bottling, to the fresh, white Vernaccia, best enjoyed young, Italian wines offer something for every wine lover, particularly in conjunction with food.

The Wine PocketList contains wine from virtually every one of Italy's 20 growing regions, including many different types: sweet, dry, red, white, sparkling, and everything in between. They run the gamut, from $30 Nebbiolo and Barbera and $15-and-under Merlot, Dolcetto and Sangiovese. However, the high quality of Italian wines is evident in the fact that no wine reviewed (in a recent Wine PocketList search), with a retail price of higher than $16, had ratings lower than an A-. And though the majority of Italian wine in the "bargain" category was graded a B+, several A- ratings appear here as well.

NUMBER FIVE: SPAIN

A Contradiction in the Premium Wine Business

With a wine industry as old and established as that of France, Spain has the most land in vineyards of any country. Even so, it is only the third-largest wine producer in the world. And though it was the first country in Europe to put laws in place to help define wine quality, its entry into the premium wine market coincides with that of relative latecomer California.

In the late 1950s, fine wines from Rioja began to signal Spain's emergence as a quality wine producer. Even so, until the 1980s its wines were better known for quantity and low price than quality.

Long known for its Sherry and red wines, Spain is also one of the world's leading exporters of very good sparkling wines. With many made in the traditional méthode Champenoise, they are often a great value. Today, the wines of Spain range from barrel-aged reds, crisp whites, rosés, and sparkling wines to the sweet wines and fortified wines of the south. Although prices continue to rise, most Spanish wines still cost much less than French wines of comparable quality.

Strict Quality Control Standards

Quality is controlled through standards imposed by the *Instituto Nacional de Denominaciónes de Origen;* similar to those of the France's *Appellation Contrôlée* and Italy's *Denominazione di Origine Controllata.* In 1932 there were only four regions (Rioja, Jerez, Montilla and Málaga) designated as DO areas; today there are over fifty. Nearly half the nation's total vineyard area is classed as DO, producing about a third of Spain's wine. The top rank is DOC *(Denominaciónes de Origen Calificada).*

Wine Making Regions

Though there are many individual regions in Spain, some of the best known include Rioja, Catalonia and Jerez. The first DOC was granted in 1991 to Rioja which, after Bordeaux in France, is arguably Europe's most important wine region. Located near France and the Basque region, Rioja's famous red wine is usually made with a blend of pale Grenache grapes, and Tempranillo, Spain's best-known native red grape.

Though Catalonia doesn't share the same world recognition as Rioja, many Spanish wines are produced there. In addition to its own traditional wines based on indigenous grapes, classic European grapes like Chardonnay, Riesling, Merlot and Cabernet are grown in Catalonia. The region also specializes in the production of high quality Cavas (sparkling wines) that are a good alternative to higher priced French Champagne.

Sherry is a staple in its birthplace, Jerez. Sherry, or "Vino de Jerez" has been called the "wine with a hundred souls." Ranging from Finos and Manzanillas to the longer-aged Amontillados and Olororosos, Sherry is a blended wine of several years, not a single vintage. The differences between types are dramatic. Traditionally thought of as an aperitif, it's the Cream Sherrys that most of us are thinking of when we think "dessert wine." But try a chilled Fino or Manzanilla with tapas, seafood, soups and a mild cheese, and you may change your thinking on Sherry for good.

"IN EUROPE WE THOUGHT OF WINE AS SOMETHING AS HEALTHY AND NORMAL AS FOOD AND ALSO A GREAT GIVER OF HAPPINESS AND WELL BEING AND DELIGHT. DRINKING WINE WAS NOT A SNOBBISM NOR A SIGN OF SOPHISTICATION NOR A CULT; IT WAS AS NATURAL AS EATING AND TO ME AS NECESSARY."

Ernest Hemingway

"A MOVEABLE FEAST"

BUYING GUIDES

HOW TO USE THE WINE POCKETLIST BUYING GUIDES

*T*he heart of the Wine PocketList Book is its buying guides. Here, you'll be able to quickly search through over 1700 wines, sorted into three primary sections.

Every wine that appears in this guide has a suggested retail price of $30 a bottle or less, and—to the best of our ability to discover the information—a minimum case production of 1000 cases for domestic (U.S.) producers, and 1000 cases imported for wines produced outside the U.S.

QUICK BUYING GUIDES

The first section is comprised of five *"Quick Buying Guides"*. First is an alphabetical listing of wineries included in this issue, plus the composite grades of its represented wines. This is followed by four guides based on the Wine PocketList exclusive categories: Widely Available Wines; Top Buy-by-the-Case Wines; Bargain Wines; and Splurge Wines.

COMPREHENSIVE BUYING GUIDES

The second section is comprised of two primary guides:

Guide by Type Wines sorted by varietal or generally known region (e.g. Bordeaux)

Guide by Region Wines sorted by country or U.S. state

UNDERSTANDING OUR SYSTEM

Entries in the Wine PocketList appear as follows:

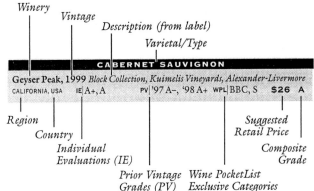

Winery

Vintage

Description (from label)

Varietal/Type

CABERNET SAUVIGNON

Geyser Peak, 1999 *Block Collection, Kuimelis Vineyards, Alexander-Livermore*
CALIFORNIA, USA   IE|A+, A   PV|'97 A–, '98 A+   WPL|BBC, S   **$26**   A

Region

Country

Individual Evaluations (IE)

Prior Vintage Grades (PV)

Wine PocketList Exclusive Categories (W, BBC, B, S)

Suggested Retail Price

Composite Grade

Winery: **Geyser Peak**

Common winery name, alphabetized (except in the case of common import prefixes, such as Chateau, first names, etc.)

Vintage: **1999**

Both the year of the actual grape harvest as well as the year the wine was made.

Description: **Block Collection, Kuimelis Vineyards...**

Label information describing the distinct makeup of a wine. E.g. Reserve, specific vineyard, county, etc.

Varietal/Type: **Cabernet Sauvignon**

The primary grape varietal from which the wine was made, or the region by which it's known.

Individual Evaluations: **IE |A, A+**

This represents the individual reviews and ratings on which the composite grade is based.

Prior Vintage Grades: **PV |'97, A- '98, A+**

When available, this designation indicates the composite grades of up to two earlier vintages of the same wine. If you're looking for a 2001 wine and only a 2002 grade is available, this can help you determine the historical quality of the wine.

Wine PocketList Exclusive Categories: **BBC, W, B, S**

There are four exclusive PocketList categories, and many wines rated by the PocketList will fall into one of these special designations.

[B] *Bargain Wines* Top-rated wines for $10 or less.

[S] *Splurge Wines* For most of us, spending more than $25 on a bottle of wine isn't something we do lightly. These are wines that, while more expensive, are well worth the price.

[BBC] *Top Buy-by-the-Case* Based on multiple high reviews, these are wines you might want to buy for your cellar.

[W] *Widely Available* These wines typically have bottling of 20,000 cases or more, making them easier to find.

Suggested Retail Price: **$26**

Prices are the suggested retail prices quoted by the wineries and distributors. Though these are close to what you'd pay at the winery, (and less than half what you'll pay at a restaurant) you'll often find discounts of 20 percent and more off these prices at retail.

Composite Grade: **A**

Grades represent a composite score developed using our proprietary system to blend wine quality and scoring information.

QUICK BUYING GUIDES TO TOP RATED WINES

WINERY LISTING

———— ✍ ————

ALPHABETIZED*

A. Rafanelli USA (A-)

Abacela USA (B+)

Abadia Retuerta SP (A-)

Acacia USA (B+, B+)

Acorn USA (A-)

J. B. Adam FR (A, B+)

Adega de Monção POR (B+)

Ch. d' Aiguilhe FR (A-)

Ch. d' Aiguilloux FR (B+)

Alban USA (A, A-, B+)

Alderbrook USA (B+)

Alexander Valley USA (B+, B+, B+)

Caves Aliança POR (A, A-, B+, B+)

Alkoomi AUS (B+)

Allan Scott NZ (A-, B+, B+)

Allandale AUS (B+, B+)

Amano IT (B+)

Amity USA (B+, B+)

Anastasia ARG (B+)

Dom. d' Andezon FR (B+)

Andretti USA (A, A-, A-, A-)

Andrew Murray USA (A, A-, A-, A-)

Andrew Rich USA (A-)

Olivier Andrieu FR (A-)

Ch. d' Angludet FR (B+)

Annie's Lane AUS (A-, A-, B+)

Antinori IT (A-)

Antonelli IT (B+)

Apaltagua CH (B+, B+)

Ch. D' Aquéria FR (B+)

Araujo USA (A)

Arbios USA (A)

Arbor Crest USA (A-, B+)

Arca Nova POR (B+)

Arcadian USA (A-)

Argyle USA (A, B+)

Marqués de Arienzo SP (A, B+, B+)

Arrowood USA (A-, A-, B+, B+)

Artadi SP (A-, A-)

Artesa USA (A, A, A-, A-, A-, B+, B+)

Astoria IT (A-, B+)

Atalon USA (A)

Atlas Peak USA (A-)

Au Bon Climat USA (A)

Dom. D' Aupilhac FR (B+)

Quinta da Aveleda POR (B+, B+)

Avila USA (B+)

Avinyo SP (B+)

Babcock USA (A, A-, B+)

Babich NZ (B+)

Clos Badon-Thunevin FR (A)

Baileyana USA (B+, B+)

Balgownie Estate AUS (A-)

Ballentine USA (B+)

Balnaves AUS (A, A-)

Castello Banfi IT (B+, B+)

Bannister USA (A-)

Baobab SA (B+)

Antonio Barbadillo SP (A-, A-, A-, B+, B+, B+)

* While U.S. wineries are listed by their full name, import wines are typically listed by their primary name, and not by common prefixes (e.g. Chateau, Caves, Domaine, etc) or first names.

Ch. de Barbe Blanche FR (B+)

Barefoot USA (A-)

Bargemone FR (B+)

Bargetto USA (B+)

Barnard Griffin USA (B+, B+)

Barnett USA (B+)

Barnwood USA (B+)

Barossa Valley AUS (A, A, B+)

Barton & Guestier FR (B+, B+)

Dr. von Bassermann-Jordan GER (A)

Beni di Batasiolo IT (A-, B+)

Bates Creek USA (A)

Dom. Des Baumard FR (A-)

Baystone USA (B+, B+)

BearBoat USA (B+)

Beaucanon USA (A-)

Beaulieu (BV) USA (A, A-, A-, A-, B+)

Ch. Beaumont FR (A-)

Ch. Beau-Site FR (A-)

Beckmen USA (A-, B+, B+)

Bedford Thompson USA (A-)

Ch. Belgrave FR (A-)

Bell USA (A-)

Bella Glos USA (A)

Bellarine AUS (B+)

Ch. Bellefont-Belcier FR (A-)

Bellenda IT (A-)

Bellevue SA (A-, B+)

Belnaves AUS (A)

Belvedere USA (A, A-)

Benjamin AUS (A+)

Benziger USA (A-, A-, B+, B+, B+)

Berberana SP (B+)

Dr. Pauly Bergweiler GER (A+, A-, A-, B+, B+)

Beringer USA (A+, A, A, A-, B+, B+, B+, B+)

Louis Bernard FR (B+, B+, B+)

Ch. W. Bernard GER (A-)

Bernardus USA (A, B+)

Best's AUS (A)

Betz Family Winery USA (A)

Ramon Bibao SP (B+, B+)

Big Fire USA (B+)

Bighorn USA (A, A)

Bodegas Bilbainas SP (A-)

Bisol IT (A-)

Blackjack Ranch USA (A-)

Dom. des Blageurs FR (A-)

Paul Blanck GER (A-)

Bolla IT (B+)

Bommarito USA (B+)

Bonair USA (A-)

Pierre Boniface FR (B+)

Dom. Borie de Maurel FR (A-, B+)

Borja SP (A-, B+)

Boscarelli IT (A-)

Boschendal SA (B+, B+)

Francesco Boschis IT (A-)

Bouchaine USA (B+)

Henri Bourgeois FR (A-, B+)

Ch. Bouscaut FR (A-)

Ch. Bousquette FR (A, B+)

Boutari GRC (A, A-, B+, B+, B+, B+, B+)

Chateau la Boutignane FR (A+, B+, B+)

Bouvet FR (B+)

Albert Boxler FR (A-)

Ch. Boyd-Cantenac FR (A-)

Brampton SA (B+)

Brancott NZ (A-)

Bodegas Breton SP (B+)

Georg Breuer GER (A-)

Bridgeview USA (B+,)

Bridlewood USA (A-)

Ch. Brillette FR (B+)

Jean-Marc Brocard FR (A)

Brogan USA (B+)

Castello di Brolio IT (B+)

Brookland Valley AUS (A-)

Broquel ARG (B+)

Bründlmayer AUT (A)

Domaine Brusset FR (B+)

de Bruyne FR (A+)

Buena Vista USA (B+, B+, B+, B+)

Buitenverwachting SA (B+)

Burgess USA (B+)

Dr. Bürklin-Wolf GER (A-)

Buttonwood USA (B+)

Buty USA (B+)

Byington USA (B+)

Byington USA (B+)

Ca' del Solo USA (A-, B+)

Ca' Montini IT (A-)

Marqués de Cáceres SP (A-)

Cairnbrae NZ (B+)

Cakebread USA (B+)

Cálem POR (A-)

Calera USA (B+)

Calina CH (B+)

Callaway USA (B+, B+, B+)

Camaraderie USA (A, B+)

Cambria USA (A+)

Ch. Camensac FR (A-)

Gould Campbell POR (A)

Campbells AUS (A)

Ch. Camplazen FR (A-)

Campo Ardosa POR (A+)

Campo Viejo SP (A-)

Ch. de Campuget FR (B+)

Cana's Feast USA (A-)

Canella IT (A-)

Canoe Ridge USA (A)

Dom. des Cantarelles FR (A-, B+)

Ch. Cantelauze FR (A-)

Ch. Cantemerle FR (A)

Ch. Cantenac FR (A-)

Ch. Cantenac-Brown FR (A)

Cantiga Wineworks USA (B+)

Canyon Road USA (B+)

Capezzana IT (A, A, A-)

Arnaldo Caprai IT (A, B+)

Ch. la Cardonne FR (A-)

Carmen CH (B+, B+)

Carmenet USA (B+)

Carneros Creek USA (A-)

Caroline Bay NZ (A-)

Carpe Diem USA (A)

Carpene Malvolti IT (B+)

Carpineto IT (A-)

Cartlidge and Browne USA (B+)

Casa de la Ermita SP (A-, B+)

Casa de Santar POR (A-)

Casa de Vila Verde POR (A, B+)

Casa do Valle POR (B+)

Casa Emma IT (A-)

Casa Julia CH (B+)

Casa Lapostolle CH (B+, B+, B+, B+)

Casa Rivas CH (B+)

Quinto do Casal Branco POR (A-)

Casanova di Neri IT (A-)

Castaño SP (A+, A)

Castillo SP (B+)

Castle USA (A-)

Castoro Cellars USA (A-)

Leone de Castris IT (B+, B+)

Catacula USA (A-)

Catena ARG (A-)

Caterina USA (A, A, B+, B+, B+, B+, B+)

Cathedral SA (A-, B+)

Cavas del Valle ARG (B+)

Cedarville USA (A)

Cellars of Canterbury NZ (A-)

Ch. Bianca USA (B+)

Ch. Julien USA (B+)

Ch. Los Boldos CH (B+)

Ch. Montelena USA (A-, B+)

Ch. Potelle USA (A-)

Ch. Reynella AUS (A)

Ch. Souverain USA (A+, A-, B+, B+, B+, B+, B+, B+)

Ch. St. Jean USA (A, A-, B+)

Ch. Ste. Michelle USA (A+, A, A, A-, A-, A-, A-, A-, A-, B+, B+, B+, B+, B+, B+)

Ch. Ste. Michelle & Dr. Loosen USA (A-)

Chalk Hill USA (A-)

Chalone USA (A, A-)

Chappellet USA (A+, A)

Dom. de la Charbonnièrre FR (A)

Charles Krug USA (B+, B+, B+)

Charles Wiffen NZ (A-)

Ch. Charmail FR (A-)

Chateau Xanadu AUS (B+)

Chatter Creek USA (A, B+)

Chehalem USA (B+)

Chiarello USA (A-)

Michele Chiarlo IT (A-)

Chinook USA (A-, A-, B+, B+)

A. Christmann GER (A+)

Jon. Jos. Christoffel GER (A)

Cinnabar USA (B+)

Claar USA (A-, B+)

Cline USA (A-)

Cloninger USA (B+)

Clos du Bois USA (A-, B+, B+, B+, B+, B+)

Clos du Val USA (B+, B+)

Clos la Chance USA (A, A-, B+, B+)

Clos Malverne SA (B+)

Clos Pegase USA (A+, B+)

Dom. du Closel FR (B+)

Cloudy Bay NZ (A)

Coldstream Hills AUS (A)

Colio CAN (B+)

Podere Colla IT (A)

Collalbrigo IT (B+)

Dom. Jean Collet FR (A)

Colpetrone IT (A)

Columbia USA (A-, B+, B+, B+, B+, B+, B+)

Columbia Crest USA (A+, A, A, A-, B+, A, A+)

Concannon USA (B+)

Concha y Toro CH (A-, A-, A-, A-, B+)

Condado de Haza SP (B+)

Conn Creek USA (A+)

Consilience USA (A-)

Conti Contini IT (A)

Coopers Creek NZ (B+)

Cordorniu SP (B+)

Coriole AUS (A+)

Le Corti IT (A-, B+)

Cosentino USA (A-, B+)

Ch. Cos-Labory FR (A-)

Dom. la Coste FR (A-)

Ch. Côte de Baleau FR (A-)

Ch. Coupe Roses FR (B+, B+)

Dom. le Couroulu FR (A-)

Covides SP (B+)

Craggy Range NZ (A-, A-)

Craneford AUS (B+)

Quinta de Crasto POR (A-)

Cristom USA (A)

Ch. la Croix du Casse FR (A+)

Ch. Croix-de-Gay FR (A-)

Ch. Croizet-Bages FR (A-)

Crusius GER (A)

Crystal Valley USA (A, A-)

Cullen AUS (A+)

Cuneo USA (B+)

Dom. de Curebeasse FR (B+)

Curtis USA (B+)

Cuvaison USA (A)

Cuvée Cle'Mente FR (A-)

CVNE (CUNE) SP (B+)

Didier Dagueneau FR (A)

Dakensig SA (B+)

Dallas Conté CH (B+)

Dão Sul POR (A, A, B+)

Dashe USA (A, A, A-, B+, B+)

Ch. Dauzac FR (A)

David Bruce USA (B+)

Davis Bynum USA (A, A, A-)

Davis Family ARG (A-)

Dom. Machard de Gramont FR (A)

De Loach USA (A, A, A-, B+, B+, B+)

De Lorimier USA (A, A-)

De Wetshof SA (A-)

Decoy USA (B+)

Deerfield Ranch USA (A, B+, B+)

Dehlinger USA (A-)

Dei IT (A)

Delas Cote-du-Ventoux FR (B+)

DeLille USA (A)

DeSante USA (B+)

Deux Amis USA (B+)

DFJ POR (A, A, A, A-, A-)

Di Majo Norante IT (B+)

Dom. Chandon USA (A-)

Dom. de la Terre Rouge USA (A+, A-, B+, B+)

Dom. Serene USA (A)

Domaine Alfred USA (B+)

Domaine Chandon USA (A-)

Dopff & Irion FR (A-)

Dow POR (A-)

Dr. Konstantin Frank USA (A)

Dry Creek USA (A, A, A-, A-, B+)

Drylands NZ (A-)

Du Preez SA (B+, B+)

Georges Duboeuf FR (A-, B+, B+, B+)

Dunnewood USA (B+, B+)

Duval-Leroy FR (A)

Easton USA (B+)

Eberle USA (B+)

Echelon USA (B+)

Vina Echeverria CH (B+)

Edgewood USA (A-, A-)

Edmeades USA (A-)

Edmeades USA (A+, A)

Edmunds St. John USA (A, B+)

Edna Valley USA (B+)

Clos l' Eglise FR (A-)

Luigi Einaudi IT (A-)

Elk Cove USA (B+, B+)

Elysian Fields AUS (A-)

Emmolo USA (B+)

Emrich-Schönleber GER (A+, A-)

Enate SP (B+)

Benoit Ente FR (A-)

EOS USA (A, B+, B+)

Equus USA (A)

Karl Erbes GER (B+)

Errazuriz CH (B+, B+)

Escudo Rojo CH (B+)

Esser Cellars USA (A-)

Estancia USA (B+)

Etude USA (A)

Evans & Tate AUS (B+)

Everett Ridge USA (B+)

EXP USA (B+)

Robert Eymael (Mönchhof) GER (A-)

Eyrie USA (B+)

Fairhall Downs NZ (A)

Fairview SA (A, A-, B+, B+)

Ch. Faizeau FR (B+)

Falesco IT (B+)

Clos Fantine FR (A-)

Remo Farina IT (A-)

Fassati IT (B+)

Felipe Rutini ARG (A-)

Livio Felluga IT (A-)

Marco Felluga IT (B+, B+, B+)

Ferrari-Carano USA (A-)

A. Esteves Ferreira POR (A+)

Fess Parker USA (B+, B+)

Fetzer USA (B+)

Feudi di San Gregorio IT (A-, A-)

Nicolas Feuillatte FR (B+)

Fife USA (A)

Fifteen FR (B+)

Firestone USA (B+)

La Fleur de Bouard FR (A-)

J. Vidal Fleury FR (B+, B+)

Flora Springs USA (A, A-, A-, A-)

Dom. Jean Foillard FR (A)

Foley USA (B+)

Folie à Deux USA (A)

Ch. Fonréaud FR (B+)

José Maria da Fonseca POR (A+, A, B+)

Fontanavecchia IT (B+)

Ch. Fontenil FR (A)

Foppiano USA (B+)

Forefathers NZ (B+)

Forest Glen USA (B+)

La Forge FR (B+)

Forgeron Cellars USA (B+)

Dom. Foulaquier FR (A-)

Fox Creek AUS (A-)

Foxen USA (A-, B+)

Framingham NZ (B+)

Francis Coppola USA (A-, B+)

Franciscan Oakville USA (A-)

Frank Family USA (B+)

Frankland AUS (A, A, B+)

Franus USA (A-, B+)

Frei Brothers USA (A-, B+)

Frescobaldi IT (B+)

Friedrich-Wilhelm-Gymnasium GER (A)

Frog's Leap USA (B+)

Castello di Gabbiano IT (A-)

Gaia GRC (A-, B+)

Gaia GRC (B+)

Gainey USA (A, A-, B+, B+)

Gallo of Sonoma USA (A, A, A-, B+, B+, B+)

Dom. Gardies FR (A-, B+, B+, B+)

Garretson USA (A)

Gary Farrell USA (A+, A, A-)

Michel Gassier FR (A)

Benoit Gautier FR (A-)

Geoff Merrill AUS (A)

Dom. Gerovassiliou GRC (A-)

Geyser Peak USA (A, A-, A-, B+, B+)

La Ghersa IT (B+)

Gibbston Valley NZ (A-)

Giesen NZ (A-)

Ch. Gigault FR (A)

Girard USA (B+)

Giribaldi IT (A, B+)

Glen Fiona USA (A)

Glenwood Ridge USA (A)

Ch. Gloria FR (B+)

Gloria Ferrer USA (A, A-, B+)

Paul Goerg FR (B+)

Dom. Cathérine le Goeuil FR (B+)

Goldwater NZ (A-)

Carl Graff GER (B+)

Gran Cermeño SP (A)

Ch. Grand Corbin-Despagne FR (A-)

Dom. Grand Nicolet FR (B+)

Dom. Grand Romane FR (A-)

Grand Veneur FR (B+)

Ch. Grande Cassagne FR (B+, B+)

Ch. Grand-Pontet FR (A+)

Ch. les Grands Maréchaux FR (B+)

Grange de Rouquettes FR (B+, B+)

Granite Springs USA (B+)

Grans-Fassian GER (A-)

Grant Burge AUS (B+)

Dom. du Grapillon d'Or FR (A)

The Green Vineyard AUS (A)

Greenwood Ridge USA (A+)

Greg Norman AUS (A)

Grgich Hills USA (A-, B+)

Groom AUS (A)

Groot Constantia SA (A+)

Alois Gross AUT (A-)

Grosset AUS (A+, A)

Dom. Jean-Pierre Grossot FR (A, A)

Groth USA (A)

Guardian Peak SA (B+, B+)

Guelbenzu SP (B+)

Guenoc USA (B+)

E. Guigal FR (A+)

Jacques Guindon FR (B+)

Johann Haart GER (A)

Hahn USA (A-)

Hamilton AUS (A)

Handley USA (A-, B+)

Hanna USA (A, A)

Hardys AUS (A, B+)

Harlequin USA (A)

Hartford USA (A)

Hartford Court USA (A-)

Hatcher Wineworks USA (B+)

Ch. Haut-Bages-Libéral FR (A+)

Ch. Haut-Batailley FR (A+)

Ch. Haut-Beauséjour FR (A-)

Haut-Carles FR (A)

Ch. Haut-Chaigneau FR (B+)

Ch. Haut-Corbin FR (A)

Ch. Haut-Maillet FR (A-)

Ch. Haut-Marbuzet FR (A-)

Hawley USA (A-)

Hedges USA (A, B+, B+)

Heggies AUS (B+)

Piper Heidsieck FR (A)

Hendry Ranch USA (A-)

Raymond Henriot FR (A+)

Henry USA (B+)

Herdade de Esporão POR (A, A-, B+, B+)

R. Lopez de Heredia SP (A-)

Heritage Road AUS (A+)

Hernder Estate CAN (A)

Hess Estate USA (B+)

Hess Select USA (B+)

Helmut Hexamer GER (A-, B+)

Hidalgo SP (A-, B+)

Highfield NZ (A, A)

Hillview Vineyards AUS (B+)

Hogue USA (A-, A-, A-, A-, B+, B+, B+, B+)

Honig USA (A, A-, B+)

Dom. de l Hortus FR (B+)

S. A. Huët FR (A, A-)

Huia NZ (A)

Hunt USA (A, A)

Huntington Cellars USA (A-, B+, B+, B+)

Inniskillin Okanagan CAN (A-)

Ionian GRC (B+)

Iron Horse USA (A, A-, A-, A-, B+)

Isabel NZ (A)

Isenhower Cellars USA (A-, A-)

Viña Izadi SP (B+)

J C USA (B+)

J.C. & Boris Leclercq FR (A-)

Jackson-Triggs CAN (A-)

Jacob's Creek AUS (B+, B+)

Jade Mountain USA (A, A-)

Jaffurs USA (B+)

Jakoby-Mathy GER (A-)

James AUS (A-, B+)

Jaume Serra SP (B+)

Jessie's Grove USA (B+)

Jest Red USA (B+)

Jim Barry AUS (B+)

JM Cellars USA (A)

Joel Gott USA (B+, B+)

Schloss Johannisberger GER (A+, A-)

Johannishof GER (A)

Pascal Jolivet FR (A-, B+)

Jordan USA (A)

Joseph Phelps USA (A, B+)

Joseph Swan USA (B+)

Joullian USA (A-)

Judd Hill USA (A-)

Daniel Junot FR (B+)

Justin USA (A-, B+, B+)

Juvé y Camps SP (A+)

Kaesler AUS (A)

Kaesler AUS (A+)

Kangarilla Road AUS (A-)

Kanonkop SA (A-)

Kanu SA (B+)

Karlsmühle GER (A-)

Katnook AUS (A-)

Kelham USA (A-)

Keller USA (A)

Kendall-Jackson USA (A, A-, A-, A-, B+)

Kenwood USA (A-, B+)

Heribert Kerpen GER (A-)

Reichsgraf von Kesselstatt GER (A-, A-)

Kestral USA (A, A-, A-)

Keyhole Ranch USA (A)

Kim Crawford NZ (A-)

King USA (A-)

King Estate USA (A-, B+)

Kiona USA (A+)

Kirsten GER (B+)

Klein Constantia SA (A-)

Staatsweingüter Kloster Eberbach GER (A, A)

Knappstein AUS (A, A-)

Baron zu Knyphäusen GER (A)

Konrad & Conrad NZ (A)

Kooyong AUS (A)

Kourtaki GRC (B+)

Krüger-Rumpf GER (A)

Ktima Kyr-Yianni GRC (A+, A-)

Kumeu River NZ (A+)

Kunde USA (A-, A-, A-, B+, B+, B+)

KWV SA (A-, B+, B+)

La Crema USA (A, A, A-, B+, B+)

La Storia USA (A-)

Dom. R. & M. Labbe FR (B+)

Laborie SA (B+)

Dom. Lacroix-Vanel FR (A-, B+)

De Ladoucette FR (A-)

Laetitia USA (A)

Lafond USA (A-, B+, B+)

Ch. Lafon-Rochet FR (A)

Ch. Lagrezette FR (A-)

Ch. la Lagune FR (A-)

Lake Breeze AUS (A)

Lake Sonoma USA (A-, A-, A-, B+)

Lakeview CAN (A)

Lambert Bridge USA (B+)

Dom. des Lambertins FR (A-)

Dom. Hubert Lamy FR (A)

Landmark USA (A)

Lane Tanner USA (A, A-, A-, A-, B+)

Langtry USA (A)

Latcham USA (B+)

Laurel Glen USA (B+)

Lazzaro SP (B+)

Leasingham AUS (A-, B+)

Leatitia USA (A-)

L'Ecole No. 41 USA (A-, A-, B+)

Leeuwin AUS (A-)

Condesa de Leganza SP (B+)

LeGrys NZ (A-)

Lemelson USA (A-, B+)

Lengs & Cooter AUS (A)

Leopold & Silvane Sommer AUT (A)

Patrick Lesec FR (B+)

Domaine de l'Harmas FR (B+)

Libelula USA (A)

LinCourt USA (A-, B+, B+)

Lindemans AUS (A, A, A-, B+)

Linden NZ (B+)

Lingenfelder GER (A-)

Liparita USA (A, A-, A-)

Carl Loewen GER (A-)

Logan AUS (A)

Lolonis USA (B+)

Longfellow USA (A-)

Longoria USA (A)

Dr. Loosen GER (A+, A+, A, A, A-, A-, A-)

Frederic Lornet FR (B+)

Louis M. Martini USA (A-, B+)

Ch. la Louvière FR (A)

Loxton USA (A-)

Luna USA (A, A-, B+)

Emilio Lustau SP (A-)

Ch. Lynch-Moussas FR (A)

Dom. de la Lyre FR (B+)

MacMurray Ranch USA (A)

MacRostie USA (A, B+, B+)

Maculan IT (B+)

Madfish AUS (B+, B+)

Madrigal USA (A, B+)

Ch. Malartic LaGravière FR (A+)

Ch. Malescasse FR (A-)

Maleta CAN (A)

Castillo de Maluenda SP (B+, B+)

Marcelina USA (B+)

Marimar Torres USA (A)

Markham USA (A+, A, A-)

Marquis Philips AUS (A-, A-, B+, B+)

Martin & Weyrich USA (A-)

Martin Ray USA (A-, B+)

Martinborough NZ (A-)

Martinelli USA (A, A-, A-)

Ch. Martinens FR (A)

Martinsancho SP (B+)

Mas Carlot FR (A-, B+, B+)

Mas de Bressades FR (B+, B+, B+)

Mas de Guiot FR (A-, B+)

Masi IT (B+)

Mason USA (A-)

Masottina IT (B+)

La Massa IT (A-)

Ch. Massamier la Mignarde FR (A)

Matariki NZ (A)

Matetic Vineyards CH (A+, B+)

Helmut Mathern GER (A)

Matua Valley NZ (A-)

Ch. de Mauvanne FR (A-)

Mayo Family USA (A-)

McCray Ridge USA (B+)

McCrea USA (A, A-, B+)

McDowell USA (B+)

McGuigan AUS (A)

McIlroy USA (B+, B+, B+)

McPherson AUS (A)

McWilliam's AUS (B+)

Meerea Park AUS (A)

Melville USA (A-, A-, B+)

Dom. Mercouri GRC (B+)

Meridian USA (A, A-, B+)

Alfred Merkelbach GER (A-)

Merryvale USA (A, A-, B+)

Meulenhof GER (A+, A, A-)

Mill Creek USA (B+)

Mills Reef NZ (A, B+)

Miner USA (A-, B+)

Régis Minet FR (A-)

Mionetto IT (A, B+, B+)

Mirassou USA (B+)

Mitchell AUS (A+)

Mitchelton AUS (A-)

Dom. des Molines FR (B+)

Feudo Monaci IT (B+)

Cantina dei Monaci IT (A)

Ch. Monbrison FR (A)

Marqués de Monistrol SP (A-, B+, B+, B+)

Castello di Monsanto IT (A-)

Mont Gras CH (B+)

Mont St. John USA (A-)

Bodegas Montecillo SP (B+)

Montecillo (A-)

Montegaredo SP (B+)

Montes CH (A-, B+, B+)

Monteviña USA (A-, A-)

Monticello USA (A+)

Montinore USA (B+)

Morandé CH (A, A, A-, A-, B+)

Dom. de la Mordoree FR (A-, B+)

Morgan USA (A-, B+, B+, B+)

Morgenhof SA (A-)

Morgenhof Estate SA (B+)

Moroder IT (A-)

Moss Wood AUS (A+)

Mount Eden USA (A, B+)

Mount Horrocks AUS (A-)

Mount Palomar USA (B+)

Mount Riley NZ (B+)

Mountford NZ (A-)

Dom. de Mourchon FR (B+)

Ch. de Mouton FR (A-)

Mt. Difficulty NZ (A+)

Mud House NZ (A-)

Muddy Water NZ (A-)

Mulderbosch SA (B+)

Murphy-Goode USA (A, A-, A-, A-, B+, B+)

Marqués de Murrieta SP (B+)

Schumann Nägler GER (A)

Nautilus NZ (A-, B+)

Dom. Navarre FR (A-)

Navarro USA (A+, A+, A-)

Navarrsotillo SP (B+)

Nino Negri IT (A-)

Neirano IT (A)

Bodega Nekeas SP (B+)

Lis Neris IT (A-)

Newlan USA (A)

Newton USA (A-, A-)

Neyers USA (A, A-, A-)

Nga Waka NZ (A+)

Fattoria Nicodemi IT (B+)

Maison Nicolas FR (A)

Peter Nicolay GER (A, A-, A-, B+)

Niepoort POR (A-, A-)

Nittnaus AUT (A-)

Nobilo NZ (A, A-)

Le Noble FR (B+)

Nociano IT (A-)

Dom. Alain Normand FR (B+)

Novella USA (B+)

Novelty Hill USA (A)

Novy USA (A-, B+)

Odfjell CH (B+)

Ojai USA (A, A-)

Okahu NZ (A, A-)

Omaka Springs NZ (A-, B+)

Ontañon SP (A)

Orlando AUS (B+)

Von Othegraven GER (A, A-, A-)

Pacific Echo USA (B+)

Paige 23 USA (A+)

Palacio de Fefinanes SP (B+)

Alvaro Palacios SP (A-)

Fattoria Il Palagio IT (B+)

Palliser NZ (B+)

Caves des Papes FR (A-)

Paracombe AUS (A-)

Paradise Ridge USA (B+)

Paringa AUS (B+)

Parxet SP (A)

Paschal USA (A-, B+)

Luis Pato POR (A, A-, A-)

Patton Valley Vineyard USA (A)

Ch. Paus Mas FR (B+)

Pazen GER (A)

Pazo de Barrantes SP (A-)

Pazo de Señorans SP (A-)

Peachy Canyon USA (B+)

Fratelli Pecchenino IT (A)

Quinta da Pedra POR (A+)

Pedroncelli USA (A, B+)

Pegasus Bay NZ (A-)

Peirano USA (A)

Pencarrow NZ (A-)

Pend d'Oreille USA (A-)

Penfolds AUS
(A, A, A, A, A-, A-, A-, B+)

Peninsula Ridge CAN (B+)

Penley AUS (A-)

Penmara AUS (B+)

Dom. de la Pépière FR (B+)

Perbacco Cellars USA (A-)

Castillo de Perelada SP (B+)

Perrin FR (A-, A-)

Perry Creek USA (A-)

Ch. Pesquié FR (B+)

Pessagno USA (A)

Petaluma AUS (B+)

Peterson USA (A-)

Ch. Peyros FR (B+)

Pezzi King USA (A-)

R. & A. Pfaffl AUT (A+, A+, A, A-)

Philip Staley USA (B+)

Ch. Pibran FR (A-)

J.-C. Pichot FR (A-)

Ch. Picque-Caillou FR (A-)

Pierro AUS (A)

Pietra Santa USA (B+)

Pikes AUS (A+, A, A-)

Pine Crest SA (B+)

Pine Ridge USA (A-, A-)

Francois Pinon FR (B+)

Pirramimma AUS (A+)

Plantagenet AUS (A)

Poggio Bertaio IT (A-)

Ch. la Pointe FR (A)

Pol Roger FR (A-)

Viñas Pomal SP (A-)

Ponte do Lima POR (B+)

Ponzi USA (A-)

Porcupine Ridge SA (B+)

Cims de Porrera SP (A-)

Portal do Fidalgo POR (B+)

Porter Creek USA (B+, B+)

Philippe Portier FR (B+)

Potel-Aviron FR (A-)

Ch. Poujeaux FR (A-)

Dom. de Pouy FR (B+)

Powers USA (A)

Prager AUT (A-)

Ch. Prieuré-Lichine FR (A)

Primo AUS (B+)

The Prisoner USA (A-)

Jon. Jos. Prüm GER (A-)

Marqués del Puerto SP (B+)

Fattoria le Pupille IT (B+)

Ch. Puygueraud FR (A-)

Dom. de la Quilla FR (B+)

Quinta do Crasto SP (A)

Compania das Quintas POR (B+)

Quintas Juntas SP (A)

Quivira USA (B+)

Qupé USA (A+, A, A-, B+)

Jean-Maurice Raffault FR (B+)

Rainoldi IT (A-, A-)

Ch. Ramafort FR (A-)

J. POR Ramos (A-, A-, B+)

Ramos-Pinto POR (B+, B+, B+)

Rancho Zabaco USA
(A, B+, B+, B+)

Raptor Ridge USA (B+)

Ravenswood USA (B+, B+)

Raymond USA (A-)

Rebuli IT (B+)

Red Hill NZ (B+)

Castell del Remei SP (A)

Remelluri SP (A)

Renwood USA (A-)

Balthasar Ress GER (B+, B+)

Pascal & Nicolas Reverdy FR (A-)

Rex Hill USA (A-, B+, B+, B+)

Reynolds AUS (B+)

Richard Hamilton AUS (A)

Ridge USA
(A, A, A, A-, A-, A-, A-, B+, B+)

Dom. Rimbert FR (B+)

Riondo IT (A-)

Marqués de Riscal SP (B+)

Trenuta di Riseccoli IT (B+)

Robert Craig USA (A-, A-)

Robert Mondavi USA (A+)

Robert Stemmler USA (A, B+)

Rocca di Fabbri IT (A-, B+)

Rocche dei Manzoni IT (A)

Dom. Rocher FR (A)

Rochioli USA (A, A-)

Rockbare AUS (B+)

Rockland USA (A-)

Rodney Strong USA
(A, A-, A-, B+, B+)

Ch. Romanin FR (A-)

Quinta de Romera POR (B+)

Quinta dos Roques POR (A-, A-)

Quinta de Roriz POR (A, B+)

Rose Vineyards USA (A-)

Rosemont AUS
(A+, A-, A-, A-, A-)

Rosenblum USA (A+, A+, A, A, A-,
A-, B+, B+, B+, B+, B+)

Ross Andrews Winery USA (A)

Rothbury AUS (A-)

Rotllan Torra SP (B+)

Ch. Rouillac FR (A-)

Rudd USA (A-)

Rufus Stone AUS (A+)

Rusack USA (A-)

Rust en Vrede SA (B+)

Rutherford Hill USA (A-)

Rutherford Oaks USA (A-)

Rutz USA (A, A, B+)

Ryan Patrick USA (A)

S. Anderson USA (A+)

Schloss Saarstein GER (B+)

Sable Ridge USA (A)

Saddleback USA (A, A)

Sagelands USA (B+)

Saint Chapelle USA
(A-, B+, B+, B+, B+)

Saint Clair NZ (A, A, A-, B+, B+)

Saint Gregory USA (B+)

Dom. de Saint-Antoine FR
(B+, B+, B+)

Saint-Cosme FR (B+)

Ch. Saint-Martin de la Garrigue
FR (A, A-, B+)

Saintsbury USA (A-, B+, B+)

Sakonnet USA (B+)

Viña Salceda SP (A-)

Prinz zu Salm-Dalberg'sches GER (B+)

Salomon (Undhof) AUT (A, A-)

Samos GRC (A-, B+)

Sandalford AUS (A, A-, B+)

Sandhill USA (A+, A-, B+, B+, B+)

Sandstone CAN (A+, A)

Dom. le Sang des Cailloux FR (A+)

Santa Anastasia IT (B+)

Santa Barbara USA (A)

Santa Carolina CH (B+)

Santa Rita CH (A, A-, B+)

Santero IT (B+)

Cooperativa Agricola de Santo, Isidro de Pegoes POR (A-)

Hnos. Sastre SP (B+)

Sausal USA (A, A-, A-, B+)

Dom. de la Sauveuse FR (B+)

Scacciadiavoli IT (B+)

Willi Schaefer GER (A-)

Scherrer USA (A)

Dom. Schlumberger FR (A, A-)

Carl Schmitt-Wagner GER (A+)

André Schneider & Fils FR (A+)

Schloss Schönborn GER (A, A, A-, A-, A-, B+)

Schug USA (A, B+, B+)

Schweiger Vineyards USA (A-)

Sebastiani USA (A-, A-, A-, A-, B+, B+, B+, B+)

Seghesio USA (A, B+, B+)

Ch. des Ségriès FR (A, B+, B+)

Selaks NZ (A, A-, B+)

Selbach-Oster GER (A+, A, A-)

Selby USA (A)

Selvapiana IT (A)

Ch. Sénèjac FR (B+)

Sequoia Grove USA (A)

Seresin NZ (A)

Faldas da Serra POR (A)

Ch. la Serre FR (A)

Seven Hills USA (B+)

Seven Peaks USA (A-)

Shaw & Smith AUS (A-)

Shea Wine Cellars USA (A-)

Shenandoah USA (A-)

Shepherds Ridge NZ (A-)

Sherwood Estates NZ (B+)

Shingle Peak NZ (A-)

Shooting Star USA (B+)

Shottesbrooke AUS (A)

Siduri USA (A)

Ch. Signac FR (A-, B+)

Silver USA (B+)

Silver Lake USA (B+)

Silverado USA (A, A-)

Simi USA (A, A, A-)

Simonsig SA (B+)

Sineann USA (A+, A, A-)

Siskiyou USA (A)

Robert Skalli FR (B+)

Skouras GRC (A)

Smith Madrone USA (A)

Snoqualmie USA (B+, B+)

Sobon USA (A, A-, B+)

Finca Sobreno SP (B+)

Jurtschitsch Sonnhof AUT (A-)

Sonnhof AUT (A-)

Sonoma-Loeb USA (A+)

Soos Creek USA (A, A-, A-)

Pierre & Yves Soulez FR (A+)

Domingos Alves Sousa SP (B+)

Pedro de Soutomaior SP (B+)

Pierre Sparr FR (A, B+, B+)

Sparrow Lane USA (A-)

Spencer Roloson USA (A-)

Spottswoode USA (A-)

Spy Valley NZ (B+, B+)

St. Clement USA (A, B+, B+)

St. Supéry USA (A-, A-, B+, B+)

St. Urbans-Hof GER (A-)

Stags' Leap Winery USA (A-, A-, A-, A-)

Steele USA (B+)

Steltzner USA (A)

Stephen Ross USA (B+)

Sticks AUS (A-)

Stone Wolf USA (B+)

Stonefly USA (A-)

Stonehedge USA (A-, B+)

Stonestreet USA (B+)

Stoney Ridge CAN (B+)

Stony Hill USA (A, B+)

J. & H. A. Strub GER (A)

Stryker Sonoma USA (A-)

Sumac Ridge CAN (A)

Summers USA (A, A-)

Summit Lake USA (A)

Susana Balbo ARG (B+)

Tagaris USA (B+, B+)

Tahbilk AUS (A)

Cave de Tain l'Hermitage FR (B+)

Talley USA (A-, A-, A)

Taltarni AUS (A-)

Tamarack Cellars USA (B+)

Tasca d'Almerita IT (A-, A-, A-)

Te Kairanga NZ (A+)

Te Mata NZ (B+)

Manfred Tement AUT (A, A)

Dom. Tempier FR (A)

Terra Mater CH (B+)

Terra Rosa ARG (B+)

Terrabianca IT (A-)

Terrace Road NZ (A)

Teruzzi & Puthod IT (B+)

Tesch GER (A-, B+)

Éric Texier FR (A-)

Dr. H. Thanisch-Erben Müller-Burggraef GER (A-, B+)

The Green Vineyard AUS (A)

Thea USA (A-)

Thelema SA (A, A, A-, B+)

Thomas Fogarty USA (A, A-)

Thorn-Clarke AUS (B+, B+)

Three Rivers Winery USA (A, A-, B+)

Thurston Wolfe USA (A, A-, A-)

Pierre-Yves Tijou FR (B+)

Tim Adams AUS (A-, A-)

Tommasi IT (A-)

Agusti Torello SP (B+, B+)

Tormaresca IT (B+)

Toro Albalá SP (A-)

Chat. la Touche FR (A-)

Ch. la Tour Carnet FR (A-)

Dom. de la Tour du Bon FR (A+)

Tour St. Martin FR (A-)

Treana USA (A+, A-)

Trefethen USA (A-, B+)

Trentadue USA (A-, B+, B+, B+)

Trevor Jones AUS (B+)

Trinchero USA (B+)

Ch. les Trois Croix FR (A-)

Truchard USA (A-, A-)

Tsantali GRC (A-)

Dom. Tselepos GRC (A-)

Tualatin USA (A-)

Dom. du Tunnel FR (A)

Turley USA (A, A, B+)

T-Vine USA (A-)

Two Oceans SA (B+)

Unti USA (B+)

Raymond Usseglio FR (A)

V. Sattui USA (A, A-)

Cave de Vacqueyras FR (B+, B+)

Val delle Rose IT (B+)

P. J. Valckenberg GER (B+)

Ch. Valcombe FR (A-)

Valdivieso USA (B+)

Valentin Bianchi ARG (B+)

Valette Fontaine CH (A-)

Vall Llach SP (A)

Valle dell'Acate IT (B+)

Valley of the Moon USA
(A-, A-, A-, B+, B+)

Vallobera SP (B+)

Varner USA (A)

Vasse Felix AUS (A)

Vega Sindoa (Nekeas) SP (B+)

Vegoritis GRC (B+)

Venge Family USA (A-)

Venta Mazzaron SP (B+)

Ventana USA (B+)

Veramonte CH (A, B+, B+)

Verget FR (A)

George Vernay FR (A+)

Castello Vicchiomaggio IT (A, A-)

Victor Hugo USA (B+)

Vie di Romans IT (A-, A-)

Vieil Armand FR (A)

Campo Viejo SP (A-)

Le Vieux Donjon FR (A+)

Les Vignerons de Villeveyrac FR
(A-, B+)

Vignobles FR (A-)

Villa Cafaggio IT (A-)

Villa Maria NZ (A+, A-, A-)

Villa Mt. Eden USA (A, B+)

Villa Sandi IT (B+)

Ch. Villeneuve FR (B+)

Paisajes y Viñedos SP (A-)

Vineland CAN (B+)

J. P. Vinhos POR (A)

Vinterra ARG (A-, A-)

Vinum Cellars USA (A-)

Castello di Volpaia IT (B+)

Voss USA (A-)

Voyager AUS (A-)

W. B. Bridgman USA (B+, B+)

W. H. Smith USA (A-)

Wairau River NZ (A-)

Wakefield AUS (B+)

Walla Walla Vintners USA (A)

Warre's POR (A, A)

Warwick SA (A+, A)

Washington Hills USA (B+, B+)

Water Wheel AUS (B+)

Waterbrook USA (A-, A-, B+, B+, B+)

Watts USA (A-)

Euguen Wehrheim GER (B+)

Robert Weil GER (A-)

Weingut Eilenz GER (B+)

Weingut Johannishof GER
(A-, A-, B+)

Weingut Karl Erbes GER (B+)

Weingut Wwe. Dr. Thanisch GER
(A-)

Wendell USA (A-)

White Oak USA (A, A, A-, B+, B+)

Whitehall Lane USA (B+, B+)

Whitehaven NZ (A-)

Whitford USA (A, A)

WillaKenzie USA (A)

Williams Selyem USA (A, A)

Willow Brook USA (A-)

Willow Crest USA (B+, B+, B+)

Windsor USA (B+)

Wirra Wirra AUS (A)

J.L. Wolf GER (A+, A+, A, A-)

Wolf Blass AUS
(A, A, A-, B+, B+, B+)

Wolff USA (A-, B+)

Woodward Canyon USA (A-)

Wynns Coonawarra AUS (A-)

Wyvern USA (A-, A-)

Xanadu AUS (A-, A-)

Yalumba AUS (A-, A-, B+)

Yarra Burn AUS (A, A-)

Yellow Hawk Cellar USA (B+)

Yerring Station AUS (A+)

Yorkville USA (A, A-, B+)
Zaca Mesa USA (A, B+)
Zardetto IT (B+)

COUNTRY DESIGNATIONS

ARG = Argentina	**GRC** = Greece
AUS = Australia	**IT** = Italy
AUT = Austria	**NZ** = New Zealand
CAN = Canada	**POR** = Portugal
CH = Chile	**SA** = South Africa
FR = France	**SP** = Spain
GER = Germany	**USA** = United States

"WINE DRINKING IS NO OCCULT ART TO BE PRACTICED
ONLY BY THE GIFTED FEW. INDEED, IT IS NOT AN ART
AT ALL. IT IS, OR SHOULD BE, THE SOBER HABIT OF
EVERY NORMAL MAN AND WOMAN BURDENED WITH NOR-
MAL RESPONSIBILITIES AND WITH A NORMAL DESIRE TO
KEEP THEIR PROBLEMS IN PERSPECTIVE AND
THEMSELVES IN GOOD HEALTH."

Allan Sichel

THE "PENGUIN BOOK OF WINES"

QUICK BUYING GUIDES TO TOP RATED WINES

BARGAIN WINES (B)

$10 A BOTTLE AND UNDER

CABERNET SAUVIGNON					
Covides, 1996 *Gran Castellflorit Reserva*					
PENEDÈS, SP	IE| B+	PV|	WPL| B	$10	B+
Condesa de Leganza, 1998 *Crianza*					
MANCHA, SP	IE| B+	PV|	WPL| B	$9	B+
KWV, 2000					
WESTERN CAPE, SA	IE| A-	PV|	WPL| B	$10	A-
Powers, 2000					
WA, USA	IE| A	PV|	WPL| B	$10	A

MERLOT					
Buena Vista, 2000					
CA, USA	IE| B+	PV|	WPL| B	$9	B+
Casa Julia, 2001					
CH	IE| B+	PV|	WPL| B	$9	B+

SYRAH/SHIRAZ					
Dom. des Blageurs, 2000 *Syrah, Vin de Pays d'Oc*					
LANGUEDOC, FR	IE| A-	PV|	WPL| B	$9	A-
Vinterra, 1999					
MENDOZA, ARG	IE| A-	PV|	WPL| B	$10	A-

TEMPRANILLO					
Campo Viejo, 1998 *Crianza*					
RIOJA, SP	IE| A-	PV|	WPL| B	$10	A-

ZINFANDEL					
Buena Vista, 2000 *Carneros*					
CA, USA	IE| B+, B+	PV|	WPL| B	$9	B+
Cline, 2000					
CA, USA	IE| B+	PV|	WPL| B	$10	B+
Ravenswood, 2000 *Vintners Blend*					
CA, USA	IE| B+	PV| 99 A-	WPL| B	$10	B+
Rosenblum, NV *Vintners Cuvée XXIV*					
CA, USA	IE| B+	PV|	WPL| B	$10	B+

OTHER RED					
Caves Aliança, 1999 *Galeria Tinta Roriz*					
DOURO, POR	IE| A-	PV|	WPL| B	$9	A-
Ca' del Solo, 2001 *Big House Red*					
CA, USA	IE| A-	PV| 00 B+	WPL| B	$10	A-

OTHER RED (CONTINUED)

Castaño, 2001 *Hecula*
YECLA, SP   IE| A   PV| 99 A-   WPL| B $9   A

DFJ, 2000 *Tinta Roriz-Merlot*
ESTREMADURA, POR   IE| A   PV| WPL| B $10   A

DFJ, 2000 *Tinta Miuda-Cabernet Sauvignon*
ESTREMADURA, POR   IE| A-   PV| WPL| B $9   A-

Clos Fantine, 1999 *Faugères*
LANGUEDOC, FR   IE| A-   PV| WPL| B $10   A-

Nociano, 1998 *Rosso IGT*
UMBRIA, IT   IE| A-   PV| WPL| B $9   A-

Ch. Saint-Martin de la Garrigue, 2000 *Cuvée Tradition, Coteaux du Languedoc*
LANGUEDOC, FR   IE| A-   PV| WPL| B $9   A-

Ch. Saint-Martin de la Garrigue, 2000 *Cuvée Réservée, Coteaux de Bessilles*
LANGUEDOC, FR   IE| A   PV| WPL| B $10   A

J. P. Vinhos, 1995 *J. P. Garrafeira, Palmela*
TERRAS DO SADO, POR   IE| A   PV| WPL| B $9   A

ALBARIÑO

Quinta da Pedra, 2001 *Alvarinho*
VINHO VERDE, POR   IE| A+   PV| 99 A+   WPL| B $10   A+

CHARDONNAY

Esser Cellars, 2001 *California*
CA, USA   IE| A-   PV| WPL| B $8   A-

Le Noble, 2001 *Vin de Pays*
SOUTH, FR   IE| B+   PV| WPL| B $7   B+

Rothbury, 2001
SOUTH EASTERN, AUS   IE| A-   PV| WPL| B $8   A-

RIESLING

Bonair, 2001 *Yakima Valley*
WA, USA   IE| A-   PV| WPL| B $10   A-

Ch. Ste. Michelle, 2001 *Dry Riesling, Columbia Valley*
WA, USA   IE| A-   PV| WPL| B $8   A-

Claar, 2001 *Late Harvest, White Bluffs, Columbia Valley*
WA, USA   IE| A-   PV| WPL| B $10   A-

Saint Chapelle, 2001 *Special Harvest Johannisberg Riesling*
ID, USA   IE| A-   PV| WPL| B $10   A-

Washington Hills, 2001 *Late Harvest, Columbia Valley*
WA, USA   IE| B+, B+   PV| 99 B+   WPL| B $9   B+

SAUVIGNON/FUMÉ BLANC

Ch. Ste. Michelle, 2001 *Columbia Valley*
WA, USA   IE| B+   PV| WPL| B $10   B+

Du Preez, 2001
GOUDINI VALLEY, SA   IE| B+   PV| WPL| B $9   B+

Hedges, 2001 *Fumé-Chardonnay, Columbia Valley*
WA, USA   IE| A   PV| WPL| B $9   A

OTHER WHITE

Casa de Vila Verde, 2001 *Senhorio d'Agras*
VINHO VERDE, POR   IE| A   PV| WPL| B $8   A

Mas Carlot, 2001 *Marsanne-Roussanne, Cuvée Tradition, Vin de Pays d'Oc*
LANGUEDOC, FR   IE| B+   PV| WPL| B $8   B+

ROSÉ

Dom. de la Mordoree, 2001 *Tavel*
RHÔNE, FR   IE| A-   PV| 99 B+   WPL| B $10   A-

Vega Sindoa (Nekeas), 2001
NAVARRA, SP   IE| B+, B+   PV| WPL| B $6   B+

SPARKLING

Astoria, NV *Extra Dry, Prosecco di Valdobbiandene*
IT   IE| A-   PV| WPL| B $9   A-

Cuvée Cle'Mente, 2000 *Brut, Blancs de Blanc, Chardonnay*
FR   IE| A-   PV| WPL| B $9   A-

Riondo, NV *ProseccoConegliano-Valdobiaddene*
VENETO, IT   IE| A-   PV| WPL| B $9   A-

"**WHAT IS THE DEFINITION OF GOOD WINE?
IT SHOULD START AND END WITH A SMILE.**"

ATTRIBUTED TO:

William Sokolin

**INCLUDED IN "BOTTLED WISDOM," COMPILED
AND EDITED BY MARK POLLMAN, 1998**

QUICK BUYING GUIDES TO TOP RATED WINES

SPLURGE WINES (S)

WORTH THE PRICE

BORDEAUX

Ch. la Croix du Casse, 2000 *Pomerol*
BORDEAUX, FR IE| A+ PV| WPL| S $30 A+

CABERNET SAUVIGNON

Concha y Toro, 1999 *Terrunyo, Maipo Valley*
CENTRAL VALLEY, CH IE| A-, A-, A PV| WPL| S,BBC $29 A-

Geyser Peak, 1999 *Block Collection, Kuimelis Vineyards, Alexander Valley-Livermore Valley*
CA, USA IE| A, A- PV| WPL| S,BBC $26 A

Sineann, 2000 *McDuffee Vineyard, Columbia Valley*
WA, USA IE| A PV| WPL| S $27 A

Thelema, 2000
STELLENBOSCH, SA IE| A PV| 99 A WPL| S $30 A

DOLCETTO

Fratelli Pecchenino, 2000 *Siri d'Jermu, Dogliani*
PIEDMONT, IT IE| A-, A PV| 99 A- WPL| S,BBC $29 A

MERLOT

Canoe Ridge, 2000 *Columbia Valley*
CA, USA IE| A, A PV| WPL| BBC $25 A

Chappellet, 2000 *Napa Valley*
CA, USA IE| A+ PV| 99 A WPL| S $26 A+

L'Ecole No. 41, 2000 *Columbia Valley*
WA, USA IE| A-, A- PV| WPL| S,BBC $30 A-

White Oak, 2000 *Napa Valley*
CA, USA IE| A, A PV| WPL| S,BBC $28 A

PETITE SIRAH

Rosenblum, 2000 *Pickett Road, Napa Valley*
CA, USA IE| A+ PV| WPL| S $28 A+

PINOT NOIR

Lane Tanner, 2000 *Bien Nacido Vineyard, Santa Maria Valley, Santa Barbara Co.*
CA, USA IE| A PV| WPL| S $28 A

SYRAH/SHIRAZ

Cline, 2000 *Los Carneros*
CA, USA IE| A, A-, A-, A- PV| WPL| S,BBC $28 A-

Edmunds St. John, 2000 *Wylie-Fenaughty, El Dorado Co., Sierra Foothills*
CA, USA   IE| A+, A-   PV| WPL| S,BBC $30   A

Jade Mountain, 2000 *Napa Valley*
CA, USA   IE| A, A   PV| WPL| S,BBC $28   A

Mills Reef, 2000 *Elspeth Syrah, Mere Road Vineyard*
HAWKES BAY, NZ   IE| A+, A   PV| 99 A-   WPL| S,BBC $30   A+

ZINFANDEL

Ridge, 2000 *Lytton Springs, Dry Creek Valley, Sonoma Co.*
CA, USA   IE| A+, B, A+, B+, A+   PV| 99 A   WPL| S,BBC $30   A

Rosenblum, 2001 *Rockpile Vineyard, Dry Creek Valley, Sonoma Co.*
CA, USA   IE| A+   PV| 00 A-   WPL| S $26   A+

Turley, 2000 *Duarte Vineyard, Contra Costa Co.*
CA, USA   IE| A+, B+, A   PV| WPL| S,BBC $30   A

Turley, 2000 *Old Vines*
CA, USA   IE| A, B, A   PV| 99 A   WPL| BBC $25   A-

OTHER RED

Columbia Crest, 1999 *Reserve Red, Columbia Valley*
WA, USA   IE| A, A   PV| WPL| S,BBC $30   A

Dom. du Grapillon d'Or, 2000 *Gigondas*
RHÔNE, FR   IE| A   PV| 99 A+   WPL| S $30   A

E. Guigal, 1999 *Châteauneuf-du-Pape*
RHÔNE, FR   IE| A+   PV| WPL| S $30   A+

Le Vieux Donjon, 2000 *Châteauneuf-du-Pape*
RHÔNE, FR   IE| A+, A   PV| 99 A-   WPL| S,BBC $30   A+

CHARDONNAY

Clos la Chance, 2001 *Vanumanutagi Vineyard, Santa Cruz Mountains*
CA, USA   IE| A, A   PV| 00 A-   WPL| S,BBC $30   A

Keller, 2000 *La Cruz Vineyard, Sonoma Coast, Sonoma Co.*
CA, USA   IE| A+, A-, A+, B+, A   PV| WPL| BBC $25   A

Martinelli, 2000 *Woolsey Road, Russian River Valley, Sonoma Co.*
CA, USA   IE| A, A   PV| WPL| S,BBC $28   A

Whitford, 2000 *Haynes Vineyard, Napa Valley*
CA, USA   IE| A, A   PV| WPL| S,BBC $28   A

RIESLING

Bründlmayer, 2001 *Steinmassel, Lagenlois*
KAMPTAL, AUT   IE| A, A+   PV| 99 A-, 00 A   WPL| BBC $25   A+

Carl Schmitt-Wagner, 2001 *Auslese, Longuicher Maximiner Herrenberg*
MOSEL-SAAR-RUWER, GER   IE| A+, A-   PV| WPL| S,BBC $26   A

Grosset, 2002 *Polish Hill, Clare Valley*
SOUTH, AUS   IE| A+   PV| 01 A   WPL| S $29   A+

J.L. Wolf, 2001 *Auslese, Wachenheimer Gerümpel*
GER   IE| A+   PV| WPL| S $30   A+

VIOGNIER

Treana, 2001 *Viognier-Marsanne Mer Soleil Vineyard, Central Coast*
CA, USA   IE| A+   PV| 99 A-, 00 A-   WPL| $25 A+

OTHER WHITE

Etude, 2000 *Pinot Blanc, Carneros*
CA, USA   IE| A   PV| 99 A   WPL| S $28 A

George Vernay, 2001 *Les Terrasses de L'Empire*
CONDRIEU, FR   IE| A+   PV| WPL| S $29 A+

Beringer, 1998 *Sauvignon Blanc/Semillon, Nightingale, Napa Valley*
CA, USA   IE| A+   PV| 99 A   WPL| S $30 A+

SPARKLING

Juvé y Camps, NV *Cava, Brut, Gran Juvé*
SP   IE| A+   PV| WPL| S $30 A+

"WINE MAKES DAILY LIVING EASIER, LESS HURRIED, WITH FEWER TENSIONS AND MORE TOLERANCE."

ATTRIBUTED TO:

Benjamin Franklin

QUICK BUYING GUIDES TO TOP RATED WINES

BUY BY THE CASE (BBC)

MULTIPLE REVIEWS, A- OR BETTER

BORDEAUX

Ch. Monbrison, 2000 *Margaux*
BORDEAUX, FR   IE| A, A-   PV| WPL| S,BBC   **$30**   A

CABERNET SAUVIGNON

Ch. Ste. Michelle, 1999 *Cold Creek Vineyard, Columbia Valley*
WA, USA   IE| A, A-   PV| WPL| S,BBC   **$29**   A

Sebastiani, 1999 *Appellation SelectionAlexander Valley, Sonoma Co.*
CA, USA   IE| A, A-, B+   PV| WPL| BBC   **$24**   A-

DOLCETTO

Francesco Boschis, 1998 *Vigna dei Prey, Dogliani*
PIEDMONT, IT   IE| A, A-   PV| WPL| BBC   **$17**   A

GAMAY

Georges Duboeuf, 2000 *Prestige, Morgon*
BEAUJOLAIS, FR   IE| A-, A-, B   PV| WPL| BBC   **$14**   A-

MERLOT

Ch. Ste. Michelle, 1999 *Canoe Ridge Estate Vineyard, Columbia Valley*
WA, USA   IE| A, A-, B   PV| WPL| BBC   **$23**   A-

Louis M. Martini, 1999 *Del Rio Vineyard, Russian River Valley, Sonoma Co.*
CA, USA   IE| A-, A-   PV| WPL| BBC   **$22**   A-

Selby, 1999 *Sonoma Co.*
CA, USA   IE| A, A, A-   PV| WPL| BBC   **$24**   A

PINOT NOIR

King , 1999 *Eugene*
OR, USA   IE| A-, B+   PV| WPL| BBC   **$20**   A-

La Crema, 2000 *Anderson Valley, Mendocino Co.*
CA, USA   IE| A, A-   PV| WPL| BBC   **$25**   A

SANGIOVESE

Capezzana, 1999 *Conte Contini Bonacossi, Carmignano*
TUSCANY, IT   IE| A-, A-   PV| WPL| BBC   **$20**   A-

SYRAH/SHIRAZ

Ch. Souverain, 2000 *Alexander Valley, Sonoma Co.*
CA, USA   IE| B+, A-, B, A+   PV| WPL| BBC   **$20**   A-

Equus, 1999 *Paso Robles, San Luis Obispo Co.*
CA, USA   IE| A, A-   PV| WPL| BBC   **$18**   A

La Crema, 2000 *Sonoma Co.*
CA, USA   IE| A-, A-   PV| WPL| BBC   **$18**   A-

Morandé, 2001 *Vitisterra Grand Reserve, Maipo Valley*
CENTRAL VALLEY, CH   IE| A-, A-   PV| WPL| BBC   **$15**   A-

Penfolds, 1999 *Shiraz, Kalimna Bin 28*
SOUTH, AUS   IE| A-, B+, A   PV| WPL| BBC   **$24**   A-

Zaca Mesa, 2000 *Santa Ynez Valley*
CA, USA   IE| A, A-   PV| WPL| BBC   **$20**   A

ZINFANDEL

Dashe, 2000 *Dry Creek Valley, Sonoma Co.*
CA, USA   IE| A, A, B   PV| 99 A-   WPL| BBC   **$20**   A-

Dry Creek, 2000 *Old Vines, Sonoma Co.*
CA, USA   IE| A, A, B+, A   PV| WPL| BBC   **$21**   A

Gallo Sonoma, 1999 *Frei Ranch Vineyard, Dry Creek Valley, Sonoma Co.*
CA, USA   IE| A, A-   PV| WPL| BBC   **$22**   A

Lake Sonoma, 2000 *Dry Creek Valley, Sonoma Co.*
CA, USA   IE| A, B, A   PV| 99 B+   WPL| BBC   **$17**   A-

CHARDONNAY

Ch. St. Jean, 2000 *Belle Terre Vineyard, Alexander Valley, Sonoma Co.*
CA, USA   IE| A, A   PV| 99 B   WPL| BBC   **$22**   A

Gloria Ferrer, 2000 *Carneros*
CA, USA   IE| A-, A-, B+, B+   PV| WPL| BBC   **$20**   A-

Hartford, 2000 *Sonoma Coast, Sonoma Co.*
CA, USA   IE| A-, A, A   PV| WPL| BBC   **$24**   A

Talley, 2000 *Oliver's Vineyard, Edna Valley, San Luis Obispo Co.*
CA, USA   IE| A, A-, A-, A- PV| WPL| BBC   **$20**   A-

GEWÜRZTRAMINER

Pierre Sparr, 2001 *Réserve*
ALSACE, FR   IE| A+, B+   PV| WPL| BBC   **$15**   A

PINOT GRIS/GRIGIO

Luna, 2001 *Napa Valley*
CA, USA   IE| A, A   PV| 00 B+   WPL| BBC   **$20**   A

RIESLING

Dr. Loosen, 2001 *Riesling Kabinett, Bernkasteler Lay*
MOSEL-SAAR-RUWER, GER   IE| A+, A- PV| WPL| BBC   **$17**   A

Grans-Fassian, 2001 *Kabinett, Trittenheirmer*
MOSEL-SAAR-RUWER, GER   IE| A-, A   PV| WPL| BBC   **$17**   A

Wolf Blass, 2001 *Gold Label, Clare Valley-Eden Valley*
SOUTH, AUS   IE| A, B+, B+   PV| WPL| BBC   **$14**   A-

SAUVIGNON/FUMÉ BLANC

Flora Springs, 2001 *Soliloquy, Napa Valley*
CA, USA   IE| A-,,A, A-   PV| 01 B   WPL| BBC $25   A-

Beringer, 2000 *Alluvium White, Knights Valley*
CA, USA   IE| A-, A-   PV| WPL| BBC $16   A-

Honig, 2001 *Napa Valley*
CA, USA   IE| A-, B+, A-   PV| 00 B+   WPL| BBC $14   A-

Isabel, 2001
MARLBOROUGH, NZ   IE| A, A   PV| WPL| BBC $18   A

St. Supéry, 2001 *Napa Valley*
CA, USA   IE| A, A, A-, B+   PV| 00 B+   WPL| W,BBC $15   A-

VIOGNIER

Treana, 2000 *Viognier-MarsanneMer Soleil Vineyard, Central Coast*
CA, USA   IE| A-, B+, A-   PV| WPL| BBC $25   A-

OTHER SWEET

Greenwood Ridge, 1999 *Late Harvest, Mendocino Ridge, Mendocino Co.*
CA, USA   IE| A+, A+   PV| WPL| BBC $24   A+

**"I MADE A MENTAL NOTE TO WATCH WHICH BOTTLE
BECAME EMPTY SOONEST, SOMETIMES A MORE TELLING
EVALUATION SYSTEM THAN ANY OTHER."**

Gerald Asher

"ON WINE," 1982

QUICK BUYING GUIDES TO TOP RATED WINES

WIDELY AVAILABLE (W)

20,000 CASES OR MORE

BORDEAUX

Ch. Beaumont, 2000 *Haut-Médoc*
BORDEAUX, FR   IE| A-   PV| WPL| W $15 A-

Ch. Beau-Site, 2000 *St.-Estéphe*
BORDEAUX, FR   IE| A-   PV| WPL| W $20 A-

Ch. Belgrave, 2000 *Haut-Médoc*
BORDEAUX, FR   IE| A-   PV| WPL| W $20 A-

Ch. Camensac, 2000 *Haut-Médoc*
BORDEAUX, FR   IE| A-   PV| WPL| W $20 A-

Ch. la Cardonne, 2000 *Médoc*
BORDEAUX, FR   IE| A-   PV| WPL| W $15 A-

CABERNET SAUVIGNON

Benziger, 1999 *Sonoma Co.*
CA, USA   IE| A-, B   PV| WPL| W $19 B+

Columbia Crest, 1999 *Valley Grand Estates, Columbia Valley*
WA, USA   IE| B+   PV| WPL| W $11 B+

Concha y Toro, 2000 *Marqués de Casa Concha, Puente Alto Vineyard, Maipo Valley*
CENTRAL VALLEY, CH   IE| A-   PV| 99 A-   WPL| W $14 A-

Marquis Philips, 2000
SOUTH EASTERN, AUS   IE| A, B+, B   PV| WPL| W $15 B+

Simi, 1999 *Alexander Valley, Sonoma Co.*
CA, USA   IE| A-   PV| WPL| W $25 A-

MALBEC

Montes, 2001 *Reserve, Colchagua Valley, Rapel Valley*
CENTRAL VALLEY, CH   IE| B+   PV| WPL| W, B $10 B+

MERLOT

Hogue, 1999 *Vinyard Selection, Columbia Valley*
WA, USA   IE| A-   PV| WPL| W $18 A-

PINOT NOIR

Acacia, 2001 *Napa Valley/Carneros*
CA, USA   IE| B+   PV| WPL| W $20 B+

Saintsbury, 2000 *Carneros*
CA, USA   IE| A, B+,B, B+ PV| WPL| W $24 B+

SANGIOVESE

Carpineto, 1998 *Riserva, Chianti Classico*
TUSCANY, IT IE| A-, A- PV| WPL| W,BBC **$22** A-

Santa Anastasia, 1999 *Passomaggio*
SICILY, IT IE| B+, A- PV| WPL| W **$14** A-

SYRAH/SHIRAZ

Lindemans, 1999 *Shiraz, Reserve, Padthaway*
SOUTH, AUS IE| B+, A-, A-, B+ PV| WPL| W,BBC **$15** A-

Penfolds, 2000 *Shiraz-Mourvèdre, Bin 2*
SOUTH EASTERN, AUS IE| A-, B+ PV| WPL| W **$11** A-

Wolf Blass, 2000 *Shiraz-Cabernet Sauvignon, Red Label*
SOUTH, AUS IE| B+, B PV| WPL| W **$12** B+

OTHER RED

Condado de Haza, 2000
RIBERA DEL DUERO, SP IE| B+ PV| WPL| W **$20** B+

Di Majo Norante, 1998 *Terra degli Osci, Ramitello*
MOLISE, IT IE| B+ PV| WPL| W **$12** B+

CHARDONNAY

Acacia, 2001 *Carneros*
CA, USA IE| B+, B+, B+ PV| 00 B WPL| W **$20** B+

Cathedral, 2001
WESTERN CAPE, SA IE| A- PV| WPL| W **$12** A-

Cellars of Canterbury, 2000 *Momona*
MARLBOROUGH, NZ IE| A- PV| WPL| W **$13** A-

Ch. Ste. Michelle, 2000 *Columbia Valley*
WA, USA IE| B+, B+, B, B+PV| WPL| W **$13**B+

Frei Brothers, 2001 *Reserve, Russian River Valley, Northern Sonoma*
CA, USA IE| A, B, A- PV| WPL| W,BBC **$20** A-

Kendall-Jackson, 2000 *Estate Series, Camelot Beach, Santa Maria Valley, Santa Barbara Co.*
CA, USA IE| A- PV| WPL| W **$17** A-

PINOT GRIS/GRIGIO

Ch. Ste. Michelle, 2002 *Pinot Gris, Columbia Valley*
WA, USA IE| B+ PV| 01 B+ WPL| W **$13** B+

Marco Felluga, 2001 *Collio*
FRIULI, IT IE| B+ PV| WPL| W **$15** B+

RIESLING

Columbia, 2002 *Cellarmaster's Reserve, Columbia Valley*
WA, USA IE| B+ PV| 99 B+ WPL| W, B **$8** B+

Hogue, 2002 *Johannnisberg Riesling, Columbia Valley*
WA, USA IE| B+ PV| 00 B+ WPL| W, B **$9** B+

SAUVIGNON/FUMÉ BLANC

Allan Scott, 2002
MARLBOROUGH, NZ   IE| B+   PV| WPL| W $11 B+

Beringer, 2000 *Appellation Collection Napa Valley*
CA, USA   IE| B+   PV| 99 B+   WPL| W $12 B+

Cakebread, 2000 *Napa Valley*
CA, USA   IE| A, B+, B   PV| WPL| W $17 B+

Cloudy Bay, 2001
MARLBOROUGH, NZ   IE| A, A   PV| 99 A-, 00 A   WPL| W,BBC $24 A

Ferrari-Carano, 2001 *Fumé Blanc, Sonoma Co.*
CA, USA   IE| A-, B+   PV| WPL| W,BBC $15 A-

Grgich Hills, 2000 *Fumé Blanc, Napa Valley*
CA, USA   IE| A-   PV| WPL| W $18 A-

OTHER WHITE

Feudi di San Gregorio, 2001 *Falanghina Sannio*
CAMPANIA, IT   IE| A-   PV| 99 B+, 00 B+ WPL| W $14 A-

SPARKLING

Piper Heidsieck, NV *Brut*
CHAMPAGNE, FR   IE| A   PV| WPL| W,S $30 A

"THE STOMACH IS THE REAL TEST-TUBE FOR WINE."

Dr. Robert Druitt

"REPORT ON CHEAP WINES," 1873

COMPREHENSIVE BUYING GUIDES TO TOP RATED WINES

WINES SORTED BY TYPE

REDS

BARBERA

La Ghersa, 1999 *Camparo*
ASTI SUPERIORE, IT   IE| B+   PV| WPL| $14 B+

Monteviña, 1999 *Terra d'Oro, Amador Co.*
CA, USA   IE| A-   PV| WPL| $18 A-

Neirano, 1998 *Le Croci, Barbara Asti d'Superiore*
PIEDMONT, IT   IE| A   PV| WPL| S $30 A

Sebastiani, 2000 *Sonoma Co.*
CA, USA   IE| B+   PV| WPL| $18 B+

BAROLO

Beni di Batasiolo, 2001 *Barolo*
BARBARA D'ALBA, IT IE| B+   PV| WPL| $18 B+

Beni di Batasiolo, 1998 *Barolo*
LA MORRA, IT   IE| A-   PV| WPL| W,S $30 A-

Michele Chiarlo, 1998 *Barolo*
PIEDMONT, IT   IE| A-   PV| WPL| S $30 A-

BORDEAUX

Ch. d' Angludet, 2000 *Margaux*
BORDEAUX, FR   IE| B+   PV| WPL| $16 B+

Clos Badon-Thunevin, 2000 *St.-Emilion*
BORDEAUX, FR   IE| A   PV| WPL| $25 A

Ch. Beaumont, 2000 *Haut-Médoc*
BORDEAUX, FR   IE| A-   PV| WPL| W $15 A-

Ch. Beau-Site, 2000 *St.-Estéphe*
BORDEAUX, FR   IE| A-   PV| WPL| W $20 A-

Ch. Belgrave, 2000 *Haut-Médoc*
BORDEAUX, FR   IE| A-   PV| WPL| W $20 A-

Ch. Bellefont-Belcier, 2000 *Saint-Emilion*
BORDEAUX, FR   IE| A-   PV| WPL| S $30 A-

Ch. Bouscaut, 2000 *Pessac-Léognan*
BORDEAUX, FR   IE| A-   PV| WPL| $20 A-

Ch. Boyd-Cantenac, 2000 *Margaux*
BORDEAUX, FR   IE| A-   PV| WPL| S $30 A-

Ch. Brillette, 2000 *Listrac & Moulis*
BORDEAUX, FR   IE| B+   PV| WPL| $15 B+

Ch. Camensac, 2000 *Haut-Médoc*
BORDEAUX, FR   IE| A-   PV| WPL| W $20 A-

BORDEAUX (CONTINUED)

Ch. Cantelauze, 2000 *Pomerol*
BORDEAUX, FR   IE| A-   PV| WPL| $25 A-

Ch. Cantemerle, 2000 *Haut-Médoc*
BORDEAUX, FR   IE| A   PV| WPL| W,S $30 A

Ch. Cantenac, 2000 *Saint-Emilion*
BORDEAUX, FR   IE| A-   PV| WPL| $15 A-

Ch. Cantenac-Brown, 2000 *Margaux*
BORDEAUX, FR   IE| A   PV| WPL| S $30 A

Ch. la Cardonne, 2000 *Médoc*
BORDEAUX, FR   IE| A-   PV| WPL| W $15 A-

Ch. Charmail, 2000 *Haut-Médoc*
BORDEAUX, FR   IE| A-   PV| WPL| $15 A-

Ch. Cos-Labory, 2000 *St.-Estéphe*
BORDEAUX, FR   IE| A-   PV| WPL| $25 A-

Ch. Côte de Baleau, 2000 *Saint-Emilion*
BORDEAUX, FR   IE| A-   PV| WPL| S $30 A-

Ch. la Croix du Casse, 2000 *Pomerol*
BORDEAUX, FR   IE| A+   PV| WPL| S $30 A+

Ch. Croix-de-Gay, 2000 *Pomerol*
BORDEAUX, FR   IE| A-   PV| WPL| S $30 A-

Ch. Croizet-Bages, 2000 *Pauillac*
BORDEAUX, FR   IE| A-   PV| WPL| $25 A-

Ch. Dauzac, 2000 *Margaux*
BORDEAUX, FR   IE| A   PV| WPL| S $30 A

Ch. Faizeau, 2000 *Séléction Vieilles Vignes, Montagne-St.-Emilion*
BORDEAUX, FR   IE| B+   PV| WPL| $15 B+

La Fleur de Bouard, 2000 *Lalande-de-Pomerol*
BORDEAUX, FR   IE| A-   PV| WPL| S $30 A-

Ch. Fonréaud, 2000 *Listrac*
BORDEAUX, FR   IE| B+   PV| WPL| $15 B+

Ch. Gigault, 2000 *Premières, Cuvée Viva, Côtes de Blaye*
BORDEAUX, FR   IE| A   PV| WPL| $25 A

Ch. Gloria, 2000 *St.-Julien*
BORDEAUX, FR   IE| A-, B   PV| WPL| W,S $30 B+

Ch. Grand Corbin-Despagne, 2000 *Saint-Emilion*
BORDEAUX, FR   IE| A-   PV| WPL| $25 A-

Ch. Grand-Pontet, 2000 *Saint-Émilion*
BORDEAUX, FR   IE| A+   PV| WPL| S $30 A+

Ch. les Grands Maréchaux, 2000 *Premières, Côtes de Blaye*
BORDEAUX, FR   IE| B+   PV| WPL| $15 B+

Ch. Haut-Bages-Libéral, 2000 *Pauillac*
BORDEAUX, FR   IE| A+   PV| WPL| S $30 A+

Ch. Haut-Batailley, 2000 *Pauillac*
BORDEAUX, FR   IE| A+   PV| WPL| S $30 A+

Ch. Haut-Beauséjour, 2000 *Saint Estèphe*
BORDEAUX, FR   IE| A-   PV| WPL| $20   A-

Ch. Haut-Chaigneau, 2000 *Lalande-de-Pomerol*
BORDEAUX, FR   IE| B+   PV| WPL| $15   B+

Ch. Haut-Corbin, 2000 *Saint-Émilion*
BORDEAUX, FR   IE| A   PV| WPL| $25   A

Ch. Haut-Maillet, 2000 *Pomerol*
BORDEAUX, FR   IE| A-   PV| WPL| $20   A-

Ch. Haut-Marbuzet, 2000 *St.-Estéphe*
BORDEAUX, FR   IE| A-   PV| WPL| W,S $30   A-

Ch. Lafon-Rochet, 2000 *St.-Estéphe*
BORDEAUX, FR   IE| A   PV| WPL| S $30   A

Ch. la Lagune, 2000 *Haut-Médoc*
BORDEAUX, FR   IE| A-   PV| WPL| S $30   A-

Ch. la Louvière, 2000 *Pessac-Léognan*
BORDEAUX, FR   IE| A   PV| WPL| $25   A

Ch. Lynch-Moussas, 2000 *Pauillac*
BORDEAUX, FR   IE| A   PV| WPL| W $25   A

Ch. Malartic LaGravière, 2000 *Pessac-Léognan*
BORDEAUX, FR   IE| A+   PV| 99 A-   WPL| S $30   A+

Ch. Malescasse, 2000 *Haut-Médoc*
BORDEAUX, FR   IE| A-   PV| WPL| $15   A-

Ch. Martinens, 2000 *Margaux*
BORDEAUX, FR   IE| A   PV| WPL| $20   A

Ch. Monbrison, 2000 *Margaux*
BORDEAUX, FR   IE| A, A-   PV| WPL| S,BBC $30   A

Ch. de Mouton, 2000 *Bordeaux Supérieur*
BORDEAUX, FR   IE| A-   PV| WPL| $15   A-

Ch. Pibran, 2000 *Pauillac*
BORDEAUX, FR   IE| A-   PV| WPL| $20   A-

Ch. Picque-Caillou, 2000 *Pessac-Léognan*
BORDEAUX, FR   IE| A-   PV| WPL| $15   A-

Ch. la Pointe, 2000 *Pomerol*
BORDEAUX, FR   IE| A   PV| WPL| $25   A

Ch. Poujeaux, 2000 *Listrac & Moulis*
BORDEAUX, FR   IE| A-   PV| WPL| W $25   A-

Ch. Prieuré-Lichine, 2000 *Margaux*
BORDEAUX, FR   IE| A   PV| WPL| S $30   A

Ch. Ramafort, 2000 *Médoc*
BORDEAUX, FR   IE| A-   PV| WPL| $20   A-

Ch. Rouillac, 2000 *Pessac-Léognan*
BORDEAUX, FR   IE| A-   PV| WPL| $16   A-

Ch. Sénèjac, 2000 *Haut-Médoc*
BORDEAUX, FR   IE| B+   PV| WPL| $15   B+

Ch. la Serre, 2000 *Saint-Emilion*
BORDEAUX, FR   IE| A   PV| WPL| $25   A

REDS
SORTED BY TYPE

Ch. la Tour Carnet, 2000 *Haut-Médoc*
BORDEAUX, FR   IE| A-   PV| WPL| $25   A-

CABERNET FRANC

Bellevue, 2001 *Umkhulu Titan*
STELLENBOSCH, SA   IE| A-   PV| WPL| $23   A-

Cana's Feast, 1999 *Red Table Wine, Red Mountain*
WA, USA   IE| A-   PV| WPL| S $30   A-

Colio, 1999 *Reserve, CEV, Lake Erie North Shore*
ONTARIO, CAN   IE| B+   PV| WPL| $15   B+

Conn Creek, 1999 *Limited Release, Napa Valley*
CA, USA   IE| A+   PV| WPL| $25   A+

Cuneo, 1999 *Columbia Valley*
WA, USA   IE| B+   PV| WPL| $15   B+

Decoy, 2000 *Migration, Napa Valley*
CA, USA   IE| B+   PV| WPL| $24   B+

Hernder Estate, 1999 *Niagara Peninsula*
ONTARIO, CAN   IE| A   PV| WPL| $11   A

Huntington Cellars, 2000 *Alexander Valley, Sonoma Co.*
CA, USA   IE| B+   PV| WPL| $18   B+

Stonefly, 1999 *Napa Valley*
CA, USA   IE| A-   PV| WPL| S $27   A-

Warwick, 2000 *Estate Reserve*
STELLENBOSCH, SA   IE| A   PV| WPL| S $29   A

Willow Crest, 1999 *Yakima Valley*
WA, USA   IE| B+   PV| WPL| $15   B+

CABERNET SAUVIGNON

Andretti, 1999 *Napa Valley*
CA, USA   IE| A   PV| WPL| S $30   A

Annie's Lane, 1999 *Cabernet Sauvignon-Merlot, Clare Valley*
SOUTH , AUS   IE| A-   PV| WPL| $15   A-

Arbios, 1999 *Alexander Valley, Sonoma Co.*
CA, USA   IE| A, A-   PV| WPL| S,BBC $30   A

Arbor Crest, *Columbia Valley*
WA, USA   IE| A-   PV| WPL| S $26   A-

Artesa, 1999 *Napa Valley*
CA, USA   IE| A   PV| WPL| S $30   A

Avila, 2000 *Santa Barbara*
CA, USA   IE| B+, B+   PV| WPL| $12   B+

Barnwood, 2000 *Santa Barbara Co.*
CA, USA   IE| A-, B   PV| WPL| $22   B-

Bates Creek, 1999 *Napa Valley*
CA, USA   IE| A   PV| WPL| $25   A

Beaulieu (BV), 1999 *Rutherford, Napa Valley*
CA, USA   IE| A-   PV| WPL| $25   A-

Benziger, 1999 *Sonoma Co.*
CA, USA   IE| A-, B   PV| WPL| W   **$19**   **A-**

Beringer, 1999 *Knights Valley, Sonoma Co.*
CA, USA   IE| A-, B   PV| WPL| S   **$26**   **A-**

Bommarito, 2000 *Napa Valley*
CA, USA   IE| B+   PV| WPL| **$20**   **B+**

Calina, 2000 *Cabernet Sauvignon-Carmenère, Coastal Vineyards, Maule Valley*
CENTRAL VALLEY, CH   IE| B+, B   PV| WPL| **$14**   **B+**

Camaraderie, 1999
WA, USA   IE| A   PV| WPL| **$22**   **A**

Casa Lapostolle, 2000 *Rapel Valley*
CENTRAL VALLEY, CH   IE| B+   PV| WPL| B   **$10**   **B+**

Caterina, 1999 *Willard Family Vineyard, Yakima Valley*
WA, USA   IE| A   PV| WPL| S   **$28**   **A**

Caterina, 1999 *Columbia Valley*
WA, USA   IE| B+   PV| WPL| **$20**   **B+**

Cathedral, 1999
COASTAL REGION, SA   IE| B+   PV| WPL| **$15**   **B+**

Ch. Los Boldos, 2000 *Vieilles Vignes, Requinoa*
CENTRAL VALLEY, CH   IE| B+   PV| WPL| **$20**   **B+**

Ch. Souverain, 1999 *Alexander Valley, Sonoma Co.*
CA, USA   IE| B+, B+   PV| WPL| W   **$20**   **B+**

Ch. Ste. Michelle, 2000 *Columbia Valley*
WA, USA   IE| B+   PV| 99 B+   WPL| W   **$15**   **B+**

Ch. Ste. Michelle, 1999 *Cold Creek Vineyard, Columbia Valley*
WA, USA   IE| A, A-   PV| WPL| S,BBC   **$29**   **A**

Columbia, 1999 *Columbia Valley*
WA, USA   IE| B+   PV| WPL| **$15**   **B+**

Columbia Crest, 2000 *Grand Estates, Columbia Valley*
WA, USA   IE| A   PV| 99 B+   WPL| **$15**   **A**

Columbia Crest, 1999 *Walter Clore Private Reserve, Columbia Valley*
WA, USA   IE| A+   PV| WPL| S   **$30**   **A+**

Columbia Crest, 1999 *Valley Grand Estates, Columbia Valley*
WA, USA   IE| B+   PV| WPL| W   **$11**   **B+**

Columbia Crest, 1999 *Reserve, Columbia Valley*
WA, USA   IE| A   PV| WPL| S   **$28**   **A**

Concha y Toro, 2000 *Marqués de Casa Concha, Puente Alto Vineyard, Maipo Valley*
CENTRAL VALLEY, CH   IE| A-   PV| 99 A-   WPL| W   **$14**   **A-**

Concha y Toro, 1999 *Terrunyo, Maipo Valley*
CENTRAL VALLEY, CH   IE| A-, A-, A   PV| WPL| S,BBC   **$29**   **A-**

Covides, 1996 *Gran Castellflorit Reserva*
PENEDÈS, SP   IE| B+   PV| WPL| B   **$10**   **B+**

Crystal Valley, 2000
CA, USA   IE| A   PV| WPL| **$16**   **A**

CABERNET SAUVIGNON (CONTINUED)

Dakensig, 2001 *Coastal*
SA   IE| B+   PV| WPL| $13   B+

Errazuriz, 1999 *Reserva Don Maximiano Estate, Valle Aconcagua*
CH   IE| B+   PV| WPL| $14   B+

Foppiano, 2000 *Russian River Valley, Sonoma Co.*
CA, USA   IE| B+   PV| WPL| $17   B+

Franciscan Oakville, 2000 *Napa Valley*
CA, USA   IE| A-   PV| WPL| S $27   A-

Gallo of Sonoma, 1999 *Reserve, Sonoma Co.*
CA, USA   IE| B+   PV| WPL| $13   B+

Gallo of Sonoma, 2000 *Reserve, Sonoma Co.*
CA, USA   IE| B+   PV| WPL| $13   B+

Geyser Peak, 1999 *Block Collection, Kuimelis Vineyards, Alexander Valley-Livermore Valley*
CA, USA   IE| A, A-   PV| WPL| S,BBC $26   A

Glenwood Ridge, 1999 *Mendocino Ridge, Philo*
CA, USA   IE| A   PV| WPL| S $30   A

Guardian Peak, 2001
STELLENBOSCH, SA IE| B+   PV| WPL| B $10   B+

Hawley, 1999 *Dry Creek Valley, Sonoma Co.*
CA, USA   IE| A-   PV| WPL| S $28   A-

Hedges, 1999 *Three Vineyards, Red Mountain, Columbia Valley*
WA, USA   IE| B+   PV| WPL| $18   B+

Heritage Road, 1999 *Reserve, Limited, Bethany Creek Vineyard, Barossa Valley*
SOUTH, AUS   IE| A+   PV| WPL| S $30   A+

Hess Estate, 1999 *Napa Valley*
CA, USA   IE| B+   PV| WPL| $20   B+

Hillview Vineyards, 1999 *Blewitt Springs, Fleurieu Peninsula*
SOUTH, AUS   IE| B+   PV| WPL| $15   B+

Hogue, 1999 *Genesis, Columbia Valley*
WA, USA   IE| B+   PV| WPL| $16   B+

Honig, 1999 *Napa Valley*
CA, USA   IE| A   PV| WPL| S $30   A

Justin, 2000 *Paso Robles, San Luis Obispo Co.*
CA, USA   IE| A-   PV| 99 A   WPL| $23   A-

Kangarilla Road, 1999 *McLaren Vale*
SOUTH, AUS   IE| A-   PV| WPL| $23   A-

Kiona, 1999
WA, USA   IE| A+   PV| WPL| $24   A+

KWV, 2000
WESTERN CAPE, SA IE| A-   PV| WPL| B $10   A-

Laborie, 2001
PAARL, SA   IE| B+   PV| WPL| $12   B+

Lazzaro, 2000
MENDOZA, SP   IE| B+   PV| WPL| **$12 B+**

Leasingham, 1999 *Cabernet Sauvignon, Bin 56, Clare Valley*
SOUTH, AUS   IE| A-, B+, B+ PV| WPL| **$19 B+**

Lindemans, 1999 *St. George, Coonawarra*
SOUTH, AUS   IE| A   PV| WPL| S   **$27 A**

Lolonis, 1999 *Redwood Valley, Mendocino Co.*
CA, USA   IE| B+   PV| WPL| **$20 B+**

Madfish, 2001 *Cabernet Sauvignon-Merlot-Cabernet Franc*
WESTERN, AUS   IE| B+   PV| WPL| **$14 B+**

Markham, 1999 *Napa Valley*
CA, USA   IE| A-   PV| WPL| S   **$26 A-**

Marquis Philips, 2001 *McLaren Vale*
SOUTH EASTERN, AUS   IE| A-   PV| WPL| **$23 A-**

Marquis Philips, 2000
SOUTH EASTERN, AUS   IE| A, B+, B PV| WPL| W   **$15 B+**

Martin Ray, 1999 *Mariage, Napa Valley, Sonoma & Mendocino*
CA, USA   IE| A-   PV| WPL| **$24 A-**

Mas Carlot, 2000 *Cabernet Sauvignon-Syrah, Vin de Pays d'Oc*
LANGUEDOC, FR   IE| A-   PV| WPL| **$12 A-**

Mas de Guiot, 2000 *Cabernet Sauvignon-Syrah, Vin de Pays du Gard*
LANGUEDOC, FR   IE| A-   PV| WPL| **$14 A-**

Morandé, 1999 *Maipo Valley*
CENTRAL VALLEY, CH   IE| A   PV| WPL| S   **$30 A**

Murphy-Goode, 2000 *Alexander Valley, Sonoma Co.*
CA, USA   IE| A   PV| WPL| **$22 A**

Pedroncelli, 1999 *Three Vineyards, Dry Creek Valley, Sonoma Co.*
CA, USA   IE| A   PV| WPL| **$12 A**

Penfolds, 2000 *Cabernet Sauvignon-Shiraz, Bin 389*
SOUTH, AUS   IE| A-   PV| WPL| S   **$26 A-**

Penfolds, 1999 *Bin 407*
SOUTH, AUS   IE| A   PV| WPL| S   **$26 A**

Perry Creek, 1999 *El Dorado Co., Sierra Foothills*
CA, USA   IE| A-   PV| WPL| **$14 A-**

Peterson, 1999 *Bradford Mountain, Dry Creek Valley, Sonoma Co.*
CA, USA   IE| A-, B+ PV| WPL| S,BBC **$28 A-**

Pine Ridge, 1999 *Rutherford, Napa Valley*
CA, USA   IE| A-   PV| WPL| S   **$30 A-**

Powers, 2000
WA, USA   IE| A   PV| WPL| B   **$10 A**

Ridge, 1999 *Santa Cruz Mountains Cabernert Sauvignon, Santa Cruz Mountains*
CA, USA   IE| A   PV| WPL| S   **$30 A**

Rodney Strong, 2000 *Sonoma Co.*
CA, USA   IE| A-   PV| WPL| **$18 A-**

Rodney Strong, 1999 *Alexander's Crown Vineyard, Alexander Valley, Sonoma Co.*
CA, USA   IE| A   PV| WPL| S   **$28 A**

REDS
SORTED BY TYPE

CABERNET SAUVIGNON (CONTINUED)

Rosemount, 2000 *Orange Vineyard,*
NEW SOUTH WALES, AUS IE| A-   PV| WPL| $24 A-

Rosemount, 2000 *Show Reserve, Coonawarra*
SOUTH, AUS   IE| A-   PV| WPL| $24 A-

Rosemount, 2000 *Hill of Gold, Mudgee*
NEW SOUTH WALES, AUS IE| A-   PV| WPL| $19 A-

Rosemount, 1999 *Cabernet Sauvignon-Merlot-Petit Verdot, Traditional, McLaren Vale-Langhorne Creek*
SOUTH, AUS   IE| A-   PV| WPL| S $26 A-

Ross Andrews Winery, 1999 *Columbia Valley*
WA, USA   IE| A   PV| WPL| $25 A

Rust en Vrede, 1999
STELLENBOSCH, SA   IE| B+   PV| WPL| $20 B+

Rutherford Hill, 1999 *25th Anniversary, Napa Valley*
CA, USA   IE| A-   PV| WPL| S $30 A-

S. Anderson, 1999 *Stags' Leap District, Napa Valley*
CA, USA   IE| A+   PV| WPL| S $30 A+

Saint Chapelle, 2000 *Winemaker's Series*
ID, USA   IE| B+   PV| WPL| B $10 B+

Sandalford, 1999 *Mount Barker, Margaret River*
WESTERN, AUS   IE| A-   PV| WPL| $22 A-

Sandhill, 1999 *Red Mountain*
USA   IE| A+   PV| WPL| $25 A+

Santa Rita, 2000 *Reserva, Maipo Valley*
CENTRAL VALLEY, CH IE| B+   PV| 99 B+   WPL| W $13 B+

Sausal, 2000 *Sonoma Co.*
CA, USA   IE| A-   PV| WPL| S $26 A-

Sebastiani, 1999 *Russian River Valley, Sonoma Co.*
CA, USA   IE| B+   PV| WPL| W $20 B+

Sebastiani, 1999 *Sonoma Co. Selection, Sonoma Co.*
CA, USA   IE| A-   PV| WPL| $17 A-

Sebastiani, 1999 *Appellation SelectionAlexander Valley, Sonoma Co.*
CA, USA   IE| A, A-, B+ PV| WPL| BBC $24 A-

Sequoia Grove, 1999 *Napa Valley*
CA, USA   IE| A   PV| WPL| S $29 A

Seven Peaks, 1999 *Cabernet Sauvignon-Shiraz, Central Coast*
CA, USA   IE| A-   PV| WPL| $20 A-

Simi, 1999 *Alexander Valley, Sonoma Co.*
CA, USA   IE| A-   PV| WPL| W $25 A-

Sineann, 2000 *McDuffee Vineyard, Columbia Valley*
WA, USA   IE| A   PV| WPL| S $27 A

Siskiyou, 2000 *La Cave Rouge*
OR, USA   IE| A   PV| WPL| $12 A

Soos Creek, 1999 *Champoux Vineyard, Columbia Valley*					
WA, USA	IE| A, B+	PV|	WPL| S,BBC	$30	A-
Soos Creek, 1999 *Columbia Valley*					
WA, USA	IE| A	PV|	WPL| S	$30	A
Sticks, 2000 *Yarra Valley*					
AUS	IE| A-	PV|	WPL|	$13	A-
Terra Rosa, 2000					
MENDOZA, ARG	IE| B+	PV|	WPL| B	$10	B+
Thelema, 2000					
STELLENBOSCH, SA	IE| A	PV| 99 A	WPL| S	$30	A
Thelema, 1999					
STELLENBOSCH, SA	IE| A	PV|	WPL| S	$30	A
Three Rivers Winery, 2000 *Columbia Valley*					
WA, USA	IE| B+	PV|	WPL|	$20	B+
Tim Adams, 1999 *Clare Valley*					
SOUTH, AUS	IE| A-	PV|	WPL|	$22	A-
Trentadue, 2000 *Sonoma Co.*					
CA, USA	IE| A-	PV|	WPL|	$22	A-
Valdivieso, 2000 *Reserve, Central Valley*					
CA, USA	IE| B+	PV|	WPL|	$20	B+
Veramonte, 2001 *Maipo Valley*					
CENTRAL VALLEY, CH	IE| B+	PV|	WPL| B	$10	B+
Villa Mt. Eden, 1999 *Grand Reserve, Napa Valley*					
CA, USA	IE| A	PV|	WPL|	$20	A
Voyager, 1999 *Margaret River*					
SOUTH, AUS	IE| A-	PV|	WPL| S	$27	A-
Wakefield, 1999 *Promised Land, Clare Valley*					
SOUTH, AUS	IE| B+	PV|	WPL|	$11	B+
Washington Hills, 2000 *Columbia Valley*					
WA, USA	IE| B+	PV|	WPL| B	$10	B+
Waterbrook, 1999 *Red Mountain*					
WA, USA	IE| B+	PV|	WPL|	$15	B+
Wolf Blass, 1999 *Grey Label Cabernet Sauvignon Shiraz, Langhorne Creek*					
SOUTH, AUS	IE| A	PV|	WPL|	$19	A
Wynns Coonawarra, 1999 *Estate Cabernet Sauvignon, Coonawarra*					
SOUTH, AUS	IE| A-	PV|	WPL|	$15	A-
Xanadu, 1999 *Margaret River*					
WESTERN, AUS	IE| A-	PV|	WPL|	$18	A-
Yarra Burn, 2000 *Yarra Valley*					
VICTORIA, AUS	IE| A-, B+	PV| 99 A	WPL| BBC	$21	A-
Yarra Burn, 1999 *Yarra Valley*					
VICTORIA, AUS	IE| A	PV|	WPL|	$20	A

REDS SORTED BY TYPE

CARMENÈRE

Apaltagua, 2001 *Carmenère, Colchagua Valley*					
CH	IE| B+	PV|	WPL| B	$10	B+

Apaltagua, 2000 *Carmenère, Colchagua Valley*
CH   IE| B+   PV| WPL| $15   B+

Carmen, 2000 *Carmenère-Cabernet Sauvignon, Reserve, Maipo Valley*
CENTRAL VALLEY, CH   IE| B+   PV| 99 B+   WPL| $15   B+

Casa Rivas, 2001 *Carmenère, Gran Reserva, Maipo Valley*
CENTRAL VALLEY, CH   IE| B+   PV| WPL| $13   B+

Concha y Toro, 2000 *Carmenère, Terrunyo, Peumo Valley, Rapel Valley*
CENTRAL VALLEY, CH   IE| A-, A-   PV| 99 A   WPL| S,BBC $29   A-

Odfjell, 2001 *Carmenère, Maipo Valley*
CENTRAL VALLEY, CH   IE| B+   PV| WPL| $15   B+

Santa Carolina, 2000 *Carmenère, Barrica Selection, Colchagua Valley, Maipo Valley*
CENTRAL VALLEY, CH   IE| B+   PV| WPL| $12   B+

Valette Fontaine, 1999 *Cabernet/Carmenère, Memorias, Maipo Valley*
CENTRAL VALLEY, CH   IE| A-   PV| WPL| S $28   A-

CHIANTI

Banfi, 1998 *Classico, Chianti Classico*
TUSCANY, IT   IE| B+   PV| WPL| $17   B+

Le Corti, 2000 *Chianti Classico*
TUSCANY, IT   IE| B+   PV| 99 B+   WPL| $14   B+

Castello di Monsanto, 1999 *Riserva, Chianti Classico*
TUSCANY, IT   IE| A-   PV| WPL| $23   A-

Castello Vicchiomaggio, 1998 *La Prima Reserva, Chianti Classico*
TUSCANY, IT   IE| A   PV| WPL| $25   A

CLARET

Andretti, 1999 *Claret*
CA, USA   IE| A-   PV| WPL| $15   A-

Francis Coppola, 2000 *Claret, Diamond Series, Black Label*
CA, USA   IE| A-   PV| WPL| $17   A-

Newton, 1999 *Claret, Napa Valley*
CA, USA   IE| A-   PV| WPL| $22   A-

Murphy-Goode, 2000 *Claret, Wild Card, Alexander Valley, Sonoma Co.*
CA, USA   IE| A-   PV| WPL| $19   A-

DOLCETTO

Abacela, 2000 *Umpqua Valley*
OR, USA   IE| B+, B   PV| WPL| $18   B+

Francesco Boschis, 1998 *Vigna dei Prey, Dogliani*
PIEDMONT, IT   IE| A, A-   PV| WPL| BBC $17   A-

Luigi Einaudi, 2000 *Vigna Tecc, Dogliani*
PIEDMONT, IT   IE| A-   PV| WPL| $21   A-

Fratelli Pecchenino, 2000 *Siri d'Jermu, Dogliani*
PIEDMONT, IT   IE| A-, A   PV| 99 A-   WPL| S,BBC $29   A

GAMAY

Georges Duboeuf, 2000 *Prestige, Morgon*
BEAUJOLAIS, FR   IE| A-, A-, B   PV| WPL| BBC $14 A-

Georges Duboeuf, 2001 *Dom. Jean Descombes, Morgon*
BEAUJOLAIS, FR   IE| B+   PV| 99 A-, 00 A- WPL| $12 B+

Georges Duboeuf, 2000 *Prestige, Brouilly*
BEAUJOLAIS, FR   IE| A-, B+, B-   PV| WPL| $14 B+

Georges Duboeuf, 2000 *Prestige, Fleurie*
BEAUJOLAIS, FR   IE| B+, B+, B, B+   PV| WPL| $13 B+

Dom. Jean Foillard, 2000 *Première, Morgon*
BEAUJOLAIS, FR   IE| A   PV| WPL| $21 A

Potel-Aviron, 2000 *Morgon*
BEAUJOLAIS, FR   IE| A-   PV| WPL| $17 A-

Sandhill, 2001 *Gamay Noir, Burrowing Owl Vineyard, Okanagan Valley*
BC, CAN   IE| B+   PV| WPL| $11 B+

Sandstone, 2000 *Reserve, Niagara Peninsula*
ONTARIO, CAN   IE| A   PV| 99 A   WPL| $19 A

GRENACHE

Beckmen, 2000 *Purisima Mountain Vineyard, Santa Ynez Valley,*
Santa Barbara Co.
CA, USA   IE| B+, B   PV| WPL| $18 B+

Borja, 2001 *Borsao, 3 Picos*
CAMPO DE BORJA, SP IE| A-   PV| 00 A-   WPL| B $10 A-

Borja, 2001 *Borsao*
CAMPO DE BORJA, SP IE| B+   PV| 00 B+   WPL| B $6 B+

Fifteen, 2001 *Vin de Pays de Pyrénées Orientales*
FR   IE| B+, B   PV| 00 A-   WPL| $15 B+

Jaffurs, 2000 *Stolpman Family Vineyard, Santa Barbara Co.*
CA, USA   IE| B+   PV| WPL| $20 B+

Castillo de Maluenda, 2001 *Viña Alarba, Old Vines*
CALATAYUD, SP   IE| B+   PV| WPL| B $6 B+

Castillo de Maluenda, 2001 *Viña Alarba*
CALATAYUD, SP   IE| B+   PV| WPL| B $6 B+

Philip Staley, 1999 *Staley Vineyard, Russian River Valley, Sonoma Co.*
CA, USA   IE| B+, B   PV| WPL| $18 B+

Dom. de Saint-Antoine, 2001 *Vin de Pays du Gard*
LANGUEDOC, FR   IE| B+   PV| WPL| B $9 B+

Yalumba, 2000 *Tricentenary Vines, Barossa Valley*
SOUTH, AUS   IE| B+   PV| WPL| S $30 B+

Yalumba, 2000 *Bush Vine, Barossa Valley*
SOUTH, AUS   IE| A-   PV| WPL| $15 A-

MALBEC

Broquel, 2000
MENDOZA, ARG   IE| B+   PV| WPL| $15 B+

REDS
SORTED BY TYPE

Cavas del Valle, 2000
MENDOZA, ARG   IE| B+   PV| WPL| $15   B+

Davis Family, 2000 *Gusto Vita*
MENDOZA, ARG   IE| A-   PV| WPL| S $30   A-

Felipe Rutini, 2000
TUPUNGATO, ARG   IE| A-   PV| WPL| $18   A-

Montes, 2001 *Reserve, Colchagua Valley, Rapel Valley*
CENTRAL VALLEY, CH   IE| B+   PV| WPL| W, B $10   B+

Susana Balbo, 2001 *Mendoza Crios*
MENDOZA, ARG   IE| B+   PV| WPL| $15   B+

Terra Mater, 1999 *Curico Valley*
CENTRAL VALLEY, CH   IE| B+   PV| WPL| B $9   B+

Vinterra, 1999
LUJAN DE CUYO, ARG   IE| A-   PV| WPL| $15   A-

MERLOT

Alexander Valley, 2000 *Alexander Valley, Sonoma Co.*
CA, USA   IE| B+   PV| WPL| $20   B+

Andretti, 1999 *Napa Valley*
CA, USA   IE| A, B+   PV| WPL| BBC $20   A-

Arrowood, 1999 *Grand Archer, Sonoma Co.*
CA, USA   IE| A-   PV| WPL| $20   A-

Atalon, 1999 *Napa Valley*
CA, USA   IE| A   PV| WPL| S $29   A

Barefoot, 1999 *Reserve, Sonoma Co.*
CA, USA   IE| A-   PV| WPL| $17   A-

Barnard Griffin, 2000 *Columbia Valley*
WA, USA   IE| B+   PV| WPL| $15   B+

Barton & Guestier, 2000 *Premium Merlot, Vin de Pays d'Oc*
LANGUEDOC, FR   IE| B+   PV| WPL| $13   B+

Beaulieu (BV), 1999 *Napa Valley*
CA, USA   IE| A-   PV| WPL| $18   A-

Benziger, 2000 *Sonoma Co.*
CA, USA   IE| B+   PV| 99 B+   WPL| $19   B+

Bolla, 2000 *Colforte*
VENETO, IT   IE| B+   PV| WPL| $15   B+

Boutari, 2000 *Merlot-Xinomavro, Imathia*
GRC   IE| B+   PV| 99 B+   WPL| $11   B+

Buena Vista, 2000
CA, USA   IE| B+   PV| WPL| B $9   B+

Canoe Ridge, 2000 *Columbia Valley*
CA, USA   IE| A, A   PV| WPL| BBC $25   A

Carmen, 2000 *Reserve, Maipo Valley*
CENTRAL VALLEY, CH   IE| B+   PV| WPL| $15   B+

Carmenet, 2000 *Dynamite, North Coast*
CA, USA   IE| B+   PV| 99 A-   WPL| W $18   B+

Casa Julia, 2001
CH   IE| B+   PV| WPL| B   **$9**   B+

Casa Lapostolle, 2001 *Rapel Valley*
CENTRAL VALLEY, CH   IE| B+   PV| WPL| **$12**   B+

Caterina, 1999 *DuBrul Vineyard, Yakima Valley*
WA, USA   IE| A   PV| WPL| S   **$30**   A

Caterina, 1999 *Columbia Valley*
WA, USA   IE| B+   PV| WPL| **$20**   B+

Ch. Souverain, 2000 *Alexander Valley, Sonoma Co.*
CA, USA   IE| B+   PV| WPL| **$18**   B+

Ch. Ste. Michelle, 1999 *Canoe Ridge Estate Vineyard, Columbia Valley*
WA, USA   IE| A, A-, B   PV| WPL| BBC   **$23**   A-

Ch. Ste. Michelle, 2000 *Canoe Ridge Estate Vineyard, Columbia Valley*
WA, USA   IE| B+, B+   PV| WPL| **$24**   B+

Chappellet, 1999 *Napa Valley*
CA, USA   IE| A+, A   PV| WPL| BBC   **$25**   A+

Chappellet, 2000 *Napa Valley*
CA, USA   IE| A+   PV| WPL| S   **$26**   A+

Cinnabar, 2000 *Paso Robles, San Luis Obispo Co.*
CA, USA   IE| B+   PV| WPL| **$14**   B+

Clos du Val, 1999 *Napa Valley*
CA, USA   IE| A-, B   PV| WPL| **$25**   B+

Clos la Chance, 2001 *Central Coast*
CA, USA   IE| A-   PV| WPL| **$18**   A-

Clos Pegase, 1999 *Mitsuko's Vineyard, Carneros, Napa Valley*
CA, USA   IE| A+   PV| WPL| **$25**   A+

Columbia Crest, 1999 *Reserve, Columbia Valley*
WA, USA   IE| A-, A   PV| WPL| S,BBC   **$28**   A

Concha y Toro, 2000 *Peuma Marques de Casa Concha*
CH   IE| B+   PV| WPL| **$14**   B+

Crystal Valley, 2000 *Reserve*
CA, USA   IE| A-   PV| WPL| **$16**   A-

Dashe, 2000 *Potter Valley, Mendocino Co.*
CA, USA   IE| A   PV| WPL| S   **$26**   A

Davis Bynum, 1999 *Laureles, Russian River Valley, Sonoma Co.*
CA, USA   IE| A   PV| WPL| S   **$28**   A

De Loach, 1999 *Estate Bottled, Russian River Valley, Sonoma Co.*
CA, USA   IE| B+   PV| WPL| **$20**   B+

Du Preez, 2000
GOUDINI VALLEY, SA   IE| B+   PV| WPL| **$11**   B+

Dunnewood, 1999 *Mendocino Co.*
CA, USA   IE| B+, B   PV| WPL| B   **$9**   B+

Estancia, 2000 *Alexander Valley, Sonoma Co.*
CA, USA   IE| B+   PV| WPL| **$16**   B+

Fetzer, 1999 *Barrel Select, Sonoma Co.*
CA, USA   IE| B+   PV| WPL| **$13**   B+

REDS
SORTED BY TYPE

MERLOT (CONTINUED)

Flora Springs, 2000 *Napa Valley*
CA, USA   IE| A   PV| WPL| $22 A

Frei Brothers, 2001 *Reserve, Dry Creek Valley, Sonoma Co.*
CA, USA   IE| B+   PV| WPL| $20 B+

Gainey, 1999 *Santa Ynez Valley, Santa Barbara Co.*
CA, USA   IE| A, B   PV| WPL| $20 B+

Hogue, 1999 *Vinyard Selection, Columbia Valley*
WA, USA   IE| A-   PV| WPL| W $18 A-

Hogue, 1999 *Reserve, Columbia Valley*
WA, USA   IE| A-   PV| WPL| S $30 A-

Huntington Cellars, 2000 *Alexander Valley, Sonoma Co.*
CA, USA   IE| A-   PV| WPL| $18 A-

Iron Horse, 1999 *T Bar T Vineyard, Alexander Valley, Sonoma Co.*
CA, USA   IE| B+   PV| WPL| S $26 B+

Isenhower Cellars, 1999 *Columbia Valley*
WA, USA   IE| A-   PV| WPL| $22 A-

Judd Hill, 1999 *Napa Valley*
CA, USA   IE| A-   PV| WPL| S $26 A-

Ktima Kyr-Yianni, 1999 *Imathia Yiannakohori*
NÁOUSSA, GRC   IE| A   PV| WPL| S $28 A

KWV, 2001
WESTERN CAPE, SA   IE| B+   PV| WPL| B $10 B+

Lakeview, 1999 *Reserve, Niagara Peninsula*
ONTARIO, CAN   IE| A   PV| WPL| $23 A

Lambert Bridge, 1999 *Sonoma Co.*
CA, USA   IE| A, A, B+, B, B   PV| WPL| $24 B+

L'Ecole No. 41, 2000 *Columbia Valley*
WA, USA   IE| A-, A-   PV| WPL| S,BBC $30 A-

Liparita, 1999 *Napa Valley*
CA, USA   IE| A   PV| WPL| S $28 A

Louis M. Martini, 1999 *Del Rio Vineyard, Russian River Valley, Sonoma Co.*
CA, USA   IE| A-, A-   PV| WPL| BBC $22 A-

MacRostie, 1999 *Carneros, Napa Valley*
CA, USA   IE| B+   PV| WPL| S $26 B+

Madrigal, 1999 *Napa Valley*
CA, USA   IE| B+, B+   PV| WPL| S $28 B+

Madrigal, 2000 *Napa Valley*
CA, USA   IE| A   PV| 99 B+   WPL| S $28 A

McCray Ridge, 1999 *Two Moon Vineyard, Dry Creek Valley, Sonoma Co.*
CA, USA   IE| B+   PV| WPL| S $29 B+

Mills Reef, 2000 *Elspeth Syrah, Mere Road Vineyard*
HAWKES BAY, NZ   IE| A   PV| WPL| S $30 A

Dom. des Molines, 2000 *Vin de Pays du Gard*
LANGUEDOC, FR   IE| B+   PV| WPL| B $10 B+

Montes, 2000 *Alpha, Apalta Vineyard, Santa Cruz*
CENTRAL VALLEY, CH   IE| A-   PV| WPL| $22   A-

Monticello, 1999 *Corley Family, Napa Valley*
CA, USA   IE| A+   PV| WPL| S $30   A+

Morandé, 2001 *Vitisterra Grand Reserve, Maipo Valley*
CENTRAL VALLEY, CH   IE| B+   PV| WPL| $15   B+

Murphy-Goode, 1999 *Alexander Valley, Sonoma Co.*
CA, USA   IE| B+, B+, B   PV| WPL| $19   B+

Murphy-Goode, 2000 *Alexander Valley, Sonoma Co.*
CA, USA   IE| A-, B+   PV| 99 B+   WPL| BBC $19   A-

Porcupine Ridge, 2001
COASTAL REGION, SA   IE| B+   PV| WPL| $13   B+

Richard Hamilton, 2000 *Lot 148, McLaren Vale*
SOUTH, AUS   IE| A   PV| WPL| $17   A

Sagelands, 2000 *Four Corners, Columbia Valley*
WA, USA   IE| A-, B   PV| WPL| $15   B+

Saint Chapelle, 2000 *Winemaker's Series*
ID, USA   IE| B+   PV| WPL| B $10   B+

Sandhill, 1999 *Red Mountain*
USA   IE| A-   PV| WPL| $20   A-

Selby, 1999 *Sonoma Co.*
CA, USA   IE| A, A, A-   PV| WPL| BBC $24   A

Robert Skalli, 2000 *Vin de Pays D'oc*
LANGUEDOC, FR   IE| B+   PV| WPL| B $10   B+

Snoqualmie, 1999 *Columbia Valley*
WA, USA   IE| B+   PV| WPL| $11   B+

Steltzner, 1999 *Stags Leap District, Napa Valley*
CA, USA   IE| A   PV| WPL| S $26   A

Stoney Ridge, 1999 *Reserve, Niagara Peninsula*
ONTARIO, CAN   IE| B+   PV| WPL| $14   B+

Sumac Ridge, 1999 *Black Sage Vineyard, Okanagan Valley*
BC, CAN   IE| A   PV| WPL| $11   A

Thelema, 1999
STELLENBOSCH, SA   IE| A-   PV| WPL| S $27   A-

Three Rivers Winery, 2000 *Columbia Valley*
WA, USA   IE| A-   PV| WPL| S $26   A-

Trefethen, 1999 *Napa Valley*
CA, USA   IE| A-   PV| WPL| S $26   A-

Trentadue, 2000 *Alexander Valley, Sonoma Co.*
CA, USA   IE| B+   PV| WPL| $20   B+

Trinchero, 1999 *French Camp Vineyard, Rutherford, Napa Valley*
CA, USA   IE| B+   PV| WPL| $25   B+

V. Sattui, 1999 *Napa Valley*
CA, USA   IE| A-   PV| WPL| $24   A-

W. B. Bridgman, 1999 *Columbia Valley*
WA, USA   IE| B+   PV| WPL| $19   B+

REDS
SORTED BY TYPE

Walla Walla Vintners, 2000 *Walla Walla Valley*
WA, USA   IE| A   PV| WPL| $25   A

Waterbrook, 1999 *Red Mountain*
WA, USA   IE| B+   PV| WPL| $15   B+

White Oak, 2000 *Napa Valley*
CA, USA   IE| A, A   PV| WPL| S,BBC $28   A

White Oak, 1999 *Sonoma Co.*
CA, USA   IE| A-   PV| WPL| $25   A-

Whitehall Lane, 1998 *Knights Valley, Sonoma Co.*
CA, USA   IE| B+   PV| WPL| $24   B+

PETITE SIRAH

David Bruce, 2000 *Paso Robles, San Luis Obispo Co.*
CA, USA   IE| B+   PV| 99 B+   WPL| $16   B+

EOS, 1999 *Reserve, Paso Robles, San Luis Obispo Co.*
CA, USA   IE| A   PV| WPL| $25   A

Markham, 1999 *Napa Valley*
CA, USA   IE| A   PV| WPL| $23   A

Novella, 2000 *Paso Robles, San Luis Obispo Co.*
CA, USA   IE| B+   PV| WPL| $13   B+

Rockland, 2000 *Napa Valley*
CA, USA   IE| A-   PV| WPL| S $30   A-

Rosenblum, 2000 *Pickett Road, Napa Valley*
CA, USA   IE| A+   PV| WPL| S $28   A+

Sable Ridge, 1999 *Russian River Valley, Sonoma Co.*
CA, USA   IE| A   PV| WPL| S $28   A

PINOT NOIR

Acacia, 2001 *Napa Valley/Carneros*
CA, USA   IE| B+   PV| WPL| W $20   B+

Amity, 2000 *Schouten Vineyard, Willamette Valley*
OR, USA   IE| B+   PV| WPL| $15   B+

Argyle, 2000 *Reserve, Willamette Valley*
OR, USA   IE| A   PV| WPL| S $30   A

Artesa, 2000 *Carneros*
CA, USA   IE| A   PV| 99 B+   WPL| $24   A

Au Bon Climat, 2001 *Santa Maria Valley, Santa Barbara Co.*
CA, USA   IE| A   PV| WPL| $20   A

Beaulieu (BV), 2000 *Carneros*
CA, USA   IE| B+   PV| WPL| $18   B+

Bella Glos, 2001 *Santa Maria Valley, Santa Barbara Co.*
CA, USA   IE| A   PV| WPL| S $30   A

Beringer, 1999 *Stanly Ranch, Los Carneros, Napa Valley*
CA, USA   IE| A   PV| WPL| S $30   A

Carneros Creek, 2000 *Los Carneros*
CA, USA   IE| A-   PV| WPL| $24   A-

Castle, 1999 *Sangiacoma Vineyard, Carneros*
CA, USA   IE| A-   PV| WPL| S $30   A-

Ch. Bianca, 2000
OR, USA   IE| B+   PV| WPL| $12   B+

Charles Krug, 1999 *Carneros, Napa Valley*
CA, USA   IE| B+   PV| WPL| $18   B+

Clos du Bois, 2001 *Sonoma Co.*
CA, USA   IE| B+   PV| WPL| $17   B+

Cosentino, 2000 *Carneros*
CA, USA   IE| A, B+   PV| WPL| S,BBC $30   A-

Davis Bynum, 2000 *Russian River Valley, Sonoma Co.*
CA, USA   IE| A-   PV| WPL| S $30   A-

Dom. Serene, 2000 *Cuvée, Carlton*
OR, USA   IE| A+, B+   PV| WPL| S,BBC $30   A

Edmeades, 1999 *Anderson Valley, Mendocino Co.*
CA, USA   IE| A-   PV| WPL| $20   A-

Edna Valley, 2001 *Paragon, Edna Valley, San Luis Obispo Co.*
CA, USA   IE| B+, A-   PV| WPL| $15   A-

Elk Cove, 2000 *Willamette Valley*
OR, USA   IE| B+   PV| WPL| $20   B+

Eyrie, 2000 *Estate Grown, Willamette Valley*
OR, USA   IE| B+   PV| WPL| $25   B+

Foxen, 2000 *Santa Maria Valley, Santa Barbara Co.*
CA, USA   IE| A-   PV| WPL| $24   A-

Francis Coppola, 2001 *Diamond Series, Monterey Co.*
CA, USA   IE| B+   PV| WPL| $17   B+

Gibbston Valley, 2001
CENTRAL OTAGO, NZ   IE| A-   PV| WPL| S $30   A-

Gloria Ferrer, 2000 *Carneros*
CA, USA   IE| A   PV| WPL| $24   A

Hatcher Wineworks, 2001 *A to Z, Willamette Valley*
OR, USA   IE| B+   PV| WPL| $19   B+

Iron Horse, 2000 *Green Valley, Sonoma Co.*
CA, USA   IE| B+, A   PV| 99 A   WPL| S $30   A-

Joseph Swan, 2000 *Cuvée de Trois, Russian River Valley, Sonoma Co.*
CA, USA   IE| B+   PV| WPL| $20   B+

Kendall-Jackson, 1999 *Great Estates, Monterey Co.*
CA, USA   IE| A   PV| WPL| S $30   A

Kenwood, 2000 *Reserve, Olivet Vineyards, Sonoma Co.*
CA, USA   IE| A-   PV| WPL| S $30   A-

Keyhole Ranch, 2000 *Sonoma Co.*
CA, USA   IE| A   PV| WPL| $25   A

King , 1999 *Eugene*
OR, USA   IE| A-, B+   PV| WPL| BBC $20   A-

King Estate, 2000
OR, USA   IE| B+   PV| WPL| $20   B+

PINOT NOIR (CONTINUED)

La Crema, 2000 *Anderson Valley, Mendocino Co.*
CA, USA   IE| A, A-   PV| WPL| BBC $25   A

La Crema, 2000 *Carneros*
CA, USA   IE| A   PV| WPL| $20   A

La Crema, 2000 *Estate, Carneros*
CA, USA   IE| B+, A-   PV| WPL| $25   A-

Laetitia, 1999 *Santa Barbara Co.*
CA, USA   IE| A   PV| WPL| $25   A

Lane Tanner, 2000 *Julia's Vineyard, Santa Maria Valley, Santa Barbara Co.*
CA, USA   IE| A, B+   PV| WPL| S,BBC $30   A-

Lane Tanner, 2000 *Bien Nicido Vineyard, Santa Maria Valley, Santa Barbara Co.*
CA, USA   IE| A   PV| WPL| S $28   A

Lane Tanner, 2000 *Santa Maria Valley, Santa Barbara Co.*
CA, USA   IE| A-   PV| WPL| $23   A-

Lane Tanner, 2000 *Melville Vineyard, Santa Ynez Valley, Santa Barbara Co.*
CA, USA   IE| A-   PV| WPL| $25   A-

Lemelson, 2001 *Rose Pinot Noir*
OR, USA   IE| B+   PV| WPL| $13   B+

Lemelson, 2000 *Thea's Selection, Willamette Valley*
OR, USA   IE| A-, A-, B+   PV| WPL| S,BBC $29   A-

Libelula, 1999 *Sonoma Coast*
CA, USA   IE| A   PV| WPL| S $28   A

LinCourt, 1999 *Santa Barbara Co.*
CA, USA   IE| A-   PV| WPL| $22   A-

Melville, 2000 *Santa Rita Hills, Santa Barbara Co.*
CA, USA   IE| A-   PV| WPL| $24   A-

Meridian, 1999 *Limited Release, Santa Barbara Co.*
CA, USA   IE| A   PV| WPL| $22   A

Mirassou, 1999 *Harvest Reserve, Monterey Co.*
CA, USA   IE| B+   PV| WPL| $15   B+

Montinore, 2000 *Winemaker's Reserve, Willamette Valley*
OR, USA   IE| B+   PV| WPL| $19   B+

Morgan, 2000 *Santa Lucia Highlands, Monterey Co.*
CA, USA   IE| A-, B+   PV| WPL| BBC $22   A-

Mountford, 2001
WAIPARA VALLEY, NZ   IE| A-   PV| WPL| S $30   A-

Nautilus, 2001
MARLBOROUGH, NZ   IE| A-   PV| WPL| $20   A-

Newton, 1999 *Sonoma Valley, Sonoma Co.*
CA, USA   IE| A-   PV| WPL| S $30   A-

Luis Pato, 2000 *Quinta do Ribeirinho Primeira Escolha*
BEIRAS, POR   IE| A-   PV| WPL| S $29   A-

Patton Valley Vineyard, 2000 *Willamette Valley*
OR, USA   IE| A   PV| WPL| S $30   A

Pedroncelli, 2000 *F. Johnson Vineyard, Dry Creek Valley, Sonoma Co.*
CA, USA   IE| B+   PV| WPL| $15   B+

Pencarrow, 2001 *Palliser Estate*
MARTINBOROUGH, NZ   IE| A-   PV| WPL| $20   A-

Rex Hill, 1999 *Willamette Valley*
OR, USA   IE| A-   PV| WPL| $24   A-

Robert Stemmler, 2000 *Sonoma Co.*
CA, USA   IE| B+   PV| WPL| S $28   B+

Rodney Strong, 1999 *Reserve, Russian River Valley, Sonoma Co.*
CA, USA   IE| A-   PV| WPL| S $30   A-

Rutz, 1999 *Martinelli Vineyard, Russian River Valley, Sonoma Co.*
CA, USA   IE| B+, B+   PV| WPL| S $30   B+

Rutz, 1999 *Dutton Ranch, Russian River Valley, Sonoma Co.*
CA, USA   IE| A   PV| WPL| S $30   A

Saint Gregory, 1999 *Mendocino Co.*
CA, USA   IE| B+   PV| WPL| $18   B+

Saintsbury, 2000 *Carneros*
CA, USA   IE| A, B+, B, B+ PV| WPL| W $24   B+

Saintsbury, 2001 *Carneros*
CA, USA   IE| B+   PV| 00 B+   WPL| $17   B+

Saintsbury, 2001 *Garnet, Carneros*
CA, USA   IE| A-   PV| 00 B   WPL| S $26   A-

Schug, 2000 *Carneros*
CA, USA   IE| B+   PV| WPL| $20   B+

Schug, 2000 *Sonoma Valley, Sonoma Co.*
CA, USA   IE| B+   PV| WPL| $15   B+

Schug, 1999 *Heritage Reserve, Carneros*
CA, USA   IE| A   PV| WPL| S $30   A

Sebastiani, 2000 *Sonoma Coast, Sonoma Co.*
CA, USA   IE| B+, B, B+, B+   PV| WPL| $15   B+

Sebastiani, 2001 *Sonoma Coast, Sonoma Co.*
CA, USA   IE| B+   PV| 00 B+   WPL| $15   B+

Siduri, 2001 *Russian River Valley, Sonoma Co.*
CA, USA   IE| A, A-   PV| WPL| S $28   A

Talley, 2000 *Arroyo Grande Valley, San Luis Obispo Co.*
CA, USA   IE| A-, A-   PV| WPL| S,BBC $28   A-

Thomas Fogarty, 1999 *Santa Cruz Mountains*
CA, USA   IE| A-, B+   PV| WPL| BBC $23   A-

W. H. Smith, 2001 *Sonoma Coast*
CA, USA   IE| A-   PV| WPL| S $28   A-

Yerring Station, 2000 *Yarra Valley*
SOUTH EASTERN, AUS   IE| A+   PV| WPL| $22   A+

SANGIOVESE

Boscarelli, 1999 *Vino Nobile, Montepulciano*
TUSCANY, IT   IE| A-   PV| WPL| S $27   A-

REDS
SORTED BY TYPE

SANGIOVESE (CONTINUED)

Castello di Brolio, 1999 *Chianti Classico*
TUSCANY, IT   IE| B+   PV| WPL| $16   B+

Capezzana, 1999 *Conte Contini Bonacossi, Carmignano*
TUSCANY, IT   IE| A-, A-   PV| WPL| BBC $20   A-

Capezzana, 1999 *Carmignano*
TUSCANY, IT   IE| A   PV| WPL| $21   A

Carpineto, 1998 *Riserva, Chianti Classico*
TUSCANY, IT   IE| A-, A-   PV| WPL| W,BBC $22   A-

Casa Emma, 1999 *Riserva, Chianti Classico*
TUSCANY, IT   IE| A-   PV| WPL| $25   A-

Columbia, 1999 *David Lake Signature Series, Willow Vineyard, Yakima Valley*
WA, USA   IE| A-   PV| WPL| $25   A-

Conti Contini, 2001 *Bonacossi, Capezzana Barco Reale, Carmignano*
TUSCANY, IT   IE| A   PV| WPL| $15   A

Le Corti, 2000 *Don Tommaso, Chianti Classico*
TUSCANY, IT   IE| A-   PV| 99 B+   WPL| S $29   A-

Dei, 1999 *Vino Nobile, Montepulciano*
TUSCANY, IT   IE| A   PV| WPL| $24   A

Flora Springs, 1999 *Napa Valley*
CA, USA   IE| A-   PV| WPL| $16   A-

Frescobaldi, 1998 *Nipozzano Riserva, Chianti Classico*
TUSCANY, IT   IE| B+   PV| WPL| $15   B+

Castello di Gabbiano, 1999 *Riserva, Chianti Classico*
TUSCANY, IT   IE| A-   PV| WPL| $17   A-

Luna, 1999 *Napa Valley*
CA, USA   IE| A, B+, B+   PV| WPL| BBC $18   A-

La Massa, 2000 *Chianti Classico*
TUSCANY, IT   IE| A-   PV| 99 A+   WPL| $23   A-

Poggio Bertaio, 2000 *Cimbolo*
UMBRIA, IT   IE| A-   PV| WPL| $20   A-

Trenuta di Riseccoli, 1999 *Chianti Classico*
TUSCANY, IT   IE| B+   PV| WPL| $12   B+

Rocca di Fabbri, 2000 *Satiro, Colli Martani*
UMBRIA, IT   IE| B+   PV| WPL| $12   B+

Saddleback, 2000 *Venge Family Reserve Sangiovese,*
Penny Lane Vineyard, Napa Valley
CA, USA   IE| A   PV| WPL| S $30   A

Santa Anastasia, 1999 *Passomaggio*
SICILY, IT   IE| B+, A-   PV| WPL| W $14   A-

Selvapiana, 1999 *Bucerchiale Riserva, Chianti Rufina*
TUSCANY, IT   IE| A.   PV| WPL| S $30   A

Thurston Wolfe, 2000 *Columbia Valley*
WA, USA   IE| A   PV| WPL| $20   A

Venge Family, 2000 *Reserve, Penny Lane Vineyard, Oakville, Napa Valley*
CA, USA   IE| A-   PV| WPL| $20 A-

Castello Vicchiomaggio, 1998 *Petri Riserva, Chianti Classico*
TUSCANY, IT   IE| A-   PV| WPL| $24 A-

Villa Cafaggio, 1999 *Riserva, Chianti Classico*
TUSCANY, IT   IE| A-   PV| WPL| S $30 A-

Castello di Volpaia, 2000 *Classico, Chianti Classico*
TUSCANY, IT   IE| B+   PV| WPL| $17 B+

Waterbrook, 2000 *Ciel du Cheval Sangiovese, Red Mountain*
USA   IE| A-   PV| WPL| S $28 A-

SYRAH/SHIRAZ

Alexander Valley, 2000 *Alexander Valley, Sonoma Co.*
CA, USA   IE| B+, B   PV| WPL| $18 B+

Allandale, 2000 *Shiraz, Mathew, Hunter Valley*
NEW SOUTH WALES, AUS IE| B+   PV| WPL| $14 B+

Dom. d' Andezon, 2001 *Côtes du Rhône*
RHÔNE, FR   IE| B+   PV| 99 B+, 00 B+ WPL| $11 B+

Andrew Murray, 2001 *Tous les Jours, Central Coast*
CA, USA   IE| A-   PV| WPL| $16 A-

Andrew Murray, 2000 *Roasted Slope Vineyard, Santa Ynez Valley,
Santa Barbara Co.*
CA, USA   IE| A   PV| WPL| S $30 A

Andrew Rich, 2000 *Les Vigneaux, Columbia Valley*
WA, USA   IE| A-   PV| WPL| $21 A-

Annie's Lane, 2001 *Clare Valley*
SOUTH, AUS   IE| B+   PV| WPL| $13 B+

Annie's Lane, 1999 *Shiraz, Clare Valley*
SOUTH, AUS   IE| A-   PV| WPL| $15 A-

Baileyana, 2000 *Paso Robles, San Luis Obispo Co.*
CA, USA   IE| B+   PV| WPL| $18 B+

Balgownie Estate, 2000 *Beningo*
AUS   IE| A-   PV| WPL| $25 A-

Barossa Valley, 2000 *Ebenezer Shiraz, Barossa Valley*
SOUTH, AUS   IE| A   PV| 99 A-   WPL| S $30 A

Barossa Valley, 1999 *Ebenezer Shiraz, Barossa Valley*
SOUTH, AUS   IE| A-, A   PV| WPL| S,BBC $30 A

Baystone, 2000 *Shiraz, Dry Creek Valley, Sonoma Co.*
CA, USA   IE| B+   PV| WPL| $24 B+

Beckmen, 2000 *Santa Ynez Valley, Santa Barbara Co.*
CA, USA   IE| A-   PV| WPL| $24 A-

Bell, 1999 *Canterbury Vineyard, Sierra Foothills*
CA, USA   IE| A-   PV| WPL| $28 A-

Belnaves, 1998 *Coonawarra*
SOUTH, AUS   IE| A   PV| WPL| S $30 A

SYRAH/SHIRAZ (CONTINUED)

Belvedere, 1999 *Healdsburg Ranches, Sonoma Co.*
CA, USA IE| A PV| WPL| S $26 A

Benziger, 2000
CA, USA IE| A- PV| WPL| $22 A-

Beringer, 1999 *Shiraz, Founders' Estate*
CA, USA IE| A-, B- PV| WPL| $12 A-

Best's, 1998 *Shiraz, Bin O, Grampians*
VICTORIA, AUS IE| A PV| WPL| S $30 A

Dom. des Blageurs, 2000 *Syrah, Vin de Pays d'Oc*
LANGUEDOC, FR IE| A- PV| WPL| B $9 A-

Bridlewood, 2000 *Central Coast*
CA, USA IE| A-, B+ PV| WPL| BBC $19 A-

Burgess, 2000 *Napa Valley*
CA, USA IE| A-, B, B+ PV| WPL| $22 B+

Campbells, 1998 *Bobby Burns Shiraz, Rutherglen*
VICTORIA, AUS IE| A PV| WPL| $20 A

Dom. des Cantarelles, 2000 *Syrah-Cabernet Sauvignon, Vin de Pays du Gard*
LANGUEDOC, FR IE| B+, B PV| WPL| $13 B+

Canyon Road, 2000 *Shiraz*
CA, USA IE| B+, B PV| WPL| B $10 B+

Cedarville, 2000 *El Dorado Co., Sierra Foothills*
CA, USA IE| A PV| 99 A WPL| $25 A

Ch. Julien, 2000 *Monterey Co.*
CA, USA IE| B+ PV| WPL| B $10 B+

Ch. Reynella, 2000 *Shiraz, Basket Pressed, McLaren Vale*
SOUTH, AUS IE| A PV| 99 B+ WPL| S $28 A

Ch. Souverain, 2000 *Alexander Valley, Sonoma Co.*
CA, USA IE| B+, A-, B, A+ PV| WPL| BBC $20 A-

Ch. Ste. Michelle, 1999 *Reserve, Columbia Valley*
WA, USA IE| A-, A- PV| WPL| S,BBC $29 A-

Ch. Ste. Michelle, 2000 *Columbia Valley*
WA, USA IE| B+ PV| WPL| $15 B+

Chateau Xanadu, 2001 *Secession Shiraz-Cabernet*
WESTERN, AUS IE| B+ PV| WPL| B $10 B+

Chatter Creek, 2000 *Jack Jones Vineyard*
WA, USA IE| B+ PV| WPL| $20 B+

Chatter Creek, 2000 *Lonesome Spring Ranch*
WA, USA IE| A PV| WPL| $20 A

Cline, 2000 *Los Carneros*
CA, USA IE| A, A-, A-, A- PV| WPL| S,BBC $28 A-

Cline, 2000 *Sonoma Co.*
CA, USA IE| B+ PV| WPL| $16 B+

Clos du Bois, 1999 *Reserve Shiraz, Alexander Valley, Sonoma Co.*
CA, USA IE| B+ PV| WPL| $16 B+

Columbia, 2000 *Columbia Valley*
WA, USA   IE| B+   PV| WPL| $15   B+

Columbia Crest, 2000 *Reserve, Columbia Valley*
WA, USA   IE| A+   PV| 99 A-   WPL| S $28   A+

Columbia Winery, 2000 *Columbia Valley*
WA, USA   IE| B+   PV| WPL| $15   B+

Concannon, 1999 *San Francisco Bay*
CA, USA   IE| B+   PV| WPL| $19   B+

Dom. la Coste, 2000 *Ultra, Coteaux d'Aix-en-Provence*
PROVENCE, FR   IE| A-   PV| WPL| S $28   A-

Dom. de la Terre Rouge, 2000 *Sierra Foothills*
CA, USA   IE| A-   PV| WPL| $15   A-

Dom. de la Terre Rouge, 2000 *California les Cotes de L'Ouest, Plymouth*
CA, USA   IE| B+   PV| WPL| $15   B+

Dom. de la Terre Rouge, 1999 *Sierra Foothills*
CA, USA   IE| A+   PV| WPL| $22   A+

Edmunds St. John, 2001
CA, USA   IE| B+   PV| WPL| $18   B+

Edmunds St. John, 2000 *Wylie-Fenaughty, El Dorado Co., Sierra Foothills*
CA, USA   IE| A+, A-   PV| WPL| S,BBC $30   A

Equus, 1999 *Paso Robles, San Luis Obispo Co.*
CA, USA   IE| A, A-   PV| WPL| BBC $18   A

EXP, 2000 *Dunnigan Hills, Yolo Co.*
CA, USA   IE| B+   PV| WPL| $14   B+

Fairview, 2000
PAARL, SA   IE| A-   PV| WPL| S $28   A-

Fife, 2000 *Mendocino Co.*
CA, USA   IE| A   PV| WPL| $20   A

Firestone, 2000 *Santa Ynez Valley, Santa Barbara Co.*
CA, USA   IE| B+   PV| WPL| $18   B+

Forest Glen, 2000 *Oak Barrel Selection*
CA, USA   IE| B+   PV| WPL| B $10   B+

La Forge, 2000 *Vin de Pays d'Oc*
LANGUEDOC, FR   IE| B+   PV| WPL| $12   B+

Fox Creek, 2000 *Shiraz-Grenache, McLaren Vale*
SOUTH, AUS   IE| A+, B+   PV| WPL| BBC $20   A

Geyser Peak, 2000 *Sonoma Co.*
CA, USA   IE| B+,A-   PV| WPL| BBC $17   A-

Glen Fiona, 1999 *Puncheon Aged, Walla Walla Valley*
WA, USA   IE| A   PV| WPL| S $30   A

Granite Springs, 1999 *Sierra Foothills, El Dorado Co.*
CA, USA   IE| B+, B   PV| WPL| $16   B+

Grant Burge, 1999 *Shiraz, Miamba, Barossa Valley*
SOUTH, AUS   IE| B+   PV| WPL| $15   B+

Greg Norman, 1999 *Estates Shiraz, Limestone Coast*
SOUTH, AUS   IE| A   PV| WPL| $20   A

REDS
SORTED BY TYPE

SYRAH/SHIRAZ (CONTINUED)

Guardian Peak, 2001
WESTERN CAPE, SA IE| B+   PV| WPL| B $9   B+

Hahn, 2001 *San Luis Obispo Co.*
CA, USA IE| A-   PV| WPL| $12   A-

Hamilton, 1999 *Fuller's Barn, Ewell Vineyard*
BAROSSA VALLEY, AUS IE| A   PV| WPL| S $30   A

Hardys, 2000 *Shiraz*
SOUTH EASTERN, AUS IE| B+   PV| WPL| B $8   B+

Harlequin, 2000 *Sundance Vineyard, Columbia Valley*
WA, USA IE| A   PV| WPL| S $30   A

Herdade de Esporão, 2000
ALENTEJO, POR IE| B+   PV| WPL| $11   B+

Hess Select, 2000 *Napa Valley*
CA, USA IE| B+   PV| WPL| $14   B+

Hogue, 1999 *Genesis, Columbia Valley*
WA, USA IE| A-   PV| WPL| $25   A-

Isenhower Cellars, 2000 *Columbia Valley*
WA, USA IE| A-   PV| WPL| $25   A-

J C, 2000 *Rodney's Vineyard, Santa Barbara Co.*
CA, USA IE| B+   PV| 99 A   WPL| S $27   B+

Jacob's Creek, 2000 *Shiraz, Reserve*
SOUTH, AUS IE| B+   PV| 99 B+   WPL| $14   B+

Jade Mountain, 2000 *Napa Valley*
CA, USA IE| A, A   PV| WPL| S,BBC   **$28**   A

Jim Barry, 2001 *The Lodge Hill Shiraz, Clare Valley*
SOUTH, AUS IE| B+   PV| WPL| $14   B+

Joseph Phelps, 2000 *Le Mistral, Napa Valley*
CA, USA IE| A   PV| WPL| $25   A

Kaesler, 2001 *Avignon Grenache Shiraz, Barossa Valley*
SOUTH, AUS IE| A+   PV| WPL| $23   A+

Kestral, 2000 *Yakima Valley*
WA, USA IE| A-   PV| WPL| S $28   A-

Knappstein, 1999 *Shiraz, Clare Valley*
SOUTH, AUS IE| A   PV| WPL| $19   A

Ktima Kyr-Yianni, 1999 *Imathia Yiannakohori*
GRC IE| A-   PV| WPL| S $28   A-

La Crema, 2000 *Sonoma Co.*
CA, USA IE| A-, A-   PV| WPL| BBC $18   A-

Lafond, 2001 *SRH, Santa Rita Hills*
CA, USA IE| B+   PV| WPL| $18   B+

Lake Breeze, 2000 *Barnoota Langhorne Creek*
AUS IE| A   PV| WPL| $19   A

Lane Tanner, 2000 *French Camp, San Luis Obispo Co.*
CA, USA IE| B+   PV| WPL| $20   B+

Leasingham, 2000 *Shiraz, Bin 61, Clare Valley*
SOUTH, AUS   IE| A-   PV| 99 A-   WPL| W $21   A-

LinCourt, 2000 *Santa Barbara Co.*
CA, USA   IE| B+   PV| WPL| $20   B+

Lindemans, 1999 *Shiraz, Reserve, Padthaway*
SOUTH, AUS   IE| B+, A-, A-, B+PV| WPL| W,BBC $15 A-

Lindemans, 1998 *Shiraz-Cabernet Sauvignon, Limestone Ridge, Coonawarra*
SOUTH, AUS   IE| A+, B, A   PV| WPL| S,BBC $27   A

Longfellow, 2001 *Dry Creek Valley*
CA, USA   IE| A-   PV| WPL| S $29   A-

Loxton, 1999 *Timbervine Ranch, Russian River Valley, Sonoma Co.*
CA, USA   IE| A-   PV| WPL| S $26   A-

MacRostie, 2000 *Blue Oaks Vineyard, Paso Robles, San Luis Obispo Co.*
CA, USA   IE| B+   PV| WPL| $19   B+

Madfish, 2001 *Shiraz*
WESTERN, AUS   IE| B+   PV| WPL| $14   B+

Marquis Philips, 2001 *Shiraz*
SOUTH EASTERN, AUS   IE| B+, B   PV| 00 B+   WPL| $15   B+

Mas Carlot, 2001 *Syrah-Grenache, Cuvée Tradition, Vin de Pays d'Oc*
LANGUEDOC, FR   IE| B+   PV| WPL| B $9   B+

Mas de Bressades, 2001 *Syrah-Grenache, Vin de Pays du Gard*
LANGUEDOC, FR   IE| B+   PV| WPL| B $10   B+

Mas de Guiot, 2001 *Syrah-Grenache, Vin de Pays du Gard*
LANGUEDOC, FR   IE| A-, B   PV| WPL| B $9   B+

Matetic Vineyards, 2001 *EQ, San Antonio*
CH   IE| A+   PV| WPL| $25   A+

McDowell, 2000 *Mendocino Co.*
CA, USA   IE| B+   PV| WPL| $12   B+

McGuigan, 1999 *Genus 4 Shiraz, Hunter Valley*
NEW SOUTH WALES, AUS IE| A   PV| WPL| $20   A

McPherson, 2000 *Reserve Shiraz, Goulburn Valley*
AUS   IE| A   PV| WPL| $19   A

McWilliam's , 2001 *Hanwood Estate*
SOUTH EASTERN, AUS   IE| B+   PV| WPL| $11   B+

Meridian, 1999 *Paso Robles, San Luis Obispo Co.*
CA, USA   IE| A-, B, B   PV| WPL| $15   B+

Mills Reef, 2000 *Elspeth Syrah, Mere Road Vineyard*
HAWKES BAY, NZ IE| A+, A   PV| 99 A-   WPL| S,BBC $30   A+

Morandé, 2001 *Vitisterra Grand Reserve, Maipo Valley*
CENTRAL VALLEY, CH   IE| A-, A-   PV| WPL| BBC $15   A-

Morgan, 2000 *Monterey Co.*
CA, USA   IE| B+, A-, B   PV| WPL| $20   B+

Neyers, 2000 *Napa Valley*
CA, USA   IE| A-   PV| WPL| S $30   A-

Novy, 2000 *Santa Lucia Highlands*
CA, USA   IE| A-, B+, B+ PV| WPL| $23   B+

SYRAH/SHIRAZ (CONTINUED)

Novy, 2001 *Santa Lucia Highlands*
CA, USA   IE| A-   PV| 00 B+   WPL| S $26 A-

Ojai, 2000 *Santa Barbara Co.*
CA, USA   IE| A-   PV| WPL| $24 A-

Paige 23, 2000 *Santa Barbara Co.*
CA, USA   IE| A+   PV| WPL| $21 A+

Paracombe, 1998 *Shiraz, Adelaide Hills*
SOUTH, AUS   IE| A, A-   PV| WPL| S,BBC $28 A

Paringa, 2001 *Shiraz, Individual Vineyard*
SOUTH, AUS   IE| A-, B+   PV| 00 B+   WPL| W,B $10 A-

Ch. Paus Mas, 2000 *Coteaux du Languedoc*
LANGUEDOC, FR   IE| B+   PV| WPL| $15 B+

Pend d'Oreille, 2000 *Columbia Valley*
WA, USA   IE| A-   PV| WPL| $23 A-

Penfolds, 2000 *Thomas Hyland Shiraz*
SOUTH, AUS   IE| A-   PV| WPL| $18 A-

Penfolds, 2000 *Shiraz-Mourvèdre, Bin 2*
SOUTH EASTERN, AUS   IE| A-, B+   PV| WPL| W $11 A-

Penfolds, 2000 *Shiraz, Kalimna Bin 28*
SOUTH, AUS   IE| A-   PV| WPL| $24 A-

Penfolds, 1999 *Shiraz, Kalimna Bin 28*
SOUTH, AUS   IE| A-, B+, A   PV| WPL| BBC $24 A-

Penfolds, 1999 *Shiraz, Bin 128, Coonawarra*
SOUTH, AUS   IE| A   PV| WPL| $23 A

Penley, 1999 *Shiraz, Hyland, Coonawarra*
SOUTH, AUS   IE| A-, A   PV| WPL| BBC $25 A-

Petaluma, 1999 *Shiraz, Bridgewater Mill*
SOUTH-VICTORIA, AUS   IE| B+, B   PV| WPL| $15 B+

Pikes, 1998 *Shiraz, Reserve, Clare Valley*
SOUTH, AUS   IE| A+   PV| WPL| $24 A+

Pirramimma, 2000 *McLaren Vale*
SOUTH, AUS   IE| A+   PV| WPL| $21 A+

Plantagenet, 1999 *Mount Barker*
WESTERN, AUS   IE| A   PV| WPL| S $30 A

Qupé, 2001 *Central Coast*
CA, USA   IE| B+   PV| 99 B+   WPL| $15 B+

Qupé, 1999 *Red Mountain*
CA, USA   IE| A+   PV| WPL| $20 A+

J. Portugal Ramos, 2001
ALENTEJO, POR   IE| A-   PV| WPL| $18 A-

Ravenswood, 2000 *Icon, Sonoma Co.*
CA, USA   IE| B+   PV| WPL| $20 B+

Ridge, 2000 *Lytton Springs, Somona Co.*
CA, USA   IE| A-   PV| WPL| S $30 A-

Robert Craig, 2000 *Central Coast*
CA, USA   IE| A-   PV| WPL| S $28 A-

Rosenblum, 2000 *England-Shaw Vineyard, Solano Co.*
CA, USA   IE| A-, B   PV| WPL| S $30 B+

Rosenblum, 2000 *Rodney's Vineyard, Santa Barbara Co.*
CA, USA   IE| B+   PV| WPL| $25 B+

Rosenblum, 2000 *Hillside Vineyards, Sonoma Co.*
CA, USA   IE| A   PV| WPL| $24 A

Rosenblum, 2001 *England-Shaw Vineyard, Solano Co.*
CA, USA   IE| A-   PV| WPL| S $30 A-

Rosenblum, 2001 *Feather Foot Man Jingalu Special Artist Series, McLaren Vale*
SOUTH, AUS   IE| A-   PV| WPL| S $28 A-

Rufus Stone, 1998 *McLaren Vale*
SOUTH, AUS   IE| A+   PV| WPL| S $30 A+

Rutherford Oaks, 2000 *Hozhoni Vineyards, Napa Valley*
CA, USA   IE| A-   PV| WPL| S $28 A-

Dom. de Saint-Antoine, 2001 *Costières de Nimes*
LANGUEDOC, FR   IE| B+   PV| WPL| $13 B+

Dom. de Saint-Antoine, 2001 *Vin de Pays du Gard*
LANGUEDOC, FR   IE| B+   PV| 00 A-   WPL| $11 B+

Saint-Cosme, 2001 *Côtes du Rhône*
RHÔNE, FR   IE| B+   PV| WPL| $12 B+

Sandalford, 2001 *Shiraz-Cabernet Sauvignon*
WESTERN, AUS   IE| B+   PV| WPL| $14 B+

Shottesbrooke, 2000 *Eliza Reserve Shiraz, McLaren Vale*
SOUTH, AUS   IE| A   PV| WPL| S $30 A

Snoqualmie, 2000 *Columbia Valley*
WA, USA   IE| B+   PV| WPL| $11 B+

Taltarni, 2000 *Shiraz, Pyrenees*
VICTORIA, AUS   IE| A-   PV| WPL| $17 A-

The Green Vineyard, 2000 *Shiraz, The Forties Old Block*
HEATHCOTE, AUS   IE| A   PV| WPL| S $30 A

Thorn-Clarke, 2000 *Shiraz, Terra , Barossa Valley*
SOUTH, AUS   IE| B+   PV| WPL| B $10 B+

Thorn-Clarke, 2000 *Shiraz, Shotfire Ridge, Barossa Valley*
SOUTH, AUS   IE| B+   PV| WPL| $14 B+

Thurston Wolfe, 2000 *Columbia Valley*
WA, USA   IE| A-   PV| WPL| $18 A-

Tim Adams, 1999 *Shiraz, Clare Valley*
SOUTH, AUS   IE| A-   PV| WPL| $24 A-

Two Oceans, 2001
WESTERN CAPE, SA   IE| B+   PV| WPL| B $7 B+

Valley of the Moon, 1999 *Sonoma Co.*
CA, USA   IE| A-   PV| WPL| $15 A-

Vasse Felix, 2000 *Shiraz, Margaret River*
WESTERN, AUS   IE| A   PV| WPL| S $30 A

REDS
SORTED BY TYPE

Ventana, 2000 *Arroyo Seco*
CA, USA   IE| B+   PV| WPL| $18 B+

Victor Hugo, 2000 *Paso Robles, San Luis Obispo Co.*
CA, USA   IE| B+   PV| WPL| $20 B+

Vinterra, 1999
MENDOZA, ARG   IE| A-   PV| WPL| B $10 A-

W. B. Bridgman, 2000 *Yakima Valley*
WA, USA   IE| B+   PV| WPL| $19 B+

Water Wheel, 2000 *Bendigo*
VICTORIA, AUS   IE| B+   PV| WPL| $15 B+

Willow Crest, 1999 *Yakima Valley*
WA, USA   IE| B+   PV| WPL| $18 B+

Wirra Wirra, 2000 *Shiraz, McLaren Vale*
SOUTH, AUS   IE| A   PV| WPL| S $27 A

Wolf Blass, 2001 *Shiraz-Cabernet Sauvignon, Red Label*
SOUTH, AUS   IE| B+, B+   PV| 00 B+   WPL| $14 B+

Wolf Blass, 2000 *Shiraz-Cabernet Sauvignon, Red Label*
SOUTH, AUS   IE| B+, B   PV| WPL| W $12 B+

Wolf Blass, 1999 *Brown Label Classic Shiraz*
SOUTH, AUS   IE| A   PV| WPL| $20 A

Wolff, 2001 *Edna Valley*
CA, USA   IE| B+   PV| WPL| $18 B+

Wyvern , 2000 *Columbia Valley*
WA, USA   IE| A-   PV| WPL| $25 A-

Zaca Mesa, 2000 *Santa Ynez Valley*
CA, USA   IE| A, A-   PV| WPL| BBC $20 A

TEMPRANILLO

Marqués de Arienzo, 1998 *Crianza*
RIOJA, SP   IE| B+   PV| WPL| B $10 B+

Artadi, 1999 *Viñas de Gain*
RIOJA, SP   IE| A-   PV| WPL| $18 A-

Ramon Bibao, 1999
RIOJA, SP   IE| B+   PV| WPL| B $10 B+

Bodegas Bilbainas, 1996 *La Vicalanda de Viña Pomal, Reserva*
RIOJA, SP   IE| A-, B+   PV| WPL| BBC $20 A-

Bodegas Breton, 1999 *Loriñon, Crianza*
RIOJA, SP   IE| B+   PV| WPL| $11 B+

CVNE (CUNE), 1996 *Viña Real, Reserva*
RIOJA, SP   IE| A, A, B, B   PV| WPL| S $29 B+

Viña Izadi, 1999 *Crianza*
RIOJA, SP   IE| B+   PV| WPL| $14 B+

Montegaredo, 1999 *Tinto*
RIBERA DEL DUERO, SP IE| B+   PV| WPL| $13 B+

Navarrsotillo, 1999 *Crianza Magister Bibendi*
RIOJA, SP   IE| B+   PV| WPL| $11 B+

Bodega Nekeas, 1999
SP IE| B+ PV| WPL| B $10 B+

Marqués del Puerto, 1999 *Crianza*
RIOJA, SP IE| B+ PV| WPL| $12 B+

Viña Salceda, 1998
RIOJA, SP IE| A- PV| WPL| $15 A-

Hnos. Sastre, 2000 *Viña Sastre*
RIBERA DEL DUERO, SP IE| B+ PV| WPL| $14 B+

Vallobera, 1999 *Crianza*
RIOJA, SP IE| B+ PV| WPL| $15 B+

Campo Viejo, 1998 *Crianza*
RIOJA, SP IE| A- PV| WPL| B $10 A-

Paisajes y Viñedos, 1999 *Paisajes V Vinas Seleccionadas*
RIOJA, SP IE| A- PV| WPL| $23 A-

REDS SORTED BY TYPE

ZINFANDEL

A. Rafanelli, 2000 *Dry Creek Valley, Sonoma Co.*
CA, USA IE| A- PV| 99 A- WPL| S $26 A-

Acorn, 2000 *Alegria Vineyards, Russian River Valley, Sonoma Co.*
CA, USA IE| A- PV| WPL| S $28 A-

Amano, 2000 *Primitivo*
PUGLIA, IT IE| B+ PV| WPL| B $10 B+

Ballentine, 1999 *Napa Valley*
CA, USA IE| B+ PV| WPL| $15 B+

Beaulieu (BV), 2000 *Beauzeaux Signet Collection, Napa Valley*
CA, USA IE| A PV| WPL| $24 A

Buena Vista, 2000 *Carneros*
CA, USA IE| B+, B+ PV| WPL| B $9 B+

Castoro Cellars, 2000 *Paso Robles, San Luis Obispo Co.*
CA, USA IE| A- PV| WPL| $14 A-

Ch. Montelena, 2000 *Primitivo, Napa Valley*
CA, USA IE| A- PV| WPL| $25 A-

Ch. Souverain, 2000 *Dry Creek Valley, Sonoma Co.*
CA, USA IE| B+ PV| WPL| $18 B+

Chiarello, 2000 *Giana, Napa Valley*
CA, USA IE| A- PV| WPL| S $28 A-

Cline, 2000 *Live Oak Vineyard, Contra Costa Co.*
CA, USA IE| A+ PV| WPL| S $28 A+

Cline, 2000
CA, USA IE| B+ PV| WPL| B $10 B+

Clos du Bois, 2000 *Reserve, Dry Creek Valley, Sonoma Co.*
CA, USA IE| A- PV| WPL| $22 A-

Clos la Chance, 2000 *Twin Rivers Vineyard, El Dorado Co., Sierra Foothills*
CA, USA IE| B PV| 99 B+ WPL| $20 B+

Dashe, 2001 *Dry Creek Valley, Sonoma Co.*
CA, USA IE| B+ PV| 99 A-, 00 A WPL| $20 B+

ZINFANDEL (CONTINUED)

Dashe, 2001 *Late Harvest, Dry Creek Valley, Sonoma Co.*
CA, USA   IE| B+   PV| WPL| $20 B+

Dashe, 2000 *Todd Brothers Ranch, Alexander Valley, Sonoma Co.*
CA, USA   IE| A   PV| 99 A-   WPL| $25 A

Dashe, 2000 *Dry Creek Valley, Sonoma Co.*
CA, USA   IE| A, A, B   PV| 99 A-   WPL| BBC $20 A-

De Loach, 2000 *Pelletti Ranch, Russian River Valley, Sonoma Co.*
CA, USA   IE| A   PV| WPL| S $28 A

De Loach, 2000 *Barbieri Ranch, Russian River Valley, Sonoma Co.*
CA, USA   IE| A   PV| 99 A-   WPL| S $28 A

Deux Amis, 2000 *Somona Co.*
CA, USA   IE| B+   PV| WPL| $19 B+

Dry Creek, 2000 *Old Vines, Sonoma Co.*
CA, USA   IE| A, A, B+, A PV| WPL| BBC $21 A

Easton, 2001 *Amador Co.*
CA, USA   IE| B+, B   PV| 99 A-   WPL| $13 B+

Edgewood, 2001 *Napa Valley*
CA, USA   IE| A-   PV| WPL| $20 A-

Edgewood, 2000 *Napa Valley*
CA, USA   IE| A-   PV| WPL| $20 A-

Edmeades, 1999 *Zeni Vineyard, Mendocino Ridge, Mendocino Co.*
CA, USA   IE| A+   PV| WPL| $25 A+

Edmeades, 1999 *Ciapusci, Mendocino Ridge, Mendocino Co.*
CA, USA   IE| A   PV| WPL| $25 A

Folie à Deux, 1999 *Bowman Vineyard, Amador Co.*
CA, USA   IE| A   PV| WPL| S $26 A

Franus, 2000 *Rancho Chimiles, Napa*
CA, USA   IE| A-   PV| WPL| S $28 A-

Franus, 2000 *Planchon Vineyard, Contra Costa Co.*
CA, USA   IE| B+   PV| WPL| $20 B+

Gallo Sonoma, 1999 *Frei Ranch Vineyard, Dry Creek Valley, Sonoma Co.*
CA, USA   IE| A, A-   PV| WPL| BBC $22 A

Gary Farrell, 2000 *Dry Creek Valley, Sonoma Co.*
CA, USA   IE| A-   PV| WPL| $24 A-

Hartford Court, 2000 *Russian River Valley, Sonoma Co.*
CA, USA   IE| A-   PV| 99 A-   WPL| S $30 A-

Hendry Ranch, 2000 *Hendry Block 28, Napa Valley*
CA, USA   IE| A-   PV| WPL| S $28 A-

Hunt, 2000 *Zinphony #2 Reserve, Paso Robles, San Luis Obispo Co.*
CA, USA   IE| A   PV| WPL| S $28 A

Hunt, 1999 *Zinphony #2 Reserve, Paso Robles, San Luis Obispo Co.*
CA, USA   IE| A   PV| WPL| $24 A

Jessie's Grove, 2001 *Vintner's Choice Old Vine, Lodi*
CA, USA   IE| B+   PV| WPL| $15 B+

Joel Gott, 2001
CA, USA   IE| B+   PV| 00 B+   WPL| $15   B+

Kendall-Jackson, 2000 *Great Estates, Mendocino Co.*
CA, USA   IE| A-   PV| WPL| S $30   A-

La Storia, 2001 *Geyserville Ranch, Alexander Valley, Sonoma Co.*
CA, USA   IE| A-   PV| WPL| S $28   A-

Lake Sonoma, 1999 *Saini Farms, Dry Creek Valley, Sonoma Co.*
CA, USA   IE| B+   PV| WPL| $20   B+

Lake Sonoma, 2000 *Russian River Valley, Sonoma Co.*
CA, USA   IE| A-   PV| WPL| $22   A-

Lake Sonoma, 2000 *Dry Creek Valley, Sonoma Co.*
CA, USA   IE| A, B, A   PV| 99 B+   WPL| BBC $17   A-

Laurel Glen, 2000 *Zazin, Old Vine, Lodi*
CA, USA   IE| A-, B+   PV| WPL| $17   A-

Markham, 2000 *Napa Valley*
CA, USA   IE| A+   PV| 99 B+   WPL| $19.75   A+

Mayo Family, 2000 *Ricci Vineyard, Russian River Valley, Sonoma Co.*
CA, USA   IE| A-   PV| WPL| S $30   A-

Mont Gras, 2001 *Limited Edition, Colchagua Valley, Rapel Valley*
CENTRAL VALLEY, CH   IE| B+   PV| WPL| $15   B+

Monteviña, 1999 *Terra d'Oro, Amador Co.*
CA, USA   IE| B+   PV| WPL| $18   B+

Monteviña, 2000 *Terra d'Oro, Deaver Vineyard, Amador Co.*
CA, USA   IE| A-   PV| WPL| $24   A-

Murphy-Goode, 2000 *Liar's Dice, Sonoma Co.*
CA, USA   IE| B+   PV| WPL| $20   B+

Newlan, 2000 *Napa Valley*
CA, USA   IE| A   PV| WPL| $22   A

Peachy Canyon, 2000 *Westside, Paso Robles, San Luis Obispo Co.*
CA, USA   IE| B+   PV| WPL| $19   B+

Pezzi King, 2000 *Maple Vineyard, Dry Creek Valley, Sonoma Co.*
CA, USA   IE| A-, A-   PV| 99 A-   WPL| S,BBC $30   A-

Rancho Zabaco, 2001 *Chiotti Vineyard, Dry Creek Valley, Sonoma Co.*
CA, USA   IE| A   PV| WPL| S $28   A

Rancho Zabaco, 2001 *Heritage Vines, Sonoma Co.*
CA, USA   IE| B+   PV| 99 A-, 00:B+   WPL| $18   B+

Rancho Zabaco, 2001 *Dancing Bull, Lodi*
CA, USA   IE| B+   PV| WPL| $12   B+

Rancho Zabaco, 2000 *Heritage Vines, Sonoma Co.*
CA, USA   IE| B+   PV| 99 A-   WPL| $14   B+

Ravenswood, 2000 *Vintners Blend*
CA, USA   IE| B+   PV| 99 A-   WPL| B $10   B+

Raymond, 1999 *Reserve, Napa Valley*
CA, USA   IE| A-   PV| WPL| $22   A-

Ridge, 2000 *Lytton Springs, Dry Creek Valley, Sonoma Co.*
CA, USA   IE| A+, B, A+, B+, A+   PV| 99 A   WPL| S,BBC $30   A

REDS
SORTED BY TYPE

ZINFANDEL (CONTINUED)

Ridge, 2000 *Paso Robles, San Luis Obispo Co.*
CA, USA   IE| A, B, B+   PV| WPL| $25 B+

Ridge, 2001 *Geyserville, Sonoma Co.*
CA, USA   IE| A-   PV| 99 A-   WPL| S $30 A-

Ridge, 2001 *Lytton Springs, Dry Creek Valley, Sonoma Co.*
CA, USA   IE| A   PV| 99 B, 00 A   WPL| S $30 A

Ridge, 2001 *Sonoma Station, Sonoma Co.*
CA, USA   IE| A-   PV| WPL| $20 A-

Ridge, 2001 *Three Valleys, Sonoma Co.*
CA, USA .   IE| B+   PV| WPL| $18 B+

Ridge, 2000 *Pagani Ranch, Sonoma Valley, Sonoma Co.*
CA, USA   IE| A-   PV| WPL| S $28 A-

Rosenblum, NV *Vintners Cuvée XXIV*
CA, USA   IE| B+   PV| WPL| B $10 B+

Rosenblum, 2001 *Rockpile Vineyard, Dry Creek Valley, Sonoma Co.*
CA, USA   IE| A+   PV| 00 A-   WPL| S $26 A+

Rosenblum, 2001 *Planchon Vineyard, San Francisco Bay*
CA, USA   IE| A   PV| 00 B+   WPL| $19 A

Rosenblum, 2000 *Continente Vineyard, San Francisco Bay*
CA, USA   IE| B+   PV| 99 B+   WPL| $20 B+

Rosenblum, 2000 *Old Vines, Russian River Valley, Sonoma Co.*
CA, USA   IE| B+   PV| WPL| $18 B+

Sausal, 1999 *Private Reserve, Alexander Valley, Sonoma Co.*
CA, USA   IE| A-   PV| WPL| $18 A-

Sausal, 2000 *Private Reserve, Alexander Valley, Sonoma Co.*
CA, USA   IE| A   PV| 99 A-   WPL| $20 A

Sausal, 2000 *Old Vine Family, Alexander Valley, Sonoma Co.*
CA, USA   IE| B+   PV| WPL| $15 B+

Scherrer, 1999 *Alexander Valley, Sonoma Co.*
CA, USA   IE| A   PV| WPL| S $28 A

Seghesio, 2000 *Cortina, Dry Creek Valley, Sonoma Co.*
CA, USA   IE| A-, B, B+   PV| WPL| S $28 B+

Seghesio, 2001 *Sonoma, Sonoma Co.*
CA, USA   IE| B+, B+   PV| 99 B+, 00 B+ WPL| $17 B+

Shenandoah, 2001 *ReZerve, Paul's Vineyard, Shenandoah Valley, Sierra Foothills*
CA, USA   IE| A-   PV| WPL| $24 A-

Sobon, 2001 *ReZerve, Shenandoah Valley, Sierra Foothills*
CA, USA   IE| A-   PV| WPL| $24 A-

Sobon, 2000 *Cougar Hill Vineyards, Shenandoah Valley, Sierra Foothills*
CA, USA   IE| B+   PV| WPL| $17 B+

Sobon, 2000 *Rocky Top, Shenandoah Valley, Sierra Foothills*
CA, USA   IE| A   PV| WPL| $15 A

Sparrow Lane, 2000 *Sonoma Co.*
CA, USA   IE| A-   PV| WPL| $24 A-

Stonehedge, 1999 *Napa Valley*
CA, USA   IE| B+   PV| WPL| **$20**   B+

Stonehedge, 2000 *Napa Valley*
CA, USA   IE| A-   PV| WPL| **$15**   A-

Stryker Sonoma, 1999 *Old Vine Estate, Alexander Valley, Sonoma Co.*
CA, USA   IE| A-   PV| WPL| **$25**   A-

Summers, 2001 *Villa Andriana Vineyard, Napa Valley*
CA, USA   IE| A   PV| WPL| **$20**   A

Summit Lake, 1999 *Howell Mountain, Napa Valley*
CA, USA   IE| A   PV| WPL| **$22**   A

Thea, 2000 *Joaquin*
CA, USA   IE| A-   PV| WPL| **$24**   A-

Trentadue, 2000 *Alexander Valley, Sonoma Co.*
CA, USA   IE| B+   PV| WPL| **$20**   B+

Turley, 2000 *Duarte Vineyard, Contra Costa Co.*
CA, USA   IE| A+, B+, A   PV| WPL| S,BBC   **$30**   A

Turley, 2000 *Old Vines*
CA, USA   IE| A, B, A   PV| 99 A   WPL| BBC   **$25**   A

Turley, 2000 *Juvenile*
CA, USA   IE| B+, B, A-   PV| WPL| **$20**   B+

T-Vine, 2000 *Napa Valley*
CA, USA   IE| A-   PV| WPL| **$25**   A-

Unti, 2000 *Dry Creek Valley, Sonoma Co.*
CA, USA   IE| B+   PV| WPL| **$20**   B+

V. Sattui, 2000 *Suzanne's Vineyard, Napa Valley*
CA, USA   IE| A   PV| WPL| **$20**   A

Valley of the Moon, 2000 *Sonoma Co.*
CA, USA   IE| A-   PV| WPL| **$15**   A-

Watts, 1999 *Old Vines, Lodi*
CA, USA   IE| A-   PV| WPL| **$14**   A-

White Oak, 2000 *Alexander Valley, Sonoma Co.*
CA, USA   IE| A   PV| 99 A-   WPL| **$24**   A

Williams Selyem, 2000 *Russian River Valley, Sonoma Co.*
CA, USA   IE| A   PV| WPL| **$25**   A

OTHER RED

Abadia Retuerta, 2001 *Rivola*
SARDON DE DUERO, SP   IE| A-   PV| 99 A-   WPL| **$12**   A-

Ch. d' Aiguilhe, 2000 *Côte de Castillon*
BORDEAUX, FR   IE| A-   PV| WPL| S   **$30**   A-

Ch. d' Aiguilloux, 1999 *Cuvée des Trois Seigneurs*
LANGUEDOC, FR   IE| B+   PV| WPL| **$11**   B+

Caves Aliança, 1999 *Galeria Tinta Roriz*
DOURO, POR   IE| A-   PV| WPL| B   **$9**   A-

Caves Aliança, 1999 *Aliança Particular, Palmela*
TERRAS DO SADO, POR   IE| B+   PV| WPL| **$15**   B+

REDS SORTED BY TYPE

OTHER RED (CONTINUED)

Caves Aliança, 1998 *Foral Grande Escolha*
DOURO, POR   IE| B+   PV| WPL| $13   B+

Caves Aliança, 1997 *Quinta da Terrugem*
ALENTEJO, POR   IE| A-   PV| WPL| $20   A-

Olivier Andrieu, 1999 *Faugères Clos Fantine Cuvée Conurtiol*
LANGUEDOC, FR   IE| A-   PV| WPL| $17   A-

Antonelli, 1999 *Rosso, Montefalco*
UMBRIA, IT   IE| B+   PV| WPL| $14   B+

Marqués de Arienzo, 1998 *Crianza*
RIOJA, SP   IE| B+   PV| WPL| B $10   B+

Artadi, 2000 *Viñas de Gain*
RIOJA, SP   IE| A-   PV| 99 A-   WPL| $22   A-

Dom. D' Aupilhac, 2001 *Vin de Pays du Mont Baudle Lou Maset*
LANGUEDOC, FR   IE| B+   PV| WPL| $14   B+

Balnaves, 1998 *The Blend, Coonawarra*
SOUTH, AUS   IE| A-   PV| WPL| $15   A-

Baobab, 2001 *Pinotage*
WESTERN CAPE, SA IE| B+   PV| WPL| B $10   B+

Ch. de Barbe Blanche, 2000 *Cuvée Henri IV, Lussac-Saint-Émillion*
BORDEAUX, FR   IE| B+   PV| WPL| $15   B+

Barton & Guestier, 2000 *Tradition, Châteauneuf-du-Pape*
RHÔNE, FR   IE| B+   PV| WPL| $20   B+

Bellevue, 2001 *Cabernet/Pinotage Atticus*
STELLENBOSCH, SA IE| B+   PV| WPL| $15   B+

Berberana, 1997 *Garnacha/Mazuelo/Tempranillo, Viña Alarde Reserva*
RIOJA, SP   IE| B+   PV| WPL| $18   B+

Louis Bernard, 2001 *Vacqueyras*
RHÔNE, FR   IE| B+   PV| WPL| $18   B+

Louis Bernard, 2001 *Gigondas*
RHÔNE, FR   IE| B+   PV| WPL| $19   B+

Louis Bernard, 2001 *Chateau Bosc la Croix, Côtes du Rhône Villages*
RHÔNE, FR   IE| B+   PV| WPL| B $10   B+

Betz Family Winery, 2000 *Clos de Betz, Columbia Valley*
WA, USA   IE| A   PV| WPL| $24   A

Dom. Borie de Maurel, 2001 *Cuvée Alex, Minervois*
LANGUEDOC, FR   IE| A-   PV| WPL| $17   A-

Dom. Borie de Maurel, 2000 *Esprit d'Automne, Minervois*
LANGUEDOC, FR   IE| B+   PV| WPL| $13   B+

Ch. Bousquette, 2000 *Saint-Chinian*
LANGUEDOC, FR   IE| B+   PV| WPL| $15   B+

Ch. Bousquette, 1999 *Cuvée Prestige, Saint-Chinian*
LANGUEDOC, FR   IE| A   PV| WPL| S $26   A

Boutari, 2000 *Goumenissa*
GRC   IE| B+   PV| WPL| $11   B+

Boutari, 1997 *Grand Reserve*
NÁOUSSA, GRC   IE| A-   PV| WPL| $15 A-

Chateau la Boutignane, 2001 *Rosé de Saignée, Corbières*
LANGUEDOC, FR   IE| B+   PV| WPL| B $10 B+

Chateau la Boutignane, 2000 *Classique Cuvée Rouge, Corbières*
LANGUEDOC, FR   IE| B+   PV| WPL| B $10 B+

Chateau la Boutignane, 1998 *Carignane, Grande Reserve Rouge, Corbières*
LANGUEDOC, FR   IE| A+   PV| WPL| $18 A+

Domaine Brusset, 2001 *Cairanne Coteaux des Travers, Côtes du Rhône Villages-Cairanne*
RHÔNE, FR   IE| B+   PV| WPL| $14 B+

Ca' del Solo, 2001 *Big House Red*
CA, USA   IE| A-   PV| 00 B+   WPL| B $10 A-

Ca' del Solo, 2000 *Big House Red, Santa Cruz Mountains*
CA, USA   IE| B+, A-   PV| WPL| B $10 A-

Ch. Camplazen, 2000 *Premium la Clape*
LANGUEDOC, FR   IE| A-   PV| WPL| S $28 A-

Campo Ardosa, 2000 *Carvalhosa*
DOURO, POR   IE| A+   PV| WPL| S $28 A+

Arnaldo Caprai, 2000 *Poggio Belvedere*
UMBRIA, IT   IE| B+   PV| WPL| $14 B+

Arnaldo Caprai, 2000 *Rosso, Montefalco*
UMBRIA, IT   IE| A   PV| WPL| $22 A

Casa de la Ermita, 2000
JUMILLA, SP   IE| B+   PV| WPL| $12 B+

Casa de la Ermita, 2000 *Tinto*
JUMILLA, SP   IE| A-   PV| 99 A-   WPL| $12 A-

Casa de Santar, 1999 *Reserva*
DÃO, POR   IE| A-   PV| WPL| $15 A-

Quinto do Casal Branco, 1999 *Castelao/Trincadeira, Falcoaria*
RIBATEJO, POR   IE| A-   PV| WPL| $15 A-

Casanova di Neri, 2000 *Rosso, Montalcino*
TUSCANY, IT   IE| A-   PV| WPL| $23 A-

Castaño, 2001 *Solanera*
YECLA, SP   IE| A+   PV| 99 A-, 00 A-   WPL| $12 A+

Castaño, 2001 *Hecula*
YECLA, SP   IE| A   PV| 99 A-   WPL| B $9 A

Castillo, 2001 *Mourvedre, Monastrell*
JUMILLA, SP   IE| B+   PV| 99 B+   WPL| B $9 B+

Leone de Castris, 1999 *Salice Salentino Riserva*
IT   IE| B+   PV| WPL| $13 B+

Leone de Castris, 1999 *Primitivo di Manduria Santera*
IT   IE| B+   PV| WPL| $15 B+

Catacula, 1999 *Cuvée, Catacula Lake, St. Helena*
CA, USA   IE| A-   PV| WPL| $19 A-

OTHER RED (CONTINUED)

Caterina, 1999 *Rosso*
WA, USA   IE| B+   PV| WPL| $15   B+

Dom. de la Charbonnièrre, 1999 *Cuvée Mourre des Perdrix*
RHONE, FR   IE| A   PV| WPL| S $30   A

Podere Colla, 1998 *Langhe Rosso Bricco*
PIEDMONT, IT   IE| A   PV| WPL| S $28   A

Colpetrone, 1999 *Rosso di Montefalco*
UMBRIA, IT   IE| A   PV| WPL| $14   A

Columbia Crest, 1999 *Reserve Red, Columbia Valley*
WA, USA   IE| A,A   PV| WPL| S,BBC $30   A

Condado de Haza, 2000
RIBERA DEL DUERO, SP IE| B+   PV| WPL| W $20   B+

Coriole, 2000 *Cabernet/Merlot/Shiraz, Redstone, McLaren Vale*
SOUTH, AUS   IE| A+   PV| WPL| $24   A+

Ch. Coupe Roses, 2001 *La Bastide, Minervois*
LANGUEDOC, FR   IE| B+   PV| WPL| B $10   B+

Ch. Coupe Roses, 2000 *Cuvée Vignals, Minervois*
LANGUEDOC, FR   IE| B+   PV| WPL| $13   B+

Dom. le Couroulu, 1999 *Cuvée Classique, Côtes du Rhône-Vacqueyras*
RHÔNE, FR   IE| A-   PV| WPL| $13   A-

Dom. de Curebeasse, 1999 *Côtes de Provence*
PROVENCE, FR   IE| B+   PV| WPL| $11   B+

Curtis, 2000 *Counoise/Grenache/Mourvedre/Syrah Heritage Cuvée, Central Coast*
CA, USA   IE| B+   PV| WPL| $14   B+

Dão Sul, 2000 *Touriga Nacional, Quinta de Cabriz*
DÃO, POR   IE| A   PV| WPL| $19   A

Dão Sul, 2000 *Quinta da Cabris Colheita Seleccionada*
DÃO, POR   IE| B+   PV| WPL| B $6   B+

Dão Sul, 1999 *Quinta de Cabriz Alfrocheiro Preto*
DÃO, POR   IE| A   PV| WPL| $16   A

Dom. Machard de Gramont, 2000 *Les Nazoires, Chambolle-Musigny*
BURGUNDY, FR   IE| A   PV| WPL| S $30   A

De Lorimier, 1999 *Mosaic, Alexander Valley, Sonoma Co.*
CA, USA   IE| A   PV| WPL| S $30   A

Delas Cote-du-Ventoux, 2000
RHÔNE, FR   IE| B+   PV| WPL| $11   B+

DFJ, 2000 *Touriga Nacional-Touriga Franca*
ESTREMADURA, POR IE| A-   PV| WPL| $23   A-

DFJ, 2000 *Touriga Nacional, Grand'Arte*
ESTREMADURA, POR IE| A   PV| WPL| S $30   A

DFJ, 2000 *Tinta Roriz-Merlot*
ESTREMADURA, POR IE| A   PV| WPL| B $10   A

DFJ, 2000 *Tinta Miuda-Cabernet Sauvignon*
ESTREMADURA, POR IE| A-   PV| WPL| B $9   A-

DFJ, 2000 *Grand'Arte Alicante Bouschet*
ESTREMADURA, POR　IE| A　　　PV|　　　　WPL|　　$20　A

Di Majo Norante, 1998 *Terra degli Osci, Ramitello*
MOLISE, IT　　IE| B+　　PV|　　　　WPL| W　$12　B+

Dom. Chandon, 2000 *Pinot Meunier, Carneros*
CA, USA　　IE| A-　　PV|　　　　WPL| S　$29　A-

Dom. de la Terre Rouge, 2000 *Mourvedre, Sierra Foothills*
CA, USA　　IE| B+　　PV|　　　　WPL|　　$20　B+

Dry Creek, 1999 *Meritage, Dry Creek Valley, Sonoma Co.*
CA, USA　　IE| A-　　PV|　　　　WPL| S　$28　A-

Clos l' Eglise, 2000 *Côtes de Castillion*
BORDEAUX, FR　IE| A-　　PV|　　　　WPL|　　$25　A-

Enate, 1999 *Crianza*
SOMONTANO, SP　IE| B+　　PV|　　　　WPL|　　$12　B+

Escudo Rojo, 2000 *Maipo Valley*
CENTRAL VALLEY, CH　IE| B+　　PV|　　　　WPL|　　$15　B+

Fairview, 2001 *Pinotage*
PAARL, SA　　IE| A　　PV| 00 B+　　WPL|　　$25　A

Fairview, 2001 *Carignane, Pegleg*
PAARL, SA　　IE| B+　　PV|　　　　WPL|　　$25　B+

Falesco, 2001 *Vitiano*
UMBRIA, IT　　IE| B+　　PV| 00 A-　　WPL| B　$10　B+

Clos Fantine, 1999 *Faugères*
LANGUEDOC, FR　IE| A-　　PV|　　　　WPL| B　$10　A-

Remo Farina, 2000 *Valpolicella Classico Superiore, Ripasso*
VENETO, IT　　IE| A-　　PV| 99 B+　　WPL|　　$19　A-

Fassati, 1999 *Vino Nobile di Montepulciano Pasiteo*
TUSCANY, IT　　IE| B+　　PV|　　　　WPL|　　$17　B+

J. Vidal Fleury, 2000 *Côtes du Rhône*
RHÔNE, FR　　IE| B+　　PV|　　　　WPL| B　$10　B+

J. Vidal Fleury, 2000 *Côtes du Ventoux*
RHÔNE, FR　　IE| B+　　PV|　　　　WPL| B　$8　B+

José Maria da Fonseca, 2000 *Domini Plus*
DOURO, POR　IE| A+　　PV|　　　　WPL|　　$25　A+

José Maria da Fonseca, 2000 *Domini*
DOURO, POR　IE| B+　　PV|　　　　WPL|　　$15　B+

Fontanavecchia, 2000 *Aglianico del Taburno*
CAMPANIA, IT　IE| B+　　PV|　　　　WPL|　　$15　B+

Ch. Fontenil, 2000 *Fronsac, Fronsac*
BORDEAUX, FR　IE| A　　PV|　　　　WPL|　　$25　A

Dom. Foulaquier, 2000 *Le Rollier, Coteaux du Languedoc-Pic Saint-Loup*
LANGUEDOC, FR　IE| A, A-　　PV|　　WPL| BBC　$17　A

Gaia, 2000 *Agiorghitiko*
NEMEA, GRC　IE| A-　　PV|　　　　WPL|　　$20　A-

Dom. Gardies, 2000 *Tautavel, Côtes du Roussillon Villages*
ROUSSILLON, FR　IE| A-　　PV| 99 A-　　WPL|　　$19　A-

OTHER RED (CONTINUED)

Dom. Gardies, 2000 *Les Milleres, Côtes du Roussillon Villages*
ROUSSILLON, FR   IE| B+   PV| 99 B+   WPL| $15   B+

Michel Gassier, 2000 *Cuvée Joseph Torrès, Ch. de Nages, Costières de Nimes*
LANGUEDOC, FR   IE| A   PV| WPL| $20   A

Giribaldi, 1999 *Barbaresco*
PIEDMONT, IT   IE| A   PV| WPL| S $28   A

Dom. Cathérine le Goeuil, 1999 *Les Beauchières, Côtes du Rhône Villages-Cairanne*
RHÔNE, FR   IE| B+   PV| WPL| $14   B+

Dom. Grand Nicolet, 2000 *Côtes du Rhône Villages-Rasteau*
RHÔNE, FR   IE| B+   PV| WPL| $12   B+

Dom. Grand Romane, 2000 *Gigondas*
RHÔNE, FR   IE| A-   PV| WPL| $18   A-

Grand Veneur, 2000 *Les Champauvins, Côtes du Rhône*
RHÔNE, FR   IE| B+   PV| WPL| $14   B+

Ch. Grande Cassagne, 2001 *S. les Rameaux, Costières de Nimes*
LANGUEDOC, FR   IE| B+   PV| 99 B+   WPL| $13   B+

Ch. Grande Cassagne, 2001 *G.S. la Civette, Costières de Nimes*
LANGUEDOC, FR   IE| B+   PV| 00 B+   WPL| B $10   B+

Dom. du Grapillon d'Or, 2000 *Gigondas*
RHÔNE, FR   IE| A   PV| 99 A+   WPL| S $30   A

Guelbenzu, 2000 *Azul*
RIBERA DEL QUEILES, SPIE| B+   PV| WPL| $13   B+

E. Guigal, 1999 *Châteauneuf-du-Pape*
RHÔNE, FR   IE| A+   PV| WPL| S $30   A+

Haut-Carles, 2000 *Fronsac*
BORDEAUX, FR   IE| A   PV| WPL| $25   A

Hedges, 2000 *Cabernet/Merlot/Franc, Columbia Valley*
WA, USA   IE| B+   PV| WPL| $18   B+

Herdade de Esporão, 2000 *Touriga Nacional*
ALENTEJO, POR   IE| A-   PV| WPL| $15   A-

Herdade de Esporão, 2000 *Esporão Reserva*
ALENTEJO, POR   IE| A   PV| WPL| $15   A

Herdade de Esporão, 2000 *Aragones*
ALENTEJO, POR   IE| B+   PV| WPL| $14   B+

Inniskillin Okanagan, 1999 *Meritage, Reserve, Niagara Peninsula*
ONTARIO, CAN   IE| A-   PV| WPL| $13   A-

Ionian, 1998 *Agiorghitiko, Veros Moriatikos*
PELOPONNESE, GRC IE| B+   PV| WPL| B $10   B+

J.C. & Boris Leclercq, 1998 *Cabernet/Merlot, Vin de Pays, d'Oc les Portes de St.-Ros*
LANGUEDOC, FR   IE| A-   PV| WPL| $15   A-

Jackson-Triggs, 1999 *Meritage Grand Reserve, Niagara Peninsula*
ONTARIO, CAN   IE| A-   PV| WPL| $17   A-

Jade Mountain, 2000 *La Provençale*
CA, USA   IE| A-   PV| WPL| $16   A-

Jest Red, NV *Red Table Wine, Belvedere Vineyard, North Coast*
CA, USA   IE| B+   PV| WPL| $11   B+

JM Cellars, 1999 *Cabernet/Merlot/Syrah, Tre Fanciulli, Columbia Valley*
WA, USA   IE| A   PV| WPL| S $28   A

Kaesler, 2001 *Stonehorse Grenache Shiraz Mourvedre, Barossa Valley*
SOUTH, AUS   IE| A   PV| WPL| $20   A

Kanonkop, 2000 *Pinotage*
STELLENBOSCH, SA   IE| A-   PV| 99 A-   WPL| S $28   A-

Ktima Kyr-Yianni, 1998 *Imathia Yiannakohori*
GRC   IE| A   PV| WPL| $19   A

Ktima Kyr-Yianni, 1997 *Xinomavro, Ramnista*
NÁOUSSA, GRC   IE| A+   PV| WPL| $15   A+

KWV, 2001 *Roodeberg*
WESTERN CAPE, SA   IE| B+   PV| WPL| $13   B+

Dom. R. & M. Labbe, 2001 *Abymes*
SAVOIE, FR   IE| B+   PV| WPL| B $9   B+

Dom. Lacroix-Vanel, 2001 *Clos Fine Amor, Coteaux du Languedoc*
LANGUEDOC, FR   IE| B+   PV| WPL| $12   B+

Dom. Lacroix-Vanel, 2000 *Clos Melanie, Coteaux du Languedoc*
LANGUEDOC, FR   IE| A-   PV| WPL| $17   A-

Ch. Lagrezette, 1998
CAHORS, FR   IE| A-   PV| WPL| $20   A-

Dom. des Lambertins, 2000 *Côtes du Rhône-Vacqueyras*
RHÔNE, FR   IE| A-   PV| WPL| $12   A-

Patrick Lesec, 2000 *Minervois Tonneaux*
LANGUEDOC, FR   IE| B+   PV| WPL| $15   B+

Domaine de l'Harmas, 2000 *Grenache-Syrah-Mourvedre, Côtes du Rhône*
RHÔNE, FR   IE| B+   PV| WPL| $11   B+

Dom. de la Lyre, 2000 *Controlee, Côtes du Rhône*
RHÔNE, FR   IE| B+   PV| WPL| B $10   B+

Maleta, 1999 *Meritage, Niagara Peninsula*
ONTARIO, CAN   IE| A   PV| WPL| $19   A

Marquis Philips, 2000 *Sarah's Blend*
SOUTH EASTERN, AUS   IE| A+, B+, B+ PV| WPL| BBC $15   A-

Ch. Massamier la Mignarde, 1999 *Domus Maximus, la Livinière, Minervois*
LANGUEDOC, FR   IE| A   PV| WPL| $25   A

Ch. de Mauvanne, 1999 *Cru Classé Cuvée, Côtes de Provence*
LANGUEDOC, FR   IE| A-   PV| WPL| $19   A-

Meerea Park, 1999 *McLaren Vale/Hunter Valley Orange*
SOUTH, AUS   IE| A   PV| WPL| $20   A

Dom. Mercouri, 1999 *Refosco*
GRC   IE| B+   PV| WPL| $15   B+

Mitchelton, 1999 *Grenache/Mourvèdre, Central Victoria Crescent*
VICTORIA, AUS   IE| A-   PV| WPL| $21   A-

REDS SORTED BY TYPE

OTHER RED (CONTINUED)

Feudo Monaci, 2000 *Salice Salentino Rosso*
IT | IE| B+ | PV| | WPL| B | $9 | B+

Marqués de Monistrol, 2000 *Cabernet/Tempranillo*
PENEDÈS, SP | IE| B+ | PV| | WPL| B | $7 | B+

Marqués de Monistrol, 1999 *Masia Monistrol Single Vineyard Reserva Especial Cabernet/Merlot*
PENEDÈS, SP | IE| A- | PV| | WPL| | $20 | A-

Marqués de Monistrol, 1998 *Reserva Privada*
PENEDÈS, SP | IE| B+ | PV| | WPL| W, B | $10 | B+

Bodegas Montecillo, 1998 *Crianza*
RIOJA, SP | IE| B+ | PV| | WPL| | $12 | B+

Moroder, 1998 *Rosso Conero Dorico Riserva*
MARCHES, IT | IE| A- | PV| | WPL| | $25 | A-

Mount Palomar, 1999 *Meritage, Temecula*
CA, USA | IE| B+ | PV| | WPL| | $18 | B+

Dom. de Mourchon, 1998 *Seguret Tradition, Côtes du Rhône Villages*
RHÔNE, FR | IE| B+ | PV| | WPL| | $13 | B+

Dom. Navarre, 1999 *Saint-Chinian*
LANGUEDOC, FR | IE| A- | PV| | WPL| | $20 | A-

Nino Negri, 1998 *Valtellina Superiore, Inferno Mazér*
LOMBARDY, IT | IE| A- | PV| | WPL| | $17 | A-

Fattoria Nicodemi, 2000 *Montepulciano*
ABRUZZI, IT | IE| B+ | PV| | WPL| | $16 | B+

Maison Nicolas, 2000 *Languedoc/Roussillon, Consensus, Coteaux du Languedoc*
LANGUEDOC, FR | IE| A | PV| | WPL| | $15 | A

Nittnaus, 2000 *Blaufränkisch/Cabernet, Qualitätswein Trocken*
BURGENLAND, AUT | IE| A- | PV| | WPL| S | $28 | A-

Nociano, 1998 *Rosso IGT*
UMBRIA, IT | IE| A- | PV| | WPL| B | $9 | A-

Okahu, 2000 *Ninety Mile*
NZ | IE| A- | PV| | WPL| | $17 | A-

Alvaro Palacios, 1999 *Les Terrasses*
PRIORAT, SP | IE| A- | PV| | WPL| | $25 | A-

Caves des Papes, 2000 *Oratorio, Gigondas*
RHÔNE, FR | IE| A- | PV| | WPL| | $23 | A-

Luis Pato, 2000 *Vinha Pan*
BEIRAS, POR | IE| A- | PV| | WPL| | $13 | A-

Luis Pato, 2000 *Vinha Barrosa Vina Velha*
BEIRAS, POR | IE| A | PV| | WPL| S | $29 | A

Castillo de Perelada, 2000 *Emporda Costa Brava Tinto Crianza*
SP | IE| B+ | PV| | WPL| B | $10 | B+

Perrin, 2000 *Côtes du Rhône-Vacqueyras*
RHÔNE, FR | IE| A- | PV| | WPL| | $21 | A-

Perrin, 1999 *Côtes du Rhône-Vacqueyras*
RHÔNE, FR   IE| A-   PV| 00 A-   WPL| **$19**   A-

Ch. Pesquié, 1999 *Quintessence, Côtes du Ventoux*
RHÔNE, FR   IE| B+   PV| WPL| **$15**   B+

Ch. Peyros, 1999 *Madiran*
PROVENCE, FR   IE| B+   PV| WPL| **$14**   B+

Cims de Porrera, 2000 *Solanes, Denominacion de Orgen*
SP   IE| A-   PV| WPL| **$24**   A-

The Prisoner, 2000 *Charbono/Petite Sirah/Syrah/Zinfandel, Napa Valley*
CA, USA   IE| A-   PV| WPL| S   **$28**   A-

Fattoria le Pupille, 2001 *Maremma Toscana*
TUSCANY, IT   IE| B+   PV| 99 A-   WPL| **$12**   B+

Ch. Puygueraud, 2000 *Côtes de Francs*
BORDEAUX, FR   IE| A-   PV| WPL| **$15**   A-

Compania das Quintas, 1999 *Quinta do Cardo Touriga*
BEIRA INTERIOR, POR   IE| B+   PV| WPL| **$14**   B+

Jean-Maurice Raffault, 2001 *Chinon les Galluches, Chinon*
LOIRE, FR   IE| B+   PV| WPL| **$14**   B+

Rainoldi, 1998 *Valtellina Superiore, Prugnolo*
LOMBARDY, IT   IE| A-   PV| WPL| **$17**   A-

Rainoldi, 1998 *Valtellina Superiore, Il Crespino*
LOMBARDY, IT   IE| A-   PV| WPL| S   **$30**   A-

J. Portugal Ramos, 2001 *Vila Santa*
ALENTEJO, POR   IE| A-   PV| 99 A-   WPL| **$20**   A-

J. Portugal Ramos, 2000 *Marques de Borba Reserva*
ALENTEJO, POR   IE| B+   PV| WPL| **$12**   B+

Castell del Remei, 2000 *Gotim Bru*
COSTERS DEL SEGRE, SP   IE| A   PV| WPL| B   **$10**   A

Remelluri, 2000
RIOJA, SP   IE| A   PV| WPL| **$24**   A

Dom. Rimbert, 2001 *Le Chant de Marjolaine, Vin de Pays d'Oc*
LANGUEDOC, FR   IE| B+   PV| 99 B+   WPL| **$13**   B+

Rocca di Fabbri, 2000 *Montefalco*
UMBRIA, IT   IE| A-   PV| WPL| **$20**   A-

Rocche dei Manzoni, 1997 *Bricco, Vino da Tavola*
PIEDMONT, IT   IE| A, A-   PV| WPL| S,BBC   **$30**   A

Dom. Rocher, 2000 *Côtes du Rhône Villages-Cairanne*
RHÔNE, FR   IE| A   PV| 99 B+   WPL| **$12**   A

Ch. Romanin, 1998 *Les Baux*
PROVENCE, FR   IE| A-   PV| WPL| **$25**   A-

Quinta de Romera, 1999 *Fronteira Reserva*
DOURO, POR   IE| B+   PV| WPL| **$11**   B+

Quinta dos Roques, 2001
DOURO, POR   IE| A-   PV| WPL| **$18**   A-

Quinta dos Roques, 2000 *Tinta Roriz*
DÃO, POR   IE| A-   PV| WPL| **$22**   A-

REDS SORTED BY TYPE

OTHER RED (CONTINUED)

Quinta de Roriz, 2001 *Prazo de Roriz*
DOURO, POR   IE| B+   PV| WPL| $13 B+

Quinta de Roriz, 2000 *Reserva*
DOURO, POR   IE| A   PV| WPL| S $29 A

Rosemont, 2000 *Grenache/Mourvedre/Shiraz , McLaren Vale/Barossa Valley*
SOUTH, AUS   IE| A+   PV| WPL| S $30 A+

Rosenblum, 2001 *Mourvedre, Continente Vineyard, San Francisco Bay*
CA, USA   IE| A-   PV| WPL| $18 A-

Rotllan Torra, 1997 *Garnacha-Carinena-Cabernet Sauvignon, Reserva*
PRIORAT, SP   IE| B+   PV| WPL| $15 B+

Ryan Patrick, 1999 *Columbia Valley*
WA, USA   IE| A   PV| WPL| S $29 A

Saddleback, 1999 *Venge Family Reserve Scouts Honor, Oakville, Napa Valley*
CA, USA   IE| A   PV| WPL| S $30 A

Ch. Saint-Martin de la Garrigue, 2000 *Cuvée Tradition, Coteaux du Languedoc*
LANGUEDOC, FR IE| A-   PV| WPL| B $9   A-

Ch. Saint-Martin de la Garrigue, 2000 *Cuvée Réservée, Coteaux de Bessilles*
LANGUEDOC, FR IE| A   PV| WPL| B $10 A

Ch. Saint-Martin de la Garrigue, 2000 *Bronzinelle*
LANGUEDOC, FR IE| B+   PV| 99 A+   WPL| $15 B+

Dom. le Sang des Cailloux, 2000 *Cuvée Azaliaïs, Côtes du Rhône-Vacqueyras*
RHÔNE, FR   IE| A+   PV| WPL| $23 A+

Cooperativa Agricola de Santo, Isidro de Pegoes, 2000 *Cabernet/Touriga Nacional, Adega de Peg'es Colheita Seleccionada*
TERRAS DO SADO, POR IE| A-   PV| WPL| $13 A-

Dom. de la Sauveuse, 1999 *Côtes de Provence*
PROVENCE, FR IE| B+   PV| WPL| $13 B+

Scacciadiavoli, 2000 *Rosso, Montefalco*
UMBRIA, IT   IE| B+   PV| WPL| $12 B+

Seghesio, 1999 *Bouquet*
PIEDMONT, IT IE| A   PV| WPL| $18 A

Ch. des Ségriès, 2001 *Cuvée Réservée, Lirac*
RHÔNE, FR   IE| B+   PV| 99 B+   WPL| B $9   B+

Ch. des Ségriès, 2001 *Clos de l'Hermitage, Côtes du Rhône*
RHÔNE, FR   IE| A   PV| WPL| $15 A

Ch. des Ségriès, 2001 *Côtes du Rhône*
RHÔNE, FR   IE| B+   PV| WPL| B $8   B+

Faldas da Serra, 2000 *Quintas das Maias Jaen*
DÃO, POR   IE| A   PV| WPL| $22 A

Shooting Star, 2001 *Blue Franc Lemberger*
WA, USA   IE| B+   PV| WPL| $12 B+

Ch. Signac, 2000 *Village Chuscian, Côtes du Rhône*
RHÔNE, FR   IE| B+   PV| WPL| $15 B+

Ch. Signac, 2000 *Cuvée Terra Amata, Côtes du Rhône Villages-Chusclan*
FR   IE| A-   PV| WPL| **$22**   A-

Skouras, 1998 *Megas Oenos*
PELOPONNESE, GRC   IE| A   PV| WPL| **$19**   A

Finca Sobreno, 2000 *Crianza*
TORO, SP   IE| B+   PV| WPL| **$12**   B+

Soos Creek, NV *Sundance Red, Columbia Valley*
WA, USA   IE| A-   PV| WPL| **$20**   A-

Tamarack Cellars, 2000 *Firehouse Red, Walla Walla Valley*
WA, USA   IE| B+   PV| WPL| **$18**   B+

Tasca d'Almerita, 1999 *Cabernet/Nero d'Avola Cygnus*
SICILY, IT   IE| A-   PV| WPL| **$21**   A-

Dom. Tempier, 2000 *Appellation Bandol controlee, Bandol*
PROVENCE, FR   IE| A   PV| WPL| S   **$27**   A

Terrabianca, 1999 *Piano del Cipresso*
TUSCANO, IT   IE| A-   PV| WPL| **$22**   A-

Thurston Wolfe, 2000 *Lemberger/Syrah, Blue Franc, Columbia Valley*
WA, USA   IE| A-   PV| WPL| **$13**   A-

Tommasi, 1998 *Valpolicella Ripasso Classico Superiore*
VENETO, IT   IE| A-   PV| WPL| **$20**   A-

Tormaresca, 2000 *Red Table Wine*
APULIA, IT   IE| B+   PV| WPL| **$11**   B+

Dom. de la Tour du Bon, 1999 *Bandol*
PROVENCE, FR   IE| A+   PV| WPL| **$24**   A+

Trentadue, 2000 *Old Patch Red Estate, Alexander Valley, Sonoma Co.*
CA, USA   IE| B+   PV| WPL| **$15**   B+

Ch. les Trois Croix, 2000 *Fronsac*
BORDEAUX, FR   IE| A-   PV| WPL| **$14**   A-

Tsantali, 1997 *Rapsani Reserve, Epilegmonos*
GRC   IE| A-   PV| WPL| **$18**   A-

Dom. Tselepos, 2000 *Agiorghitiko*
NEMEA, GRC   IE| A-   PV| WPL| **$15**   A-

Dom. du Tunnel, 2000 *Cuvée Prestige, Cornas*
RHÔNE, FR   IE| A   PV| WPL| S   **$30**   A

Raymond Usseglio, 2000 *Châteauneuf-du-Pape*
RHÔNE, FR   IE| A   PV| WPL| S   **$30**   A

Cave de Vacqueyras, 2001 *Domaine Mas du Bouquet, Vacqueyras*
RHÔNE, FR   IE| B+   PV| WPL| **$12**   B+

Cave de Vacqueyras, 2001 *Chateau des Hautes Ribes, Vacqueyras*
RHÔNE, FR   IE| B+   PV| WPL| **$12**   B+

Val delle Rose, 1999 *Morellino di Scansano*
TUSCANY, IT   IE| B+   PV| WPL| **$14**   B+

Ch. Valcombe, 2000 *Cuvée Prestige, Costières de Nimes*
LANGUEDOC, FR   IE| A, B   PV| WPL| **$12**   A-

Vall Llach, 1999 *Embruix,*
PRIORAT, SP   IE| A   PV| WPL| **$25**   A

REDS SORTED BY TYPE

OTHER RED (CONTINUED)

Valle dell'Acate, 2001 *Nero d'Avola, Poggio Bidini*
SICILY, IT   IE| B+   PV| WPL| B $9   B+

Valley of the Moon, 1999 *Cuvée de la Luna, Sonoma Co.*
CA, USA   IE| A-   PV| WPL| S $28 A-

Venta Mazzaron, 2001
TORO, SP   IE| B+   PV| WPL| B $10 B+

Veramonte, 1999 *Cabernet/Carmenère, Primus, Alto, Casablanca Valley*
CENTRAL VALLEY, CH   IE| A   PV| WPL| $22 A

Le Vieux Donjon, 2000 *Châteauneuf-du-Pape*
RHÔNE, FR   IE| A+, A   PV| 99 A-   WPL| S,BBC $30 A+

Les Vignerons de Villeveyrac, 2000 *Moulin de Gassac Elise, Vieilles Vignes, Vin de Pays de l'Herault*
LANGUEDOC, FR   IE| B+   PV| WPL| $11 B+

Les Vignerons de Villeveyrac, 2000 *Moulin de Gassac Albaran, Vieilles Vignes, Vin de Pays de l'Herault*
LANGUEDOC, FR   IE| A-   PV| WPL| $11 A-

Vignobles, 2000 *Jean Royer Cuvèe Prestige*
RHÔNE, FR   IE| A-   PV| WPL| $23 A-

J. P. Vinhos, 1995 *J. P. Garrafeira, Palmela*
TERRAS DO SADO, POR IE| A   PV| WPL| B $9   A

Warwick, 2000 *Cabernet/Merlot/Pinotage Three Cape Ladies*
STELLENBOSCH, SA   IE| A+   PV| WPL| $23 A+

Waterbrook, 2001 *Cabernet Sauvignon/Merlot/Sangiovese/Syrah Melange,, Columbia Valley*
WA, USA   IE| B+   PV| WPL| $13 B+

Zaca Mesa, 1999 *Mourvedre, Chapel Vineyard, Santa Barbara Co.*
CA, USA   IE| B+   PV| WPL| $15 B+

WHITES

ALBARIÑO

Adega de Monção, 2001 *Alvarinho*
VINHO VERDE, POR   IE| B+   PV| WPL| $11 B+

A. Esteves Ferreira, 2001 *Alvarinho, Soalheiro*
VINHO VERDE, POR   IE| A+   PV| 99 A   WPL| $14 A+

Palacio de Fefinanes, 2001
RÍAS BAIXAS, SP   IE| B+   PV| WPL| $15 B+

Pazo de Barrantes, 2001
RÍAS BAIXAS, SP   IE| A-   PV| WPL| $15 A-

Pazo de Señorans, 2001
RÍAS BAIXAS, SP   IE| A-   PV| 99 A+, 00 A-   WPL| $15 A-

Quinta da Pedra, 2001 *Alvarinho*
VINHO VERDE, POR   IE| A+   PV| 99 A+   WPL| B $10 A+

Portal do Fidalgo, 2001 *Alvarinho*
VINHO VERDE, POR   IE| B+   PV| 99 A-, 00 A-   WPL| $15 B+

Pedro de Soutomaior, 2000
RÍAS BAIXAS, SP   IE| B+   PV| 99 A-   WPL| $15   B+

CHARDONNAY

Acacia, 2001 *Carneros*
CA, USA   IE| B+, B+, B+   PV| 00 B   WPL| W $20   B+

Alderbrook, 2000 *Dry Creek Valley, Sonoma Co.*
CA, USA   IE| B+   PV| WPL| $20   B+

Allandale, 2000 *Hunter Valley*
NEW SOUTH WALES, AUS IE| B+   PV| WPL| $15   B+

Anastasia, 2001
MENDOZA, ARG   IE| B+   PV| WPL| B $10   B+

Andretti, 2001 *Napa Valley*
CA, USA   IE| A-   PV| WPL| $16   A-

Arbor Crest, 2000 *Columbia Valley*
WA, USA   IE| B+   PV| WPL| $14   B+

Arrowood, 2001 *Somona Co.*
CA, USA   IE| A, B   PV| WPL| S $29   B+

Artesa, 2000 *Carneros*
CA, USA   IE| B+,   PV| 99 B+   WPL| $23   B+

Artesa, 2000 *Reserve, Carneros*
CA, USA   IE| A   PV| WPL| S $30   A

Babcock, 2000 *Santa Ynez Valley, Santa Barbara Co.*
CA, USA   IE| A-   PV| WPL| $25   A-

Bargetto, 2000 *Regan Vineyard, Santa Cruz Mountains*
CA, USA   IE| B+   PV| WPL| $20   B+

Barnard Griffin, 2000 *Reserve, Columbia Valley*
WA, USA   IE| B+   PV| WPL| $19   B+

Barnett, 2000 *Napa Valley*
CA, USA   IE| B+   PV| WPL| $25   B+

Barossa Valley, 2002 *Barossa Valley*
SOUTH, AUS   IE| B+   PV| WPL| B $10   B+

Baystone, 2000 *Dijon Clones 76 & 96, Saralee's Vineyard, Russian River Valley, Sonoma Co.*
CA, USA   IE| B+   PV| WPL| $20   B+

BearBoat, 2001 *Russian River Valley, Sonoma Co.*
CA, USA   IE| B+   PV| 99 A-   WPL| $17   B+

Beaulieu (BV), 2000 *Carneros Reserve, Napa Valley*
CA, USA   IE| A-   PV| WPL| S $28   A-

Bedford Thompson, 2000 *Santa Barbara Co.*
CA, USA   IE| A-   PV| WPL| $18   A-

Bellarine, 2000 *James' Paddock*
VICTORIA, AUS   IE| B+   PV| WPL| $15   B+

Beringer, 2000 *Appellation Collection Napa Valley*
CA, USA   IE| A   PV| WPL| $16   A

CHARDONNAY (CONTINUED)

Bernardus, 2000 *Monterey Co.*
CA, USA   IE| B+   PV| WPL| $20   B+

Bouchaine, 2001 *Carneros*
CA, USA   IE| B+, B+   PV| 99 A-   WPL| $18   B+

Bridgeview, 2000
OR, USA   IE| B+   PV| WPL| B $7   B+

Bridgeview, 2000 *Blue Moon*
OR, USA   IE| B+   PV| WPL| B $10   B+

Jean-Marc Brocard, 2000 *Côte de Jouan*
CHABLIS, FR   IE| A   PV| 99 A-   WPL| $25   A

Benoit Ente, 1999 *Puligny-Montrachet*
BURGUNDY, FR   IE| A-   PV| WPL| S $30   A-

Brookland Valley, 2000 *Margaret River*
SOUTH WEST, AUS   IE| A-   PV| WPL| $24   A-

Buitenverwachting, 2001
CONSTANTIA, SA   IE| B+   PV| WPL| $15   B+

Byington, 2001 *Sonoma Co.*
CA, USA   IE| B+   PV| WPL| $18   B+

Byington, 2000 *Sonoma Co.*
CA, USA   IE| B+   PV| 99 B+   WPL| $18   B+

Calera, 2000 *Central Coast*
CA, USA   IE| B+   PV| WPL| $18   B+

Callaway, 2001 *Reserve, Coastal*
CA, USA   IE| B+   PV| 99 B+   WPL| $15   B+

Callaway, 2000 *Reserve, Coastal, Santa Maria Valley, Santa Barbara Co.*
CA, USA   IE| B+   PV| 99 B+   WPL| $16   B+

Cambria, 2001 *Katherine's Vineyard, Santa Maria Valley, Santa Barbara Co.*
CA, USA   IE| A+   PV| 99 A, 00 A-   WPL| $20   A+

Cantiga Wineworks, 2000 *Monterey Co.*
CA, USA   IE| B+   PV| WPL| $20   B+

Carpe Diem, 2000 *Firepeak Vineyard, Edna Valley, San Luis Obispo Co.*
CA, USA   IE| A   PV| WPL| $25   A

Cartlidge and Browne, 2001
CA, USA   IE| B+   PV| WPL| B $10   B+

Casa Lapostolle, 2001 *Casablanca Valley*
CH   IE| B+   PV| WPL| B $10   B+

Catena, 2001 *Agrelo Vineyards*
MENDOZA, ARG   IE| A-   PV| WPL| $20   A-

Caterina, 2000 *Columbia Valley*
WA, USA   IE| B+   PV| WPL| $13   B+

Cathedral, 2001
WESTERN CAPE, SA   IE| A-   PV| WPL| W $12   A-

Cellars of Canterbury, 2000 *Momona*
MARLBOROUGH, NZ   IE| A-   PV| WPL| W $13   A-

Ch. Souverain, 2000 *Winemaker's Reserve, Russian River Valley, Sonoma Co.*
CA, USA   IE| B+   PV| 99 A   WPL| **$20**   B+

Ch. Souverain, 2001 *Sonoma Co.*
CA, USA   IE| B+, B   PV| 00 A-   WPL| W   **$14**   B+

Ch. Souverain, 2001 *Winemaker's Reserve, Russian River Valley, Sonoma Co.*
CA, USA   IE| A+   PV| 99 A, 00 B+   WPL| **$25**   A+

Ch. St. Jean, 2000 *Durell Vineyard, Carneros*
CA, USA   IE| A-, A   PV| 99 B   WPL| BBC   **$24**   A

Ch. St. Jean, 2000 *Belle Terre Vineyard, Alexander Valley, Sonoma Co.*
CA, USA   IE| A, A   PV| 99 B   WPL| BBC   **$22**   A

Ch. Ste. Michelle, 2000 *Columbia Valley*
WA, USA   IE| B+, B+, B, B+   PV| WPL| W   **$13**   B+

Ch. Ste. Michelle, 2000 *Cold Creek Vineyard, Columbia Valley*
WA, USA   IE| A-, A-   PV| 99 A-   WPL| S,BBC   **$26**   A-

Ch. Ste. Michelle, 2000 *Indian Wells Vineyards, Columbia Valley*
WA, USA   IE| A-, A   PV| 99 A-, 00 B+   WPL| BBC   **$21**   A

Ch. Ste. Michelle, 2000 *Canoe Ridge Vineyard, Columbia Valley*
WA, USA   IE| A-   PV| 99 A-   WPL| **$20**   A-

Ch. Ste. Michelle, 2000 *Reserve, Columbia Valley*
WA, USA   IE| A+   PV| 99 A-   WPL| S   **$29**   A+

Charles Krug, 2000 *Napa Valley*
CA, USA   IE| B+, B   PV| WPL| **$15**   B+

Charles Krug, 2001 *Napa Valley*
CA, USA   IE| B+   PV| 00 B+   WPL| **$17**   B+

Cloninger, 2000 *Estate Grown, Santa Lucia Highlands*
CA, USA   IE| B+   PV| WPL| **$16**   B+

Clos du Bois, 2000 *Calciare Vineyard, Alexander Valley, Sonoma Co.*
CA, USA   IE| A-, B   PV| WPL| **$22**   B+

Clos du Val, 2001 *Carneros, Napa Valley*
CA, USA   IE| B+, B+   PV| WPL| **$21**   B+

Clos la Chance, 2000 *Santa Cruz Mountains*
CA, USA   IE| B+   PV| WPL| **$19**   B+

Clos la Chance, 2001 *Vanumanutagi Vineyard, Santa Cruz Mountains*
CA, USA   IE| A, A   PV| 00 A-   WPL| S,BBC   **$30**   A

Coldstream Hills, 1998 *Reserve, Yarra Valley*
VICTORIA, AUS   IE| A   PV| WPL| **$20**   A

Dom. Jean Collet, 2000 *Montèe de Tonnerre*
CHABLIS, FR   IE| A   PV| WPL| S   **$29**   A

Concha y Toro, 2001 *Marqués de Casa Concha, Puente Alto Vineyard, Maipo Valley*
CENTRAL VALLEY, CH   IE| A-   PV| 00 A   WPL| **$14**   A-

Cristom, 2001 *Germaine Vineyard, Willamette Valley*
OR, USA   IE| A   PV| WPL| **$19**   A

Cuvaison, 2001 *Carneros, Napa Valley*
CA, USA   IE| A   PV| 00 A-   WPL| **$22**   A

WHITES
SORTED BY TYPE

CHARDONNAY (CONTINUED)

Dallas Conté, 2002 *Casablanca Valley*
CENTRAL VALLEY, CH   IE| B+   PV| WPL| B $10   B+

Davis Bynum, 2000 *Limited Edition, Russian River Valley, Sonoma Co.*
CA, USA   IE| A   PV| WPL| S $30   A

De Loach, 2000 *Russian River Valley, Sonoma Co.*
CA, USA   IE| B+, B+   PV| WPL| W $18   B+

De Wetshof, 2001 *Bon Vallon*
ROBERTSON, SA   IE| A-   PV| 00 B+   WPL| $14   A-

Dehlinger, 2000 *Estate, Russian River Valley, Sonoma Co.*
CA, USA   IE| A-   PV| 99 A-   WPL| S $27   A-

Dom. Alain Normand, 2000 *La Roche Vineuse, Mâcon*
BURGUNDY, FR   IE| B+   PV| WPL| $13   B+

Domaine Alfred, 2001 *Chamisal Vineyards, Edna Valley*
CA, USA   IE| A, B   PV| WPL| $22   B+

Domaine Chandon, 2000 *Carneros*
CA, USA   IE| A-   PV| WPL| $19   A-

Errazuriz, 2001 *Casablanca Valley*
CH   IE| B+, B   PV| WPL| B $10   B+

Esser Cellars, 2001 *California*
CA, USA   IE| A-   PV| WPL| B $8   A-

Evans & Tate, 2001 *Margaret River*
WESTERN, AUS   IE| B+, B+   PV| WPL| $15   B+

Everett Ridge, 2000 *Hawk Hill Vineyard, Russian River Valley, Sonoma Co.*
CA, USA   IE| B+   PV| WPL| $20   B+

Fess Parker, 2000 *Santa Barbara Co.*
CA, USA   IE| B+   PV| WPL| $18   B+

Flora Springs, 2001 *Barrel Fermented Reserve, Napa Valley*
CA, USA   IE| A-   PV| WPL| S $26   A-

Forgeron Cellars, 2001 *Columbia Valley*
WA, USA   IE| B+   PV| WPL| $19   B+

Frank Family, 2000 *Napa Valley*
CA, USA   IE| B+, A-   PV| WPL| S $29   A-

Frei Brothers, 2001 *Reserve, Russian River Valley, Northern Sonoma*
CA, USA   IE| A, B, A-   PV| WPL| W,BBC $20   A-

Gainey, 2000 *Santa Barbara Co.*
CA, USA   IE| A-   PV| WPL| $18   A-

Gallo Sonoma, 2000 *Laguna Ranch Vineyard, Russian River Valley, Sonoma Co.*
CA, USA   IE| A-   PV| WPL| $24   A-

Gary Farrell, 2000 *Russian River Valley, Sonoma Co.*
CA, USA   IE| A+   PV| WPL| S $29   A+

Geyser Peak, 2001 *Sonoma Co.*
CA, USA   IE| B+   PV| WPL| $12   B+

Geyser Peak, 2001 *Block Collection, Ricci Vineyard, Carneros*
CA, USA   IE| B+, A-, B+   PV| 00 A-   WPL| $21   B+

Girard, 2001 *Russian River Valley, Sonoma Co.*
CA, USA   IE| B+   PV| WPL| $20   B+

Gloria Ferrer, 2000 *Carneros*
CA, USA   IE| A-, A-, B+, B+   PV| WPL| BBC $20   A-

Dom. Jean-Pierre Grossot, 2000 *Vaucoupins*
CHABLIS, FR   IE| A   PV| WPL| $25   A

Dom. Jean-Pierre Grossot, 2000 *Mont de Milieu*
CHABLIS, FR   IE| A   PV| WPL| S $30   A

Handley, 2000 *Estates, Anderson Valley, Mendocino Co.*
CA, USA   IE| B+   PV| WPL| $16   B+

Hanna, 2001 *Estate, Russian River Valley, Sonoma Co.*
CA, USA   IE| A   PV| WPL| $18   A

Hardys, 2001 *Eileen Hardy*
SOUTH, AUS   IE| A   PV| WPL| $20   A

Hartford, 2000 *Sonoma Coast, Sonoma Co.*
CA, USA   IE| A-, A, A   PV| WPL| BBC $24   A

Heggies, 2001 *Eden Valley*
SOUTH, AUS   IE| B+   PV| WPL| $20   B+

Huntington Cellars, 2000 *Russian River Valley, Sonoma Co.*
CA, USA   IE| B+   PV| WPL| $15   B+

Iron Horse, 2000 *Sonoma Co.*
CA, USA   IE| A   PV| WPL| S $26   A

Jacob's Creek, 2001 *Reserve*
SOUTH, AUS   IE| B+   PV| WPL| $14   B+

James, 2000 *Compass, Hunter Valley*
NEW SOUTH WALES, AUS IE| A-   PV| WPL| $13   A-

James, 2000 *Chardonnay-Semillon, Sundara, Hunter Valley*
NEW SOUTH WALES, AUS IE| B+   PV| WPL| B $9   B+

Jordan, 2000 *Russian River Valley, Sonoma Co.*
CA, USA   IE| A   PV| WPL| S $26   A

Joullian, 2000 *Monterey Co.*
CA, USA   IE| B+, A-   PV| WPL| BBC $16   A-

Daniel Junot, 2001
BURGUNDY, FR   IE| B+   PV| WPL| $11   B+

Justin, 2000 *Paso Robles, San Luis Obispo Co.*
CA, USA   IE| A, B-   PV| WPL| $19   B+

Katnook, 2000 *Coonawarra*
SOUTH, AUS   IE| A-   PV| WPL| $17   A-

Keller, 2000 *La Cruz Vineyard, Sonoma Coast, Sonoma Co.*
CA, USA   IE| A+, A-, A+, B+, A PV| WPL| BBC $25   A

Kendall-Jackson, 2000 *Grand Reserve*
CA, USA   IE| B+   PV| 99 B+   WPL| W $18   B+

Kendall-Jackson, 2000 *Estate Series, Camelot Beach, Santa Maria Valley, Santa Barbara Co.*
CA, USA   IE| A-   PV| WPL| W $17   A-

CHARDONNAY (CONTINUED)

Kenwood, 2001 *Reserve, Russian River Valley, Sonoma Co.*
CA, USA   IE| B+   PV| WPL| **$20**   **B+**

Kooyong, 2000 *Mornington Penninsula*
AUS   IE| A   PV| WPL| **$25**   **A**

Kumeu River, 2000 *Kumeu River*
AUCKLAND, NZ   IE| A+   PV| 99 A-   WPL| **$22**   **A+**

Kunde, 2000 *C. S. Ridge, Sonoma Valley, Sonoma Co.*
CA, USA   IE| A-   PV| WPL| **$22**   **A-**

Kunde, 2000 *Kinneybrook Vineyard, Sonoma Valley, Sonoma Co.*
CA, USA   IE| B+, B+   PV| WPL| **$20**   **B+**

Kunde, 2000 *Wildwood Vineyard, Sonoma Valley, Sonoma Co.*
CA, USA   IE| B+, A   PV| WPL| BBC   **$20**   **A-**

La Crema, 2001 *Sonoma Coast, Sonoma Co.*
CA, USA   IE| B+   PV| WPL| W   **$16**   **B+**

Lafond, 2000 *Santa Ynez Valley, Santa Barbara Co.*
CA, USA   IE| B+   PV| WPL| **$18**   **B+**

Lafond, 2000 *Sweeny Canyon Vineyard, Santa Ynez Valley, Santa Barbara Co.*
CA, USA   IE| A-   PV| WPL| S   **$28**   **A-**

Dom. Hubert Lamy, 2000 *Les Frionnes, Saint-Aubin*
BURGUNDY, FR   IE| A   PV| WPL| S   **$28**   **A**

Landmark, 2000 *Overlook, Sonoma Co.-Santa Barbara Co.-Monterey Coounty*
CA, USA   IE| A   PV| 99 A-   WPL| **$25**   **A**

Leatitia, 2001 *Estate, Arroyo Grande Valley, San Luis Obispo Co.*
CA, USA   IE| A-   PV| 99 B+   WPL| **$18**   **A-**

LinCourt, 2000 *LinCourt Vineyards, Santa Barbara Co.*
CA, USA   IE| B+, B   PV| 99 A-   WPL| **$19**   **B+**

Linden, 2000 *Hawkes Bay, Esk Valley*
HAWKES BAY, NZ   IE| B+   PV| WPL| B   **$10**   **B+**

Liparita, 2000 *Reserve, Lake Vineyard, Carneros*
CA, USA   IE| A-   PV| WPL| S   **$30**   **A-**

Logan, 1999 *Reserve, Orange*
AUS   IE| A   PV| WPL| **$21**   **A**

Longoria, 2000 *Santa Rita Hills*
CA, USA   IE| A   PV| WPL| **$25**   **A**

MacRostie, 2001 *Carneros*
CA, USA   IE| A   PV| 00 A-   WPL| **$20**   **A**

Marcelina, 2001 *Carneros*
CA, USA   IE| B+   PV| WPL| **$25**   **B+**

Marimar Torres, 2000 *Don Miguel Vineyard, Russian River Valley, Sonoma Co.*
CA, USA   IE| A   PV| 99 A-   WPL| S   **$26**   **A**

Martin Ray, 2000 *Mariage, Russian River Valley, Sonoma Co.*
CA, USA   IE| B+   PV| WPL| **$18**   **B+**

Martinelli, 2000 *Woolsey Road, Russian River Valley, Sonoma Co.*
CA, USA   IE| A, A   PV| WPL| S,BBC   **$28**   **A**

Martinelli, 2000 *Gold Ridge, Russian River Valley, Sonoma Co.*
CA, USA   IE| A-   PV| WPL| $25 A-

McCrea, 2000 *Elerding Vineyard, Yakima Valley*
WA, USA   IE| A-   PV| WPL| S $30 A-

McIlroy, 2000 *Aquarius Ranch, Russian River Valley, Sonoma Co.*
CA, USA   IE| B+   PV| WPL| $20 B+

Melville, 2000 *Santa Rita Hills, Santa Barbara Co.*
CA, USA   IE| B+   PV| WPL| $20 B+

Melville, 2000 *Clone 76, Inox, Santa Rita Hills, Santa Barbara Co.*
CA, USA   IE| A-   PV| WPL| $25 A-

Merryvale, 2000 *Dutton Ranch, Russian River Valley, Sonoma Co.*
CA, USA   IE| A   PV| WPL| S $29 A

Miner, 2000 *Napa Valley*
CA, USA   IE| A-   PV| WPL| S $30 A-

Mont St. John, 2000 *Madonna Estate, Carneros*
CA, USA   IE| A-, A-   PV| WPL| BBC $16 A-

Montes, 2002 *Reserve, Barrel Fermented, Curicó Valley*
CENTRAL VALLEY, CH   IE| B+   PV| WPL| B $10 B+

Morgenhof, 1999
STELLENBOSCH, SA   IE| A-   PV| WPL| $14 A-

Mount Eden, 2000 *MacGregor Vineyard, Edna Valley, San Luis Obispo Co.*
CA, USA   IE| A   PV| WPL| $18 A

Muddy Water, 2000
WAIPARA VALLEY, NZ   IE| A-   PV| WPL| $20 A-

Navarro, 2001 *Première Reserve, Anderson Valley, Mendocino Co.*
CA, USA   IE| A+   PV| WPL| $18 A+

Neyers, 2000 *Napa Valley*
CA, USA   IE| A, A-, B+, B+   PV| 99 A   WPL| S,BBC $30 A-

Neyers, 2000 *Carneros*
CA, USA   IE| A   PV| 00 A   WPL| S $26 A

Nga Waka, 2000
MARTINBOROUGH, NZ   IE| A+   PV| WPL| $25 A+

Le Noble, 2001 *Vin de Pays*
SOUTH, FR   IE| B+   PV| WPL| B $7 B+

Ojai, 2000 *Talley-Rincon Vineyard, Arroyo Grande Valley, San Luis Obispo Co.*
CA, USA   IE| A   PV| WPL| S $27 A

Okahu, 2000
NORTHLAND CHIFTON, NZIE| A   PV| WPL| $17 A

Paschal, 2000 *Rogue Valley*
OR, USA   IE| B+   PV| WPL| $18 B+

Pegasus Bay, 2000
WAIPARA VALLEY, NZ   IE| A, B+   PV| 99 A   WPL| S,BBC $30 A-

Penmara, 2000 *Reserve*
NEW SOUTH WALES, AUS IE| B+   PV| WPL| $13 B+

Perbacco Cellars, 2000 *La Linda Vineyard, Edna Valley*
CA, USA   IE| A-   PV| WPL| $18 A-

CHARDONNAY (CONTINUED)

Pessagno, 2000 *Sleepy Hollow Vineyard, Santa Lucia Highlands*
CA, USA   IE| A   PV| WPL| S $30   A

Pietra Santa, 2001 *Cienega Valley*
CA, USA   IE| B+   PV| WPL| $13   B+

Pine Crest, 2000
FRANSCHHOEK, SA   IE| B+   PV| WPL| $13   B+

Pine Ridge, 2001 *Dijon Clones, Carneros, Napa Valley*
CA, USA   IE| A-   PV| 00 A-   WPL| S $27   A-

Porter Creek, 2000 *George's Hill, Russian River Valley, Sonoma Co.*
CA, USA   IE| B+   PV| 99 A   WPL| $18   B+

Qupé, 2000 *Reserve, Bien Nacido Vineyard, Santa Maria Valley, Santa Barbara Co.*
CA, USA   IE| A   PV| 99 A-   WPL| $25   A

Qupé, 2001 *Reserve Block Eleven, Bien Nacido Vineyard, Santa Maria Valley, Santa Barbara Co.*
CA, USA   IE| A-   PV| 00 A   WPL| $25   A-

Reynolds, 2001
NEW SOUTH WALES, AUS   IE| B+   PV| WPL| B $10   B+

Robert Craig, 2001 *Russian River Valley, Sonoma Co.*
CA, USA   IE| A-   PV| WPL| $24   A-

Robert Mondavi, 2000 *Napa Valley*
CA, USA   IE| A+   PV| WPL| $24   A+

Robert Stemmler, 2000 *Sonoma Co.*
CA, USA   IE| A, A   PV| WPL| BBC $20   A

Rochioli, 2000 *Estate, Russian River Valley, Sonoma Co.*
CA, USA   IE| A   PV| WPL| S $30   A

Rockbare, 2002 *McLaren Vale*
SOUTH, AUS   IE| B+   PV| WPL| $12   B+

Rodney Strong, 2001 *Sonoma Co.*
CA, USA   IE| B+   PV| 99 B+   WPL| $14   B+

Rothbury, 2001
SOUTH EASTERN, AUS   IE| A-   PV| WPL| B $8   A-

Rusack, 2001 *Santa Barbara Co.*
CA, USA   IE| A-   PV| WPL| $18   A-

Saint Clair, 2001 *Unoaked*
MARLBOROUGH, NZ   IE| B+   PV| WPL| $15   B+

Saint Clair, 2001
MARLBOROUGH, NZ   IE| A-, B   PV| WPL| $15   B+

Sandalford, 2001 *Margaret River*
AUS   IE| A   PV| WPL| $25   A

Sandhill, 2001 *Burrowing Owl Vineyard, Okanagan Valley*
BC, CAN   IE| B+   PV| WPL| $11   B+

Santa Barbara, 2000 *Reserve, Santa Ynez Valley, Santa Barbara Co.*
CA, USA   IE| A   PV| WPL| $22   A

Santa Rita, 2002 *Reserva, Casablanca Valley*
CENTRAL VALLEY, CH   IE| A-   PV| WPL| $12 A-

Schweiger Vineyards, 2000 *Spring Mountain, Napa Valley*
CA, USA   IE| A-   PV| WPL| S $30 A-

Shea Wine Cellars, 2000 *Shea Vineyard, Willamette Valley*
OR, USA   IE| A-   PV| WPL| $25 A-

Silver Lake, 2000 *Reserve, Columbia Valley*
WA, USA   IE| B+   PV| WPL| $14 B+

Silverado, 2000 *Napa Valley*
CA, USA   IE| A   PV| WPL| $20 A

Simonsig, 2000
STELLENBOSCH, SA   IE| B+, B, B, B+ PV| WPL| B $10 B+

Smith Madrone, 2000 *Napa Valley*
CA, USA   IE| A-, A   PV| WPL| BBC $25 A

Sonoma-Loeb, 2001 *Private Reserve, Sonoma Co.*
CA, USA   IE| A+   PV| WPL| S $27 A+

St. Clement, 2001 *Napa Valley*
CA, USA   IE| B+   PV| WPL| $16 B+

St. Clement, 2000 *Abbotts Vineyard, Carneros, Napa Valley*
CA, USA   IE| A   PV| 99 A-   WPL| $20 A

St. Supéry, 2000 *Napa Valley*
CA, USA   IE| B+   PV| 99 B+   WPL| W $19 B+

Stags' Leap Winery, 2001 *Napa Valley*
CA, USA   IE| A-   PV| WPL| $22 A-

Stephen Ross, 2000 *Edna Ranch, Edna Valley*
CA, USA   IE| B+   PV| WPL| $20 B+

Talley, 2000 *Arroyo Grande Valley, San Luis Obispo Co.*
CA, USA   IE| A   PV| 99 A-   WPL| $24 A

Talley, 2000 *Oliver's Vineyard, Edna Valley, San Luis Obispo Co.*
CA, USA   IE| A, A-, A-, A- PV| WPL| BBC $20 A-

Te Mata, 2000
HAWKES BAY, NZ   IE| B+   PV| WPL| $18 B+

Truchard, 2000 *Carneros, Napa Valley*
CA, USA   IE| A-, B+, B, B+, A, A- PV| 99 A- WPL| S,BBC $30 A-

Truchard, 2001 *Carneros, Napa Valley*
CA, USA   IE| A-   PV| WPL| S $30 A-

Valley of the Moon, 2001 *Sonoma Co.*
CA, USA   IE| B+   PV| WPL| $15 B+

Varner, 2001 *Amphitheater Block, Santa Cruz Mountains*
CA, USA   IE| A   PV| WPL| S $30 A

Verget, 2000 *Cuvèe des 10 Ans*
CHABLIS, FR   IE| A   PV| WPL| S $30 A

Vie di Romans, 2000 *Isonzo*
FRIULI, IT   IE| A-   PV| WPL| S $28 A-

White Oak, 2000 *Russian River Valley, Sonoma Co.*
CA, USA   IE| B+, B+, B, A-   PV| 99 A- WPL| $16 B+

Whitford, 2000 *Haynes Vineyard, Napa Valley*
CA, USA   IE| A, A   PV| WPL| S,BBC $28   A

Williams Selyem, 2000 *Russian River Valley, Sonoma Co.*
CA, USA   IE| A   PV| WPL| S $30   A

Willow Brook, 2001 *Oak Ridge Vineyard, Russian River Valley, Sonoma Co.*
CA, USA   IE| A-   PV| WPL| S $28   A-

Windsor, 2000 *Reserve, Signature Series, Russian River Valley, Sonoma Co.*
CA, USA   IE| B+   PV| WPL| $20   B+

Wolf Blass, 2002
SOUTH, AUS   IE| B+   PV| WPL| $14   B+

Wolff, 2001 *Old Vines, Edna Valley*
CA, USA   IE| A-   PV| WPL| $19   A-

Xanadu, 2000 *Margaret River*
WESTERN, AUS   IE| A-   PV| WPL| $15   A-

CHENIN BLANC

Dom. Des Baumard, 2000 *Clos de Papillon, Savennieres*
LOIRE, FR   IE| A-   PV| WPL| $23   A-

Chalone, 2001 *Chalone Estate*
CA, USA   IE| A   PV| 00 A-   WPL| $22   A

Benoit Gautier, 2001 *Vouvray*
LOIRE, FR   IE| A-   PV| WPL| $11   A-

S. A. Huët, 2000 *Sec, Clos du Bourg, Vouvray*
LOIRE, FR   IE| A-   PV| WPL| $20   A-

S. A. Huët, 2000 *Demi Sec, Clos du Bourg, Vouvray*
LOIRE, FR   IE| A   PV| WPL| $20   A

L'Ecole No. 41, 2001 *Walla Voila, Walla Walla Co.*
WA, USA   IE| B+   PV| WPL| $12   B+

Mulderbosch, 2002
STELLENBOSCH, SA   IE| B+   PV| WPL| $14   B+

J.-C. Pichot, 2002 *Vouvray, Dom. Le Peu de la Moriette*
LOIRE, FR   IE| A-   PV| WPL| $11   A-

Pierre & Yves Soulez, 1999 *Cuvée d'Avant, Ch. de Chamboureau, Savennières-Roche aux Moines Doux*
LOIRE, FR   IE| A+   PV| WPL| S $29   A+

Ch. Villeneuve, 2001 *Samur*
LOIRE, FR   IE| B+   PV| WPL| $11   B+

GEWÜRZTRAMINER

Alexander Valley, 2001 *New Gewürz, North Coast*
CA, USA   IE| B+   PV| WPL| B $9   B+

Arrowood, 2001 *Saralee's Vineyard, Russian River Valley, Sonoma Co.*
CA, USA   IE| B+   PV| WPL| $20   B+

Dr. Konstantin Frank, 2001 *Finger Lakes*
NY, USA   IE| A   PV| WPL| $16   A

Hogue, 2001 *Columbia Valley*
WA, USA   IE| B+   PV| WPL| B $10   B+

Louis M. Martini, 2000 *Del Rio Vineyard, Russian River Valley, Sonoma Co.*
CA, USA   IE| B+   PV| WPL| $15 B+

McIlroy, 2000 *Late Harvest, Aquarius Ranch, Russian River Valley, Sonoma Co.*
CA, USA   IE| B+   PV| WPL| $13 B+

Navarro, 2001 *Dry, Anderson Valley, Mendocino Co.*
CA, USA   IE| A-   PV| 00 A+   WPL| $15 A-

Saint Chapelle, 2001 *Dry Gewurztraminer*
ID, USA   IE| B+   PV| WPL| B $6 B+

Sineann, 2001 *Celilo Vineyard, Columbia Valley*
WA, USA   IE| A+   PV| WPL| $18 A+

Pierre Sparr, 2001
ALSACE, FR   IE| B+, B+   PV| WPL| $13 B+

Pierre Sparr, 2001 *Réserve*
ALSACE, FR   IE| A+, B+   PV| WPL| BBC $15 A

Spy Valley, 2001
MARLBOROUGH, NZ   IE| B+, B+   PV| WPL| $12 B+

Stony Hill, 2000 *Napa Valley*
CA, USA   IE| B+   PV| WPL| $15 B+

Thomas Fogarty, 2001 *Monterey Co.*
CA, USA   IE| A   PV| 00 B+   WPL| $15 A

Three Rivers Winery, 2001 *Late Harvest Biscuit Ridge, Walla Walla Valley*
WA, USA   IE| A   PV| WPL| $23 A

PINOT GRIS/GRIGIO

J. B. Adam, 2001 *Réserve*
ALSACE, FR   IE| B+   PV| WPL| $13 B+

Babcock, 2001 *Santa Barbara Co.*
CA, USA   IE| B+   PV| WPL| $13 B+

Castello Banfi, 2001 *Pinot Grigio, San Angelo*
TUSCANY, IT   IE| B+   PV| WPL| $15 B+

Big Fire, 2001
OR, USA   IE| B+   PV| WPL| $14 B+

Albert Boxler, 2000 *Tokay Pinot Gris*
ALSACE, FR   IE| A-   PV| WPL| $23 A-

Bridgeview, 2000 *Pinot Gris, Reserve*
OR, USA   IE| B+, B+   PV| WPL| $15 B+

Ca' Montini, 2001 *Trentino*
TRENTINO-ALTO ADIGE, IT   IE| A-   PV| WPL| $15 A-

Ch. Ste. Michelle, 2002 *Pinot Gris, Columbia Valley*
WA, USA   IE| B+   PV| 01 B+   WPL| W $13 B+

Ch. Ste. Michelle, 2001 *Pinot Gris, Columbia Valley*
WA, USA   IE| B+   PV| WPL| $13 B+

Chehalem, 2001 *Willamette Valley*
OR, USA   IE| B+   PV| WPL| $15 B+

Elk Cove, 2001 *Pinot Gris, Willamette Valley*
OR, USA   IE| B+   PV| 99 A-, 00 B+   WPL| $15 B+

PINOT GRIS/GRIGIO (CONTINUED)

Marco Felluga, 2001 *Collio*
FRIULI, IT   IE| B+   PV| WPL| W $15   B+

King Estate, 2001 *Pinot Gris, Reserve, Eugene*
OR, USA   IE| A-   PV| 00 B+   WPL| $20   A-

Luna, 2000 *Pinot Grigio, Napa Valley*
CA, USA   IE| A-; B+   PV| 99 A-   WPL| $18   B+

Luna, 2001 *Napa Valley*
CA, USA   IE| A, A   PV| 00 B+   WPL| BBC $20   A

MacMurray Ranch, 2001 *Russian River Valley, Sonoma Co.*
CA, USA   IE| A   PV| WPL| $23   A

Morgan, 2001 *Santa Lucia Highlands R&D, Franscioni Vineyard, Monterey Co.*
CA, USA   IE| B+   PV| WPL| $15   B+

Navarro, 2001 *Pinot Gris, Anderson Valley, Mendocino Co.*
CA, USA   IE| A+   PV| 00 A   WPL| $16   A+

Lis Neris, 2000
FRIULI, IT   IE| A-   PV| WPL| S $28   A-

Raptor Ridge, 2001 *Pinot Gris, Yamhill Vineyard, Willamette Valley*
OR, USA   IE| B+   PV| WPL| $15   B+

Rex Hill, 2000 *Pinot Gris, Reserve*
OR, USA   IE| A-, B   PV| WPL| $18   B+

Rex Hill, 2001 *Pinot Gris, Reserve*
OR, USA   IE| B+   PV| 00 B+   WPL| $18   B+

Sineann, 2001
OR, USA   IE| A-   PV| WPL| $15   A-

Pierre Sparr, 2001
ALSACE, FR   IE| B+   PV| WPL| $13   B+

Stone Wolf, 2001
OR, USA   IE| B+   PV| WPL| B $10   B+

Vie di Romans, 2000 *Dessimis, Isonzo*
FRIULI, IT   IE| A-   PV| WPL| S $28   A-

Vieil Armand, 2000 *Tokay, Grand Cru Ollviller*
ALSACE, FR   IE| A   PV| WPL| $22   A

WillaKenzie, 2001 *Pinot Gris*
OR, USA   IE| A   PV| 99 A-, 00 A-   WPL| $20   A

RIESLING

J. B. Adam, 2001 *Cuvée Jean-Baptiste, Kaefferkopf*
ALSACE, FR   IE| A   PV| WPL| $20   A

Dr. von Bassermann-Jordan, 2001 *Spätlese trocken, Forster Ungeheuer*
PFALZ, GER   IE| A   PV| WPL| $22   A

Dr. Pauly Bergweiler, 20001 *Kabinett, Graacher Himmelreich*
MOSEL-SAAR-RUWER, GER   IE| B+   PV| WPL| $14   B+

Dr. Pauly Bergweiler, 2001 *Noble House Riesling QbA*
MOSEL-SAAR-RUWER, GER   IE| B+   PV| WPL| B $8   B+

Dr. Pauly Bergweiler, 2001 *Kabinett, Bernkasteler alte Badstube am Doctorberg*
MOSEL-SAAR-RUWER, GER   IE| A+   PV| WPL| $16 A+

Dr. Pauly Bergweiler, 2001 *Kabinett, Bernkasteler Badstube*
MOSEL-SAAR-RUWER, GER   IE| A-   PV| WPL| $14 A-

Dr. Pauly Bergweiler, 2001 *Auslese, Wehlener Sonnenuhr*
MOSEL-SAAR-RUWER, GER   IE| A-   PV| WPL| S $26 A-

Ch. W. Bernard, 2001 *Kabinett, Hackenheimer Kirchberg*
RHEINHESSEN, GER   IE| A-   PV| WPL| $16 A-

Bonair, 2001 *Yakima Valley*
WA, USA   IE| A-   PV| WPL| B $10 A-

Georg Breuer, 2001 *Terra Montosa QbA*
MOSEL-SAAR-RUWER, GER   IE| A-   PV| WPL| $20 A-

Bründlmayer, 2001 *Steinmassel, Lagenlois*
KAMPTAL, AUT   IE| A, A+   PV| 99 A-, 00 A   WPL| BBC $25 A

Dr. Bürklin-Wolf, 2001 *Bürklin Estate QbA*
MOSEL-SAAR-RUWER, GER   IE| A-   PV| WPL| $16 A-

Ch. Montelena, 2001 *Potter Valley, Mendocino Co.*
CA, USA   IE| B+, B   PV| 99 B+   WPL| $15 B+

Ch. Ste. Michelle, 2001 *Cold Creek Vineyard, Columbia Valley*
WA, USA   IE| A-   PV| WPL| $14 A-

Ch. Ste. Michelle, 2001 *Eroica Riesling, Columbia Valley*
WA, USA   IE| A   PV| 99 B+   WPL| $20 A

Ch. Ste. Michelle, 2001 *Dry Riesling, Columbia Valley*
WA, USA   IE| A-   PV| WPL| B $8 A-

Ch. Ste. Michelle & Dr. Loosen, 2001 *Eroica, Columbia Valley*
WA, USA   IE| A-   PV| 99 A-, 00 B+   WPL| $20 A-

A. Christmann, 2001 *Auslese, Ruppertsberger Reiterpfad*
GER   IE| A+   PV| WPL| S $30 A+

Jon. Jos. Christoffel, 2001 *Kabinett, Erdener Treppchen*
MOSEL-SAAR-RUWER, GER   IE| A   PV| WPL| $23 A

Claar, 2001 *Late Harvest, White Bluffs, Columbia Valley*
WA, USA   IE| A-   PV| WPL| B $10 A-

Columbia, 2002 *Cellarmaster's Reserve, Columbia Valley*
WA, USA   IE| B+   PV| 99 B+   WPL| W, B $8 B+

Craneford, 2001 *Eden Valley*
SOUTH, AUS   IE| B+   PV| WPL| $12 B+

Crusius, 2001 *Kabinett, Traiser Rotelfels*
NAHE, GER   IE| A   PV| WPL| $22 A

Dopff & Irion, 2001 *Dom. de Ch. de Riquewihr, Les Murailles*
ALSACE, FR   IE| A-   PV| WPL| $19 A-

Elysian Fields, 2001 *Clare Valley*
SOUTH, AUS   IE| A-   PV| WPL| $20 A-

Emrich-Schönleber, 2001 *Kabinett Halbtrocken, Monzinger Halenberg*
NAHE, GER   IE| A-   PV| WPL| $16 A-

Emrich-Schönleber, 2001 *Kabinett, Monzinger Frülingsplätzchen*
NAHE, GER   IE| A+   PV| WPL| $16 A+

RIESLING (CONTINUED)

Karl Erbes, 2001 *Spätlese, Urziger Würzgarten*
MOSEL-SAAR-RUWER, GER   IE| B+   PV| WPL| $14   B+

Robert Eymael (Mönchhof), 2001 *QbA*
MOSEL-SAAR-RUWER, GER   IE| A-   PV| WPL| $14   A-

Frankland, 2001 *Isolation Ridge, Frankland River*
WESTERN, AUS   IE| B+   PV| WPL| $15   B+

Frankland, 2001 *Poison Hill, Frankland River*
WESTERN, AUS   IE| A   PV| WPL| $15   A

Frankland, 2001 *Cooladerra, Frankland River*
WESTERN, AUS   IE| A   PV| WPL| $15   A

Friedrich-Wilhelm-Gymnasium, 2001 *Spätlese, Graacher Himmelreich*
MOSEL-SAAR-RUWER, GER   IE| A   PV| WPL| $18   A

Giesen, 2001
CANTERBURY, NZ   IE| A-   PV| 00 B+   WPL| $13   A-

Carl Graff, 2001 *Auslese, Erdener Prälat*
MOSEL-SAAR-RUWER, GER   IE| B+   PV| WPL| $14   B+

Grans-Fassian, 2001 *Kabinett, Trittenheirmer*
MOSEL-SAAR-RUWER, GER   IE| A-,A PV| WPL| BBC $17   A

Grosset, 2002 *Polish Hill, Clare Valley*
SOUTH, AUS   IE| A+   PV| 01 A   WPL| S $29   A+

Grosset, 2002 *Watervale, Clare Valley*
SOUTH, AUS   IE| A   PV| WPL| $24   A

Johann Haart, 2001 *Spätlese, Piesporter Goldtröpfchen*
MOSEL-SAAR-RUWER, GER   IE| A   PV| WPL| $20   A

Helmut Hexamer, 2001 *Spätlese, Meddersheimer Rheingrafenberg*
NAHE, GER   IE| A-,A- PV| WPL| BBC $19   A-

Helmut Hexamer, 2001 *Kabinett, Meddersheimer Rheingrafenberg*
NAHE, GER   IE| B+   PV| WPL| $16   B+

Hogue, 2002 *Johannisberg Riesling, Columbia Valley*
WA, USA   IE| B+   PV| 00 B+   WPL| W, B $9   B+

Jakoby-Mathy, 2001 *Riesling Kabinett, Kinheimer Rosenberg*
MOSEL-SAAR-RUWER, GER   IE| A-   PV| WPL| $13   A-

Schloss Johannisberger, 2001 *Spätlese*
RHEINGAU, GER   IE| A+   PV| WPL| S $28   A+

Schloss Johannisberger, 2001 *QbA*
RHEINGAU, GER   IE| A-   PV| 00 A-   WPL| $18   A-

Johannishof, 2001 *Spätlese, Rudesheimer Berg Rottland*
RHEINGAU, GER   IE| A   PV| WPL| $22   A

Karlsmühle, 2001 *Kabinett, Kaseler Nies'chen*
MOSEL-SAAR-RUWER, GER   IE| A-   PV| WPL| $20   A-

Heribert Kerpen, 2001 *Kabinett, Wehlener Sonnenuhr*
MOSEL-SAAR-RUWER, GER   IE| A-   PV| WPL| $19   A-

Reichsgraf von Kesselstatt, 2001 *Spätlese, Scharzhofberger*
MOSEL-SAAR-RUWER, GER   IE| A-   PV| WPL| $25   A-

Reichsgraf von Kesselstatt, 2001 *Spätlese, Piesporter Goldtröpfchen*
MOSEL-SAAR-RUWER, GER IE| A- PV| WPL| $24 A-

Kirsten, 1998 *Riesling Brut*
MOSEL, GER IE| B+ PV| WPL| $16 B+

Staatsweingüter Kloster Eberbach, 2001 *Kabinett, Erbacher Marcobrunn*
RHEINGAU, GER IE| A PV| WPL| $19 A

Staatsweingüter Kloster Eberbach, 2001 *Kabinett, Steinberger*
RHEINGAU, GER IE| A PV| WPL| $18 A

Knappstein, 2001 *Handpicked Riesling, Clare Valley*
SOUTH, AUS IE| A- PV| WPL| $14 A-

Baron zu Knyphäusen, 2001 *Spätlese, Erbacher Steinmorgen*
RHEINGAU, GER IE| A PV| WPL| $22 A

Krüger-Rumpf, 2001 *Kabinett, Münsterer Pittersberg*
NAHE, GER IE| A PV| 99 A- WPL| $17 A

Leeuwin, 2001 *Art Series Margaret River*
WESTERN, AUS IE| A- PV| 00 A- WPL| $20 A-

Lengs & Cooter, 2001 *Clare Valley*
SOUTH, AUS IE| A PV| WPL| $16 A

Lingenfelder, 2001 *QbA Bird Label*
PFALZ, GER IE| A- PV| WPL| $13 A-

Carl Loewen, 2001 *Spätlese, Thörnicher Ritsch*
MOSEL-SAAR-RUWER, GER IE| A- PV| WPL| $20 A-

Dr. Loosen, 2001 *Spätlese, Erdener Treppchen*
MOSEL-SAAR-RUWER, GER IE| A- PV| WPL| $25 A-

Dr. Loosen, 2001 *Spätlese, Ürziger Würzgarten*
MOSEL-SAAR-RUWER, GER IE| A- PV| WPL| $25 A-

Dr. Loosen, 2001 *Spätlese, Wehlener Sonnenuhr*
MOSEL-SAAR-RUWER, GER IE| A PV| WPL| $25 A

Dr. Loosen, 2001 *Riesling Kabinett, Bernkasteler Lay*
MOSEL-SAAR-RUWER, GER IE| A+, A- PV| WPL| BBC $17 A+

Dr. Loosen, 2001 *Riesling Spätlese, Graacher Himmelreich*
MOSEL-SAAR-RUWER, GER IE| A+ PV| WPL| $25 A+

Dr. Loosen, 2001 *Riesling Kabinett, Wehlener Sonnenuhr*
MOSEL-SAAR-RUWER, GER IE| A+ PV| WPL| $18 A+

Dr. Loosen, 2001 *Kabinett, Erdener Treppchen*
MOSEL-SAAR-RUWER, GER IE| A- PV| WPL| $18 A-

Martinborough, 2001
MARTINBOROUGH, NZ IE| A- PV| 99 B+ WPL| $15 A-

Helmut Mathern, 2001 *Kabinett, Niederhäuser Felsensteyer*
NAHE, GER IE| PV| WPL| $18 A

Alfred Merkelbach, 2001 *Spätlese, Ürziger Würzgarten Fuder 11*
MOSEL-SAAR-RUWER, GER IE| A- PV| WPL| $17 A-

Meulenhof, 2001 *Riesling Kabinett, Erdener Treppchen*
MOSEL-SAAR-RUWER, GER IE| A PV| WPL| $16 A

Meulenhof, 2001 *Kabinett, Wehlener Sonnenuhr*
MOSEL-SAAR-RUWER, GER IE| A- PV| 99 B+ WPL| $16 A-

RIESLING (CONTINUED)

Meulenhof, 2001 *Auslese, Wehlener Sonnenuhr*
MOSEL-SAAR-RUWER, GER　IE| A+　PV|　　　WPL|　　$24　A+

Mitchell, 2001 *Watervale, Clare Valley*
SOUTH, AUS　　　IE| A+　PV|　　　WPL|　　$18　A+

Mount Horrocks, 2002 *Clare Valley*
SOUTH, AUS　　　IE| A-　PV|　　　WPL|　　$20　A-

Schumann Nägler, 2001 *Kabinett, Johannisberger Erntebringer*
RHEINGAU, GER　　IE| A　PV|　　　WPL|　　$15　A

Peter Nicolay, 2001 *Spätlese, Bernkasteler alte Badstube am Doctorberg*
MOSEL-SAAR-RUWER, GER　IE| A-　PV| 00 B+　WPL| S　$28　A-

Peter Nicolay, 2001 *Spätlese, Urziger Goldwingert*
MOSEL-SAAR-RUWER, GER　IE| A　PV|　　　WPL| S　$26　A

Peter Nicolay, 2001 *Kabinett, Berkasteler Badstube*
MOSEL-SAAR-RUWER, GER　IE| B+　PV|　　　WPL|　　$15　B+

Omaka Springs, 2002
MARLBOROUGH, NZ　　IE| B+　PV| 00 A-　WPL|　　$14　B+

Orlando, 2002 *Reserve, Jacobs Creek*
SOUTH, AUS　　　IE| B+　PV|　　　WPL|　　$15　B+

Von Othegraven, 2001 *QbA Riesling, Kanzemer Althenberg*
MOSEL-SAAR-RUWER, GER　IE| A　PV|　　　WPL| S　$27　A

Von Othegraven, 2001 *Ockfen Bockstein*
MOSEL-SAAR-RUWER, GER　IE| A-　PV|　　　WPL|　　$24　A-

Von Othegraven, 2001 *Maria v. O. Riesling QbA*
MOSEL-SAAR-RUWER, GER　IE| A-　PV|　　　WPL|　　$15　A-

Pazen, 2001 *Kabinett, Zeltinger Himmelreich*
MOSEL-SAAR-RUWER, GER　IE| A　PV|　　　WPL|　　$14　A

Penfolds, 2002 *Reserve Bin, Eden Valley*
SOUTH, AUS　　　IE| A　PV|　　　WPL|　　$18　A

R. & A. Pfaffl, 2001 *Terrassen Sonnleiten Riesling*
WEINVIERTEL, AUT　　IE| A+　PV|　　　WPL|　　$18　A+

Pikes, 2002 *Clare Valley*
SOUTH, AUS　　　IE| A-　PV|　　　WPL|　　$16　A-

Pikes, 2001 *Reserve, Clare Valley*
SOUTH, AUS　　　IE| A　PV|　　　WPL|　　$22　A

Prager, 1998 *Federspiel, Weissenkirchen Steinriegl*
WACHAU, AUT　　　IE| A-　PV|　　　WPL|　　$22　A-

Jon. Jos. Prüm, 2001 *Kabinett, Wehlener Sonnenuhr*
MOSEL-SAAR-RUWER, GER　IE| A-　PV|　　　WPL|　　$25　A-

Balthasar Ress, 2001 *Kabinett, Schloss Reichartshausen*
RHEINGAU, GER　　IE| B+　PV|　　　WPL|　　$14　B+

Balthasar Ress, 2001 *Kabinett, Hattenheimer Schützenhaus*
RHEINGAU, GER　　IE| B+　PV|　　　WPL|　　$12　B+

Schloss Saarstein, 2001 *QbA, Trocken*
MOSEL-SAAR-RUWER, GER　IE| B+　PV|　　　WPL|　　$11　B+

Saint Chapelle, 2001 *Special Harvest Johannisberg Riesling*
ID, USA   IE| A-   PV| WPL| B $10   A-

Saint Chapelle, 2001 *Johannisberg Riesling*
ID, USA   IE| B+   PV| WPL| B $6   B+

Saint Clair, 2001
MARLBOROUGH, NZ   IE| A-   PV| 99 B+   WPL| $13   A-

Prinz zu Salm-Dalberg'sches, 2001 *Kabinett, Schloss Wallhausen*
NAHE, GER   IE| B+   PV| WPL| $15   B+

Weingut Salomon (Undhof), 2001 *Pfaffenberg*
KREMSTAL, AUT   IE| A   PV| WPL| $18   A

Weingut Salomon (Undhof), 2001 *Kremser Koegl*
KREMSTAL, AUT   IE| A-   PV| WPL| $23   A-

Sandstone, 2000 *Select Late Harvest, Niagara Peninsula*
ONTARIO, CAN   IE| A+   PV| WPL| $14   A+

Willi Schaefer, 2001 *Kabinett, Wehlener Sonnenuhr*
MOSEL-SAAR-RUWER, GER   IE| A-   PV| WPL| $20   A-

Dom. Schlumberger, 1998 *Les Princes Abbés*
ALSACE, FR   IE| A-, B+   PV| WPL| BBC $16   A-

Carl Schmitt-Wagner, 2001 *Auslese, Longuicher Maximiner Herrenberg*
MOSEL-SAAR-RUWER, GER   IE| A+, A-   PV| WPL| S,BBC $26   A+

André Schneider & Fils, 1998
ALSACE, FR   IE| A+   PV| WPL| $12   A+

Schloss Schönborn, 2001 *Spätlese, Domanenweingut Hattenheimer Pfaffenberg*
RHEINGAU, GER   IE| A-   PV| WPL| S $28   A-

Schloss Schönborn, 2001 *Spätlese, Erbacher Marcobrunn*
RHEINGAU, GER   IE| A   PV| 00 A-   WPL| $23   A

Schloss Schönborn, 2001 *Spätlese, Hattenheimer Pfaffenberg*
RHEINGAU, GER   IE| A   PV| WPL| $17   A

Schloss Schönborn, 2001 *Kabinett, Erbacher Marcobrunn*
RHEINGAU, GER   IE| A-   PV| WPL| $14   A-

Schloss Schönborn, 2001 *Kabinett, Hattenheimer Pfaffenberg*
RHEINGAU, GER   IE| A-   PV| WPL| $12   A-

Schloss Schönborn, 2001 *Kabinett,*
RHEINGAU, GER   IE| B+   PV| WPL| B $10   B+

Selbach-Oster, 2001 *Kabinett, Zeltinger Schlossberg*
MOSEL-SAAR-RUWER, GER   IE| A   PV| WPL| S $27   A

Selbach-Oster, 2001 *Kabinett, Bernkasteler Badstube*
MOSEL-SAAR-RUWER, GER   IE| A-   PV| WPL| $19   A-

Selbach-Oster, 1999 *Auslese, Zeltinger Sonnenuhr*
MOSEL-SAAR-RUWER, GER   IE| A+   PV| WPL| $17   A+

Seven Hills, 2001 *Riesling, Columbia Valley*
WA, USA   IE| B+   PV| 99 B+   WPL| B $10   B+

Sonnhof, 2001 *Qualitätswein Trocken, Zoebinger Heiligensteirn*
KAMPTAL, AUT   IE| A-, A-   PV| WPL| S,BBC $28   A-

St. Urbans-Hof, 2001 *QbA*
MOSEL-SAAR-RUWER, GER   IE| A-   PV| WPL| B $10   A-

RIESLING (CONTINUED)

J. & H. A. Strub, 2001 *Spätlese, Niersteiner Paterberg Three Star*
RHEINHESSEN, GER   IE| A   PV| WPL| S   **$27**   A

Tagaris, 2001 *Reserve Johannisberg Riesling, Columbia Valley*
WA, USA   IE| B+   PV| WPL| B   **$8**   B+

Tagaris, 2001 *Johannisberg Riesling, Columbia Valley*
WA, USA   IE| B+   PV| WPL| B   **$7**   B+

Tesch, 2001 *Kabinett, Langenlonsheimer Löhrer Berg*
NAHE, GER   IE| B+   PV| WPL| **$15**   B+

Tesch, 2001 *Auslese, Langenlonsheimer Löhrer Berg*
NAHE, GER   IE| A-   PV| WPL| S   **$30**   A-

Dr. H. Thanisch-Erben Müller-Burggraef, 2001 *Kabinett, Berncasteler Doctor*
MOSEL-SAAR-RUWER, GER   IE| A-   PV| WPL| S   **$27**   A-

Dr. H. Thanisch-Erben Müller-Burggraef, 2001 *Kabinett, Wehlener Sonnenuhr*
MOSEL-SAAR-RUWER, GER   IE| B+   PV| WPL| **$15**   B+

Trefethen, 2001 *Napa Valley*
CA, USA   IE| B+   PV| WPL| **$15**   B+

P. J. Valckenberg, 2001 *QbA, Trocken*
RHEINHESSEN, GER   IE| B+   PV| WPL| B   **$10**   B+

Washington Hills, 2001 *Late Harvest, Columbia Valley*
WA, USA   IE| B+, B+   PV| 99 B+   WPL| B   **$9**   B+

Euguen Wehrheim, 2001 *Spätlese, Niersteiner Orbel*
RHEINHESSEN, GER   IE| B+   PV| WPL| **$15**   B+

Robert Weil, 2001 *Kabinett,*
RHEINGAU, GER   IE| A-   PV| WPL| **$25**   A-

Weingut Eilenz, 2001 *Kabinett, Ayler Kupp Riesling*
MOSEL-SAAR-RUWER, GER   IE| B+   PV| WPL| **$12**   B+

Weingut Johannishof, 2001 *Kabinett, Johannisberger Goldatzel*
RHEINGAU, GER   IE| B+   PV| WPL| **$11**   B+

Weingut Johannishof, 2001 *Kabinett, Johannisberger Vogelsang*
RHEINGAU, GER   IE| A-   PV| WPL| **$11**   A-

Weingut Johannishof, 2001 *Charta QbA*
RHEINGAU, GER   IE| A-   PV| WPL| **$14**   A-

Weingut Karl Erbes, 2001 *Kabinett, Urziger Wurzgarten*
MOSEL-SAAR-RUWER, GER   IE| B+   PV| WPL| **$12**   B+

Weingut Wwe. Dr. Thanisch, 2001 *Kabinett, Bercasteler Doctor*
MOSEL-SAAR-RUWER, GER   IE| A-   PV| WPL| S   **$27**   A-

J.L. Wolf, 2001 *Spätlese Trocken, Ruppertsberger Hoheburg*
PFALZ, GER   IE| A+   PV| WPL| S   **$27**   A+

J.L. Wolf, 2001 *Spätlese Trocken, Wachenheimer Gerümpel*
PFALZ, GER   IE| A   PV| WPL| **$18**   A

J.L. Wolf, 2001 *Qualitätswein Trocken, Forster Pechstein*
PFALZ, GER   IE| A-   PV| WPL| **$14**   A-

J.L. Wolf, 2001 *Auslese, Wachenheimer Gerümpel*
GER — IE| A+ — PV| — WPL| S — $30 — A+

Wolf Blass, 2001 *Gold Label, Clare Valley-Eden Valley*
SOUTH, AUS — IE| A, B+, B+ — PV| — WPL| — $14 — A-

SAUVIGNON/FUMÉ BLANC

Allan Scott, 2002
MARLBOROUGH, NZ — IE| B+ — PV| — WPL| W — $11 — B+

Allan Scott, 2002 *Vintage Select*
MARLBOROUGH, NZ — IE| A- — PV| — WPL| — $11 — A-

Allan Scott, 2001
MARLBOROUGH, NZ — IE| B+ — PV| — WPL| — $15 — B+

Araujo, 2000 *Eisele Vineyard, Napa Valley*
CA, USA — IE| A — PV| — WPL| S — $30 — A

Artesa, 2000 *Reserve, Napa Valley*
CA, USA — IE| A-, B+ — PV| 99 A- — WPL| BBC — $19 — A-

Babich, 2002
MARLBOROUGH, NZ — IE| B+ — PV| — WPL| W — $12 — B+

Baileyana, 2001 *Paragon Vineyard, Edna Valley, San Luis Obispo Co.*
CA, USA — IE| B+ — PV| — WPL| — $13 — B+

Beckmen, 2001 *Santa Ynez Valley, Santa Barbara Co.*
CA, USA — IE| B+ — PV| — WPL| — $16 — B+

Benziger, 2000 *Sonoma Mountain, Sonoma Co.*
CA, USA — IE| A- — PV| — WPL| — $22 — A-

Beringer, 2000 *Appellation Collection Napa Valley*
CA, USA — IE| B+ — PV| 99 B+ — WPL| W — $12 — B+

Beringer, 2000 *Alluvium White, Knights Valley*
CA, USA — IE| A-, A- — PV| — WPL| BBC — $16 — A-

Bernardus, 2001 *Griva Vineyard, Arroyo Seco, Monterey Co.*
CA, USA — IE| A — PV| — WPL| — $20 — A

Boschendal, 2002
COASTAL REGION, SA — IE| B+ — PV| — WPL| — $12 — B+

Boschendal, 2002 *Grande Cuvée*
COASTAL REGION, SA — IE| B+ — PV| 99 B+ — WPL| — $14 — B+

Henri Bourgeois, 2001 *La Porte du Caillou, Sancerre*
LOIRE, FR — IE| A- — PV| — WPL| — $18 — A-

Henri Bourgeois, 2000 *Haute Victoire, Quincy*
LOIRE, FR — IE| B+ — PV| — WPL| B — $10 — B+

Brampton, 2002
COASTAL, SA — IE| B+ — PV| — WPL| B — $10 — B+

Brancott, 2001 *Reserve*
MARLBOROUGH, NZ — IE| A-, B — PV| — WPL| BBC — $18 — B+

Brogan, 2001 *Russian River Valley, Sonoma Co.*
CA, USA — IE| B+ — PV| — WPL| — $20 — B+

Buena Vista, 2001 *Lake Co.*
CA, USA — IE| B+ — PV| — WPL| B — $7 — B+

WHITES
SORTED BY TYPE

SAUVIGNON/FUMÉ BLANC (CONTINUED)

Cairnbrae, 2002 *The Stones*
MARLBOROUGH, NZ   IE| B+   PV| 00 B+, 01 B+ WPL| **$14** B+

Cakebread, 2000 *Napa Valley*
CA, USA   IE| A, B+, B   PV| WPL| W   **$17** B+

Caroline Bay, 2001
MARLBOROUGH, NZ   IE| A-   PV| 00 A-   WPL| **$20** A-

Caterina, 2001 *Columbia Valley*
WA, USA   IE| B+   PV| WPL| B   **$10** B+

Ch. Potelle, 2000 *Napa Valley*
CA, USA   IE| A,B   PV| 99 B+   WPL| BBC   **$15** B+

Ch. Souverain, 2001 *Alexander Valley, Sonoma Co.*
CA, USA   IE| B+, B, B+   PV| 99 B+   WPL| **$12** B+

Ch. Ste. Michelle, 2001 *Columbia Valley*
WA, USA   IE| B+   PV| WPL| B   **$10** B+

Chalk Hill, 2000 *Chalk Hill, Sonoma Co.*
CA, USA   IE| A-   PV| WPL| S   **$29** A-

Charles Wiffen, 2002
MARLBOROUGH, NZ   IE| A-   PV| WPL| **$15** A-

Chinook, 2000 *Yakima Valley*
WA, USA   IE| A-   PV| WPL| **$15** A-

Clos Malverne, 2001
STELLENBOSCH, SA   IE| A, B, B+   PV| WPL| **$15** B+

Clos Pegase, 2001 *Carneros Mitsuko's Vineyard Q Block, Napa Valley*
CA, USA   IE| B+   PV| WPL| **$18** B+

Cloudy Bay, 2001
MARLBOROUGH, NZ   IE| A, A   PV| 99 A-, 00 A WPL| W,BBC **$24** A

Coopers Creek, 2001 *Reserve*
MARLBOROUGH, NZ   IE| B+   PV| 99 A-   WPL| **$15** B+

Cosentino, 2000 *The Novelist*
CA, USA   IE| B+   PV| WPL| **$16** B+

Craggy Range, 2002 *Te Muna Road Vineyard, Martinborough*
MARLBOROUGH, NZ   IE| A-   PV| WPL| **$19** A-

Craggy Range, 2001 *Old Renwick Vineyard*
MARLBOROUGH, NZ   IE| A-   PV| WPL| **$17** A-

Didier Dagueneau, 2000 *En Chailloux, Pouilly Fumé*
LOIRE, FR   IE| A   PV| WPL| S   **$26** A

De Lorimier, 2000 *Spectrum Res, Alexander Valley, Sonoma Co.*
CA, USA   IE| A-   PV| WPL| **$16** A-

Deerfield Ranch, 2001 *Peterson Vineyard, Sonoma Valley, Sonoma Co.*
CA, USA   IE| B+   PV| WPL| **$18** B+

Deerfield Ranch, 2000 *Peterson Vineyard, Sonoma Valley, Sonoma Co.*
CA, USA   IE| B+   PV| WPL| **$18** B+

DeSante, 2001 *Napa Valley*
CA, USA   IE| B+   PV| WPL| **$18** B+

Dry Creek, 2001 *Fumé Blanc, DCV3, Dry Creek Valley, Sonoma Co.*
CA, USA IE| B+, B, A-, A PV| WPL| BBC **$18** A-

Dry Creek, 2001 *Fumé Blanc, Sonoma Co.*
CA, USA IE| B+ WPL| **$13** B+

Dry Creek, 2000 *Fumé Blanc, Reserve, Dry Creek Valley, Sonoma Co.*
CA, USA IE| A PV| 99 B+ WPL| **$18** A

Drylands, 2001 *Winemaker's Reserve*
MARLBOROUGH, NZ IE| A- PV| WPL| **$19** A-

Du Preez, 2001
GOUDINI VALLEY, SA IE| B+ PV| WPL| B **$9** B+

Vina Echeverria, 1999 *Late Harvest Special Selection, Molina, Curico Valley*
CENTRAL VALLEY, CH IE| B+ PV| WPL| **$19** B+

Emmolo, 2001 *Napa Valley*
CA, USA IE| B+ PV| WPL| **$16** B+

EOS, 2000 *Paso Robles, San Luis Obispo Co.*
CA, USA IE| A-, B PV| WPL| **$14** B+

EOS, 2000 *Fumé Blanc, Reserve, Paso Robles, San Luis Obispo Co.*
CA, USA IE| B+ PV| WPL| **$19** A-

Fairhall Downs, 2001
MARLBOROUGH, NZ IE| A PV| WPL| **$18** A

Ferrari-Carano, 2001 *Fumé Blanc, Sonoma Co.*
CA, USA IE| A-, B+ PV| WPL| W,BBC **$15** A-

Flora Springs, 2001 *Soliloquy, Napa Valley*
CA, USA IE| A-,A, A- PV| 01 B WPL| BBC **$25** A-

Foley, 2000 *Santa Barbara Co.*
CA, USA IE| B+, B PV| WPL| **$16** B+

Forefathers, 2002
MARLBOROUGH, NZ IE| B+ PV| 00 B+ WPL| **$14** B+

Framingham, 2001
MARLBOROUGH, NZ IE| B+ PV| WPL| **$14** B+

Frog's Leap, 2001 *Rutherford, Napa Valley*
CA, USA IE| B+, B, B PV| WPL| W **$16** B+

Gainey, 2001 *Limited Selection, Santa Ynez Valley, Santa Barbara Co.*
CA, USA IE| B+ PV| WPL| **$20** B+

Gary Farrell, 2002 *Redwood Ranch, Sonoma Co.*
CA, USA IE| A PV| WPL| **$21** A

Geyser Peak, 2001 *Sonoma Co.*
CA, USA IE| A- PV| 00 B WPL| **$15** A-

Goldwater, 2002 *Dog Point*
MARLBOROUGH, NZ IE| A- PV| 99 A-, 00 A- WPL| S **$30** A-

Grgich Hills, 2000 *Fumé Blanc, Napa Valley*
CA, USA IE| A- PV| WPL| W **$18** A-

Grgich Hills, 2001 *Fumé Blanc, Napa Valley*
CA, USA IE| B+, B+ PV| 00 A- WPL| **$18** B+

Groom, 2002 *Adelaide Hills*
SOUTH, AUS IE| A PV| WPL| **$16** A

SAUVIGNON/FUMÉ BLANC (CONTINUED)

Groot Constantia, 2001
CONSTANTIA, SA   IE| A+   PV| WPL| $15   A+

Alois Gross, 1999 *Sulz*
AUT   IE| A-   PV| WPL| S $30   A-

Groth, 2001 *Napa Valley*
CA, USA   IE| A   PV| WPL| $15   A

Guenoc, 2001 *Lake Co.*
CA, USA   IE| B+, B+   PV| WPL| $15   B+

Handley, 2001 *Ferrington Vineyard, Anderson Valley, Mendocino Co.*
CA, USA   IE| A-, B+   PV| 99 B+   WPL| BBC $15   A-

Hanna, 2001 *Slusser Vineyard, Russian River Valley, Sonoma Co.*
CA, USA   IE| A   PV| 00 B+   WPL| $16   A

Hedges, 2001 *Fumé-Chardonnay, Columbia Valley*
WA, USA   IE| A   PV| WPL| B $9   A

Highfield, 2002
MARLBOROUGH, NZ   IE| A   PV| WPL| $18   A

Highland, 2001
MARLBOROUGH, NZ   IE| A   PV| WPL| $17   A

Honig, 2001 *Napa Valley*
CA, USA   IE| A-, B+, A-   PV| 00 B+   WPL| BBC $14   A-

Honig, 2001 *Reserve, Napa Valley*
CA, USA   IE| B+   PV| 99 A-, 00 A-   WPL| $20   B+

Huia, 2002
MARLBOROUGH, NZ   IE| A   PV| 01 B+   WPL| $16   A

Huntington Cellars, 2002 *Earthquake, Napa Valley*
CA, USA   IE| B+   PV| WPL| $12   B+

Iron Horse, 2001 *Cuvée, T Bar T Vineyard, Alexander Valley, Sonoma Co.*
CA, USA   IE| B+   PV| 00 B+   WPL| $19   B+

Isabel, 2001
MARLBOROUGH, NZ   IE| A, A   PV| WPL| BBC $18   A

Joel Gott, 2001 *Two Ranches, Napa Valley*
CA, USA   IE| B+   PV| WPL| $17   B+

Pascal Jolivet, 2001 *Ch. du Nozay, Sancerre*
LOIRE, FR   IE| A-   PV| WPL| $23   A-

Pascal Jolivet, 2000 *Les Caillottes, Sancerre*
LOIRE, FR   IE| A-, B, A-   PV| WPL| $22   B+

Joseph Phelps, 2001 *Napa Valley*
CA, USA   IE| A+, B, B   PV| 00 A-   WPL| $20   B+

Justin, 2001 *Edna Valley*
CA, USA   IE| B+   PV| WPL| $14   B+

Kanu, 2002 *Limited Release*
STELLENBOSCH, SA   IE| B+   PV| WPL| $13   B+

Kelham, 2000 *Oakville*
CA, USA   IE| A-   PV| WPL| $22   A-

Kim Crawford, 2002
MARLBOROUGH, NZ — IE| A-   PV| WPL| $18 A-

Klein Constantia, 2001
CONSTANTIA, SA — IE| A+, B   PV| WPL| BBC $15 A-

Kunde, 2002 *Magnolia Lane, Sonoma Valley, Sonoma Co.*
CA, USA — IE| B+   PV| WPL| $15 B+

Langtry, 2001 *Meritage, Guenoc Valley, Lake Co.*
CA, USA — IE| A   PV| WPL| $24 A

Latcham, 2000 *El Dorado Co., Sierra Foothills*
CA, USA — IE| B+   PV| WPL| $12 B+

LeGrys, 2001
MARLBOROUGH, NZ — IE| A-   PV| 00 A-   WPL| $15 A-

Liparita, 2001 *Oakville, Napa Valley*
CA, USA — IE| B+, A-   PV| 99 A-, 00 B+ WPL| BBC $18 A-

Martinelli, 2000 *Martinelli Vineyard, Russian River Valley, Sonoma Co.*
CA, USA — IE| A-   PV| WPL| $18 A-

Mason, 2001 *Napa Valley*
CA, USA — IE| B+, B+, A PV| 99 A-, 00 A- WPL| BBC $17 A-

Matariki, 2001
HAWKES BAY, NZ — IE| A   PV| 99 A-   WPL| $15 A

Matetic Vineyards, 2001 *EQ, San Antonio*
CH — IE| B+   PV| WPL| $12 B+

Matua Valley, 2002
MARLBOROUGH, NZ — IE| A-, B+   PV| WPL| BBC $13 A-

Merryvale, 2001 *Juliana Vineyards, Napa Valley*
CA, USA — IE| B+   PV| WPL| $20 B+

Merryvale, 2001 *Starmont, Napa Valley*
CA, USA — IE| A-   PV| WPL| $17 A-

Mill Creek, 2001 *Dry Creek Valley, Sonoma Co.*
CA, USA — IE| B+   PV| WPL| $16 B+

Mills Reef, 2001 *Reserve*
HAWKES BAY, NZ — IE| B+   PV| WPL| $15 B+

Morandé, 2001 *Terrarum Reserve, Casablanca Valley*
CENTRAL VALLEY, CH — IE| A   PV| WPL| $11 A

Morgan, 2001 *Monterey Co.*
CA, USA — IE| B+   PV| WPL| $14 B+

Morgenhof Estate, 2002 *Simonsberg*
STELLENBOSCH, SA — IE| B+   PV| WPL| $12 B+

Mount Riley, 2001
MARLBOROUGH, NZ — IE| A-, B+   PV| WPL| $15 A-

Mt. Difficulty, 2001
CENTRAL OTAGO, NZ — IE| A+   PV| 00 B+   WPL| $16 A+

Mud House, 2001
MARLBOROUGH, NZ — IE| A-   PV| 00 A-   WPL| $15 A-

Murphy-Goode, 2000 *Reserve, Fumé, Alexander Valley, Sonoma Co.*
CA, USA — IE| A-, B, A   PV| WPL| BBC $17 A-

SAUVIGNON/FUMÉ BLANC (CONTINUED)

Nautilus, 2002
MARLBOROUGH, NZ   IE| A-, B   PV| WPL| $17   B+

Nobilo, 2002 *Icon Series*
MARLBOROUGH, NZ   IE| A   PV| 01:A-   WPL| $19   A

Nobilo, 2001 *Icon Series*
MARLBOROUGH, NZ   IE| A-   PV| WPL| $19   A-

Novelty Hill, 2000 *Klipsun Vineyard, Red Mountain*
USA   IE| A   PV| WPL| $19   A

Omaka Springs, 2002
MARLBOROUGH, NZ   IE| A-   PV| 00 B+   WPL| W $17   A-

Fattoria Il Palagio, 2001 *Sauvignon*
TOSCANA, IT   IE| B+   PV| WPL| $12   B+

Palliser, 2001
MARLBOROUGH, NZ   IE| A-, B, A   PV| WPL| $18   A-

Paradise Ridge, 2002 *Grandview Vineyard, Sonoma Co.*
CA, USA   IE| B+   PV| WPL| $15   B+

Porter Creek, 2000 *Poplar Vineyard, Russian River Valley, Sonoma Co.*
CA, USA   IE| B+   PV| WPL| $16   B+

Philippe Portier, 2000 *Quincy*
LOIRE, FR   IE| B+   PV| WPL| $14   B+

Quivira, 2001 *Fig Tree Vineyard, Dry Creek Valley, Sonoma Co.*
CA, USA   IE| B+   PV| 99 B+   WPL| $16   B+

Red Hill, 2002
MARLBOROUGH, NZ   IE| B+   PV| WPL| $11   B+

Pascal & Nicolas Reverdy, 2000 *Vieilles Vignes, Sancerre*
LOIRE, FR   IE| A-   PV| WPL| $24   A-

Rex Hill, 2000 *Willamette Valley*
OR, USA   IE| B+   PV| WPL| $12   B+

Rochioli, 2001 *Russian River Valley, Sonoma Co.*
CA, USA   IE| A+, A-, B+,B, A- PV| 99 B+, 00 A- WPL| BBC $24   A-

Rodney Strong, 2001 *Charlotte's Home, Sonoma Co.*
CA, USA   IE| B+, B+   PV| WPL| $15   B+

Rose Vineyards, 2000 *Napa Valley*
CA, USA   IE| A-   PV| WPL| $18   A-

Rudd, 2001 *Napa Valley*
CA, USA   IE| A-, A-   PV| 00 A-   WPL| S,BBC $28   A-

Saint Clair, 2001
MARLBOROUGH, NZ   IE| A   PV| 00 B+   WPL| $14   A

Saint Clair, 2001 *Reserve, Wairau Valley*
MARLBOROUGH, NZ   IE| A   PV| WPL| $18   A

Santa Rita, 2002 *Reserva*
CASABLANCA VALLEY, CH IE| A   PV| WPL| $12   A

Sebastiani, 2001 *Cole Vineyard, Russian River Valley, Sonoma Co.*
CA, USA   IE| A-   PV| WPL| $18   A-

Selaks, 2001
MARLBOROUGH, NZ   IE| A   PV| 99 B+, 00 B+ WPL| $14 A

Selaks, 2001 *Premium Selection*
MARLBOROUGH, NZ   IE| B+   PV| WPL| $14 B+

Seresin, 2001
MARLBOROUGH, NZ   IE| A   PV| WPL| $20 A

Shaw & Smith, 2002 *Adelaide Hills*
SOUTH, AUS   IE| A-   PV| 01 A   WPL| $17 A-

Shepherds Ridge, 2001
MARLBOROUGH, NZ   IE| A-   PV| 99 A-   WPL| $15 A-

Sherwood Estates, 2001
MARLBOROUGH, NZ   IE| B+   PV| WPL| $11 B+

Shingle Peak, 2001
MARLBOROUGH, NZ   IE| A-   PV| 99 B+   WPL| $12 A-

Silverado, 2000 *Napa Valley*
CA, USA   IE| A-   PV| WPL| $14 A-

Simi, 2000 *Sauvignon Blanc/Semillon, Sendal Reserve, Sonoma Co.*
CA, USA   IE| A   PV| WPL| $20 A

Spottswoode, 2001 *Napa Valley*
CA, USA   IE| A-   PV| WPL| S $27 A-

Spy Valley, 2001
MARLBOROUGH, NZ   IE| B+   PV| WPL| $13 B+

St. Clement, 2001 *Napa Valley*
CA, USA   IE| B+   PV| 00 B+   WPL| $13 B+

St. Supéry, 2001 *Napa Valley*
CA, USA   IE| A, A, A-, B+ PV| 00 B+ WPL| W,BCC $15 A-

St. Supéry, 2002 *Napa Valley*
CA, USA   IE| A-   PV| 00 B+, 01 A- WPL| $16 A-

Stags' Leap Winery, 2001 *Napa Valley*
CA, USA   IE| B+, A- PV| WPL| BCC $20 A-

Stonestreet, 2000 *Upper Barn Vineyard, Alexander Valley, Sonoma Co.*
CA, USA   IE| B+   PV| 99 B+   WPL| $22 B+

Te Kairanga, 2001
MARLBOROUGH, NZ   IE| A+   PV| 99 A   WPL| $14 A+

Manfred Tement, 2001 *Zieregg*
SUDSTEIERMARK, AUT IE| A   PV| WPL| $25 A

Manfred Tement, 2001 *Grassnitzberg*
SUDSTEIERMARK, AUT IE| A   PV| WPL| S $30 A

Terrace Road, 2001
MARLBOROUGH, NZ   IE| A   PV| WPL| $17 A

Thelema, 2002
STELLENBOSCH, SA IE| B+   PV| WPL| $16 B+

Tour St. Martin, 2000 *Menetou Salon-Morogues*
LOIRE, FR   IE| B+   PV| WPL| $15 B+

Valentin Bianchi, 2002
MENDOZA, ARG   IE| B+   PV| WPL| $12 B+

Veramonte, 2002 *Casablanca Valley*
CH   IE| B+   PV| WPL| B $10 B+

Villa Maria, 2002 *Cellar Selection*
MARLBOROUGH, NZ   IE| A-   PV| 00 A-   WPL| $22 A-

Villa Maria, 2001 *Reserve, Clifford Bay, Awatere Valley*
MARLBOROUGH, NZ   IE| A+   PV| WPL| S $29 A+

Villa Maria, 2001 *Private Bin, Dillons Point*
MARLBOROUGH, NZ   IE| A-   PV| WPL| $15 A-

Voss, 2001 *Napa Valley*
CA, USA   IE| B+, B+, A   PV| 99 A-, 00 B+   WPL| BBC $18 A-

Wairau River, 2000 *Reserve*
MARLBOROUGH, NZ   IE| A-, A-, B+   PV| WPL| BBC $16 A-

Waterbrook, 2001 *Columbia Valley*
WA, USA   IE| B+   PV| WPL| B $9 B+

White Oak, 2001 *Napa Valley*
CA, USA   IE| B+   PV| 00 B+   WPL| $18 B+

Whitehall Lane, 2001 *Napa Valley*
CA, USA   IE| B+   PV| WPL| $15 B+

Whitehaven, 2001
MARLBOROUGH, NZ   IE| A-   PV| WPL| $16 A-

VIOGNIER

Alban, 2001 *Central Coast*
CA, USA   IE| B+   PV| 99 B+   WPL| $20 B+

Alban, 2001 *Estate, Edna Valley, San Luis Obispo Co.*
CA, USA   IE| A   PV| 00 A-   WPL| S $28 A

Andrew Murray, 2001 *Santa Ynez Valley, Santa Barbara Co.*
CA, USA   IE| A   PV| WPL| $25 A

Arrowood, 2001 *Saralee's Vineyard, Russian River Valley, Sonoma Co.*
CA, USA   IE| A-   PV| 99 A-   WPL| S $30 A-

Callaway, 2001 *Coastal Reserve*
CA, USA   IE| B+   PV| WPL| $15 B+

Ch. de Campuget, 2001 *Vin de Pays du Gard*
LANGUEDOC, FR   IE| B+   PV| WPL| $11 B+

Dom. Des Cantarelles, 2001 *Vin de Pays du Gard*
LANGUEDOC, FR   IE| A-   PV| 00 A-   WPL| $13 A-

Consilience, 2000 *Santa Barbara Co.*
CA, USA   IE| A-   PV| WPL| $21 A-

De Loach, 2001 *Russian River Valley, Sonoma Co.*
CA, USA   IE| B+   PV| WPL| $20 B+

Eberle, 2001 *Mill Road Vineyard, Paso Robles, San Luis Obispo Co.*
CA, USA   IE| B+, A-   PV| WPL| $18 B+

Echelon, 2001 *Esperanza Vineyards*
CA, USA   IE| B+   PV| WPL| $13 B+

Fess Parker, 2001 *Santa Barbara Co.*
CA, USA   IE| B+   PV| 00 A-   WPL| $20 B+

Garretson, 2001 *Table 62, Vogelzang Vineyard, Santa Ynez Valley, Santa Barbara Co.*
CA, USA   IE| A   PV| WPL| S $30   A

Hogue, 2001 *Genesis, Columbia Valley*
WA, USA   IE| A-   PV| 00 B+   WPL| $16   A-

Kunde, 2001 *Sonoma Valley, Sonoma Co.*
CA, USA   IE| A-   PV| WPL| $23   A-

McCrea, 2000 *Yakima Valley*
WA, USA   IE| A   PV| 99 B+   WPL| $22   A

Miner, 2001 *Simpson Vineyard*
CA, USA   IE| B+   PV| WPL| $20   B+

Renwood, 2000 *Shenandoah Valley*
CA, USA   IE| A-   PV| WPL| $25   A-

Silver, 2001 *Vogelzang Vineyards, Santa Barbara Co.*
CA, USA   IE| B+   PV| WPL| $22   B+

Spencer Roloson, 2001 *Skellenger Vineyard, Rutherford/Napa Valley*
CA, USA   IE| A-   PV| WPL| S $26   A-

Stags' Leap Winery, 2001 *Napa Valley*
CA, USA   IE| A-   PV| WPL| $25   A-

Summers, 2000 *Monterey Co.*
CA, USA   IE| A-   PV| WPL| $18   A-

Treana, 2000 *Viognier-MarsanneMer Soleil Vineyard, Central Coast*
CA, USA   IE| A-, B+, A-   PV| WPL| BBC $25   A-

Treana, 2001 *Viognier-MarsanneMer Soleil Vineyard, Central Coast*
CA, USA   IE| A+   PV| 99 A-, 00 A-   WPL| $25   A+

Vinum Cellars, 2000 *Vista Verde Vineyard, San Benito Co.*
CA, USA   IE| A-   PV| WPL| $22   A-

Waterbrook, 2001 *Viognier, Columbia Valley*
WA, USA   IE| A-   PV| WPL| $20   A-

Wendell, 2001 *Edna Valley*
CA, USA   IE| A-   PV| WPL| $21   A-

OTHER WHITE

Alkoomi, 2001 *Semillon-Chenin Blanc-Sauvignon Blanc*
WESTERN, AUS   IE| B+   PV| WPL| $11   B+

Amity, 2001 *Pinot Blanc*
OR, USA   IE| B+   PV| WPL| $12   B+

Andrew Murray, 2001 *Marsanne, Enchante, Santa Ynez Valley, Santa Barbara Co.*
CA, USA   IE| A-   PV| WPL| $22   A-

Antinori, 2001 *Vermentino, Guado al Tasso, Bolgheri*
TUSCANY, IT   IE| A, B+   PV| WPL| BBC $18   A-

Arca Nova, 2001
VINHO VERDE, POR   IE| B+   PV| 00 A   WPL| B $6   B+

Quinta da Aveleda, 2001 *Trajadura*
VINHO VERDE, POR   IE| B+   PV| WPL| B $8   B+

WHITES
SORTED BY TYPE

OTHER WHITE (CONTINUED)

Quinta da Aveleda, 2001 *Loureiro*
VINHO VERDE, POR   IE| B+   PV| WPL| B $8   B+

Beringer, 2001 *Alluvium Blanc, Knights Valley, Sonoma Co.*
CA, USA   IE| B+   PV| 00 B+   WPL| $16 B+

Paul Blanck, 2001 *Pinot Blanc*
ALSACE, GER   IE| A-   PV| WPL| $11 A-

Pierre Boniface, 2001 *Apremont*
SAVOIE, FR   IE| B+   PV| WPL| B $9   B+

Boutari, 2001 *Moschofilero*
ARCADIA, GRC   IE| B+   PV| WPL| $12 B+

Boutari, 2001 *Kallisti*
SANTORINI, GRC   IE| B+   PV| 99 A, 00 A   WPL| $15 B+

Boutari, 2000 *Kallisti*
SANTORINI, GRC   IE| A   PV| 99 A   WPL| $17 A

Boutari, 2000
NEMEA, GRC   IE| B+   PV| WPL| B $10 B+

Cantina dei Monaci, 2001 *Greco*
CAMPANIA, IT   IE| A   PV| WPL| $14 A

Casa de Vila Verde, 2001 *Senhorio d'Agras*
VINHO VERDE, POR IE| A   PV| WPL| B $8   A

Casa de Vila Verde, 2001
VINHO VERDE, POR IE| B+   PV| WPL| B $7   B+

Casa do Valle, 2001
VINHO VERDE, POR IE| B+   PV| WPL| B $6   B+

Casa Lapostolle, 2001 *Tanao*
CH   IE| B+   PV| WPL| $14 B+

Dom. du Closel, 2001 *Les Caillardieres*
LOIRE, FR   IE| B+   PV| WPL| $16 B+

Cullen, 2001 *Semillon-Sauvignon Blanc, Margaret River*
WESTERN, AUS   IE| A+   PV| WPL| S $30 A+

DeLille, 2000 *Chaleur Estate Blanc, Columbia Valley*
WA, USA   IE| A   PV| WPL| $25 A

Etude, 2000 *Pinot Blanc, Carneros*
CA, USA   IE| A   PV| 99 A   WPL| S $28 A

Fairview, 2001 *Semillon, Oom Pagel*
PAARL, SA   IE| B+   PV| WPL| $25 B+

Marco Felluga, 2001 *Tocai Friulano, Colli*
FRIULI, IT   IE| B+   PV| WPL| $14 B+

Marco Felluga, 2001 *Molamatta, Pinot Bianco/Ribolla Gialla/Tocai Friulano, Collio*
FRIULI, IT   IE| B+   PV| WPL| $15 B+

Livio Felluga, 2001 *del Friuli Tocai Friulano, Colli Orientali*
FRIULI, IT   IE| A-   PV| WPL| $24 A-

Feudi di San Gregorio, 2001 *Greco di Tufo, Tufo*
CAMPANIA, IT   IE| A-   PV| WPL| W $18   A-

Feudi di San Gregorio, 2001 *Falanghina Sannio*
CAMPANIA, IT   IE| A-   PV| 99 B+, 00 B+   WPL| W $14   A-

Dom. Gardies, 2001 *Muscat Sec, Vin de Pays de Côtes Catalanes*
ROUSSILLON, FR   IE| B+   PV| WPL| $12   B+

Dom. Gerovassiliou, 2001 *White*
THESSALONIKI, GRC   IE| A-   PV| WPL| $13   A-

Grange de Rouquettes, 2001 *Marsanne-Viognier, Vin de Pays d'Oc*
LANGUEDOC, FR   IE| B+   PV| WPL| $12   B+

Grange de Rouquettes, 2001 *Le Pelican, Vin de Pays d'Oc*
LANGUEDOC, FR   IE| B+   PV| WPL| $15   B+

Jacques Guindon, 2001 *Muscadet des Coteaux du Loire*
LOIRE, FR   IE| B+   PV| WPL| B $9   B+

Henry, 2001 *Müller Thurgau, Umpqua Valley*
OR, USA   IE| B+   PV| WPL| B $9   B+

Dom. de l' Hortus, 2001 *Cuvée Classique, La Bergerie de l'Hortus, Vin de Pays du Val de Montferrand*
LANGUEDOC, FR   IE| B+   PV| WPL| $12   B+

Kourtaki, 2000 *Assyrtiko*
SANTORINI, GRC   IE| B+   PV| WPL| $11   B+

De Ladoucette, 2000 *Pouiilly-Fume*
LOIRE, FR   IE| A-   PV| WPL| S $30   A-

Leopold & Silvane Sommer, 2001 *Grüner Veltliner*
NEUSIEDLERSEE, AUT   IE| A   PV| WPL| $13   A

Maculan, 2001 *Pinot & Toi*
VENETO, IT   IE| B+   PV| WPL| $11   B+

Martinsancho, 2001 *Verdejo*
RUEDA, SP   IE| B+   PV| WPL| B $10   B+

Mas Carlot, 2001 *Marsanne-Roussanne, Cuvée Tradition, Vin de Pays d'Oc*
LANGUEDOC, FR   IE| B+   PV| WPL| B $8   B+

Mas de Bressades, 2001 *Roussanne-Viognier, Vin de Pays du Gard*
LANGUEDOC, FR   IE| B+   PV| WPL| $14   B+

Masi, 2001 *Bianco Garganega/Sauvignon, Veneto Serego Alighieri Possessioni*
VENETO, IT   IE| B+   PV| WPL| $12   B+

McCrea, 2000 *Chardonnay/Viognier, la Mer, Yakima Valley*
WA, USA   IE| B+   PV| WPL| $18   B+

Moss Wood, 2001 *Semillon, Margaret River*
WESTERN, AUS   IE| A+   PV| WPL| $20   A+

Marqués de Murrieta, 1997 *Ygay, Capellania*
RIOJA, SP   IE| B+   PV| WPL| $15   B+

Paschal, 2000 *Pinot Blanc, Rogue Valley*
OR, USA   IE| A-   PV| WPL| $16   A-

Dom. de la Pépière, 2001 *Sur Lie, Cuvée Vieilles Vignes, Clos des Briords, Muscadet de Sèvre et Maine*
LOIRE, FR   IE| B+   PV| WPL| $12   B+

OTHER WHITE (CONTINUED)

R. & A. Pfaffl, 2001 *Grüner Veltliner; Goldjoch*
WEINVIERTEL, AUT   IE| A+   PV| WPL| $18   A+

R. & A. Pfaffl, 2001 *Grüner Veltliner, Trocken, Hundsleiten/Sandtal*
WEINVIERTEL, AUT   IE| A-   PV| WPL| $18   A-

R. & A. Pfaffl, 2000 *Grüner Veltliner; Hundsleiten/Sandtal*
WEINVIERTEL, AUT   IE| A   PV| WPL| $18   A

Pierro, 2000 *Semillon-Sauvignon Blanc, Margaret River*
WESTERN, AUS   IE| A   PV| WPL| $20   A

Francois Pinon, 2001 *Cuvée Tradition*
LOIRE, FR   IE| B+   PV| WPL| $12   B+

Ponte do Lima, 2001 *Loureiro, Encostas do Lima*
VINHO VERDE, POR   IE| B+   PV| WPL| B $6   B+

Dom. de Pouy, 2001 *Vin de Pays des Côtes de Gascogne*
SOUTHWEST, FR   IE| B+   PV| 99 B+, 00 B+   WPL| B $7   B+

Primo, 2002 *Colombard, la Biondina, Adelabe*
SOUTH, AUS   IE| B+   PV| WPL| $13   B+

Dom. de la Quilla, 2000 *Sur Lie, Muscadet de Sèvre et Maine*
LOIRE, FR   IE| B+   PV| WPL| B $10   B+

Samos, 2000 *Grand Cru Vin Doux Naturel*
SAMOS, GRC   IE| B+   PV| WPL| B $10   B+

Sandhill, 2001 *Semillon, Burrowing Owl Vineyard, Okanagan Valley*
BC, CAN   IE| B+   PV| WPL| $14   B+

Jurtschitsch Sonnhof, 2001 *Grüner Veltliner, Schenkenbichl*
KAMPTAL, AUT   IE| A-   PV| WPL| $25   A-

Cave de Tain l'Hermitage, 2001 *White Nobles Rives, Crozes-Hermitage*
RHÔNE, FR   IE| B+   PV| WPL| $12   B+

Tasca d'Almerita, 2000 *Inzolia/Sauvignon Blanc, Nozze d'Oro*
SICILY, IT   IE| A-   PV| WPL| $23   A-

Teruzzi & Puthod, 2001 *Terre di Tufi*
TUSCANY, IT   IE| B+   PV| WPL| W $20   B+

Chat. la Touche, 2000 *Muscadet Sur Lie Cuvée Choisie*
LOIRE, FR   IE| A-   PV| WPL| $15   A-

Trevor Jones, 2001 *Boots, Barossa Valley*
SOUTH, AUS   IE| B+   PV| WPL| $15   B+

Vegoritis, 2000 *Florina Samaropetra*
GRC   IE| B+   PV| WPL| $13   B+

George Vernay, 2001 *Les Terrasses de L'Empire*
CONDRIEU, FR   IE| A+   PV| WPL| S $29   A+

Woodward Canyon, 2000 *Charbonneau Blanc, Walla Walla Co.*
WA, USA   IE| A-   PV| 99 A-   WPL| S $28   A-

SPARKLING

Astoria, NV *Prosecco di Conegliano*						
IT	IE| B+	PV|	WPL|		$13	B+
Astoria, NV *Extra Dry, Prosecco di Valdobbiandene*						
IT	IE| A-	PV|	WPL| B		$9	A-
Avinyo, NV *Cava, Brut*						
SP	IE| B+	PV|	WPL|		$13	B+
Bellenda, 2000 *Prosecco, Brut, Conegliano-Valdobiaddene*						
VENETO, IT	IE| A-	PV|	WPL|		$12	A-
Bisol, NV *Crede, Prosecco di Valdobbiadene*						
IT	IE| A-	PV|	WPL|		$12	A-
Bouvet, NV *Signature Brut, Saumur*						
LOIRE, FR	IE| B+	PV|	WPL|		$13	B+
de Bruyne, *Cuvée Absolue NV, à-Sezanne*						
FR	IE| A+	PV|	WPL| S		$27	A+
Canella, NV *Prosecco, Extra Dry, Prosecco di Conegliano*						
IT	IE| A-	PV|	WPL|		$11	A-
Carpene Malvolti, NV *ProseccoProsecco di Conegliano*						
IT	IE| B+	PV|	WPL|		$12	B+
Collalbrigo, NV *Prosecco, Brut, Conegliano*						
VENETO, IT	IE| B+	PV|	WPL|		$12	B+
Cordorniu, NV *Cava, Brut, Pinot Noir*						
SP	IE| B+	PV|	WPL|		$11	B+
Cuvée Cle'Mente, 2000 *Brut, Blancs de Blanc, Chardonnay*						
FR	IE| A-	PV|	WPL| B		$9	A-
Duval-Leroy, NV *Brut*						
CHAMPAGNE, FR	IE| A	PV|	WPL| S		$28	A
Giribaldi, NV *Selezioni Rodellesi Dolce Brachetto*						
PIEDMONT, IT	IE| B+	PV|	WPL|		$15	B+
Gloria Ferrer, NV *Sparkling Brut, Sonoma Co.*						
CA, USA	IE| B+	PV|	WPL| W		$18	B+
Paul Goerg, NV *Brut Rose Champagne*						
CHAMPAGNE, FR	IE| B+	PV|	WPL| S		$29	B+
Piper Heidsieck , NV *Brut*						
CHAMPAGNE, FR	IE| A	PV|	WPL| W,S		$30	A
Raymond Henriot, NV *Brut*						
CHAMPAGNE, FR	IE| A+	PV|	WPL|		$21	A+
Iron Horse, 1997 *Russian Cuvée, Green Valley, Sonoma Co.*						
CA, USA	IE| A-	PV|	WPL| S		$28	A-
Iron Horse, 1997 *Classic Vintage Brut, Green Valley, Sonoma Co.*						
CA, USA	IE| A-	PV|	WPL| S		$28	A-
Jaume Serra, NV *Cava, Extra Dry, Cristalino*						
SP	IE| B+	PV|	WPL| B		$9	B+

Juvé y Camps, NV *Cava, Brut, Gran Juvé*
SP   IE| A+   PV| WPL| S $30 A+

Frederic Lornet, NV *Cremant de Jura Rosa*
FR   IE| B+   PV| WPL| B $10 B+

Masottina, NV *Prosecco Prosecco di Conegliano Valdobbiadene*
IT   IE| B+   PV| WPL| $14 B+

Mionetto, NV *Spumante Brut, Prosecco*
VENETO, IT   IE| B+   PV| WPL| $11 B+

Mionetto, NV *Sergio Extra Dry, Prosecco di Valdobbiandene*
VENETO, IT   IE| A   PV| WPL| $16 A

Mionetto, NV *Brut, Prosecco*
VENETO, IT   IE| B+   PV| WPL| B $10 B+

Marqués de Monistrol, NV *Reserva Brut (Cava)*
SP   IE| B+   PV| WPL| B $9 B+

Nicolas Feuillatte, NV *Brut*
CHAMPAGNE, FR   IE| B+   PV| WPL| W $25 B+

Pacific Echo, NV *Brut, Mendocino Co.*
CA, USA   IE| B+   PV| WPL| W $19 B+

Parxet, NV *Cava, Pinot Noir, Cuvée Dessert*
SP   IE| A   PV| WPL| $17 A

Pol Roger, NV *Brut*
CHAMPAGNE, FR   IE| A-   PV| WPL| S $30 A-

Rebuli, NV *Prosecco, Brut, Cuvèe d'Oro, Conegliano-Valdobiaddene*
VENETO, IT   IE| B+   PV| WPL| $11 B+

Riondo, NV *Prosecco Conegliano-Valdobiaddene*
VENETO, IT   IE| A-   PV| WPL| B $9 A-

Santero, NV *Prosecco, Brut*
VENETO, IT   IE| B+   PV| WPL| B $9 B+

Agusti Torello, 1999 *Cava, Brut Reserva*
SP   IE| B+   PV| WPL| $12 B+

Agusti Torello, 1998 *Cava, Gran Reserva Extra Brut*
SP   IE| B+   PV| WPL| $16 B+

Tualatin, 2001 *Muscat, Semi-Sparkling, Willamette Valley*
OR, USA   IE| A-   PV| 99 A-, 00 B+   WPL| $16 A-

Villa Sandi, NV *Cuvée, Prosecco di Valdobbiadene*
IT   IE| B+   PV| WPL| $15 B+

Zardetto, NV *Prosecco, Brut*
VENETO, IT   IE| B+, B, B+   PV| WPL| $11 B+

ROSÉ WINES

Ch. d' Aquéria, 2001 *Tavel*
RHÔNE, FR   IE| B+   PV| WPL| $15 B+

Bargemone, 2001 *Coteaux d'Aix en Provence*
PROVENCE, FR   IE| B+   PV| WPL| B $10 B+

Chinook, 2001 *Cabernet Franc Rosé, Yakima Valley*
WA, USA   IE| B+   PV| 99 A-   WPL| **$15 B+**

Gaia, 2001 *14-18th*
PELOPONNESE, GRC   IE| B+   PV| WPL| B   **$8 B+**

Mas de Bressades, 2001 *Costières de Nîmes*
LANGUEDOC, FR   IE| B+   PV| WPL| B   **$10 B+**

Dom. de la Mordoree, 2001 *Côtes du Rhône*
RHÔNE, FR   IE| B+   PV| WPL| B   **$10 B+**

Dom. de la Mordoree, 2001 *Tavel*
RHÔNE, FR   IE| A-   PV| 99 B+   WPL| B   **$10 A-**

Peninsula Ridge, 2000 *Cabernet Franc, Niagara Peninsula*
ONTARIO, CAN   IE| B+   PV| WPL| B   **$8 B+**

Tasca d'Almerita, 2001 *Nerrello Mascalese/Nero d'Avola, Rosé di Regaleali*
SICILY, IT   IE| A-   PV| WPL| **$11 A-**

Vega Sindoa (Nekeas), 2001
NAVARRA, SP   IE| B+, B+   PV| WPL| B   **$6 B+**

Vineland, 2000 *Niagara Peninsula*
ONTARIO, CAN   IE| B+   PV| WPL| B   **$9 B+**

SWEET WINES

PORT

Cálem, 1997 *LBV Port, Bottled 2002*
DOURO, POR   IE| A-   PV| WPL| **$23 A-**

Gould Campbell, 1996 *LBV Port, Bottled 2002*
DOURO, POR   IE| A   PV| WPL| **$20 A**

Quinta de Crasto, 1996 *LBV Port, Bottled 2000*
DOURO, POR   IE| A-   PV| WPL| **$20 A-**

Dow, 1996 *LBV Port, Bottled 2002*
DOURO, POR   IE| A-   PV| WPL| **$20 A-**

José Maria da Fonseca, 1996 *Late Bottled Vintage*
DOURO, POR   IE| A-, A   PV| WPL| BBC   **$21 A**

Niepoort, 1998 *LBV Port, Bottled 2002*
DOURO, POR   IE| A-   PV| WPL| **$22 A-**

Niepoort, 1997 *LBV Port, Bottled 2001*
DOURO, POR   IE| A-   PV| WPL| **$20 A-**

Ramos-Pinto, NV *Urtiga*
POR   IE| B+   PV| WPL| **$16 B+**

Ramos-Pinto, 1996 *Late Bottle Vintage*
POR   IE| B+   PV| WPL| **$15 B+**

Ramos-Pinto, 1995 *LBV Port, Bottled 1999*
DOURO, POR   IE| B+   PV| WPL| **$15 B+**

Rosemount, NV *Tawny, Old Benson, Solare Aged*
SOUTH EASTERN, AUS   IE| A-   PV| WPL| **$25 A-**

Warre's, NV *Tawny, 10-Year-Old, Optima*
DOURO, POR   IE| A   PV| WPL| **$25 A**

ROSÉ SORTED BY TYPE

SWEET SORTED BY TYPE

Yalumba, NV *Antique Tawny Port, Museum Release*
NEW SOUTH WALES, AUS IE| A, B+   PV| WPL| BBC   **$17** **A-**

SHERRY

Antonio Barbadillo, NV *Pedro Ximénez, Extra Rich*
JEREZ, SP   IE| B+   PV| WPL| **$15** **B+**

Antonio Barbadillo, NV *Oloroso, Seco Cuco*
JEREZ, SP   IE| A-   PV| WPL| S   **$30** **A-**

Antonio Barbadillo, NV *Oloroso, Full Dry*
JEREZ, SP   IE| B+   PV| WPL| W, B   **$9** **B+**

Antonio Barbadillo, NV *Cream, Eva*
JEREZ, SP   IE| A-   PV| WPL| **$12** **A-**

Hidalgo, NV *Cream, Napoléon*
JEREZ, SP   IE| B+   PV| WPL| **$12** **B+**

Hildago, NV *Pedro Ximénez, Viejo*
JEREZ, SP   IE| A-   PV| WPL| **$18** **A-**

Emilio Lustau, NV *East India Solera*
JEREZ, SP   IE| A-   PV| WPL| **$18** **A-**

Toro Albalá, 1975 *Pedro Ximénez, Don Gran Reserva*
MONTILLA-MORILES, SP IE| A-   PV| WPL| S   **$28** **A-**

OTHER SWEET

Caves Aliance, 1999 *Single Estate, Quinta dos Quatro Ventos*
DOURO, SP   IE| A   PV| WPL| S   **$30** **A**

Antonio Barbadillo, NV *Moscatel, Laura*
JEREZ, SP   IE| A-   PV| WPL| **$22** **A-**

Benjamin, NV *Muscat, Museum Release*
VICTORIA, AUS   IE| A+   PV| WPL| **$16** **A+**

Beringer, 1998 *Sauvignon Blanc/Semillon, Nightingale, Napa Valley*
CA, USA   IE| A+   PV| 99 A   WPL| S   **$30** **A+**

Buty, 2000 *Sauvignon Blanc/Semillon Columbia Valley*
WA, USA   IE| B+   PV| WPL| **$18** **B+**

Tenuta di Capezzana, 1996 *Vin Santo di Carmignano, Reserva, Carmignano*
TUSCANY, IT   IE| A   PV| WPL| S   **$27** **A**

Chinook, 2000 *Semillon Yakima Valley*
WA, USA   IE| B+, B+   PV| WPL| **$14** **B+**

Dom. Gardies, 2000 *Muscat Muscat di Rivesaltes*
ROUSSILLON, FR   IE| B+   PV| WPL| **$14** **B+**

Greenwood Ridge, 1999 *Late Harvest, Mendocino Ridge, Mendocino Co.*
CA, USA   IE| A+, A+   PV| WPL| BBC   **$24** **A+**

Konrad & Conrad, 2001 *Riesling, Late Harvest, Noble*
MARLBOROUGH, NZ   IE| A   PV| WPL| **$20** **A**

L'Ecole No. 41, 2000 *Semillon, Wahluke Slope, Fries Vineyard*
WA, USA   IE| A-, B+   PV| WPL| BBC   **$20** **A-**

Régis Minet, 2001 *Pouilly-Fumé, Vieilles Vignes*
LOIRE, FR   IE| A-   PV| WPL| **$17** **A-**

Morandé, 2000 *Edición Limitada, Golden Harvest, Casablanca Valley*
CH   IE| A-   PV| WPL| $25 A-

Quinta do Crasto, 1998 *Reserva*
DOURO, SP   IE| A   PV| WPL| S $28 A

Quintas Juntas, 2000 *Reserva*
DOURO, SP   IE| A   PV| WPL| $20 A

Samos, 2000 *Muscat, Grand Cru*
GRC   IE| A-   PV| WPL| $20 A-

Selaks, 2001 *Ice Wine*
MARLBOROUGH, NZ IE| A-   PV| WPL| $15 A-

Domingos Alves Sousa, 2001 *Quinta do Vale da Raposa*
DOURO, SP   IE| B+   PV| WPL| B $9   B+

St. Supéry, 2001 *Moscato*
CA, USA   IE| B+, B   PV| WPL| $15 B+

Éric Texier, 1999 *Nôble Rot Botrytis*
FR   IE| A-   PV| WPL| S $30 A-

Pierre-Yves Tijou, 2001 *Ch. Soucherie, Coteaux du Layon-Chaume*
LOIRE, FR   IE| B+   PV| WPL| $16 B+

Willow Crest, 2001 *Black Muscat, Yakima Valley*
WA, USA   IE| B+   PV| WPL| B $8   B+

Yellow Hawk Cellar, 2001 *Muscat Canelli, Columbia Valley*
WA, USA   IE| B+   PV| WPL| $12 B+

**"AS A WINE DRINKER, BUT NOT AS A WINE EXPERT,
ONE'S TASTES ARE CONSTANTLY CHANGING."**

Elizabeth David

"AN OMELET AND A GLASS OF WINE," 1873

"IN WINE TASTING AND IN WINE TALK, THERE
IS AN ENORMOUS AMOUNT OF HUMBUG."

"THE ESSENTIAL WINE BUFF,"
EDITED BY JENNIFER TAYLOR, 1996

COMPREHENSIVE BUYING GUIDES TO TOP RATED WINES

WINES SORTED BY COUNTRY: UNITED STATES

REDS

BARBERA

Monteviña, 1999 *Terra d'Oro, Amador Co.*
CA, USA   IE| A-   PV| WPL| $18   A-

Sebastiani, 2000 *Sonoma Co.*
CA, USA   IE| B+   PV| WPL| $18   B+

CABERNET FRANC

Cana's Feast, 1999 *Red Table Wine, Red Mountain*
WA, USA   IE| A-   PV| WPL| S $30   A-

Conn Creek, 1999 *Limited Release, Napa Valley*
CA, USA   IE| A+   PV| WPL| $25   A+

Cuneo, 1999 *Columbia Valley*
WA, USA   IE| B+   PV| WPL| $15   B+

Decoy, 2000 *Migration, Napa Valley*
CA, USA   IE| B+   PV| WPL| $24   B+

Huntington Cellars, 2000 *Alexander Valley, Sonoma Co.*
CA, USA   IE| B+   PV| WPL| $18   B+

Stonefly, 1999 *Napa Valley*
CA, USA   IE| A-   PV| WPL| S $27   A-

Willow Crest, 1999 *Yakima Valley*
WA, USA   IE| B+   PV| WPL| $15   B+

CABERNET SAUVIGNON

Andretti, 1999 *Napa Valley*
CA, USA   IE| A   PV| WPL| S $30   A

Arbios, 1999 *Alexander Valley, Sonoma Co.*
CA, USA   IE| A, A-   PV| WPL| S,BBC $30   A

Arbor Crest, *Columbia Valley*
WA, USA   IE| A-   PV| WPL| S $26   A-

Artesa, 1999 *Napa Valley*
CA, USA   IE| A   PV| WPL| S $30   A

Avila, 2000 *Santa Barbara*
CA, USA   IE| B+, B+   PV| WPL| $12   B+

Barnwood, 2000 *Santa Barbara Co.*
CA, USA   IE| A-, B   PV| WPL| $22   B+

Bates Creek, 1999 *Napa Valley*
CA, USA   IE| A   PV| WPL| $25   A

CABERNET SAUVIGNON (CONTINUED)

Beaulieu (BV), 1999 *Rutherford, Napa Valley*
CA, USA   IE| A-   PV| WPL| $25 A-

Benziger, 1999 *Sonoma Co.*
CA, USA   IE| A-, B   PV| WPL| W $19 B+

Beringer, 1999 *Knights Valley, Sonoma Co.*
CA, USA   IE| A-, B   PV| WPL| S $26 B+

Bommarito, 2000 *Napa Valley*
CA, USA   IE| B+   PV| WPL| $20 B+

Camaraderie, 1999
WA, USA   IE| A   PV| WPL| $22 A

Caterina, 1999 *Columbia Valley*
WA, USA   IE| B+   PV| WPL| $20 B+

Caterina, 1999 *Willard Family Vineyard, Yakima Valley*
WA, USA   IE| A   PV| WPL| S $28 A

Ch. Souverain, 1999 *Alexander Valley, Sonoma Co.*
CA, USA   IE| B+, B+   PV| WPL| W $20 B+

Ch. Ste. Michelle, 2000 *Columbia Valley*
WA, USA   IE| B+   PV| 99 B+   WPL| W $15 B+

Ch. Ste. Michelle, 1999 *Cold Creek Vineyard, Columbia Valley*
WA, USA   IE| A, A-   PV| WPL| S,BBC $29 A

Claar, 1998 *White Bluffs, Columbia Valley*
WA, USA   IE| B+   PV| WPL| $11 B+

Columbia, 1999 *Columbia Valley*
WA, USA   IE| B+   PV| WPL| $15 B+

Columbia Crest, 2000 *Grand Estates, Columbia Valley*
WA, USA   IE| A   PV| 99 B+   WPL| $15 A

Columbia Crest, 1999 *Reserve, Columbia Valley*
WA, USA   IE| A   PV| WPL| S $28 A

Columbia Crest, 1999 *Valley Grand Estates, Columbia Valley*
WA, USA   IE| B+   PV| WPL| W $11 B+

Columbia Crest, 1999 *Walter Clore Private Reserve, Columbia Valley*
WA, USA   IE| A+   PV| WPL| S $30 A+

Crystal Valley, 2000
CA, USA   IE| A   PV| WPL| $16 A

Foppiano, 2000 *Russian River Valley, Sonoma Co.*
CA, USA   IE| B+   PV| WPL| $17 B+

Franciscan Oakville, 2000 *Napa Valley*
CA, USA   IE| A-   PV| WPL| S $27 A-

Gallo of Sonoma, 2000 *Reserve, Sonoma Co.*
CA, USA   IE| B+   PV| WPL| $13 B+

Gallo of Sonoma, 1999 *Reserve, Sonoma Co.*
CA, USA   IE| B+   PV| WPL| $13 B+

Geyser Peak, 1999 *Block Collection, Kuimelis Vineyards, Alexander Valley-Livermore Valley*
CA, USA   IE| A, A-   PV| WPL| S,BBC   **$26**   A

Glenwood Ridge, 1999 *Mendocino Ridge, Philo*
CA, USA   IE| A   PV| WPL| S   **$30**   A

Hawley, 1999 *Dry Creek Valley, Sonoma Co.*
CA, USA   IE| A-   PV| WPL| S   **$28**   A-

Hedges, 1999 *Three Vineyards, Red Mountain, Columbia Valley*
WA, USA   IE| B+   PV| WPL| **$18**   B+

Hess Estate, 1999 *Napa Valley*
CA, USA   IE| B+   PV| WPL| **$20**   B+

Hogue, 1999 *Genesis, Columbia Valley*
WA, USA   IE| B+   PV| WPL| **$16**   B+

Honig, 1999 *Napa Valley*
CA, USA   IE| A   PV| WPL| S   **$30**   A

Justin, 2000 *Paso Robles, San Luis Obispo Co.*
CA, USA   IE| A-   PV| 99 A   WPL| **$23**   A-

Kiona, 1999
WA, USA   IE| A+   PV| WPL| **$24**   A+

Lolonis, 1999 *Redwood Valley, Mendocino Co.*
CA, USA   IE| B+   PV| WPL| **$20**   B+

Markham, 1999 *Napa Valley*
CA, USA   IE| A-   PV| WPL| S   **$26**   A-

Martin Ray, 1999 *Mariage, Napa Valley, Sonoma & Mendocino*
CA, USA   IE| A-   PV| WPL| **$24**   A-

Murphy-Goode, 2000 *Alexander Valley, Sonoma Co.*
CA, USA   IE| A   PV| WPL| **$22**   A

Pedroncelli, 1999 *Three Vineyards, Dry Creek Valley, Sonoma Co.*
CA, USA   IE| A   PV| WPL| **$12**   A

Perry Creek, 1999 *El Dorado Co., Sierra Foothills*
CA, USA   IE| A-   PV| WPL| **$14**   A-

Peterson, 1999 *Bradford Mountain, Dry Creek Valley, Sonoma Co.*
CA, USA   IE| A-, B+   PV| WPL| S,BBC   **$28**   A-

Pine Ridge, 1999 *Rutherford, Napa Valley*
CA, USA   IE| A-   PV| WPL| S   **$30**   A-

Powers, 2000
WA, USA   IE| A   PV| WPL| B   **$10**   A

Ridge, 1999 *Santa Cruz Mountains Cabernert Sauvignon, Santa Cruz Mountains*
CA, USA   IE| A   PV| WPL| S   **$30**   A

Rodney Strong, 2000 *Sonoma Co.*
CA, USA   IE| A-   PV| WPL| **$18**   A-

Rodney Strong, 1999 *Alexander's Crown Vineyard, Alexander Valley, Sonoma Co.*
CA, USA   IE| A   PV| WPL| S   **$28**   A

Ross Andrews Winery, 1999 *Columbia Valley*
WA, USA   IE| A   PV| WPL| **$25**   A

CABERNET SAUVIGNON (CONTINUED)

Rutherford Hill, 1999 *25th Anniversary, Napa Valley*
CA, USA   IE| A-   PV| WPL| S   **$30 A-**

S. Anderson, 1999 *Stags' Leap District, Napa Valley*
CA, USA   IE| A+   PV| WPL| S   **$30 A+**

Saint Chapelle, 2000 *Winemaker's Series*
ID, USA   IE| B+   PV| WPL| B   **$10 B+**

Sandhill, 1999 *Red Mountain*
USA   IE| A+   PV| WPL| **$25 A+**

Sausal, 2000 *Sonoma Co.*
CA, USA   IE| A-   PV| WPL| S   **$26 A-**

Sebastiani, 1999 *Appellation SelectionAlexander Valley, Sonoma Co.*
CA, USA   IE| A, A-, B+   PV| WPL| BBC   **$24 A-**

Sebastiani, 1999 *Russian River Valley, Sonoma Co.*
CA, USA   IE| B+   PV| WPL| W   **$20 B+**

Sebastiani, 1999 *Sonoma Co. Selection, Sonoma Co.*
CA, USA   IE| A-   PV| WPL| **$17 A-**

Sequoia Grove, 1999 *Napa Valley*
CA, USA   IE| A   PV| WPL| S   **$29 A**

Seven Peaks, 1999 *Cabernet Sauvignon-Shiraz, Central Coast*
CA, USA   IE| A-   PV| WPL| **$20 A-**

Simi, 1999 *Alexander Valley, Sonoma Co.*
CA, USA   IE| A-   PV| WPL| W   **$25 A-**

Sineann, 2000 *McDuffee Vineyard, Columbia Valley*
WA, USA   IE| A   PV| WPL| S   **$27 A**

Siskiyou, 2000 *La Cave Rouge*
OR, USA   IE| A   PV| WPL| **$12 A**

Soos Creek, 1999 *Champoux Vineyard, Columbia Valley*
WA, USA   IE| A, B+   PV| WPL| S,BBC   **$30 A-**

Soos Creek, 1999 *Columbia Valley*
WA, USA   IE| A   PV| WPL| S   **$30 A**

Three Rivers Winery, 2000 *Columbia Valley*
WA, USA   IE| B+   PV| WPL| **$20 B+**

Trentadue, 2000 *Sonoma Co.*
CA, USA   IE| A-   PV| WPL| **$22 A-**

Valdivieso, 2000 *Reserve, Central Valley*
CA, USA   IE| B+   PV| WPL| **$20 B+**

Villa Mt. Eden, 1999 *Grand Reserve, Napa Valley*
CA, USA   IE| A   PV| WPL| **$20 A**

Washington Hills, 2000 *Columbia Valley*
WA, USA   IE| B+   PV| WPL| B   **$10 B+**

Waterbrook, 1999 *Red Mountain*
WA, USA   IE| B+   PV| WPL| **$15 B+**

CLARET

Andretti, 1999 *Claret*
CA, USA · IE| A- · PV| · WPL| · $15 · A-

Francis Coppola, 2000 *Claret, Diamond Series, Black Label*
CA, USA · IE| A- · PV| · WPL| · $17 · A-

Murphy-Goode, 2000 *Claret, Wild Card, Alexander Valley, Sonoma Co.*
CA, USA · IE| A- · PV| · WPL| · $19 · A-

Newton, 1999 *Claret, Napa Valley*
CA, USA · IE| A- · PV| · WPL| · $22 · A-

DOLCETTO

Abacela, 2000 *Umpqua Valley*
OR, USA · IE| B+, B · PV| · WPL| · $18 · B+

GRENACHE

Beckmen, 2000 *Purisima Mountain Vineyard, Santa Ynez Valley, Santa Barbara Co.*
CA, USA · IE| B+, B · PV| · WPL| · $18 · B+

Jaffurs, 2000 *Stolpman Family Vineyard, Santa Barbara Co.*
CA, USA · IE| B+ · PV| · WPL| · $20 · B+

Philip Staley, 1999 *Staley Vineyard, Russian River Valley, Sonoma Co.*
CA, USA · IE| B+, B · PV| · WPL| · $18 · B+

MERLOT

Alexander Valley, 2000 *Alexander Valley, Sonoma Co.*
CA, USA · IE| B+ · PV| · WPL| · $20 · B+

Andretti, 1999 *Napa Valley*
CA, USA · IE| A, B+ · PV| · WPL| BBC · $20 · A-

Arrowood, 1999 *Grand Archer, Sonoma Co.*
CA, USA · IE| A- · PV| · WPL| · $20 · A-

Atalon, 1999 *Napa Valley*
CA, USA · IE| A · PV| · WPL| S · $29 · A

Barefoot, 1999 *Reserve, Sonoma Co.*
CA, USA · IE| A- · PV| · WPL| · $17 · A-

Barnard Griffin, 2000 *Columbia Valley*
WA, USA · IE| B+ · PV| · WPL| · $15 · B+

Beaulieu (BV), 1999 *Napa Valley*
CA, USA · IE| A- · PV| · WPL| · $18 · A-

Benziger, 2000 *Sonoma Co.*
CA, USA · IE| B+ · PV| 99 B+ · WPL| · $19 · B+

Buena Vista, 2000
CA, USA · IE| B+ · PV| · WPL| B · $9 · B+

Canoe Ridge, 2000 *Columbia Valley*
CA, USA · IE| A, A · PV| · WPL| BBC · $25 · A

Carmenet, 2000 *Dynamite, North Coast*
CA, USA · IE| B+ · PV| 99 A- · WPL| W · $18 · B+

MERLOT (CONTINUED)

Caterina, 1999 *Columbia Valley*
| WA, USA | IE| B+ | PV| | WPL| | $20 | B+ |

Caterina, 1999 *DuBrul Vineyard, Yakima Valley*
| WA, USA | IE| A | PV| | WPL| S | $30 | A |

Ch. Souverain, 2000 *Alexander Valley, Sonoma Co.*
| CA, USA | IE| B+ | PV| | WPL| | $18 | B+ |

Ch. Ste. Michelle, 2000 *Canoe Ridge Estate Vineyard, Columbia Valley*
| WA, USA | IE| B+, B+ | PV| | WPL| | $24 | B+ |

Ch. Ste. Michelle, 1999 *Canoe Ridge Estate Vineyard, Columbia Valley*
| WA, USA | IE| A, A-, B | PV| | WPL| BBC | $23 | A- |

Chappellet, 2000 *Napa Valley*
| CA, USA | IE| A+ | PV| | WPL| S | $26 | A+ |

Chappellet, 1999 *Napa Valley*
| CA, USA | IE| A+, A | PV| | WPL| BBC | $25 | A |

Cinnabar, 2000 *Paso Robles, San Luis Obispo Co.*
| CA, USA | IE| B+ | PV| | WPL| | $14 | B+ |

Clos du Val, 1999 *Napa Valley*
| CA, USA | IE| A-, B | PV| | WPL| | $25 | B+ |

Clos la Chance, 2001 *Central Coast*
| CA, USA | IE| A- | PV| | WPL| | $18 | A- |

Clos Pegase, 1999 *Mitsuko's Vineyard, Carneros, Napa Valley*
| CA, USA | IE| A+ | PV| | WPL| | $25 | A+ |

Columbia Crest, 1999 *Reserve, Columbia Valley*
| WA, USA | IE| A-, A | PV| | WPL| S,BBC | $28 | A |

Crystal Valley, 2000 *Reserve*
| CA, USA | IE| A- | PV| | WPL| | $16 | A- |

Dashe, 2000 *Potter Valley, Mendocino Co.*
| CA, USA | IE| A | PV| | WPL| S | $26 | A |

Davis Bynum, 1999 *Laureles, Russian River Valley, Sonoma Co.*
| CA, USA | IE| A | PV| | WPL| S | $28 | A |

De Loach, 1999 *Estate Bottled, Russian River Valley, Sonoma Co.*
| CA, USA | IE| B+ | PV| | WPL| | $20 | B+ |

Dunnewood, 1999 *Mendocino Co.*
| CA, USA | IE| B+, B | PV| | WPL| B | $9 | B+ |

Estancia, 2000 *Alexander Valley, Sonoma Co.*
| CA, USA | IE| B+ | PV| | WPL| | $16 | B+ |

Fetzer, 1999 *Barrel Select, Sonoma Co.*
| CA, USA | IE| B+ | PV| | WPL| | $13 | B+ |

Flora Springs, 2000 *Napa Valley*
| CA, USA | IE| A | PV| | WPL| | $22 | A |

Frei Brothers, 2001 *Reserve, Dry Creek Valley, Sonoma Co.*
| CA, USA | IE| B+ | PV| | WPL| | $20 | B+ |

Gainey, 1999 *Santa Ynez Valley, Santa Barbara Co.*
| CA, USA | IE| A, B | PV| | WPL| | $20 | A- |

Hogue, 1999 *Vinyard Selection, Columbia Valley*
WA, USA   IE| A-   PV| WPL| W $18 A-

Hogue, 1999 *Reserve, Columbia Valley*
WA, USA   IE| A-   PV| WPL| S $30 A-

Huntington Cellars, 2000 *Alexander Valley, Sonoma Co.*
CA, USA   IE| A-   PV| WPL| $18 A-

Iron Horse, 1999 *T Bar T Vineyard, Alexander Valley, Sonoma Co.*
CA, USA   IE| B+   PV| WPL| S $26 B+

Isenhower Cellars, 1999 *Columbia Valley*
WA, USA   IE| A-   PV| WPL| $22 A-

Judd Hill, 1999 *Napa Valley*
CA, USA   IE| A-   PV| WPL| S $26 A-

Lambert Bridge, 1999 *Sonoma Co.*
CA, USA   IE| A, A, B+, B, B   PV| WPL| $24 B+

L'Ecole No. 41, 2000 *Columbia Valley*
WA, USA   IE| A-, A-   PV| WPL| S,BBC $30 A-

Liparita, 1999 *Napa Valley*
CA, USA   IE| A   PV| WPL| S $28 A

Louis M. Martini, 1999 *Del Rio Vineyard, Russian River Valley, Sonoma Co.*
CA, USA   IE| A-, A-   PV| WPL| BBC $22 A-

MacRostie, 1999 *Carneros, Napa Valley*
CA, USA   IE| B+   PV| WPL| S $26 B+

Madrigal, 1999 *Napa Valley*
CA, USA   IE| B+, B+   PV| WPL| S $28 B+

Madrigal, 2000 *Napa Valley*
CA, USA   IE| A   PV| 99 B+   WPL| S $28 A

McCray Ridge, 1999 *Two Moon Vineyard, Dry Creek Valley, Sonoma Co.*
CA, USA   IE| B+   PV| WPL| S $29 B+

Monticello, 1999 *Corley Family, Napa Valley*
CA, USA   IE| A+   PV| WPL| S $30 A+

Murphy-Goode, 2000 *Alexander Valley, Sonoma Co.*
CA, USA   IE| A-, B+   PV| 99 B+   WPL| BBC $19 A-

Murphy-Goode, 1999 *Alexander Valley, Sonoma Co.*
CA, USA   IE| B+, B+, B   PV| WPL| $19 B+

Sagelands, 2000 *Four Corners, Columbia Valley*
WA, USA   IE| A-, B   PV| WPL| $15 B+

Saint Chapelle, 2000 *Winemaker's Series*
ID, USA   IE| B+   PV| WPL| B $10 B+

Sandhill, 1999 *Red Mountain*
USA   IE| A-   PV| WPL| $20 A-

Selby, 1999 *Sonoma Co.*
CA, USA   IE| A, A, A-   PV| WPL| BBC $24 A

Snoqualmie, 1999 *Columbia Valley*
WA, USA   IE| B+   PV| WPL| $11 B+

Steltzner, 1999 *Stags Leap District, Napa Valley*
CA, USA   IE| A   PV| WPL| S $26 A

MERLOT (CONTINUED)

Three Rivers Winery, 2000 *Columbia Valley*
WA, USA   IE| A-   PV| WPL| S $26 A-

Trefethen, 1999 *Napa Valley*
CA, USA   IE| A-   PV| WPL| S $26 A-

Trentadue, 2000 *Alexander Valley, Sonoma Co.*
CA, USA   IE| B+   PV| WPL| $20 B+

Trinchero, 1999 *French Camp Vineyard, Rutherford, Napa Valley*
CA, USA   IE| B+   PV| WPL| $25 B+

V. Sattui, 1999 *Napa Valley*
CA, USA   IE| A-   PV| WPL| $24 A-

W. B. Bridgman, 1999 *Columbia Valley*
WA, USA   IE| B+   PV| WPL| $19 B+

Walla Walla Vintners, 2000 *Walla Walla Valley*
WA, USA   IE| A   PV| WPL| $25 A

Waterbrook, 1999 *Red Mountain*
WA, USA   IE| B+   PV| WPL| $15 B+

White Oak, 2000 *Napa Valley*
CA, USA   IE| A, A   PV| WPL| S,BBC $28 A

White Oak, 1999 *Sonoma Co.*
CA, USA   IE| A-   PV| WPL| $25 A-

Whitehall Lane, 1998 *Knights Valley, Sonoma Co.*
CA, USA   IE| B+   PV| WPL| $24 B+

PETITE SIRAH

David Bruce, 2000 *Paso Robles, San Luis Obispo Co.*
CA, USA   IE| B+   PV| 99 B+   WPL| $16 B+

EOS, 1999 *Reserve, Paso Robles, San Luis Obispo Co.*
CA, USA   IE| A   PV| WPL| $25 A

Markham, 1999 *Napa Valley*
CA, USA   IE| A   PV| WPL| $23 A

Novella, 2000 *Paso Robles, San Luis Obispo Co.*
CA, USA   IE| B+   PV| WPL| $13 B+

Rockland, 2000 *Napa Valley*
CA, USA   IE| A-   PV| WPL| S $30 A-

Rosenblum, 2000 *Pickett Road, Napa Valley*
CA, USA   IE| A+   PV| WPL| S $28 A+

Sable Ridge, 1999 *Russian River Valley, Sonoma Co.*
CA, USA   IE| A   PV| WPL| S $28 A

PINOT NOIR

Acacia, 2001 *Napa Valley/Carneros*
CA, USA   IE| B+   PV| WPL| W $20 B+

Amity, 2000 *Schouten Vineyard, Willamette Valley*
OR, USA   IE| B+   PV| WPL| $15 B+

Argyle, 2000 *Reserve, Willamette Valley*
OR, USA   IE| A   PV| WPL| S $30   A

Artesa, 2000 *Carneros*
CA, USA   IE| A   PV| 99 B+   WPL| $24   A

Au Bon Climat, 2001 *Santa Maria Valley, Santa Barbara Co.*
CA, USA   IE| A   PV| WPL| $20   A

Beaulieu (BV), 2000 *Carneros*
CA, USA   IE| B+   PV| WPL| $18   B+

Bella Glos, 2001 *Santa Maria Valley, Santa Barbara Co.*
CA, USA   IE| A   PV| WPL| S $30   A

Beringer, 1999 *Stanly Ranch, Los Carneros, Napa Valley*
CA, USA   IE| A   PV| WPL| S $30   A

Carneros Creek, 2000 *Los Carneros*
CA, USA   IE| A-   PV| WPL| $24   A-

Castle, 1999 *Sangiacoma Vineyard, Carneros*
CA, USA   IE| A-   PV| WPL| S $30   A-

Ch. Bianca, 2000
OR, USA   IE| B+   PV| WPL| $12   B+

Charles Krug, 1999 *Carneros, Napa Valley*
CA, USA   IE| B+   PV| WPL| $18   B+

Clos du Bois, 2001 *Sonoma Co.*
CA, USA   IE| B+   PV| WPL| $17   B+

Cosentino, 2000 *Carneros*
CA, USA   IE| A, B+   PV| WPL| S,BBC $30   A-

Davis Bynum, 2000 *Russian River Valley, Sonoma Co.*
CA, USA   IE| A-   PV| WPL| S $30   A-

Dom. Serene, 2000 *Cuvée, Carlton*
OR, USA   IE| A+, B+   PV| WPL| S,BBC $30   A

Edmeades, 1999 *Anderson Valley, Mendocino Co.*
CA, USA   IE| A-   PV| WPL| $20   A-

Edna Valley, 2001 *Paragon, Edna Valley, San Luis Obispo Co.*
CA, USA   IE| B+, A-   PV| WPL| $15   A-

Elk Cove, 2000 *Willamette Valley*
OR, USA   IE| B+   PV| WPL| $20   B+

Eyrie, 2000 *Estate Grown, Willamette Valley*
OR, USA   IE| B+   PV| WPL| $25   B+

Foxen, 2000 *Santa Maria Valley, Santa Barbara Co.*
CA, USA   IE| A-   PV| WPL| $24   A-

Francis Coppola, 2001 *Diamond Series, Monterey Co.*
CA, USA   IE| B+   PV| WPL| $17   B+

Gloria Ferrer, 2000 *Carneros*
CA, USA   IE| A   PV| WPL| $24   A

Hatcher Wineworks, 2001 *A to Z, Willamette Valley*
OR, USA   IE| B+   PV| WPL| $19   B+

Iron Horse, 2000 *Green Valley, Sonoma Co.*
CA, USA   IE| B+, A   PV| 99 A   WPL| S $30   A-

PINOT NOIR (CONTINUED)

Joseph Swan, 2000 *Cuvée de Trois, Russian River Valley, Sonoma Co.*
CA, USA   IE| B+   PV| WPL| $20   B+

Kendall-Jackson, 1999 *Great Estates, Monterey Co.*
CA, USA   IE| A   PV| WPL| S $30   A

Kenwood, 2000 *Reserve, Olivet Vineyards, Sonoma Co.*
CA, USA   IE| A-   PV| WPL| S $30   A-

Keyhole Ranch, 2000 *Sonoma Co.*
CA, USA   IE| A   PV| WPL| $25   A

King Estate, 2000
OR, USA   IE| B+   PV| WPL| $20   B+

King , 1999 *Eugene*
OR, USA   IE| A-, B+   PV| WPL| BBC $20   A-

La Crema, 2000 *Anderson Valley, Mendocino Co.*
CA, USA   IE| A, A-   PV| WPL| BBC $25   A

La Crema, 2000 *Carneros*
CA, USA   IE| A   PV| WPL| $20   A

La Crema, 2000 *Estate, Carneros*
CA, USA   IE| B+, A-   PV| WPL| $25   A-

Laetitia, 1999 *Santa Barbara Co.*
CA, USA   IE| A   PV| WPL| $25   A

Lane Tanner, 2000 *Bien Nacido Vineyard, Santa Maria Valley, Santa Barbara Co.*
CA, USA   IE| A   PV| WPL| S $28   A

Lane Tanner, 2000 *Julia's Vineyard, Santa Maria Valley, Santa Barbara Co.*
CA, USA   IE| A, B+   PV| WPL| S,BBC $30   A-

Lane Tanner, 2000 *Melville Vineyard, Santa Ynez Valley, Santa Barbara Co.*
CA, USA   IE| A-   PV| WPL| $25   A-

Lane Tanner, 2000 *Santa Maria Valley, Santa Barbara Co.*
CA, USA   IE| A-   PV| WPL| $23   A-

Lemelson, 2001 *Rose Pinot Noir*
OR, USA   IE| B+   PV| WPL| $13   B+

Lemelson, 2000 *Thea's Selection, Willamette Valley*
OR, USA   IE| A-, A-, B+ PV| WPL| S,BBC $29   A-

Libelula, 1999 *Sonoma Coast*
CA, USA   IE| A   PV| WPL| S $28   A

LinCourt, 1999 *Santa Barbara Co.*
CA, USA   IE| A-   PV| WPL| $22   A-

Melville, 2000 *Santa Rita Hills, Santa Barbara Co.*
CA, USA   IE| A-   PV| WPL| $24   A-

Meridian, 1999 *Limited Release, Santa Barbara Co.*
CA, USA   IE| A   PV| WPL| $22   A

Mirassou, 1999 *Harvest Reserve, Monterey Co.*
CA, USA   IE| B+   PV| WPL| $15   B+

Montinore, 2000 *Winemaker's Reserve, Willamette Valley*
OR, USA   IE| B+   PV| WPL| $19   B+

Morgan, 2000 *Santa Lucia Highlands, Monterey Co.*
CA, USA　　　　IE| A-, B+　　PV|　　　　　　WPL| BBC　　$22　A-

Newton, 1999 *Sonoma Valley, Sonoma Co.*
CA, USA　　　　IE| A-　　　　PV|　　　　　　WPL| S　　　$30　A-

Patton Valley Vineyard, 2000 *Willamette Valley*
OR, USA　　　　IE| A　　　　PV|　　　　　　WPL| S　　　$30　A

Pedroncelli, 2000 *F. Johnson Vineyard, Dry Creek Valley, Sonoma Co.*
CA, USA　　　　IE| B+　　　　PV|　　　　　　WPL|　　　　$15　B+

Rex Hill, 1999 *Willamette Valley*
OR, USA　　　　IE| A-　　　　PV|　　　　　　WPL|　　　　$24　A-

Robert Stemmler, 2000 *Sonoma Co.*
CA, USA　　　　IE| B+　　　　PV|　　　　　　WPL| S　　　$28　B+

Rodney Strong, 1999 *Reserve, Russian River Valley, Sonoma Co.*
CA, USA　　　　IE| A-　　　　PV|　　　　　　WPL| S　　　$30　A-

Rutz, 1999 *Martinelli Vineyard, Russian River Valley, Sonoma Co.*
CA, USA　　　　IE| B+, B+　　PV|　　　　　　WPL| S　　　$30　B+

Rutz, 1999 *Dutton Ranch, Russian River Valley, Sonoma Co.*
CA, USA　　　　IE| A　　　　PV|　　　　　　WPL| S　　　$30　A

Saint Gregory, 1999 *Mendocino Co.*
CA, USA　　　　IE| B+　　　　PV|　　　　　　WPL|　　　　$18　B+

Saintsbury, 2001 *Carneros*
CA, USA　　　　IE| B+　　　　PV| 00 B+　　　WPL|　　　　$17　B+

Saintsbury, 2001 *Garnet, Carneros*
CA, USA　　　　IE| A-　　　　PV| 00 B　　　WPL| S　　　$26　A-

Saintsbury, 2000 *Carneros*
CA, USA　　　　IE| A, B+,B, B+ PV|　　　　　WPL| W　　　$24　B+

Schug, 2000 *Carneros*
CA, USA　　　　IE| B+　　　　PV|　　　　　　WPL|　　　　$20　B+

Schug, 2000 *Sonoma Valley, Sonoma Co.*
CA, USA　　　　IE| B+　　　　PV|　　　　　　WPL|　　　　$15　B+

Schug, 1999 *Heritage Reserve, Carneros*
CA, USA　　　　IE| A　　　　PV|　　　　　　WPL| S　　　$30　A

Sebastiani, 2001 *Sonoma Coast, Sonoma Co.*
CA, USA　　　　IE| B+　　　　PV| 00 B+　　　WPL|　　　　$15　B+

Sebastiani, 2000 *Sonoma Coast, Sonoma Co.*
CA, USA　　　　IE| B+, B, B+, B+　　PV|　　WPL|　　　　$15　B+

Siduri, 2001 *Russian River Valley, Sonoma Co.*
CA, USA　　　　IE| A, A-　　PV|　　　　　　WPL| S　　　$28　A

Talley, 2000 *Arroyo Grande Valley, San Luis Obispo Co.*
CA, USA　　　　IE| A-, A-　　PV|　　　　　WPL| S,BBC　$28　A-

Thomas Fogarty, 1999 *Santa Cruz Mountains*
CA, USA　　　　IE| A-, B+　　PV|　　　　　WPL| BBC　　$23　A-

W. H. Smith, 2001 *Sonoma Coast*
CA, USA　　　　IE| A-　　　　PV|　　　　　　WPL| S　　　$28　A-

SANGIOVESE

Columbia, 1999 *David Lake Signature Series, Willow Vineyard, Yakima Valley*
WA, USA   IE| A-   PV| WPL| $25 A-

Flora Springs, 1999 *Napa Valley*
CA, USA   IE| A-   PV| WPL| $16 A-

Luna, 1999 *Napa Valley*
CA, USA   IE| A, B+, B+   PV| WPL| BBC $18 A-

Saddleback, 2000 *Venge Family Reserve Sangiovese, Penny Lane Vineyard, Napa Valley*
CA, USA   IE| A   PV| WPL| S $30 A

Thurston Wolfe, 2000 *Columbia Valley*
WA, USA   IE| A   PV| WPL| $20 A

Valley of the Moon, 1998 *Sonoma Co.*
CA, USA   IE| A-, B   PV| WPL| $16 B+

Venge Family, 2000 *Reserve, Penny Lane Vineyard, Oakville, Napa Valley*
CA, USA   IE| A-   PV| WPL| $20 A-

Waterbrook, 2000 *Ciel du Cheval Sangiovese, Red Mountain*
USA   IE| A-   PV| WPL| S $28 A-

SYRAH/SHIRAZ

Alexander Valley, 2000 *Alexander Valley, Sonoma Co.*
CA, USA   IE| B+, B   PV| WPL| $18 B+

Andrew Murray, 2001 *Tous les Jours, Central Coast*
CA, USA   IE| A-   PV| WPL| $16 A-

Andrew Murray, 2000 *Roasted Slope Vineyard, Santa Ynez Valley, Santa Barbara Co.*
CA, USA   IE| A   PV| WPL| S $30 A

Andrew Rich, 2000 *Les Vigneaux, Columbia Valley*
WA, USA   IE| A-   PV| WPL| $21 A-

Baileyana, 2000 *Paso Robles, San Luis Obispo Co.*
CA, USA   IE| B+   PV| WPL| $18 B+

Baystone, 2000 *Shiraz, Dry Creek Valley, Sonoma Co.*
CA, USA   IE| B+   PV| WPL| $24 B+

Beckmen, 2000 *Santa Ynez Valley, Santa Barbara Co.*
CA, USA   IE| A-   PV| WPL| $24 A-

Bell, 1999 *Canterbury Vineyard, Sierra Foothills*
CA, USA   IE| A-   PV| WPL| S $28 A-

Belvedere, 1999 *Healdsburg Ranches, Sonoma Co.*
CA, USA   IE| A   PV| WPL| S $26 A

Benziger, 2000
CA, USA   IE| A-   PV| WPL| $22 A-

Beringer, 1999 *Shiraz, Founders' Estate*
CA, USA   IE| A-, B-   PV| WPL| $12 A

Bridlewood, 2000 *Central Coast*
CA, USA   IE| A-, B+   PV| WPL| BBC $19 A-

Burgess, 2000 *Napa Valley*
CA, USA　　IE| A-, B, B+　　PV|　　　　WPL|　　　　$22　B+

Canyon Road, 2000 *Shiraz*
CA, USA　　IE| B+, B　　PV|　　　　WPL| B　　　　$10　B+

Cedarville, 2000 *El Dorado Co., Sierra Foothills*
CA, USA　　IE| A　　PV| 99 A　　WPL|　　　　$25　A

Ch. Julien, 2000 *Monterey Co.*
CA, USA　　IE| B+　　PV|　　　　WPL| B　　　　$10　B+

Ch. Souverain, 2000 *Alexander Valley, Sonoma Co.*
CA, USA　　IE| B+, A-, B, A+PV|　　　　WPL|　　BBC　$20A-

Ch. Ste. Michelle, 2000 *Columbia Valley*
WA, USA　　IE| B+　　PV|　　　　WPL|　　　　$15　B+

Ch. Ste. Michelle, 1999 *Reserve, Columbia Valley*
WA, USA　　IE| A-, A-　　PV|　　　　WPL| S,BBC　$29　A-

Chatter Creek, 2000 *Jack Jones Vineyard*
WA, USA　　IE| B+　　PV|　　　　WPL|　　　　$20　B+

Chatter Creek, 2000 *Lonesome Spring Ranch*
WA, USA　　IE| A　　PV|　　　　WPL|　　　　$20　A

Cline, 2000 *Los Carneros*
CA, USA　　IE| A, A-, A-, A-PV|　　　　WPL| S,BBC　$28　A-

Cline, 2000 *Sonoma Co.*
CA, USA　　IE| B+　　PV|　　　　WPL|　　　　$16　B+

Clos du Bois, 1999 *Reserve Shiraz, Alexander Valley, Sonoma Co.*
CA, USA　　IE| B+　　PV|　　　　WPL|　　　　$16　B+

Columbia, 2000 *Columbia Valley*
WA, USA　　IE| B+　　PV|　　　　WPL|　　　　$15　B+

Columbia Crest, 2000 *Reserve, Columbia Valley*
WA, USA　　IE| A+　　PV| 99 A-　　WPL| S　　　　$28　A+

Concannon, 1999 *San Francisco Bay*
CA, USA　　IE| B+　　PV|　　　　WPL|　　　　$19　B+

Dom. de la Terre Rouge, 2000 *California les Cotes de L'Ouest, Plymouth*
CA, USA　　IE| B+　　PV|　　　　WPL|　　　　$15　B+

Dom. de la Terre Rouge, 2000 *Sierra Foothills*
CA, USA　　IE| A-　　PV|　　　　WPL|　　　　$15　A-

Dom. de la Terre Rouge, 1999 *Sierra Foothills*
CA, USA　　IE| A+　　PV|　　　　WPL|　　　　$22　A+

Edmunds St. John, 2001
CA, USA　　IE| B+　　PV|　　　　WPL|　　　　$18　B+

Edmunds St. John, 2000 *Wylie-Fenaughty, El Dorado Co., Sierra Foothills*
CA, USA　　IE| A+, A-　　PV|　　　　WPL| S,BBC　$30　A

Equus, 1999 *Paso Robles, San Luis Obispo Co.*
CA, USA　　IE| A, A-　　PV|　　　　WPL| BBC　$18　A

EXP, 2000 *Dunnigan Hills, Yolo Co.*
CA, USA　　IE| B+　　PV|　　　　WPL|　　　　$14　B+

Fife, 2000 *Mendocino Co.*
CA, USA　　IE| A　　PV|　　　　WPL|　　　　$20　A

SYRAH/SHIRAZ (CONTINUED)

Firestone, 2000 *Santa Ynez Valley, Santa Barbara Co.*
| CA, USA | IE| B+ | PV| | WPL| | $18 | B+ |

Forest Glen, 2000 *Oak Barrel Selection*
| CA, USA | IE| B+ | PV| | WPL| B | $10 | B+ |

Geyser Peak, 2000 *Sonoma Co.*
| CA, USA | IE| B+,A- | PV| | WPL| BBC | $17 | A- |

Glen Fiona, 1999 *Puncheon Aged, Walla Walla Valley*
| WA, USA | IE| A | PV| | WPL| S | $30 | A |

Granite Springs, 1999 *Sierra Foothills, El Dorado Co.*
| CA, USA | IE| B+, B | PV| | WPL| | $16 | B+ |

Hahn, 2001 *San Luis Obispo Co.*
| CA, USA | IE| A- | PV| | WPL| | $12 | A- |

Harlequin, 2000 *Sundance Vineyard, Columbia Valley*
| WA, USA | IE| A | PV| | WPL| S | $30 | A |

Hess Select, 2000 *Napa Valley*
| CA, USA | IE| B+ | PV| | WPL| | $14 | B+ |

Hogue, 1999 *Genesis, Columbia Valley*
| WA, USA | IE| A- | PV| | WPL| | $25 | A- |

Isenhower Cellars, 2000 *Columbia Valley*
| WA, USA | IE| A- | PV| | WPL| | $25 | A- |

J C, 2000 *Rodney's Vineyard, Santa Barbara Co.*
| CA, USA | IE| B+ | PV| 99 A | WPL| S | $27 | B+ |

Jade Mountain, 2000 *Napa Valley*
| CA, USA | IE| A, A | PV| | WPL| S,BBC | $28 | A |

Joseph Phelps, 2000 *Le Mistral, Napa Valley*
| CA, USA | IE| A | PV| | WPL| | $25 | A |

Kestral, 2000 *Yakima Valley*
| WA, USA | IE| A- | PV| | WPL| S | $28 | A- |

La Crema, 2000 *Sonoma Co.*
| CA, USA | IE| A-, A- | PV| | WPL| BBC | $18 | A- |

Lafond, 2001 *SRH, Santa Rita Hills*
| CA, USA | IE| B+ | PV| | WPL| | $18 | B+ |

Lane Tanner, 2000 *French Camp, San Luis Obispo Co.*
| CA, USA | IE| B+ | PV| | WPL| | $20 | B+ |

LinCourt, 2000 *Santa Barbara Co.*
| CA, USA | IE| B+ | PV| | WPL| | $20 | B+ |

Longfellow, 2001 *Dry Creek Valley*
| CA, USA | IE| A- | PV| | WPL| S | $29 | A- |

Loxton, 1999 *Timbervine Ranch, Russian River Valley, Sonoma Co.*
| CA, USA | IE| A- | PV| | WPL| S | $26 | A- |

MacRostie, 2000 *Blue Oaks Vineyard, Paso Robles, San Luis Obispo Co.*
| CA, USA | IE| B+ | PV| | WPL| | $19 | B+ |

McDowell, 2000 *Mendocino Co.*
| CA, USA | IE| B+ | PV| | WPL| | $12 | B+ |

Meridian, 1999 *Paso Robles, San Luis Obispo Co.*
CA, USA   IE| A-, B, B   PV| WPL| $15 B+

Morgan, 2000 *Monterey Co.*
CA, USA   IE| B+, A-, B   PV| WPL| $20 B+

Neyers, 2000 *Napa Valley*
CA, USA   IE| A-   PV| WPL| S $30 A-

Novy, 2000 *Santa Lucia Highlands*
CA, USA   IE| A-, B+, B+   PV| WPL| $23 B+

Novy, 2001 *Santa Lucia Highlands*
CA, USA   IE| A-   PV| 00 B+   WPL| S $26 A-

Ojai, 2000 *Santa Barbara Co.*
CA, USA   IE| A-   PV| WPL| $24 A-

Paige 23, 2000 *Santa Barbara Co.*
CA, USA   IE| A+   PV| WPL| $21 A+

Pend d'Oreille, 2000 *Columbia Valley*
WA, USA   IE| A-   PV| WPL| $23 A-

Qupé, 2001 *Central Coast*
CA, USA   IE| B+   PV| 99 B+   WPL| $15 B+

Qupé, 1999 *Red Mountain*
CA, USA   IE| A+   PV| WPL| $20 A+

Ravenswood, 2000 *Icon, Sonoma Co.*
CA, USA   IE| B+   PV| WPL| $20 B+

Ridge, 2000 *Lytton Springs, Somona Co.*
CA, USA   IE| A-   PV| WPL| S $30 A-

Robert Craig, 2000 *Central Coast*
CA, USA   IE| A-   PV| WPL| S $28 A-

Rosenblum, 2001 *England-Shaw Vineyard, Solano Co.*
CA, USA   IE| A-   PV| WPL| S $30 A-

Rosenblum, 2000 *England-Shaw Vineyard, Solano Co.*
CA, USA   IE| A-, B   PV| WPL| S $30 B+

Rosenblum, 2000 *Hillside Vineyards, Sonoma Co.*
CA, USA   IE| A   PV| WPL| $24 A

Rosenblum, 2000 *Rodney's Vineyard, Santa Barbara Co.*
CA, USA   IE| B+   PV| WPL| $25 B+

Rutherford Oaks, 2000 *Hozhoni Vineyards, Napa Valley*
CA, USA   IE| A-   PV| WPL| S $28 A-

Snoqualmie, 2000 *Columbia Valley*
WA, USA   IE| B+   PV| WPL| $11 B+

Thurston Wolfe, 2000 *Columbia Valley*
WA, USA   IE| A-   PV| WPL| $18 A-

Valley of the Moon, 1999 *Sonoma Co.*
CA, USA   IE| A-   PV| WPL| $15 A-

Ventana, 2000 *Arroyo Seco*
CA, USA   IE| B+   PV| WPL| $18 B+

Victor Hugo, 2000 *Paso Robles, San Luis Obispo Co.*
CA, USA   IE| B+   PV| WPL| $20 B+

ZINFANDEL

W. B. Bridgman, 2000 *Yakima Valley*
WA, USA   IE| B+   PV| WPL| $19   B+

Willow Crest, 1999 *Yakima Valley*
WA, USA   IE| B+   PV| WPL| $18   B+

Wolff, 2001 *Edna Valley*
CA, USA   IE| B+   PV| WPL| $18   B+

Wyvern , 2000 *Columbia Valley*
WA, USA   IE| A-   PV| WPL| $25   A-

Zaca Mesa, 2000 *Santa Ynez Valley*
CA, USA   IE| A, A-   PV| WPL| BBC $20   A

A. Rafanelli, 2000 *Dry Creek Valley, Sonoma Co.*
CA, USA   IE| A-   PV| 99 A-   WPL| S $26   A-

Acorn, 2000 *Alegria Vineyards, Russian River Valley, Sonoma Co.*
CA, USA   IE| A-   PV| WPL| S $28   A-

Ballentine, 1999 *Napa Valley*
CA, USA   IE| B+   PV| WPL| $15   B+

Beaulieu (BV), 2000 *Beauzeaux Signet Collection, Napa Valley*
CA, USA   IE| A   PV| WPL| $24   A

Buena Vista, 2000 *Carneros*
CA, USA   IE| B+, B+   PV| WPL| B $9   B+

Castoro Cellars, 2000 *Paso Robles, San Luis Obispo Co.*
CA, USA   IE| A-   PV| WPL| $14   A-

Ch. Montelena, 2000 *Primitivo, Napa Valley*
CA, USA   IE| A-   PV| WPL| $25   A-

Ch. Souverain, 2000 *Dry Creek Valley, Sonoma Co.*
CA, USA   IE| B+   PV| WPL| $18   B+

Chiarello, 2000 *Giana, Napa Valley*
CA, USA   IE| A-   PV| WPL| S $28   A-

Cline, 2000
CA, USA   IE| B+   PV| WPL| B $10   B+

Cline, 2000 *Live Oak Vineyard, Contra Costa Co.*
CA, USA   IE| A+   PV| WPL| S $28   A+

Clos du Bois, 2000 *Reserve, Dry Creek Valley, Sonoma Co.*
CA, USA   IE| A-   PV| WPL| $22   A-

Clos la Chance, 2000 *Twin Rivers Vineyard, El Dorado Co., Sierra Foothills*
CA, USA   IE| B   PV| 99 B+   WPL| $20   B+

Dashe, 2001 *Late Harvest, Dry Creek Valley, Sonoma Co.*
CA, USA   IE| B+   PV| WPL| $20   B+

Dashe, 2001 *Dry Creek Valley, Sonoma Co.*
CA, USA   IE| B+   PV| 99 A-, 00 A   WPL| $20   B+

Dashe, 2000 *Dry Creek Valley, Sonoma Co.*
CA, USA   IE| A, A, B   PV| 99 A-   WPL| BBC $20   A-

Dashe, 2000 *Todd Brothers Ranch, Alexander Valley, Sonoma Co.*
CA, USA   IE| A   PV| 99 A-   WPL| $25   A

De Loach, 2000 *Barbieri Ranch, Russian River Valley, Sonoma Co.*
CA, USA　　　　IE| A　　　PV| 99 A-　　　WPL| S　　　$28　A

De Loach, 2000 *Pelletti Ranch, Russian River Valley, Sonoma Co.*
CA, USA　　　　IE| A　　　PV|　　　　　　WPL| S　　　$28　A

Deux Amis, 2000 *Somona Co.*
CA, USA　　　　IE| B+　　PV|　　　　　　WPL|　　　　$19　B+

Dry Creek, 2000 *Old Vines, Sonoma Co.*
CA, USA　　　　IE| A, A, B+, A　PV|　　　WPL| BBC　$21　A

Easton, 2001 *Amador Co.*
CA, USA　　　　IE| B+, B　PV| 99 A-　　　WPL|　　　$13　B+

Edgewood, 2001 *Napa Valley*
CA, USA　　　　IE| A-　　PV|　　　　　　WPL|　　　$20　A-

Edgewood, 2000 *Napa Valley*
CA, USA　　　　IE| A-　　PV|　　　　　　WPL|　　　$20　A-

Edmeades, 1999 *Ciapusci, Mendocino Ridge, Mendocino Co.*
CA, USA　　　　IE| A　　　PV|　　　　　　WPL|　　　$25　A

Edmeades, 1999 *Zeni Vineyard, Mendocino Ridge, Mendocino Co.*
CA, USA　　　　IE| A+　　PV|　　　　　　WPL|　　　$25　A+

Folie à Deux, 1999 *Bowman Vineyard, Amador Co.*
CA, USA　　　　IE| A　　　PV|　　　　　　WPL| S　　　$26　A

Franus, 2000 *Planchon Vineyard, Contra Costa Co.*
CA, USA　　　　IE| B+　　PV|　　　　　　WPL|　　　$20　B+

Franus, 2000 *Rancho Chimiles, Napa*
CA, USA　　　　IE| A-　　PV|　　　　　　WPL| S　　　$28　A-

Gallo Sonoma, 1999 *Frei Ranch Vineyard, Dry Creek Valley, Sonoma Co.*
CA, USA　　　　IE| A, A-　PV|　　　　　WPL| BBC　$22　A

Gary Farrell, 2000 *Dry Creek Valley, Sonoma Co.*
CA, USA　　　　IE| A-　　PV|　　　　　　WPL|　　　$24　A-

Hartford Court, 2000 *Russian River Valley, Sonoma Co.*
CA, USA　　　　IE| A-　　PV| 99 A-　　　WPL| S　　　$30　A-

Hendry Ranch, 2000 *Hendry Block 28, Napa Valley*
CA, USA　　　　IE| A-　　PV|　　　　　　WPL| S　　　$28　A-

Hunt, 2000 *Zinphony #2 Reserve, Paso Robles, San Luis Obispo Co.*
CA, USA　　　　IE| A　　　PV|　　　　　　WPL| S　　　$28　A

Hunt, 1999 *Zinphony #2 Reserve, Paso Robles, San Luis Obispo Co.*
CA, USA　　　　IE| A　　　PV|　　　　　　WPL|　　　$24　A

Jessie's Grove, 2001 *Vintner's Choice Old Vine, Lodi*
CA, USA　　　　IE| B+　　PV|　　　　　　WPL|　　　$15　B+

Joel Gott, 2001
CA, USA　　　　IE| B+　　PV| 00 B+　　　WPL|　　　$15　B+

Kendall-Jackson, 2000 *Great Estates, Mendocino Co.*
CA, USA　　　　IE| A-　　PV|　　　　　　WPL| S　　　$30　A-

La Storia, 2001 *Geyserville Ranch, Alexander Valley, Sonoma Co.*
CA, USA　　　　IE| A-　　PV|　　　　　　WPL| S　　　$28　A-

Lake Sonoma, 2000 *Dry Creek Valley, Sonoma Co.*
CA, USA　　　　IE| A, B, A　PV| 99 B+　　WPL| BBC　$17　A-

ZINFANDEL (CONTINUED)

Lake Sonoma, 2000 *Russian River Valley, Sonoma Co.*
CA, USA   IE| A-   PV| WPL| $22 A-

Lake Sonoma, 1999 *Saini Farms, Dry Creek Valley, Sonoma Co.*
CA, USA   IE| B+   PV| WPL| $20 B+

Laurel Glen, 2000 *Zazin, Old Vine, Lodi*
CA, USA   IE| A-, B+   PV| WPL| $17 A

Markham, 2000 *Napa Valley*
CA, USA   IE| A+   PV| 99 B+   WPL| $20 A+

Mayo Family, 2000 *Ricci Vineyard, Russian River Valley, Sonoma Co.*
CA, USA   IE| A-   PV| WPL| S $30 A-

Monteviña, 1999 *Terra d'Oro, Amador Co.*
CA, USA   IE| B+   PV| WPL| $18 B+

Monteviña, 2000 *Terra d'Oro, Deaver Vineyard, Amador Co.*
CA, USA   IE| A-   PV| WPL| $24 A-

Murphy-Goode, 2000 *Liar's Dice, Sonoma Co.*
CA, USA   IE| B+   PV| WPL| $20 B+

Newlan, 2000 *Napa Valley*
CA, USA   IE| A   PV| WPL| $22 A

Peachy Canyon, 2000 *Westside, Paso Robles, San Luis Obispo Co.*
CA, USA   IE| B+   PV| WPL| $19 B+

Pezzi King, 2000 *Maple Vineyard, Dry Creek Valley, Sonoma Co.*
CA, USA   IE| A-, A-   PV| 99 A-   WPL| S,BBC $30 A-

Rancho Zabaco, 2001 *Dancing Bull, Lodi*
CA, USA   IE| B+   PV| WPL| $12 B+

Rancho Zabaco, 2001 *Heritage Vines, Sonoma Co.*
CA, USA   IE| B+   PV| 99 A-, 00:B+ WPL| $18 B+

Rancho Zabaco, 2001 *Chiotti Vineyard, Dry Creek Valley, Sonoma Co.*
CA, USA   IE| A   PV| WPL| S $28 A

Rancho Zabaco, 2000 *Heritage Vines, Sonoma Co.*
CA, USA   IE| B+   PV| 99 A-   WPL| $14 B+

Ravenswood, 2000 *Vintners Blend*
CA, USA   IE| B+   PV| 99 A-   WPL| B $10 B+

Raymond, 1999 *Reserve, Napa Valley*
CA, USA   IE| A-   PV| WPL| $22 A-

Ridge, 2001 *Geyserville, Sonoma Co.*
CA, USA   IE| A-   PV| 99 A-   WPL| S $30 A-

Ridge, 2001 *Lytton Springs, Dry Creek Valley, Sonoma Co.*
CA, USA   IE| PV| 99 B, 00 A   WPL| S $30 A

Ridge, 2001 *Sonoma Station, Sonoma Co.*
CA, USA   IE| A-   PV| WPL| $20 A-

Ridge, 2001 *Three Valleys, Sonoma Co.*
CA, USA   IE| B+   PV| WPL| $18 B+

Ridge, 2000 *Lytton Springs, Dry Creek Valley, Sonoma Co.*
CA, USA   IE| A+, B, A+, B+, A+   PV| 99 A   WPL| S,BBC $30 A

Ridge, 2000 *Pagani Ranch, Sonoma Valley, Sonoma Co.*
CA, USA   IE| A-   PV| WPL| S $28 A-

Ridge, 2000 *Paso Robles, San Luis Obispo Co.*
CA, USA   IE| A, B, B+   PV| WPL| $25 B+

Rosenblum, NV *Vintners Cuvée XXIV*
CA, USA   IE| B+   PV| WPL| B $10 B+

Rosenblum, 2001 *Planchon Vineyard, San Francisco Bay*
CA, USA   IE| A   PV| 00 B+   WPL| $19 A

Rosenblum, 2001 *Rockpile Vineyard, Dry Creek Valley, Sonoma Co.*
CA, USA   IE| A+   PV| 00 A-   WPL| S $26 A+

Rosenblum, 2000 *Continente Vineyard, San Francisco Bay*
CA, USA   IE| B+   PV| 99 B+   WPL| $20 B+

Rosenblum, 2000 *Old Vines, Russian River Valley, Sonoma Co.*
CA, USA   IE| B+   PV| WPL| $18 B+

Sausal, 2000 *Old Vine Family, Alexander Valley, Sonoma Co.*
CA, USA   IE| B+   PV| WPL| $15 B+

Sausal, 2000 *Private Reserve, Alexander Valley, Sonoma Co.*
CA, USA   IE| A   PV| 99 A-   WPL| $20 A

Sausal, 1999 *Private Reserve, Alexander Valley, Sonoma Co.*
CA, USA   IE| A-   PV| WPL| $18 A-

Scherrer, 1999 *Alexander Valley, Sonoma Co.*
CA, USA   IE| A   PV| WPL| S $28 A

Seghesio, 2001 *Sonoma, Sonoma Co.*
CA, USA   IE| B+, B+   PV| 99 B+, 00 B+ WPL| $17 B+

Seghesio, 2000 *Cortina, Dry Creek Valley, Sonoma Co.*
CA, USA   IE| A-, B, B+   PV| WPL| S $28 B+

Shenandoah, 2001 *ReZerve, Paul's Vineyard, Shenandoah Valley, Sierra Foothills*
CA, USA   IE| A-   PV| WPL| $24 A-

Sobon, 2001 *ReZerve, Shenandoah Valley, Sierra Foothills*
CA, USA   IE| A-   PV| WPL| $24 A-

Sobon, 2000 *Cougar Hill Vineyards, Shenandoah Valley, Sierra Foothills*
CA, USA   IE| B+   PV| WPL| $17 B+

Sobon, 2000 *Rocky Top, Shenandoah Valley, Sierra Foothills*
CA, USA   IE| A   PV| WPL| $15 A

Sparrow Lane, 2000 *Sonoma Co.*
CA, USA   IE| A-   PV| WPL| $24 A-

Stonehedge, 2000 *Napa Valley*
CA, USA   IE| A-   PV| WPL| $15 A-

Stonehedge, 1999 *Napa Valley*
CA, USA   IE| B+   PV| WPL| $20 B+

Stryker Sonoma, 1999 *Old Vine Estate, Alexander Valley, Sonoma Co.*
CA, USA   IE| A-   PV| WPL| $25 A-

Summers, 2001 *Villa Andriana Vineyard, Napa Valley*
CA, USA   IE| A   PV| WPL| $20 A

Summit Lake, 1999 *Howell Mountain, Napa Valley*
CA, USA   IE| A   PV| WPL| $22 A

ZINFANDEL (CONTINUED)

Thea, 2000 *Joaquin*
CA, USA   IE| A-   PV| WPL| $24 A-

Trentadue, 2000 *Alexander Valley, Sonoma Co.*
CA, USA   IE| B+   PV| WPL| $20 B+

Turley, 2000 *Duarte Vineyard, Contra Costa Co.*
CA, USA   IE| A+, B+, A   PV| WPL| S,BBC $30 A

Turley, 2000 *Juvenile*
CA, USA   IE| B+, B, A-   PV| WPL| $20 B+

Turley, 2000 *Old Vines*
CA, USA   IE| A, B, A   PV| 99 A   WPL| BBC $25 A-

T-Vine, 2000 *Napa Valley*
CA, USA   IE| A-   PV| WPL| $25 A-

Unti, 2000 *Dry Creek Valley, Sonoma Co.*
CA, USA   IE| B+   PV| WPL| $20 B+

V. Sattui, 2000 *Suzanne's Vineyard, Napa Valley*
CA, USA   IE| A   PV| WPL| $20 A

Valley of the Moon, 2000 *Sonoma Co.*
CA, USA   IE| A-   PV| WPL| $15 A-

Watts, 1999 *Old Vines, Lodi*
CA, USA   IE| A-   PV| WPL| $14 A-

White Oak, 2000 *Alexander Valley, Sonoma Co.*
CA, USA   IE| A   PV| 99 A-   WPL| $24 A

Williams Selyem, 2000 *Russian River Valley, Sonoma Co.*
CA, USA   IE| A   PV| WPL| $25 A

OTHER RED

Betz Family Winery, 2000 *Clos de Betz, Columbia Valley*
WA, USA   IE| A   PV| WPL| $24 A

Ca' del Solo, 2001 *Big House Red*
CA, USA   IE| A-   PV| 00 B+   WPL| B $10 A-

Ca' del Solo, 2000 *Big House Red, Santa Cruz Mountains*
CA, USA   IE| B+, A-   PV| WPL| B $10 A-

Catacula, 1999 *Cuvée, Catacula Lake, St. Helena*
CA, USA   IE| A-   PV| WPL| $19 A-

Caterina, 1999 *Rosso*
WA, USA   IE| B+   PV| WPL| $15 B+

Columbia Crest, 1999 *Reserve Red, Columbia Valley*
WA, USA   IE| A, A   PV| WPL| S,BBC $30 A

Curtis, 2000 *Counoise/Grenache/Mourvedre/Syrah Heritage Cuvée, Central Coast*
CA, USA   IE| B+   PV| WPL| $14 B+

De Lorimier, 1999 *Mosaic, Alexander Valley, Sonoma Co.*
CA, USA   IE| A   PV| WPL| S $30 A

Dom. Chandon, 2000 *Pinot Meunier, Carneros*
CA, USA   IE| A-   PV| WPL| S $29 A-

Dom. de la Terre Rouge, 2000 *Mourvedre, Sierra Foothills*
CA, USA   IE| B+   PV| WPL| $20   B+

Dry Creek, 1999 *Meritage, Dry Creek Valley, Sonoma Co.*
CA, USA   IE| A-   PV| WPL| S $28   A-

Hedges, 2000 *Cabernet/Merlot/Franc, Columbia Valley*
WA, USA   IE| B+   PV| WPL| $18   B+

Jade Mountain, 2000 *La Provençale*
CA, USA   IE| A-   PV| WPL| $16   A-

Jest Red, NV *Red Table Wine, Belvedere Vineyard, North Coast*
CA, USA   IE| B+   PV| WPL| $11   B+

JM Cellars, 1999 *Cabernet/Merlot/Syrah, Tre Fanciulli, Columbia Valley*
WA, USA   IE| A   PV| WPL| S $28   A

Mount Palomar, 1999 *Meritage, Temecula*
CA, USA   IE| B+   PV| WPL| $18   B+

Rosenblum, 2001 *Mourvedre, Continente Vineyard, San Francisco Bay*
CA, USA   IE| A-   PV| WPL| $18   A-

Ryan Patrick, 1999 *Columbia Valley*
WA, USA   IE| A   PV| WPL| S $29   A

Saddleback, 1999 *Venge Family Reserve Scouts Honor, Oakville, Napa Valley*
CA, USA   IE| A   PV| WPL| S $30   A

Shooting Star, 2001 *Blue Franc Lemberger*
WA, USA   IE| B+   PV| WPL| $12   B+

Soos Creek, NV *Sundance Red, Columbia Valley*
WA, USA   IE| A-   PV| WPL| $20   A-

Tamarack Cellars, 2000 *Firehouse Red, Walla Walla Valley*
WA, USA   IE| B+   PV| WPL| $18   B+

The Prisoner, 2000 *Charbono/Petite Sirah/Syrah/Zinfandel, Napa Valley*
CA, USA   IE| A-   PV| WPL| S $28   A-

Thurston Wolfe, 2000 *Lemberger/Syrah, Blue Franc, Columbia Valley*
WA, USA   IE| A-   PV| WPL| $13   A-

Trentadue, 2000 *Old Patch Red Estate, Alexander Valley, Sonoma Co.*
CA, USA   IE| B+   PV| WPL| $15   B+

Valley of the Moon, 1999 *Cuvée de la Luna, Sonoma Co.*
CA, USA   IE| A-   PV| WPL| S $28   A-

Waterbrook, 2001 *Cabernet Sauvignon/Merlot/Sangiovese/Syrah Melange, , Columbia Valley*
WA, USA   IE| B+   PV| WPL| $13   B+

Zaca Mesa, 1999 *Mourvedre, Chapel Vineyard, Santa Barbara Co.*
CA, USA   IE| B+   PV| WPL| $15   B+

WHITES

CHARDONNAY

Acacia, 2001 *Carneros*
CA, USA   IE| B+, B+, B+   PV| 00 B   WPL| W $20   B+

Alderbrook, 2000 *Dry Creek Valley, Sonoma Co.*
CA, USA   IE| B+   PV| WPL| $20   B+

Andretti, 2001 *Napa Valley*
CA, USA   IE| A-   PV| WPL| $16   A-

Arbor Crest, 2000 *Columbia Valley*
WA, USA   IE| B+   PV| WPL| $14   B+

Arrowood, 2001 *Somona Co.*
CA, USA   IE| A, B   PV| WPL| S $29   B+

Artesa, 2000 *Reserve, Carneros*
CA, USA   IE| A   PV| WPL| S $30   A

Artesa, 2000 *Carneros*
CA, USA   IE| B+,   PV| 99 B+   WPL| $23   B+

Babcock, 2000 *Santa Ynez Valley, Santa Barbara Co.*
CA, USA   IE| A-   PV| WPL| $25   A-

Bargetto, 2000 *Regan Vineyard, Santa Cruz Mountains*
CA, USA   IE| B+   PV| WPL| $20   B+

Barnard Griffin, 2000 *Reserve, Columbia Valley*
WA, USA   IE| B+   PV| WPL| $19   B+

Barnett, 2000 *Napa Valley*
CA, USA   IE| B+   PV| WPL| $25   B+

Baystone, 2000 *Dijon Clones 76 & 96, Saralee's Vineyard, Russian River Valley, Sonoma Co.*
CA, USA   IE| B+   PV| WPL| $20   B+

BearBoat, 2001 *Russian River Valley, Sonoma Co.*
CA, USA   IE| B+   PV| 99 A-   WPL| $17   B+

Beaulieu (BV), 2000 *Carneros Reserve, Napa Valley*
CA, USA   IE| A-   PV| WPL| S $28   A-

Bedford Thompson, 2000 *Santa Barbara Co.*
CA, USA   IE| A-   PV| WPL| $18   A-

Beringer, 2000 *Appellation Collection Napa Valley*
CA, USA   IE| A   PV| WPL| $16   A

Bernardus, 2000 *Monterey Co.*
CA, USA   IE| B+   PV| WPL| $20   B+

Bouchaine, 2001 *Carneros*
CA, USA   IE| B+, B+   PV| 99 A-   WPL| $18   B+

Bridgeview, 2000 *Blue Moon*
OR, USA   IE| B+   PV| WPL| B $10   B+

Bridgeview, 2000
OR, USA   IE| B+   PV| WPL| B $7   B+

Byington, 2001 *Sonoma Co.*
CA, USA   IE| B+   PV| WPL| $18   B+

Byington, 2000 *Sonoma Co.*
CA, USA   IE| B+   PV| 99 B+   WPL| $18   B+

Calera, 2000 *Central Coast*
CA, USA   IE| B+   PV| WPL| $18   B+

Callaway, 2001 *Reserve, Coastal*
CA, USA   IE| B+   PV| 99 B+   WPL| $15   B+

Callaway, 2000 *Reserve, Coastal, Santa Maria Valley, Santa Barbara Co.*
CA, USA   IE| B+   PV| 99 B+   WPL| $16   B+

Cambria, 2001 *Katherine's Vineyard, Santa Maria Valley, Santa Barbara Co.*
CA, USA   IE| A+   PV| 99 A, 00 A-   WPL| $20   A+

Cantiga Wineworks, 2000 *Monterey Co.*
CA, USA   IE| B+   PV| WPL| $20   B+

Carpe Diem, 2000 *Firepeak Vineyard, Edna Valley, San Luis Obispo Co.*
CA, USA   IE| A   PV| WPL| $25   A

Cartlidge and Browne, 2001
CA, USA   IE| B+   PV| WPL| B $10   B+

Caterina, 2000 *Columbia Valley*
WA, USA   IE| B+   PV| WPL| $13   B+

Ch. Souverain, 2001 *Sonoma Co.*
CA, USA   IE| B+, B   PV| 00 A-   WPL| W $14   B+

Ch. Souverain, 2001 *Winemaker's Reserve, Russian River Valley, Sonoma Co.*
CA, USA   IE| A+   PV| 99 A, 00 B+   WPL| $25   A+

Ch. Souverain, 2000 *Winemaker's Reserve, Russian River Valley, Sonoma Co.*
CA, USA   IE| B+   PV| 99 A   WPL| $20   B+

Ch. St. Jean, 2000 *Belle Terre Vineyard, Alexander Valley, Sonoma Co.*
CA, USA   IE| A, A   PV| 99 B   WPL| BBC $22   A

Ch. St. Jean, 2000 *Durell Vineyard, Carneros*
CA, USA   IE| A-, A   PV| 99 B   WPL| BBC $24   A

Ch. Ste. Michelle, 2000 *Canoe Ridge Vineyard, Columbia Valley*
WA, USA   IE| A-   PV| 99 A-   WPL| $20   A-

Ch. Ste. Michelle, 2000 *Cold Creek Vineyard, Columbia Valley*
WA, USA   IE| A-, A-   PV| 99 A-   WPL| S,BBC $26   A-

Ch. Ste. Michelle, 2000 *Columbia Valley*
WA, USA   IE| B+, B+, B, B+   PV| WPL| W $13   B+

Ch. Ste. Michelle, 2000 *Indian Wells Vineyards, Columbia Valley*
WA, USA   IE| A-, A   PV| 99 A-, 00 B+   WPL| BBC $21   A

Ch. Ste. Michelle, 2000 *Reserve, Columbia Valley*
WA, USA   IE| A+   PV| 99 A-   WPL| S $29   A+

Charles Krug, 2001 *Napa Valley*
CA, USA   IE| B+   PV| 00 B+   WPL| $17   B+

Charles Krug, 2000 *Napa Valley*
CA, USA   IE| B+, B   PV| WPL| $15   B+

Cloninger, 2000 *Estate Grown, Santa Lucia Highlands*
CA, USA   IE| B+   PV| WPL| $16   B+

Clos du Bois, 2000 *Calciare Vineyard, Alexander Valley, Sonoma Co.*
CA, USA   IE| A-, B   PV| WPL| $22   B+

Clos du Val, 2001 *Carneros, Napa Valley*
CA, USA   IE| B+, B+   PV| WPL| $21   B+

Clos la Chance, 2001 *Vanumanutagi Vineyard, Santa Cruz Mountains*
CA, USA   IE| A, A   PV| 00 A-   WPL| S,BBC $30   A

CHARDONNAY (CONTINUED)

Clos la Chance, 2000 *Santa Cruz Mountains*
CA, USA   IE| B+   PV| WPL| $19   B+

Cristom, 2001 *Germaine Vineyard, Willamette Valley*
OR, USA   IE| A   PV| WPL| $19   A

Cuvaison, 2001 *Carneros, Napa Valley*
CA, USA   IE| A   PV| 00 A-   WPL| $22   A

Davis Bynum, 2000 *Limited Edition, Russian River Valley, Sonoma Co.*
CA, USA   IE| A   PV| WPL| S $30   A

De Loach, 2000 *Russian River Valley, Sonoma Co.*
CA, USA   IE| B+, B+   PV| WPL| W $18   B+

Dehlinger, 2000 *Estate, Russian River Valley, Sonoma Co.*
CA, USA   IE| A-   PV| 99 A-   WPL| S $27   A-

Domaine Alfred, 2001 *Chamisal Vineyards, Edna Valley*
CA, USA   IE| A, B   PV| WPL| $22   B+

Domaine Chandon, 2000 *Carneros*
CA, USA   IE| A-   PV| WPL| $19   A-

Esser Cellars, 2001 *California*
CA, USA   IE| A-   PV| WPL| B $8   A-

Everett Ridge, 2000 *Hawk Hill Vineyard, Russian River Valley, Sonoma Co.*
CA, USA   IE| B+   PV| WPL| $20   B+

Fess Parker, 2000 *Santa Barbara Co.*
CA, USA   IE| B+   PV| WPL| $18   B+

Flora Springs, 2001 *Barrel Fermented Reserve, Napa Valley*
CA, USA   IE| A-   PV| WPL| S $26   A-

Forgeron Cellars, 2001 *Columbia Valley*
WA, USA   IE| B+   PV| WPL| $19   B+

Frank Family, 2000 *Napa Valley*
CA, USA   IE| B+, A-   PV| WPL| S $29   B+

Frei Brothers, 2001 *Reserve, Russian River Valley, Northern Sonoma*
CA, USA   IE| A, B, A-   PV| WPL| W,BBC $20   A-

Gainey, 2000 *Santa Barbara Co.*
CA, USA   IE| A-   PV| WPL| $18   A-

Gallo Sonoma, 2000 *Laguna Ranch Vineyard, Russian River Valley, Sonoma Co.*
CA, USA   IE| A-   PV| WPL| $24   A-

Gary Farrell, 2000 *Russian River Valley, Sonoma Co.*
CA, USA   IE| A+   PV| WPL| S $29   A+

Geyser Peak, 2001 *Block Collection, Ricci Vineyard, Carneros*
CA, USA   IE| B+, A-, B+   PV| 00 A-   WPL| $21   B+

Geyser Peak, 2001 *Sonoma Co.*
CA, USA   IE| B+   PV| WPL| $12   B+

Girard, 2001 *Russian River Valley, Sonoma Co.*
CA, USA   IE| B+   PV| WPL| $20   B+

Gloria Ferrer, 2000 *Carneros*
CA, USA   IE| A-, A-, B+, B+   PV| WPL| BBC $20   A-

Handley, 2000 *Estates, Anderson Valley, Mendocino Co.*
CA, USA   IE| B+   PV| WPL| $16   B+

Hanna, 2001 *Estate, Russian River Valley, Sonoma Co.*
CA, USA   IE| A   PV| WPL| $18   A

Hartford, 2000 *Sonoma Coast, Sonoma Co.*
CA, USA   IE| A-, A, A   PV| WPL| BBC $24   A

Huntington Cellars, 2000 *Russian River Valley, Sonoma Co.*
CA, USA   IE| B+   PV| WPL| $15   B+

Iron Horse, 2000 *Sonoma Co.*
CA, USA   IE| A   PV| WPL| S $26   A

Jordan, 2000 *Russian River Valley, Sonoma Co.*
CA, USA   IE| A   PV| WPL| S $26   A

Joullian, 2000 *Monterey Co.*
CA, USA   IE| B+, A-   PV| WPL| BBC $16   A-

Justin, 2000 *Paso Robles, San Luis Obispo Co.*
CA, USA   IE| A, B-   PV| WPL| $19   B+

Keller, 2000 *La Cruz Vineyard, Sonoma Coast, Sonoma Co.*
CA, USA   IE| A+, A-, A+, B+, A   PV| WPL| BBC $25   A

Kendall-Jackson, 2000 *Estate Series, Camelot Beach, Santa Maria Valley, Santa Barbara Co.*
CA, USA   IE| A-   PV| WPL| W $17   A-

Kendall-Jackson, 2000 *Grand Reserve*
CA, USA   IE| B+   PV| 99 B+   WPL| W $18   B+

Kenwood, 2001 *Reserve, Russian River Valley, Sonoma Co.*
CA, USA   IE| B+   PV| WPL| $20   B+

Kunde, 2000 *Wildwood Vineyard, Sonoma Valley, Sonoma Co.*
CA, USA   IE| B+, A   PV| WPL| BBC $20   A-

Kunde, 2000 *Kinneybrook Vineyard, Sonoma Valley, Sonoma Co.*
CA, USA   IE| B+, B+   PV| WPL| $20   B+

Kunde, 2000 *C. S. Ridge, Sonoma Valley, Sonoma Co.*
CA, USA   IE| A-   PV| WPL| $22   A-

La Crema, 2001 *Sonoma Coast, Sonoma Co.*
CA, USA   IE| B+   PV| WPL| W $16   B+

Lafond, 2000 *Santa Ynez Valley, Santa Barbara Co.*
CA, USA   IE| B+   PV| WPL| $18   B+

Lafond, 2000 *Sweeny Canyon Vineyard, Santa Ynez Valley, Santa Barbara Co.*
CA, USA   IE| A-   PV| WPL| S $28   A-

Landmark, 2000 *Overlook, Sonoma Co.-Santa Barbara Co.-Monterey Coounty*
CA, USA   IE| A   PV| 99 A   WPL| $25   A

Leatitia, 2001 *Estate, Arroyo Grande Valley, San Luis Obispo Co.*
CA, USA   IE| A-   PV| 99 B+   WPL| $18   A-

LinCourt, 2000 *LinCourt Vineyards, Santa Barbara Co.*
CA, USA   IE| B+, B   PV| 99 A-   WPL| $19   B+

Liparita, 2000 *Reserve, Lake Vineyard, Carneros*
CA, USA   IE| A-   PV| WPL| S $30   A-

CHARDONNAY (CONTINUED)

Longoria, 2000 *Santa Rita Hills*
CA, USA   IE| A   PV| WPL| $25 A

MacRostie, 2001 *Carneros*
CA, USA   IE| A   PV| 00 A-   WPL| $20 A

Marcelina, 2001 *Carneros*
CA, USA   IE| B+   PV| WPL| $25 B+

Marimar Torres, 2000 *Don Miguel Vineyard, Russian River Valley, Sonoma Co.*
CA, USA   IE| A   PV| 99 A-   WPL| S $26 A

Martin & Weyrich, 1999 *Edna Valley, San Luis Obispo Co.*
CA, USA   IE| A-   PV| 99 A-   WPL| $18 A-

Martin Ray, 2000 *Mariage, Russian River Valley, Sonoma Co.*
CA, USA   IE| B+   PV| WPL| $18 B+

Martinelli, 2000 *Woolsey Road, Russian River Valley, Sonoma Co.*
CA, USA   IE| A, A   PV| WPL| S,BBC $28 A

Martinelli, 2000 *Gold Ridge, Russian River Valley, Sonoma Co.*
CA, USA   IE| A-   PV| WPL| $25 A-

McCrea, 2000 *Elerding Vineyard, Yakima Valley*
WA, USA   IE| A-   PV| WPL| S $30 A-

McIlroy, 2000 *Aquarius Ranch, Russian River Valley, Sonoma Co.*
CA, USA   IE| B+   PV| WPL| $20 B+

Melville, 2000 *Clone 76, Inox, Santa Rita Hills, Santa Barbara Co.*
CA, USA   IE| A-   PV| WPL| $25 A-

Melville, 2000 *Santa Rita Hills, Santa Barbara Co.*
CA, USA   IE| B+   PV| WPL| $20 B+

Merryvale, 2000 *Dutton Ranch, Russian River Valley, Sonoma Co.*
CA, USA   IE| A   PV| WPL| S $29 A

Miner, 2000 *Napa Valley*
CA, USA   IE| A-   PV| WPL| S $30 A-

Mont St. John, 2000 *Madonna Estate, Carneros*
CA, USA   IE| A-, A-   PV| WPL| BBC $16 A-

Mount Eden, 2000 *MacGregor Vineyard, Edna Valley, San Luis Obispo Co.*
CA, USA   IE| A   PV| WPL| $18 A

Navarro, 2001 *Première Reserve, Anderson Valley, Mendocino Co.*
CA, USA   IE| A+   PV| WPL| $18 A+

Neyers, 2000 *Napa Valley*
CA, USA   IE| A, A-, B+, B+   PV| 99 A   WPL| S,BBC $30 A-

Neyers, 2000 *Carneros*
CA, USA   IE| A   PV| 00 A   WPL| S $26 A

Ojai, 2000 *Talley-Rincon Vineyard, Arroyo Grande Valley, San Luis Obispo Co.*
CA, USA   IE| A   PV| WPL| S $27 A

Paschal, 2000 *Rogue Valley*
OR, USA   IE| B+   PV| WPL| $18 B+

Perbacco Cellars, 2000 *La Linda Vineyard, Edna Valley*
CA, USA   IE| A-   PV| WPL| $18 A-

Pessagno, 2000 *Sleepy Hollow Vineyard, Santa Lucia Highlands*
CA, USA   IE| A   PV| WPL| S $30 A

Pietra Santa, 2001 *Cienega Valley*
CA, USA   IE| B+   PV| WPL| $13 B+

Pine Ridge, 2001 *Dijon Clones, Carneros, Napa Valley*
CA, USA   IE| A-   PV| 00 A-   WPL| S $27 A-

Porter Creek, 2000 *George's Hill, Russian River Valley, Sonoma Co.*
CA, USA   IE| B+   PV| 99 A   WPL| $18 B+

Qupé, 2001 *Reserve Block Eleven, Bien Nacido Vineyard, Santa Maria Valley,
Santa Barbara Co.*
CA, USA   IE| A-   PV| 00 A   WPL| $25 A-

Qupé, 2000 *Reserve, Bien Nacido Vineyard, Santa Maria Valley, Santa Barbara Co.*
CA, USA   IE| A   PV| 99 A-   WPL| $25 A

Robert Craig, 2001 *Russian River Valley, Sonoma Co.*
CA, USA   IE| A-   PV| WPL| $24 A-

Robert Mondavi, 2000 *Napa Valley*
CA, USA   IE| A+   PV| WPL| $24 A+

Robert Stemmler, 2000 *Sonoma Co.*
CA, USA   IE| A, A   PV| WPL| BBC $20 A

Rochioli, 2000 *Estate, Russian River Valley, Sonoma Co.*
CA, USA   IE| A   PV| WPL| S $30 A

Rodney Strong, 2001 *Sonoma Co.*
CA, USA   IE| B+   PV| 99 B+   WPL| $14 B+

Rusack, 2001 *Santa Barbara Co.*
CA, USA   IE| A-   PV| WPL| $18 A-

Santa Barbara, 2000 *Reserve, Santa Ynez Valley, Santa Barbara Co.*
CA, USA   IE| A   PV| WPL| $22 A

Schweiger Vineyards, 2000 *Spring Mountain, Napa Valley*
CA, USA   IE| A-   PV| WPL| S $30 A-

Shea Wine Cellars, 2000 *Shea Vineyard, Willamette Valley*
OR, USA   IE| A-   PV| WPL| $25 A-

Silver Lake, 2000 *Reserve, Columbia Valley*
WA, USA   IE| B+   PV| WPL| $14 B+

Silverado, 2000 *Napa Valley*
CA, USA   IE| A   PV| WPL| $20 A

Smith Madrone, 2000 *Napa Valley*
CA, USA   IE| A-, A   PV| WPL| BBC $25 A

Sonoma-Loeb, 2001 *Private Reserve, Sonoma Co.*
CA, USA   IE| A+   PV| WPL| S $27 A+

St. Clement, 2001 *Napa Valley*
CA, USA   IE| B+   PV| WPL| $16 B+

St. Clement, 2000 *Abbotts Vineyard, Carneros, Napa Valley*
CA, USA   IE| A   PV| 99 A-   WPL| $20 A

St. Supéry, 2000 *Napa Valley*
CA, USA   IE| B+   PV| 99 B+   WPL| W $19 B+

CHARDONNAY (CONTINUED)

Stags' Leap Winery, 2001 *Napa Valley*
CA, USA   IE| A-   PV| WPL| $22   A-

Stephen Ross, 2000 *Edna Ranch, Edna Valley*
CA, USA   IE| B+   PV| WPL| $20   B+

Talley, 2000 *Oliver's Vineyard, Edna Valley, San Luis Obispo Co.*
CA, USA   IE| A, A-, A-, A- PV| WPL| BBC $20   A-

Talley, 2000 *Arroyo Grande Valley, San Luis Obispo Co.*
CA, USA   IE| A   PV| 99 A-   WPL| $24   A

Truchard, 2001 *Carneros, Napa Valley*
CA, USA   IE| A-   PV| WPL| S $30   A-

Truchard, 2000 *Carneros, Napa Valley*
CA, USA   IE| A-, B+, B, B+, A, A-PV| 99 A- WPL| S,BBC $30   A-

Valley of the Moon, 2001 *Sonoma Co.*
CA, USA   IE| B+   PV| WPL| $15   B+

Varner, 2001 *Amphitheater Block, Santa Cruz Mountains*
CA, USA   IE| A   PV| WPL| S $30   A

White Oak, 2000 *Russian River Valley, Sonoma Co.*
CA, USA   IE| B+, B+, B, A-   PV| 99 A-   WPL| $16   B+

Whitford, 2000 *Haynes Vineyard, Napa Valley*
CA, USA   IE| A, A   PV| WPL| S,BBC $28   A

Williams Selyem, 2000 *Russian River Valley, Sonoma Co.*
CA, USA   IE| A   PV| WPL| S $30   A

Willow Brook, 2001 *Oak Ridge Vineyard, Russian River Valley, Sonoma Co.*
CA, USA   IE| A-   PV| WPL| S $28   A-

Windsor, 2000 *Reserve, Signature Series, Russian River Valley, Sonoma Co.*
CA, USA   IE| B+   PV| WPL| $20   B+

Wolff, 2001 *Old Vines, Edna Valley*
CA, USA   IE| A-   PV| WPL| $19   A-

CHENIN BLANC

Chalone, 2001 *Chalone Estate*
CA, USA   IE| A   PV| 00 A-   WPL| $22   A

L'Ecole No. 41, 2001 *Walla Voila, Walla Walla Co.*
WA, USA   IE| B+   PV| WPL| $12   B+

GEWÜRZTRAMINER

Alexander Valley, 2001 *New Gewürz, North Coast*
CA, USA   IE| B+   PV| WPL| B $9   B+

Arrowood, 2001 *Saralee's Vineyard, Russian River Valley, Sonoma Co.*
CA, USA   IE| B+   PV| WPL| $20   B+

Dr. Konstantin Frank, 2001 *Finger Lakes*
NY, USA   IE| A   PV| WPL| $16   A

Hogue, 2001 *Columbia Valley*
WA, USA   IE| B+   PV| WPL| B $10   B+

Louis M. Martini, 2000 *Del Rio Vineyard, Russian River Valley, Sonoma Co.*
CA, USA   IE| B+   PV| WPL| $15   B+

McIlroy, 2000 *Late Harvest, Aquarius Ranch, Russian River Valley, Sonoma Co.*
CA, USA   IE| B+   PV| WPL| $13   B+

Navarro, 2001 *Dry, Anderson Valley, Mendocino Co.*
CA, USA   IE| A-   PV| 00 A+   WPL| $15   A-

Saint Chapelle, 2001 *Dry Gewurztraminer*
ID, USA   IE| B+   PV| WPL| B $6   B+

Sineann, 2001 *Celilo Vineyard, Columbia Valley*
WA, USA   IE| A+   PV| WPL| $18   A+

Stony Hill, 2000 *Napa Valley*
CA, USA   IE| B+   PV| WPL| $15   B+

Thomas Fogarty, 2001 *Monterey Co.*
CA, USA   IE| A   PV| 00 B+   WPL| $15   A

Three Rivers Winery, 2001 *Late HarvestBiscuit Ridge, Walla Walla Valley*
WA, USA   IE| A   PV| WPL| $23   A

PINOT GRIS/GRIGIO

Babcock, 2001 *Santa Barbara Co.*
CA, USA   IE| B+   PV| WPL| $13   B+

Big Fire, 2001
OR, USA   IE| B+   PV| WPL| $14   B+

Bridgeview, 2000 *Pinot Gris, Reserve*
OR, USA   IE| B+, B+   PV| WPL| $15   B+

Ch. Ste. Michelle, 2002 *Pinot Gris, Columbia Valley*
WA, USA   IE| B+   PV| 01 B+   WPL| W $13   B+

Ch. Ste. Michelle, 2001 *Pinot Gris, Columbia Valley*
WA, USA   IE| B+   PV| WPL| $13   B+

Chehalem, 2001 *Willamette Valley*
OR, USA   IE| B+   PV| WPL| $15   B+

Elk Cove, 2001 *Pinot Gris, Willamette Valley*
OR, USA   IE| B+   PV| 99 A-, 00 B+ WPL| $15   B+

King Estate, 2001 *Pinot Gris, Reserve, Eugene*
OR, USA   IE| A-   PV| 00 B+   WPL| $20   A-

Luna, 2001 *Napa Valley*
CA, USA   IE| A, A   PV| 00 B+   WPL| BBC $20   A

Luna, 2000 *Pinot Grigio, Napa Valley*
CA, USA   IE| A-, B+   PV| 99 A-   WPL| $18   B+

MacMurray Ranch, 2001 *Russian River Valley, Sonoma Co.*
CA, USA   IE| A   PV| WPL| $23   A

Morgan, 2001 *Santa Lucia Highlands R&D, Franscioni Vineyard, Monterey Co.*
CA, USA   IE| B+   PV| WPL| $15   B+

Navarro, 2001 *Pinot Gris, Anderson Valley, Mendocino Co.*
CA, USA   IE| A+   PV| 00 A   WPL| $16   A+

Raptor Ridge, 2001 *Pinot Gris, Yamhill Vineyard, Willamette Valley*
OR, USA   IE| B+   PV| WPL| $15   B+

PINOT GRIS/GRIGIO (CONTINUED)

Rex Hill, 2001 *Pinot Gris, Reserve*
OR, USA   IE| B+   PV| 00 B+   WPL| $18   B+

Rex Hill, 2000 *Pinot Gris, Reserve*
OR, USA   IE| A-, B   PV| WPL| $18   B+

Sineann, 2001
OR, USA   IE| A-   PV| WPL| $15   A-

Stone Wolf, 2001
OR, USA   IE| B+   PV| WPL| B $10   B+

WillaKenzie, 2001 *Pinot Gris*
OR, USA   IE| A   PV| 99 A-, 00 A-   WPL| $20   A

RIESLING

Bonair, 2001 *Yakima Valley*
WA, USA   IE| A-   PV| WPL| B $10   A-

Ch. Montelena, 2001 *Potter Valley, Mendocino Co.*
CA, USA   IE| B+, B   PV| 99 B+   WPL| $15   B+

Ch. Ste. Michelle, 2001 *Cold Creek Vineyard, Columbia Valley*
WA, USA   IE| A-   PV| WPL| $14   A-

Ch. Ste. Michelle, 2001 *Dry Riesling, Columbia Valley*
WA, USA   IE| A-   PV| WPL| B $8   A-

Ch. Ste. Michelle, 2001 *Eroica Riesling, Columbia Valley*
WA, USA   IE| A   PV| 99 B+   WPL| $20   A

Ch. Ste. Michelle & Dr. Loosen, 2001 *Eroica, Columbia Valley*
WA, USA   IE| A-   PV| 99 A-, 00 B+   WPL| $20   A-

Claar, 2001 *Late Harvest, White Bluffs, Columbia Valley*
WA, USA   IE| A-   PV| WPL| B $10   A-

Columbia, 2002 *Cellarmaster's Reserve, Columbia Valley*
WA, USA   IE| B+   PV| 99 B+   WPL| W, B $8   B+

Hogue, 2002 *Johannnisberg Riesling, Columbia Valley*
WA, USA   IE| B+   PV| 00 B+   WPL| W, B $9   B+

Saint Chapelle, 2001 *Johannisberg Riesling*
ID, USA   IE| B+   PV| WPL| B $6   B+

Saint Chapelle, 2001 *Special Harvest Johannisberg Riesling*
ID, USA   IE| A-   PV| WPL| B $10   A-

Seven Hills, 2001 *Riesling, Columbia Valley*
WA, USA   IE| B+   PV| 99 B+   WPL| B $10   B+

Tagaris, 2001 *Johannisberg Riesling, Columbia Valley*
WA, USA   IE| B+   PV| WPL| B $7   B+

Tagaris, 2001 *Reserve Johannisberg Riesling, Columbia Valley*
WA, USA   IE| B+   PV| WPL| B $8   B+

Trefethen, 2001 *Napa Valley*
CA, USA   IE| B+   PV| WPL| $15   B+

Washington Hills, 2001 *Late Harvest, Columbia Valley*
WA, USA   IE| B+, B+   PV| 99 B+   WPL| B $9   B+

SAUVIGNON/FUMÉ BLANC

Araujo, 2000 *Eisele Vineyard, Napa Valley*
CA, USA   IE| A   PV| WPL| S $30   A

Artesa, 2000 *Reserve, Napa Valley*
CA, USA   IE| A-, B+   PV| 99 A-   WPL| BBC $19   A-

Baileyana, 2001 *Paragon Vineyard, Edna Valley, San Luis Obispo Co.*
CA, USA   IE| B+   PV| WPL| $13   B+

Beckmen, 2001 *Santa Ynez Valley, Santa Barbara Co.*
CA, USA   IE| B+   PV| WPL| $16   B+

Benziger, 2000 *Sonoma Mountain, Sonoma Co.*
CA, USA   IE| A-   PV| WPL| $22   A-

Beringer, 2000 *Alluvium White, Knights Valley*
CA, USA   IE| A-, A-   PV| WPL| BBC $16   A-

Beringer, 2000 *Appellation Collection Napa Valley*
CA, USA   IE| B+   PV| 99 B+   WPL| W $12   B+

Bernardus, 2001 *Griva Vineyard, Arroyo Seco, Monterey Co.*
CA, USA   IE| A   PV| WPL| $20   A

Brogan, 2001 *Russian River Valley, Sonoma Co.*
CA, USA   IE| B+   PV| WPL| $20   B+

Buena Vista, 2001 *Lake Co.*
CA, USA   IE| B+   PV| WPL| B $7   B+

Cakebread, 2000 *Napa Valley*
CA, USA   IE| A, B+, B   PV| WPL| W $17   B+

Caterina, 2001 *Columbia Valley*
WA, USA   IE| B+   PV| WPL| B $10   B+

Ch. Potelle, 2000 *Napa Valley*
CA, USA   IE| A, B   PV| 99 B+   WPL| BBC $15   A-

Ch. Souverain, 2001 *Alexander Valley, Sonoma Co.*
CA, USA   IE| B+, B, B+   PV| 99 B+   WPL| $12   B+

Ch. Ste. Michelle, 2001 *Columbia Valley*
WA, USA   IE| B+   PV| WPL| B $10   B+

Chalk Hill, 2000 *Chalk Hill, Sonoma Co.*
CA, USA   IE| A-   PV| WPL| S $29   A-

Chinook, 2000 *Yakima Valley*
WA, USA   IE| A-   PV| WPL| $15   A-

Clos Pegase, 2001 *Carneros Mitsuko's Vineyard Q Block, Napa Valley*
CA, USA   IE| B+   PV| WPL| $18   B+

Cosentino, 2000 *The Novelist*
CA, USA   IE| B+   PV| WPL| $16   B+

De Lorimier, 2000 *Spectrum Res, Alexander Valley, Sonoma Co.*
CA, USA   IE| A-   PV| WPL| $16   A-

Deerfield Ranch, 2001 *Peterson Vineyard, Sonoma Valley, Sonoma Co.*
CA, USA   IE| B+   PV| WPL| $18   B+

Deerfield Ranch, 2000 *Peterson Vineyard, Sonoma Valley, Sonoma Co.*
CA, USA   IE| B+   PV| WPL| $18   B+

SAUVIGNON/FUMÉ BLANC (CONTINUED)

DeSante, 2001 *Napa Valley*
CA, USA   IE| B+   PV| WPL| $18   B+

Dry Creek, 2001 *Fumé Blanc, DCV3, Dry Creek Valley, Sonoma Co.*
CA, USA   IE| B+, B, A-, A PV| WPL| BBC $18   A-

Dry Creek, 2001 *Fumé Blanc, Sonoma Co.*
CA, USA   IE| B+   PV| WPL| $13   B+

Dry Creek, 2000 *Fumé Blanc, Reserve, Dry Creek Valley, Sonoma Co.*
CA, USA   IE| A   PV| 99 B+   WPL| $18   A

Emmolo, 2001 *Napa Valley*
CA, USA   IE| B+   PV| WPL| $16   B+

EOS, 2000 *Fumé Blanc, Reserve, Paso Robles, San Luis Obispo Co.*
CA, USA   IE| B+   PV| WPL| $19   B+

EOS, 2000 *Paso Robles, San Luis Obispo Co.*
CA, USA   IE| A-, B   PV| WPL| $14   B+

Ferrari-Carano, 2001 *Fumé Blanc, Sonoma Co.*
CA, USA   IE| A-, B+   PV| WPL| W,BBC $15   A-

Flora Springs, 2001 *Soliloquy, Napa Valley*
CA, USA   IE| A-,A, A-   PV| 01 B   WPL| BBC $25   A-

Foley, 2000 *Santa Barbara Co.*
CA, USA   IE| B+, B   PV| WPL| $16   B+

Gainey, 2001 *Limited Selection, Santa Ynez Valley, Santa Barbara Co.*
CA, USA   IE| B+   PV| WPL| $20   B+

Gary Farrell, 2002 *Redwood Ranch, Sonoma Co.*
CA, USA   IE| A   PV| WPL| $21   A

Geyser Peak, 2001 *Sonoma Co.*
CA, USA   IE| A-   PV| 00 B   WPL| $15   A-

Grgich Hills, 2001 *Fumé Blanc, Napa Valley*
CA, USA   IE| B+, B+   PV| 00 A-   WPL| $18   B+

Grgich Hills, 2000 *Fumé Blanc, Napa Valley*
CA, USA   IE| A-   PV| WPL| W $18   A-

Groth, 2001 *Napa Valley*
CA, USA   IE| A   PV| WPL| $15   A

Guenoc, 2001 *Lake Co.*
CA, USA   IE| B+, B+   PV| WPL| $15   B+

Handley, 2001 *Ferrington Vineyard, Anderson Valley, Mendocino Co.*
CA, USA   IE| A-, B+   PV| 99 B+   WPL| BBC $15   A-

Hanna, 2001 *Slusser Vineyard, Russian River Valley, Sonoma Co.*
CA, USA   IE| A   PV| 00 B+   WPL| $16   A

Hedges, 2001 *Fumé-Chardonnay, Columbia Valley*
WA, USA   IE| A   PV| WPL| B $9   A

Honig, 2001 *Napa Valley*
CA, USA   IE| A-, B+, A-   PV| 00 B+   WPL| BBC $14   A-

Honig, 2001 *Reserve, Napa Valley*
CA, USA   IE| B+   PV| 99 A-, 00:A-   WPL| $20   B+

Huntington Cellars, 2002 *Earthquake, Napa Valley*
CA, USA   IE| B+   PV| WPL| $12   B+

Iron Horse, 2001 *Cuvée, T Bar T Vineyard, Alexander Valley, Sonoma Co.*
CA, USA   IE| B+   PV| 00 B+   WPL| $19   B+

Joel Gott, 2001 *Two Ranches, Napa Valley*
CA, USA   IE| B+   PV| WPL| $17   B+

Joseph Phelps, 2001 *Napa Valley*
CA, USA   IE| A+, B, B   PV| 00 A-   WPL| $20   B+

Justin, 2001 *Edna Valley*
CA, USA   IE| B+   PV| WPL| $14   B+

Kelham, 2000 *Oakville*
CA, USA   IE| A-   PV| WPL| $22   A-

Kunde, 2002 *Magnolia Lane, Sonoma Valley, Sonoma Co.*
CA, USA   IE| B+   PV| WPL| $15   B+

Langtry, 2001 *Meritage, Guenoc Valley, Lake Co.*
CA, USA   IE| A   PV| WPL| $24   A

Latcham, 2000 *El Dorado Co., Sierra Foothills*
CA, USA   IE| B+   PV| WPL| $12   B+

Liparita, 2001 *Oakville, Napa Valley*
CA, USA   IE| B+, A-   PV| 99 A-, 00 B+   WPL| BBC $18   A-

Martinelli, 2000 *Martinelli Vineyard, Russian River Valley, Sonoma Co.*
CA, USA   IE| A-   PV| WPL| $18   A-

Mason, 2001 *Napa Valley*
CA, USA   IE| B+, B+, A   PV| 99 A-, 00 A-   WPL| BBC $17   A-

Merryvale, 2001 *Juliana Vineyards, Napa Valley*
CA, USA   IE| B+   PV| WPL| $20   B+

Merryvale, 2001 *Starmont, Napa Valley*
CA, USA   IE| A-   PV| WPL| $17   A-

Mill Creek, 2001 *Dry Creek Valley, Sonoma Co.*
CA, USA   IE| B+   PV| WPL| $16   B+

Morgan, 2001 *Monterey Co.*
CA, USA   IE| B+   PV| WPL| $14   B+

Murphy-Goode, 2000 *Reserve, Fumé, Alexander Valley, Sonoma Co.*
CA, USA   IE| A-, B, A   PV| WPL| BBC $17   A-

Novelty Hill, 2000 *Klipsun Vineyard, Red Mountain*
USA   IE| A   PV| WPL| $19   A

Paradise Ridge, 2002 *Grandview Vineyard, Sonoma Co.*
CA, USA   IE| B+   PV| WPL| $15   B+

Porter Creek, 2000 *Poplar Vineyard, Russian River Valley, Sonoma Co.*
CA, USA   IE| B+   PV| WPL| $16   B+

Quivira, 2001 *Fig Tree Vineyard, Dry Creek Valley, Sonoma Co.*
CA, USA   IE| B+   PV| 99 B+   WPL| $16   B+

Rex Hill, 2000 *Willamette Valley*
OR, USA   IE| B+   PV| WPL| $12   B+

Rochioli, 2001 *Russian River Valley, Sonoma Co.*
CA, USA   IE|A+, A-, B+,B, A-   PV|99 B+, 00 A-   WPL| BBC $24   A-

SAUVIGNON/FUMÉ BLANC (CONTINUED)

Rodney Strong, 2001 *Charlotte's Home, Sonoma Co.*
CA, USA   IE| B+, B+   PV| WPL| $15 B+

Rose Vineyards, 2000 *Napa Valley*
CA, USA   IE| A-   PV| WPL| $18 A-

Rudd, 2001 *Napa Valley*
CA, USA   IE| A-, A-   PV| 00 A-   WPL| S,BBC $28 A-

Sebastiani, 2001 *Cole Vineyard, Russian River Valley, Sonoma Co.*
CA, USA   IE| A-   PV| WPL| $18 A-

Silverado, 2000 *Napa Valley*
CA, USA   IE| A-   PV| WPL| $14 A-

Simi, 2000 *Sauvignon Blanc/Semillon, Sendal Reserve, Sonoma Co.*
CA, USA   IE| A   PV| WPL| $20 A

Spottswoode, 2001 *Napa Valley*
CA, USA   IE| A-   PV| WPL| S $27 A-

St. Clement, 2001 *Napa Valley*
CA, USA   IE| B+   PV| 00 B+   WPL| $13 B+

St. Supéry, 2002 *Napa Valley*
CA, USA   IE| A-   PV| 00 B+, 01 A- WPL| $16 A-

St. Supéry, 2001 *Napa Valley*
CA, USA   IE| A, A, A-, B+ PV| 00 B+   WPL| W,BBC $15 A-

Stags' Leap Winery, 2001 *Napa Valley*
CA, USA   IE| B+, A-   PV| WPL| BBC $20 A-

Stonestreet, 2000 *Upper Barn Vineyard, Alexander Valley, Sonoma Co.*
CA, USA   IE| B+   PV| 99 B+   WPL| $22 B+

Voss, 2001 *Napa Valley*
CA, USA   IE| B+, B+, A   PV| 99 A-, 00 B+ WPL| BBC $18 A-

Waterbrook, 2001 *Columbia Valley*
WA, USA   IE| B+   PV| WPL| B $9 B+

White Oak, 2001 *Napa Valley*
CA, USA   IE| B+   PV| 00 B+   WPL| $18 B+

Whitehall Lane, 2001 *Napa Valley*
CA, USA   IE| B+   PV| WPL| $15 B+

VIOGNIER

Alban, 2001 *Central Coast*
CA, USA   IE| B+   PV| 99 B+   WPL| $20 B+

Alban, 2001 *Estate, Edna Valley, San Luis Obispo Co.*
CA, USA   IE| A   PV| 00 A-   WPL| S $28 A

Andrew Murray, 2001 *Santa Ynez Valley, Santa Barbara Co.*
CA, USA   IE| A   PV| WPL| $25 A

Arrowood, 2001 *Saralee's Vineyard, Russian River Valley, Sonoma Co.*
CA, USA   IE| A-   PV| 99 A-   WPL| S $30 A-

Callaway, 2001 *Coastal Reserve*
CA, USA   IE| B+   PV| WPL| $15 B+

Consilience, 2000 *Santa Barbara Co.*
CA, USA   IE| A-   PV| WPL| $21 A-

De Loach, 2001 *Russian River Valley, Sonoma Co.*
CA, USA   IE| B+   PV| WPL| $20 B+

Eberle, 2001 *Mill Road Vineyard, Paso Robles, San Luis Obispo Co.*
CA, USA   IE| B+, A-   PV| WPL| $18 A-

Echelon, 2001 *Esperanza Vineyards*
CA, USA   IE| B+   PV| WPL| $13 B+

Fess Parker, 2001 *Santa Barbara Co.*
CA, USA   IE| B+   PV| 00 A-   WPL| $20 B+

Garretson, 2001 *Table 62, Vogelzang Vineyard, Santa Ynez Valley, Santa Barbara Co.*
CA, USA   IE| A   PV| WPL| S $30 A

Hogue, 2001 *Genesis, Columbia Valley*
WA, USA   IE| A-   PV| 00 B+   WPL| $16 A-

Kunde, 2001 *Sonoma Valley, Sonoma Co.*
CA, USA   IE| A-   PV| WPL| $23 A-

McCrea, 2000 *Yakima Valley*
WA, USA   IE| A   PV| 99 B+   WPL| $22 A

Miner, 2001 *Simpson Vineyard*
CA, USA   IE| B+   PV| WPL| $20 B+

Renwood, 2000 *Shenandoah Valley*
CA, USA   IE| A-   PV| WPL| $25 A-

Silver, 2001 *Vogelzang Vineyards, Santa Barbara Co.*
CA, USA   IE| B+   PV| WPL| $22 B+

Spencer Roloson, 2001 *Skellenger Vineyard, Rutherford/Napa Valley*
CA, USA   IE| A-   PV| WPL| S $26 A-

Stags' Leap Winery, 2001 *Napa Valley*
CA, USA   IE| A-   PV| WPL| $25 A-

Summers, 2000 *Monterey Co.*
CA, USA   IE| A-   PV| WPL| $18 A-

Treana, 2001 *Viognier-MarsanneMer Soleil Vineyard, Central Coast*
CA, USA   IE| A+   PV| 99 A-, 00 A-   WPL| $25 A+

Treana, 2000 *Viognier-MarsanneMer Soleil Vineyard, Central Coast*
CA, USA   IE| A-, B+, A- PV| WPL| BBC $25 A-

Vinum Cellars, 2000 *Vista Verde Vineyard, San Benito Co.*
CA, USA   IE| A-   PV| WPL| $22 A-

Waterbrook, 2001 *Viognier, Columbia Valley*
WA, USA   IE| A-   PV| WPL| $20 A-

Wendell, 2001 *Edna Valley*
CA, USA   IE| A-   PV| WPL| $21 A-

OTHER WHITE

Amity, 2001 *Pinot Blanc*
OR, USA   IE| B+   PV| WPL| $12 B+

OTHER WHITE (CONTINUED)

Andrew Murray, 2001 *Marsanne, Enchante, Santa Ynez Valley, Santa Barbara Co.*
CA, USA   IE| A-   PV| WPL| $22 A-

Beringer, 2001 *Alluvium Blanc, Knights Valley, Sonoma Co.*
CA, USA   IE| B+   PV| 00 B+   WPL| $16 B+

DeLille, 2000 *Chaleur Estate Blanc, Columbia Valley*
WA, USA   IE| A   PV| WPL| $25 A

Etude, 2000 *Pinot Blanc, Carneros*
CA, USA   IE| A   PV| 99 A   WPL| S $28 A

Henry, 2001 *Müller Thurgau, Umpqua Valley*
OR, USA   IE| B+   PV| WPL| B $9 B+

McCrea, 2000 *Chardonnay/Viognier, La Mer, Yakima Valley*
WA, USA   IE| B+   PV| WPL| $18 B+

Paschal, 2000 *Pinot Blanc, Rogue Valley*
OR, USA   IE| A-   PV| WPL| $16 A-

Woodward Canyon, 2000 *Charbonneau Blanc, Walla Walla Co.*
WA, USA   IE| A-   PV| 99 A-   WPL| S $28 A-

ROSÉ

Chinook, 2001 *Cabernet Franc Rosé, Yakima Valley*
WA, USA   IE| B+   PV| 99 A-   WPL| $15 B+

SPARKLING

Gloria Ferrer, NV *Sparkling Brut, Sonoma Co.*
CA, USA   IE| B+   PV| WPL| W $18 B+

Iron Horse, 1997 *Classic Vintage Brut, Green Valley, Sonoma Co.*
CA, USA   IE| A-   PV| WPL| S $28 A-

Iron Horse, 1997 *Russian Cuvée, Green Valley, Sonoma Co.*
CA, USA   IE| A-   PV| WPL| S $28 A-

Pacific Echo, NV *Brut, Mendocino Co.*
CA, USA   IE| B+   PV| WPL| W $19 B+

Tualatin, 2001 *Muscat, Semi-Sparkling, Willamette Valley*
OR, USA   IE| A-   PV| 99 A-, 00 B+   WPL| $16 A-

SWEET

Beringer, 1998 *Sauvignon Blanc/Semillon, Nightingale, Napa Valley*
CA, USA   IE| A+   PV| 99 A   WPL| S $30 A+

Buty, 2000 *Sauvignon Blanc/Semillon Columbia Valley*
WA, USA   IE| B+   PV| WPL| $18 B+

Chinook, 2000 *Semillon Yakima Valley*
WA, USA   IE| B+, B+   PV| WPL| $14 B+

Greenwood Ridge, 1999 *Late Harvest, Mendocino Ridge, Mendocino Co.*
CA, USA   IE| A+, A+   PV| WPL| BBC $24 A+

L'Ecole No. 41, 2000 *Semillon, Wahluke Slope, Fries Vineyard*
WA, USA   IE| A-, B+   PV| WPL| BBC $20   A-

St. Supéry, 2001 *Moscato*
CA, USA   IE| B+, B   PV| WPL| $15   B+

Willow Crest, 2001 *Black Muscat, Yakima Valley*
WA, USA   IE| B+   PV| WPL| B $8   B+

Yellow Hawk Cellar, 2001 *Muscat Canelli, Columbia Valley*
WA, USA   IE| B+   PV| WPL| $12   B+

"WHEN IT COMES TO WINE, I TELL PEOPLE TO
THROW AWAY THE VINTAGE CHARTS AND INVEST
IN A CORKSCREW. THE BEST WAY TO LEARN
ABOUT WINE IS THE DRINKING."

Alex Lichine

COMPREHENSIVE BUYING GUIDES TO TOP RATED WINES

AUSTRALIA

REDS

CABERNET SAUVIGNON

Annie's Lane, 1999 *Cabernet Sauvignon-Merlot, Clare Valley*
SOUTH , AUS   IE| A-   PV| WPL| $15   A-

Heritage Road, 1999 *Reserve, Limited, Bethany Creek Vineyard, Barossa Valley*
SOUTH , AUS   IE| A+   PV| WPL| S $30   A+

Hillview Vineyards, 1999 *Blewitt Springs, Fleurieu Peninsula*
SOUTH , AUS   IE| B+   PV| WPL| $15   B+

Kangarilla Road, 1999 *McLaren Vale*
SOUTH , AUS   IE| A-   PV| WPL| $23   A-

Leasingham, 1999 *Cabernet Sauvignon, Bin 56, Clare Valley*
SOUTH , AUS   IE| A-, B+, B+   PV| WPL| $19   B+

Lindemans, 1999 *St. George, Coonawarra*
SOUTH , AUS   IE| A   PV| WPL| S $27   A

Madfish, 2001 *Cabernet Sauvignon-Merlot-Cabernet Franc*
WESTERN , AUS   IE| B+   PV| WPL| $14   B+

Marquis Philips, 2001 *McLaren Vale*
SOUTH EASTERN, AUS   IE| A-   PV| WPL| $23   A-

Marquis Philips, 2000
SOUTH EASTERN, AUS   IE| A, B+, B   PV| WPL| W $15   B+

Penfolds, 2000 *Cabernet Sauvignon-Shiraz, Bin 389*
SOUTH , AUS   IE| A-   PV| WPL| S $26   A-

Penfolds, 1999 *Bin 407*
SOUTH , AUS   IE| A   PV| WPL| S $26   A

Rosemount, 2000 *Hill of Gold, Mudgee*
NEW SOUTH WALES, AUS IE| A-   PV| WPL| $19   A-

Rosemount, 2000 *Show Reserve, Coonawarra*
SOUTH , AUS   IE| A-   PV| WPL| $24   A-

Rosemount, 2000 *Orange Vineyard,*
NEW SOUTH WALES, AUS IE| A-   PV| WPL| $24   A-

Rosemount, 1999 *Cabernet Sauvignon-Merlot-Petit Verdot, Traditional, McLaren Vale-Langhorne Creek*
SOUTH , AUS   IE| A-   PV| WPL| S $26   A-

Sandalford, 1999 *Mount Barker, Margaret River*
WESTERN, AUS   IE| A-   PV| WPL| $22   A-

Sticks, 2000 *Yarra Valley*
AUS   IE| A-   PV| WPL| $13   A-

Tim Adams, 1999 *Clare Valley*
SOUTH , AUS   IE| A-   PV| WPL| $22   A-

Voyager, 1999 *Margaret River*
SOUTH, AUS   IE| A-   PV| WPL| S $27 A-

Wakefield, 1999 *Promised Land, Clare Valley*
SOUTH, AUS   IE| B+   PV| WPL| $11 B+

Wolf Blass, 1999 *Grey Label Cabernet Sauvignon Shiraz, Langhorne Creek*
SOUTH, AUS   IE| A   PV| WPL| $19 A

Wynns Coonawarra, 1999 *Estate Cabernet Sauvignon, Coonawarra*
SOUTH, AUS   IE| A-   PV| WPL| $15 A-

Xanadu, 1999 *Margaret River*
WESTERN, AUS   IE| A-   PV| WPL| $18 A-

Yarra Burn, 2000 *Yarra Valley*
VICTORIA, AUS   IE| A-, B+   PV| 99 A   WPL| BBC $21 A-

Yarra Burn, 1999 *Yarra Valley*
VICTORIA, AUS   IE| A   PV| WPL| $20 A

GRENACHE

Yalumba, 2000 *Bush Vine, Barossa Valley*
SOUTH, AUS   IE| A-   PV| WPL| $15 A-

Yalumba, 2000 *Tricentenary Vines, Barossa Valley*
SOUTH, AUS   IE| B+   PV| WPL| S $30 B+

MERLOT

Richard Hamilton, 2000 *Lot 148, McLaren Vale*
SOUTH, AUS   IE| A   PV| WPL| $17 A

PINOT NOIR

Yerring Station, 2000 *Yarra Valley*
SOUTH EASTERN, AUS   IE| A+   PV| WPL| $22 A+

SYRAH/SHIRAZ

Allandale, 2000 *Shiraz, Mathew, Hunter Valley*
NEW SOUTH WALES, AUS IE| B+   PV| WPL| $14 B+

Annie's Lane, 2001 *Clare Valley*
SOUTH, AUS   IE| B+   PV| WPL| $13 B+

Annie's Lane, 1999 *Shiraz, Clare Valley*
SOUTH, AUS   IE| A-   PV| WPL| $15 A-

Balgownie Estate, 2000 *Beningo*
AUS   IE| A-   PV| WPL| $25 A-

Barossa Valley, 2000 *Ebenezer Shiraz, Barossa Valley*
SOUTH, AUS   IE| A   PV| 99 A-   WPL| S $30 A

Barossa Valley, 1999 *Ebenezer Shiraz, Barossa Valley*
SOUTH, AUS   IE| A-, A   PV| WPL| S,BBC $30 A

Ch. Reynella, 2000 *Shiraz, Basket Pressed, McLaren Vale*
SOUTH, AUS   IE| A   PV| 99 B+   WPL| S $28 A

Chateau Xanadu, 2001 *Secession Shiraz-Cabernet*
WESTERN, AUS   IE| B+   PV| WPL| B $10 B+

AUSTRALIA

SYRAH/SHIRAZ (CONTINUED)

Fox Creek, 2000 *Shiraz-Grenache, McLaren Vale*
SOUTH, AUS   IE| A+, B+   PV| WPL| BBC $20   A

Grant Burge, 1999 *Shiraz, Miamba , Barossa Valley*
SOUTH, AUS   IE| B+   PV| WPL| $15   B+

Greg Norman, 1999 *Estates Shiraz, Limestone Coast*
SOUTH, AUS   IE| A   PV| WPL| $20   A

Hamilton, 1999 *Fuller's Barn, Ewell Vineyard*
BAROSSA VALLEY, AUS   IE| A   PV| WPL| S $30   A

Hardys, 2000 *Shiraz*
SOUTH EASTERN, AUS   IE| B+   PV| WPL| B $8   B+

Jacob's Creek, 2000 *Shiraz, Reserve*
SOUTH, AUS   IE| B+   PV| 99 B+   WPL| $14   B+

Jim Barry, 2001 *The Lodge Hill Shiraz, Clare Valley*
SOUTH, AUS   IE| B+   PV| WPL| $14   B+

Kaesler, 2001 *Avignon Grenache Shiraz, Barossa Valley*
SOUTH, AUS   IE| A+   PV| WPL| $23   A+

Knappstein, 1999 *Shiraz, Clare Valley*
SOUTH, AUS   IE| A   PV| WPL| $19   A

Lake Breeze, 2000 *Barnoota Langhorne Creek*
AUS   IE| A   PV| WPL| $19   A

Leasingham, 2000 *Shiraz, Bin 61, Clare Valley*
SOUTH, AUS   IE| A-   PV| 99 A-   WPL| W $21   A-

Lindemans, 1999 *Shiraz, Reserve, Padthaway*
SOUTH, AUS   IE| B+, A-, A-, B+   PV| WPL| W,BBC $15   A-

Madfish, 2001 *Shiraz*
WESTERN, AUS   IE| B+   PV| WPL| $14   B+

Marquis Philips, 2001 *Shiraz*
SOUTH EASTERN, AUS   IE| B+, B   PV| 00 B+   WPL| $15   B+

McGuigan, 1999 *Genus 4 Shiraz, Hunter Valley*
NEW SOUTH WALES, AUS IE| A   PV| WPL| $20   A

McPherson, 2000 *Reserve Shiraz, Goulburn Valley*
AUS   IE| A   PV| WPL| $19   A

McWilliam's , 2001 *Hanwood Estate*
SOUTH EASTERN, AUS   IE| B+   PV| WPL| $11   B+

Paringa, 2001 *Shiraz, Individual Vineyard*
SOUTH, AUS   IE| A-, B+   PV| 00 B+   WPL| W,B $10   A-

Penfolds, 2000 *Shiraz, Kalimna Bin 28*
SOUTH, AUS   IE| A-   PV| WPL| $24   A-

Penfolds, 2000 *Shiraz-Mourvèdre, Bin 2*
SOUTH EASTERN, AUS   IE| A-, B+   PV| WPL| W $11   A-

Penfolds, 2000 *Thomas Hyland Shiraz*
SOUTH, AUS   IE| A-   PV| WPL| $18   A-

Penfolds, 1999 *Shiraz, Bin 128, Coonawarra*
SOUTH, AUS   IE| A   PV| WPL| $23   A

Penfolds, 1999 *Shiraz, Kalimna Bin 28*
SOUTH, AUS   IE| A-, B+, A   PV| WPL| BBC $24   A-

Penley, 1999 *Shiraz, Hyland, Coonawarra*
SOUTH, AUS   IE| A-, A   PV| WPL| BBC $25   A

Petaluma, 1999 *Shiraz, Bridgewater Mill*
SOUTH-VICTORIA, AUS   IE| B+, B   PV| WPL| $15   B+

Pikes, 1998 *Shiraz, Reserve, Clare Valley*
SOUTH, AUS   IE| A+   PV| WPL| $24   A+

Pirramimma, 2000 *McLaren Vale*
SOUTH, AUS   IE| A+   PV| WPL| $21   A+

Plantagenet, 1999 *Mount Barker*
WESTERN, AUS   IE| A   PV| WPL| S $30   A

Rosenblum, 2001 *Feather Foot Man Jingalu Special Artist Series, McLaren Vale*
SOUTH, AUS   IE| A-   PV| WPL| S $28   A-

Sandalford, 2001 *Shiraz-Cabernet Sauvignon*
WESTERN, AUS   IE| B+   PV| WPL| $14   B+

Shottesbrooke, 2000 *Eliza Reserve Shiraz, McLaren Vale*
SOUTH, AUS   IE| A   PV| WPL| S $30   A

Taltarni, 2000 *Shiraz, Pyrenees*
VICTORIA, AUS   IE| A-   PV| WPL| $17   A-

The Green Vineyard, 2000 *Shiraz, The Forties Old Block*
HEATHCOTE, AUS   IE| A   PV| WPL| S $30   A

Thorn-Clarke, 2000 *Shiraz, Shotfire Ridge, Barossa Valley*
SOUTH, AUS   IE| B+   PV| WPL| $14   B+

Thorn-Clarke, 2000 *Shiraz, Terra , Barossa Valley*
SOUTH, AUS   IE| B+   PV| WPL| B $10   B+

Tim Adams, 1999 *Shiraz, Clare Valley*
SOUTH, AUS   IE| A-   PV| WPL| $24   A-

Vasse Felix, 2000 *Shiraz, Margaret River*
WESTERN, AUS   IE| A   PV| WPL| S $30   A

Water Wheel, 2000 *Bendigo*
VICTORIA, AUS   IE| B+   PV| WPL| $15   B+

Wirra Wirra, 2000 *Shiraz, McLaren Vale*
SOUTH, AUS   IE| A   PV| WPL| S $27   A

Wolf Blass, 2001 *Shiraz-Cabernet Sauvignon, Red Label*
SOUTH, AUS   IE| B+, B+   PV| 00 B+   WPL| $14   B+

Wolf Blass, 2000 *Shiraz-Cabernet Sauvignon, Red Label*
SOUTH, AUS   IE| B+, B   PV| WPL| W $12   B+

Wolf Blass, 1999 *Brown Label Classic Shiraz*
SOUTH, AUS   IE| A   PV| WPL| $20   A

OTHER RED

Coriole, 2000 *Cabernet/Merlot/Shiraz, Redstone, McLaren Vale*
SOUTH, AUS   IE| A+   PV| WPL| $24   A+

Kaesler, 2001 *Stonehorse Grenache Shiraz Mourvedre, Barossa Valley*
SOUTH, AUS   IE| A   PV| WPL| $20   A

AUSTRALIA

Marquis Philips, 2000 *Sarah's Blend*
SOUTH EASTERN, AUS   IE| A+, B+, B+   PV| WPL| BBC $15   A-

Meerea Park, 1999 *McLaren Vale/Hunter Valley Orange*
SOUTH, AUS   IE| A   PV| WPL| $20   A

Mitchelton, 1999 *Grenache/Mourvèdre, Central Victoria Crescent*
VICTORIA, AUS   IE| A-   PV| WPL| $21   A-

Rosemont, 2000 *Grenache/Mourvedre/Shiraz , McLaren Vale/Barossa Valley*
SOUTH, AUS   IE| A+   PV| WPL| S $30   A+

WHITES

CHARDONNAY

Allandale, 2000 *Hunter Valley*
NEW SOUTH WALES, AUS IE| B+   PV| WPL| $15   B+

Barossa Valley, 2002 *Barossa Valley*
SOUTH, AUS   IE| B+   PV| WPL| B $10   B+

Bellarine, 2000 *James' Paddock*
VICTORIA, AUS   IE| B+   PV| WPL| $15   B+

Brookland Valley, 2000 *Margaret River*
SOUTH WEST , AUS   IE| A-   PV| WPL| $24   A-

Evans & Tate, 2001 *Margaret River*
WESTERN, AUS   IE| B+, B+   PV| WPL| $15   B+

Hardys, 2001 *Eileen Hardy*
SOUTH, AUS   IE| A   PV| WPL| $20   A

Heggies, 2001 *Eden Valley*
SOUTH, AUS   IE| B+   PV| WPL| $20   B+

Jacob's Creek, 2001 *Reserve*
SOUTH, AUS   IE| B+   PV| WPL| $14   B+

James, 2000 *Chardonnay-Semillon, Sundara, Hunter Valley*
NEW SOUTH WALES, AUS IE| B+   PV| WPL| B $9   B+

James, 2000 *Compass, Hunter Valley*
NEW SOUTH WALES, AUS IE| A-   PV| WPL| $13   A-

Katnook, 2000 *Coonawarra*
SOUTH, AUS   IE| A-   PV| WPL| $17   A-

Kooyong, 2000 *Mornington Penninsula*
AUS   IE| A   PV| WPL| $25   A

Penmara, 2000 *Reserve*
NEW SOUTH WALES, AUS IE| B+   PV| WPL| $13   B+

Reynolds, 2001
NEW SOUTH WALES, AUS IE| B+   PV| WPL| B $10   B+

Rockbare, 2002 *McLaren Vale*
SOUTH, AUS   IE| B+   PV| WPL| $12   B+

Rothbury, 2001
SOUTH EASTERN, AUS   IE| A-   PV| WPL| B $8   A-

Sandalford, 2001 *Margaret River*
AUS   IE| A   PV| WPL| $25   A

Wolf Blass, 2002
SOUTH, AUS	IE| B+	PV|	WPL|	$14	B+

Xanadu, 2000 *Margaret River*
WESTERN, AUS	IE| A-	PV|	WPL|	$15	A-

RIESLING

Craneford, 2001 *Eden Valley*
SOUTH, AUS	IE| B+	PV|	WPL|	$12	B+

Elysian Fields, 2001 *Clare Valley*
SOUTH, AUS	IE| A-	PV|	WPL|	$20	A-

Frankland, 2001 *Cooladerra, Frankland River*
WESTERN, AUS	IE| A	PV|	WPL|	$15	A

Frankland, 2001 *Poison Hill, Frankland River*
WESTERN, AUS	IE| A	PV|	WPL|	$15	A

Frankland, 2001 *Isolation Ridge, Frankland River*
WESTERN, AUS	IE| B+	PV|	WPL|	$15	B+

Grosset, 2002 *Watervale, Clare Valley*
SOUTH, AUS	IE| A	PV|	WPL|	$24	A

Grosset, 2002 *Polish Hill, Clare Valley*
SOUTH, AUS	IE| A+	PV| 01 A	WPL| S	$29	A+

Knappstein, 2001 *Handpicked Riesling, Clare Valley*
SOUTH, AUS	IE| A-	PV|	WPL|	$14	A-

Leeuwin, 2001 *Art Series Margaret River*
WESTERN, AUS	IE| A-	PV| 00 A-	WPL|	$20	A-

Lengs & Cooter, 2001 *Clare Valley*
SOUTH, AUS	IE| A	PV|	WPL|	$16	A

Mitchell, 2001 *Watervale, Clare Valley*
SOUTH, AUS	IE| A+	PV|	WPL|	$18	A+

Mount Horrocks, 2002 *Clare Valley*
SOUTH, AUS	IE| A-	PV|	WPL|	$20	A-

Orlando, 2002 *Reserve, Jacobs Creek*
SOUTH, AUS	IE| B+	PV|	WPL|	$15	B+

Penfolds, 2002 *Reserve Bin, Eden Valley*
SOUTH, AUS	IE| A	PV|	WPL|	$18	A

Pikes, 2002 *Clare Valley*
SOUTH, AUS	IE| A-	PV|	WPL|	$16	A-

Pikes, 2001 *Reserve, Clare Valley*
SOUTH, AUS	IE| A	PV|	WPL|	$22	A

Wolf Blass, 2001 *Gold Label, Clare Valley-Eden Valley*
SOUTH, AUS	IE| A, B+, B+	PV|	WPL|	$14	A-

SAUVIGNON/FUMÉ BLANC

Groom, 2002 *Adelaide Hills*
SOUTH, AUS	IE| A	PV|	WPL|	$16	A

Shaw & Smith, 2002 *Adelaide Hills*
SOUTH, AUS	IE| A-	PV| 01 A	WPL|	$17	A-

AUSTRALIA

OTHER WHITE

Alkoomi, 2001 *Semillon-Chenin Blanc-Sauvignon Blanc*
WESTERN, AUS   IE| B+   PV| WPL| $11   B+

Cullen, 2001 *Semillon-Sauvignon Blanc, Margaret River*
WESTERN, AUS   IE| A+   PV| WPL| S $30   A+

Moss Wood, 2001 *Semillon, Margaret River*
WESTERN, AUS   IE| A+   PV| WPL| $20   A+

Pierro, 2000 *Semillon-Sauvignon Blanc, Margaret River*
WESTERN, AUS   IE| A   PV| WPL| $20   A

Primo, 2002 *Colombard, La Biondina, Adelaide*
SOUTH, AUS   IE| B+   PV| WPL| $13   B+

Trevor Jones, 2001 *Boots, Barossa Valley*
SOUTH, AUS   IE| B+   PV| WPL| $15   B+

SWEET

PORT

Rosemount, NV *Tawny, Old Benson, Solare Aged*
SOUTH EASTERN, AUS   IE| A-   PV| WPL| $25   A-

Yalumba, NV *Antique Tawny Port, Museum Release*
NEW SOUTH WALES, AUS IE| A, B+   PV| WPL| BBC $17   A-

OTHER SWEET

Benjamin, NV *Muscat, Museum Release*
VICTORIA, AUS   IE| A+   PV| WPL| $16   A+

WINE: DEF. "…3: SOMETHING THAT INVIGORATES OR INTOXICATES."

WEBSTER'S DICTIONARY

COMPREHENSIVE BUYING GUIDES TO TOP RATED WINES

CHILE

REDS

CABERNET SAUVIGNON

Calina, 2000 *Cabernet Sauvignon-Carmenère, Coastal Vineyards, Maule Valley*
CENTRAL VALLEY, CH   IE| B+, B   PV| WPL| $14   B+

Casa Lapostolle, 2000 *Rapel Valley*
CENTRAL VALLEY, CH   IE| B+   PV| WPL| B $10   B+

Ch. Los Boldos, 2000 *Vieilles Vignes, Requinoa*
CENTRAL VALLEY, CH   IE| B+   PV| WPL| $20   B+

Concha y Toro, 2000 *Marqués de Casa Concha, Puente Alto Vineyard, Maipo Valley*
CENTRAL VALLEY, CH   IE| A-   PV| 99 A-   WPL| W $14   A-

Concha y Toro, 1999 *Terrunyo, Maipo Valley*
CENTRAL VALLEY, CH   IE| A-, A-, A   PV| WPL| S,BBC $29   A-

Errazuriz, 1999 *Reserva Don Maximiano Estate, Valle Aconcagua*
CH   IE| B+   PV| WPL| $14   B+

Morandé, 1999 *Maipo Valley*
CENTRAL VALLEY, CH   IE| A   PV| WPL| S $30   A

Santa Rita, 2000 *Reserva, Maipo Valley*
CENTRAL VALLEY, CH   IE| B+   PV| 99 B+   WPL| W $13   B+

Veramonte, 2001 *Maipo Valley*
CENTRAL VALLEY, CH   IE| B+   PV| WPL| B $10   B+

CARMENÈRE

Apaltagua, 2001 *Carmenère, Colchagua Valley*
CH   IE| B+   PV| WPL| B $10   B+

Apaltagua, 2000 *Carmenère, Colchagua Valley*
CH   IE| B+   PV| WPL| $15   B+

Carmen, 2000 *Carmenère-Cabernet Sauvignon, Reserve, Maipo Valley*
CENTRAL VALLEY, CH   IE| B+   PV| 99 B+   WPL| $15   B+

Casa Rivas, 2001 *Carmenère, Gran Reserva, Maipo Valley*
CENTRAL VALLEY, CH   IE| B+   PV| WPL| $13   B+

Concha y Toro, 2000 *Carmenère, Terrunyo, Peumo Valley, Rapel Valley*
CENTRAL VALLEY, CH   IE| A-, A-   PV| 99 A   WPL| S,BBC $29   A-

Odfjell, 2001 *Carmenère, Maipo Valley*
CENTRAL VALLEY, CH   IE| B+   PV| WPL| $15   B+

Santa Carolina, 2000 *Carmenère, Barrica Selection, Colchagua Valley, Maipo Valley*
CENTRAL VALLEY, CH   IE| B+   PV| WPL| $12   B+

MALBEC

Montes, 2001 *Reserve, Colchagua Valley, Rapel Valley*
CENTRAL VALLEY, CH   IE| B+   PV| WPL| W, B $10 B+

Terra Mater, 1999 *Curico Valley*
CENTRAL VALLEY, CH   IE| B+   PV| WPL| B $9 B+

MERLOT

Carmen, 2000 *Reserve, Maipo Valley*
CENTRAL VALLEY, CH   IE| B+   PV| WPL| $15 B+

Casa Julia, 2001
CH   IE| B+   PV| WPL| B $9 B+

Casa Lapostolle, 2001 *Rapel Valley*
CENTRAL VALLEY, CH   IE| B+   PV| WPL| $12 B+

Concha y Toro, 2000 *Peuma Marques de Casa Concha*
CH   IE| B+   PV| WPL| $14 B+

Montes, 2000 *Alpha, Apalta Vineyard, Santa Cruz*
CENTRAL VALLEY, CH   IE| A-   PV| WPL| $22 A-

Morandé, 2001 *Vitisterra Grand Reserve, Maipo Valley*
CENTRAL VALLEY, CH   IE| B+   PV| WPL| $15 B+

SYRAH/SHIRAZ

Matetic Vineyards, 2001 *EQ, San Antonio*
CH   IE| A+   PV| WPL| $25 A+

Morandé, 2001 *Vitisterra Grand Reserve, Maipo Valley*
CENTRAL VALLEY, CH   IE| A-, A-   PV| WPL| BBC $15 A-

ZINFANDEL

Mont Gras, 2001 *Limited Edition, Colchagua Valley, Rapel Valley*
CENTRAL VALLEY, CH   IE| B+   PV| WPL| $15 B+

OTHER RED

Escudo Rojo, 2000 *Maipo Valley*
CENTRAL VALLEY, CH   IE| B+   PV| WPL| $15 B+

Valette Fontaine, 1999 *Cabernet/Carmenère, Memorias, Maipo Valley*
CENTRAL VALLEY, CH   IE| A-   PV| WPL| S $28 A-

Veramonte, 1999 *Cabernet/Carmenère, Primus, Alto, Casablanca Valley*
CENTRAL VALLEY, CH   IE| A   PV| WPL| $22 A

WHITES

CHARDONNAY

Casa Lapostolle, 2001 *Casablanca Valley*
CH   IE| B+   PV| WPL| B $10 B+

Concha y Toro, 2001 *Marqués de Casa Concha, Puente Alto Vineyard, Maipo Valley*
CENTRAL VALLEY, CH   IE| A-   PV| 00 A   WPL| $14 A-

Dallas Conté, 2002 *Casablanca Valley*
CENTRAL VALLEY, CH IE| B+ PV| WPL| B $10 B+

Errazuriz, 2001 *Casablanca Valley*
CH IE| B+, B PV| WPL| B $10 B+

Montes, 2002 *Reserve, Barrel Fermented, Curicó Valley*
CENTRAL VALLEY, CH IE| B+ PV| WPL| B $10 B+

Santa Rita, 2002 *Reserva, Casablanca Valley*
CENTRAL VALLEY, CH IE| A- PV| WPL| $12 A-

SAUVIGNON/FUMÉ BLANC

Matetic Vineyards, 2001 *EQ, San Antonio*
CH IE| B+ PV| WPL| $12 B+

Morandé, 2001 *Terrarum Reserve, Casablanca Valley*
CENTRAL VALLEY, CH IE| A PV| WPL| $11 A

Santa Rita, 2002 *Reserva*
CASABLANCA VALLEY, CH IE| A PV| WPL| $12 A

Veramonte, 2002 *Casablanca Valley*
CH IE| B+ PV| WPL| B $10 B+

OTHER WHITE

Casa Lapostolle, 2001 *Tanao*
CH IE| B+ PV| WPL| $14 B+

SWEET

OTHER SWEET

Morandé, 2000 *Edición Limitada, Golden Harvest, Casablanca Valley*
CH IE| A- PV| WPL| $25 A-

Vina Echeverria, 1999 *Late Harvest Special Selection, Molina, Curico Valley*
CENTRAL VALLEY, CH IE| B+ PV| WPL| $19 B+

CHILE

"WINE IS A LITTLE LIKE LOVE. WHEN THE RIGHT
ONE COMES ALONG, YOU KNOW IT!"

Bolla Wines

CBS TV, AUGUST 26, 1973

COMPREHENSIVE BUYING GUIDES TO TOP RATED WINES

FRANCE

REDS

BORDEAUX

Ch. d' Angludet, 2000 *Margaux*
BORDEAUX, FR   IE| B+   PV| WPL| $16   B+

Clos Badon-Thunevin, 2000 *St.-Emilion*
BORDEAUX, FR   IE| A   PV| WPL| $25   A

Ch. Beaumont, 2000 *Haut-Médoc*
BORDEAUX, FR   IE| A-   PV| WPL| W $15   A-

Ch. Beau-Site, 2000 *St.-Estéphe*
BORDEAUX, FR   IE| A-   PV| WPL| W $20   A-

Ch. Belgrave, 2000 *Haut-Médoc*
BORDEAUX, FR   IE| A-   PV| WPL| W $20   A-

Ch. Bellefont-Belcier, 2000 *Saint-Emilion*
BORDEAUX, FR   IE| A-   PV| WPL| S $30   A-

Ch. Bouscaut, 2000 *Pessac-Léognan*
BORDEAUX, FR   IE| A-   PV| WPL| $20   A-

Ch. Boyd-Cantenac, 2000 *Margaux*
BORDEAUX, FR   IE| A-   PV| WPL| S $30   A-

Ch. Brillette, 2000 *Listrac & Moulis*
BORDEAUX, FR   IE| B+   PV| WPL| $15   B+

Ch. Camensac, 2000 *Haut-Médoc*
BORDEAUX, FR   IE| A-   PV| WPL| W $20   A-

Ch. Cantelauze, 2000 *Pomerol*
BORDEAUX, FR   IE| A-   PV| WPL| $25   A-

Ch. Cantemerle, 2000 *Haut-Médoc*
BORDEAUX, FR   IE| A   PV| WPL| W,S $30   A

Ch. Cantenac, 2000 *Saint-Emilion*
BORDEAUX, FR   IE| A-   PV| WPL| $15   A-

Ch. Cantenac-Brown, 2000 *Margaux*
BORDEAUX, FR   IE| A   PV| WPL| S $30   A

Ch. la Cardonne, 2000 *Médoc*
BORDEAUX, FR   IE| A-   PV| WPL| W $15   A-

Ch. Charmail, 2000 *Haut-Médoc*
BORDEAUX, FR   IE| A-   PV| WPL| $15   A-

Ch. Cos-Labory, 2000 *St.-Estéphe*
BORDEAUX, FR   IE| A-   PV| WPL| $25   A-

Ch. Côte de Baleau, 2000 *Saint-Emilion*
BORDEAUX, FR   IE| A-   PV| WPL| S $30   A-

Ch. la Croix du Casse, 2000 *Pomerol*
BORDEAUX, FR   IE| A+   PV| WPL| S $30   A+

Ch. Croix-de-Gay, 2000 *Pomerol*
BORDEAUX, FR   IE| A-   PV| WPL| S $30   A-

Ch. Croizet-Bages, 2000 *Pauillac*
BORDEAUX, FR   IE| A-   PV| WPL| $25   A-

Ch. Dauzac, 2000 *Margaux*
BORDEAUX, FR   IE| A   PV| WPL| S $30   A

Ch. Faizeau, 2000 *Séléction Vieilles Vignes, Montagne-St.-Emilion*
BORDEAUX, FR   IE| B+   PV| WPL| $15   B+

La Fleur de Bouard, 2000 *Lalande-de-Pomerol*
BORDEAUX, FR   IE| A-   PV| WPL| S $30   A-

Ch. Fonréaud, 2000 *Listrac*
BORDEAUX, FR   IE| B+   PV| WPL| $15   B+

Ch. Gigault, 2000 *Premières, Cuvée Viva, Côtes de Blaye*
BORDEAUX, FR   IE| A   PV| WPL| $25   A

Ch. Gloria, 2000 *St.-Julien*
BORDEAUX, FR   IE| A-, B   PV| WPL| W,S $30   B+

Ch. Grand Corbin-Despagne, 2000 *Saint-Emilion*
BORDEAUX, FR   IE| A-   PV| WPL| $25   A-

Ch. Grand-Pontet, 2000 *Saint-Émilion*
BORDEAUX, FR   IE| A+   PV| WPL| S $30   A+

Ch. les Grands Maréchaux, 2000 *Premières, Côtes de Blaye*
BORDEAUX, FR   IE| B+   PV| WPL| $15   B+

Ch. Haut-Bages-Libéral, 2000 *Pauillac*
BORDEAUX, FR   IE| A+   PV| WPL| S $30   A+

Ch. Haut-Batailley, 2000 *Pauillac*
BORDEAUX, FR   IE| A+   PV| WPL| S $30   A+

Ch. Haut-Beauséjour, 2000 *Saint Estèphe*
BORDEAUX, FR   IE| A-   PV| WPL| $20   A-

Ch. Haut-Chaigneau, 2000 *Lalande-de-Pomerol*
BORDEAUX, FR   IE| B+   PV| WPL| $15   B+

Ch. Haut-Corbin, 2000 *Saint-Émilion*
BORDEAUX, FR   IE| A   PV| WPL| $25   A

Ch. Haut-Maillet, 2000 *Pomerol*
BORDEAUX, FR   IE| A-   PV| WPL| $20   A-

Ch. Haut-Marbuzet, 2000 *St.-Estéphe*
BORDEAUX, FR   IE| A-   PV| WPL| W,S $30   A-

Ch. Lafon-Rochet, 2000 *St.-Estéphe*
BORDEAUX, FR   IE| A   PV| WPL| S $30   A

Ch. la Lagune, 2000 *Haut-Médoc*
BORDEAUX, FR   IE| A-   PV| WPL| S $30   A-

Ch. la Louvière, 2000 *Pessac-Léognan*
BORDEAUX, FR   IE| A   PV| WPL| $25   A

Ch. Lynch-Moussas, 2000 *Pauillac*
BORDEAUX, FR   IE| A   PV| WPL| W $25   A

Ch. Malartic LaGravière, 2000 *Pessac-Léognan*
BORDEAUX, FR   IE| A+   PV| 99 A-   WPL| S $30   A+

FRANCE

BORDEAUX (CONTINUED)

Ch. Malescasse, 2000 *Haut-Médoc*
BORDEAUX, FR   IE| A-   PV| WPL| $15   A-

Ch. Martinens, 2000 *Margaux*
BORDEAUX, FR   IE| A   PV| WPL| $20   A

Ch. Monbrison, 2000 *Margaux*
BORDEAUX, FR   IE| A, A-   PV| WPL| S,BBC $30   A

Ch. de Mouton, 2000 *Bordeaux Supérieur*
BORDEAUX, FR   IE| A-   PV| WPL| $15   A-

Ch. Pibran, 2000 *Pauillac*
BORDEAUX, FR   IE| A-   PV| WPL| $20   A-

Ch. Picque-Caillou, 2000 *Pessac-Léognan*
BORDEAUX, FR   IE| A-   PV| WPL| $15   A-

Ch. la Pointe, 2000 *Pomerol*
BORDEAUX, FR   IE| A   PV| WPL| $25   A

Ch. Poujeaux, 2000 *Listrac & Moulis*
BORDEAUX, FR   IE| A-   PV| WPL| W $25   A-

Ch. Prieuré-Lichine, 2000 *Margaux*
BORDEAUX, FR   IE| A   PV| WPL| S $30   A

Ch. Ramafort, 2000 *Médoc*
BORDEAUX, FR   IE| A-   PV| WPL| $20   A-

Ch. Rouillac, 2000 *Pessac-Léognan*
BORDEAUX, FR   IE| A-   PV| WPL| $16   A-

Ch. Sénèjac, 2000 *Haut-Médoc*
BORDEAUX, FR   IE| B+   PV| WPL| $15   B+

Ch. la Serre, 2000 *Saint-Emilion*
BORDEAUX, FR   IE| A   PV| WPL| $25   A

Ch. la Tour Carnet, 2000 *Haut-Médoc*
BORDEAUX, FR   IE| A-   PV| WPL| $25   A-

CABERNET SAUVIGNON

Mas Carlot, 2000 *Cabernet Sauvignon-Syrah, Vin de Pays d'Oc*
LANGUEDOC, FR   IE| A-   PV| WPL| $12   A-

Mas de Guiot, 2000 *Cabernet Sauvignon-Syrah, Vin de Pays du Gard*
LANGUEDOC, FR   IE| A-   PV| WPL| $14   A-

GAMAY

Georges Duboeuf, 2000 *Prestige, Morgon*
BEAUJOLAIS, FR   IE| A-, A-, B   PV| WPL| BBC $14   A-

Georges Duboeuf, 2001 *Dom. Jean Descombes, Morgon*
BEAUJOLAIS, FR   IE| B+   PV| 99 A-, 00 A-   WPL| $12   B+

Georges Duboeuf, 2000 *Prestige, Fleurie*
BEAUJOLAIS, FR   IE| B+, B+, B, B+   PV| WPL| $13   B+

Georges Duboeuf, 2000 *Prestige, Brouilly*
BEAUJOLAIS, FR   IE| A-, B+, B-   PV| WPL| $14   B+

Dom. Jean Foillard, 2000 *Première, Morgon*
BEAUJOLAIS, FR   IE| A   PV| WPL| **$21**   A

Potel-Aviron, 2000 *Morgon*
BEAUJOLAIS, FR   IE| A-   PV| WPL| **$17**   A-

GRENACHE

Fifteen, 2001 *Vin de Pays de Pyrénées Orientales*
FR   IE| B+, B   PV| 00 A-   WPL| **$15**   B+

Dom. de Saint-Antoine, 2001 *Vin de Pays du Gard*
LANGUEDOC, FR   IE| B+   PV| WPL| B   **$9**   B+

MERLOT

Barton & Guestier, 2000 *Premium Merlot, Vin de Pays d'Oc*
LANGUEDOC, FR   IE| B+   PV| WPL| **$13**   B+

Dom. des Molines, 2000 *Vin de Pays du Gard*
LANGUEDOC, FR   IE| B+   PV| WPL| B   **$10**   B+

Robert Skalli, 2000 *Vin de Pays D'oc*
LANGUEDOC, FR   IE| B+   PV| WPL| B   **$10**   B+

SYRAH/SHIRAZ

Dom. d' Andezon, 2001 *Côtes du Rhône*
RHÔNE, FR   IE| B+   PV| 99 B+, 00 B+   WPL| **$11**   B+

Dom. des Blageurs, 2000 *Syrah, Vin de Pays d'Oc*
LANGUEDOC, FR   IE| A-   PV| WPL| B   **$9**   A-

Dom. des Cantarelles, 2000 *Syrah-Cabernet Sauvignon, Vin de Pays du Gard*
LANGUEDOC, FR   IE| B+, B   PV| WPL| **$13**   B+

Dom. la Coste, 2000 *Ultra, Coteaux d'Aix-en-Provence*
PROVENCE, FR   IE| A-   PV| WPL| S   **$28**   A-

La Forge, 2000 *Vin de Pays d'Oc*
LANGUEDOC, FR   IE| B+   PV| WPL| **$12**   B+

Mas Carlot, 2001 *Syrah-Grenache, Cuvée Tradition, Vin de Pays d'Oc*
LANGUEDOC, FR   IE| B+   PV| WPL| B   **$9**   B+

Mas de Bressades, 2001 *Syrah-Grenache, Vin de Pays du Gard*
LANGUEDOC, FR   IE| B+   PV| WPL| B   **$10**   B+

Mas de Guiot, 2001 *Syrah-Grenache, Vin de Pays du Gard*
LANGUEDOC, FR   IE| A-, B   PV| WPL| B   **$9**   B+

Ch. Paus Mas, 2000 *Coteaux du Languedoc*
LANGUEDOC, FR   IE| B+   PV| WPL| **$15**   B+

Dom. de Saint-Antoine, 2001 *Vin de Pays du Gard*
LANGUEDOC, FR   IE| B+   PV| 00 A-   WPL| **$11**   B+

Dom. de Saint-Antoine, 2001 *Costières de Nimes*
LANGUEDOC, FR   IE| B+   PV| WPL| **$13**   B+

Saint-Cosme, 2001 *Côtes du Rhône*
RHÔNE, FR   IE| B+   PV| WPL| **$12**   B+

FRANCE

OTHER RED

Ch. d' Aiguilhe, 2000 *Côte de Castillion*
BORDEAUX, FR   IE| A-   PV| WPL| S $30   A-

Ch. d' Aiguilloux, 1999 *Cuvée des Trois Seigneurs*
LANGUEDOC, FR   IE| B+   PV| WPL| $11   B+

Olivier Andrieu, 1999 *Faugères Clos Fantine Cuvée Conurtiol*
LANGUEDOC, FR   IE| A-   PV| WPL| $17   A-

Dom. D' Aupilhac, 2001 *Vin de Pays du Mont Baudle Lou Maset*
LANGUEDOC, FR   IE| B+   PV| WPL| $14   B+

Ch. de Barbe Blanche, 2000 *Cuvée Henri IV, Lussac-Saint-Émillion*
BORDEAUX, FR   IE| B+   PV| WPL| $15   B+

Barton & Guestier, 2000 *Tradition, Châteauneuf-du-Pape*
RHÔNE, FR   IE| B+   PV| WPL| $20   B+

Louis Bernard, 2001 *Chateau Bosc la Croix, Côtes du Rhône Villages*
RHÔNE, FR   IE| B+   PV| WPL| B $10   B+

Louis Bernard, 2001 *Gigondas*
RHÔNE, FR   IE| B+   PV| WPL| $19   B+

Louis Bernard, 2001 *Vacqueyras*
RHÔNE, FR   IE| B+   PV| WPL| $18   B+

Dom. Borie de Maurel, 2001 *Cuvée Alex, Minervois*
LANGUEDOC, FR   IE| A-   PV| WPL| $17   A-

Dom. Borie de Maurel, 2000 *Esprit d'Automne, Minervois*
LANGUEDOC, FR   IE| B+   PV| WPL| $13   B+

Ch. Bousquette, 2000 *Saint-Chinian*
LANGUEDOC, FR   IE| B+   PV| WPL| $15   B+

Ch. Bousquette, 1999 *Cuvée Prestige, Saint-Chinian*
LANGUEDOC, FR   IE| A   PV| WPL| S $26   A

Chateau la Boutignane, 2001 *Rosé de Saignée, Corbières*
LANGUEDOC, FR   IE| B+   PV| WPL| B $10   B+

Chateau la Boutignane, 2000 *Classique Cuvée Rouge, Corbières*
LANGUEDOC, FR   IE| B+   PV| WPL| B $10   B+

Chateau la Boutignane, 1998 *Carignane, Grande Reserve Rouge, Corbières*
LANGUEDOC, FR   IE| A+   PV| WPL| $18   A+

Domaine Brusset, 2001 *Cairanne Coteaux des Travers, Côtes du Rhône Villages-Cairanne*
RHÔNE, FR   IE| B+   PV| WPL| $14   B+

Ch. Camplazen, 2000 *Premium la Clape*
LANGUEDOC, FR   IE| A-   PV| WPL| S $28   A-

Dom. de la Charbonnièrre, 1999 *Cuvée Mourre des Perdrix*
RHÔNE, FR   IE| A   PV| WPL| S $30   A

Ch. Coupe Roses, 2001 *La Bastide, Minervois*
LANGUEDOC, FR   IE| B+   PV| WPL| B $10   B+

Ch. Coupe Roses, 2000 *Cuvée Vignals, Minervois*
LANGUEDOC, FR   IE| B+   PV| WPL| $13   B+

Dom. le Couroulu, 1999 *Cuvée Classique, Côtes du Rhône-Vacqueyras*
RHÔNE, FR   IE| A-   PV| WPL| $13   A-

Dom. de Curebeasse, 1999 *Côtes de Provence*
PROVENCE, FR   IE| B+   PV| WPL| $11   B+

Dom. Machard de Gramont, 2000 *Les Nazoires, Chambolle-Musigny*
BURGUNDY, FR   IE| A   PV| WPL| S $30   A

Delas Cote-du-Ventoux, 2000
RHÔNE, FR   IE| B+   PV| WPL| $11   B+

Clos l' Eglise, 2000 *Côtes de Castillon*
BORDEAUX, FR   IE| A-   PV| WPL| $25   A-

Clos Fantine, 1999 *Faugères*
LANGUEDOC, FR   IE| A-   PV| WPL| B $10   A-

J. Vidal Fleury, 2000 *Côtes du Ventoux*
RHÔNE, FR   IE| B+   PV| WPL| B $8   B+

J. Vidal Fleury, 2000 *Côtes du Rhône*
RHÔNE, FR   IE| B+   PV| WPL| B $10   B+

Ch. Fontenil, 2000 *Fronsac, Fronsac*
BORDEAUX, FR   IE| A   PV| WPL| $25   A

Dom. Foulaquier, 2000 *Le Rollier, Coteaux du Languedoc-Pic Saint-Loup*
LANGUEDOC, FR   IE| A, A-   PV| WPL| BBC $17   A-

Dom. Gardies, 2000 *Les Milleres, Côtes du Roussillon Villages*
ROUSSILLON, FR   IE| B+   PV| 99 B+   WPL| $15   B+

Dom. Gardies, 2000 *Tautavel, Côtes du Roussillon Villages*
ROUSSILLON, FR   IE| A-   PV| 99 A-   WPL| $19   A-

Michel Gassier, 2000 *Cuvée Joseph Torrès, Ch. de Nages, Costières de Nimes*
LANGUEDOC, FR   IE| A   PV| WPL| $20   A

Dom. Cathérine le Goeuil, 1999 *Les Beauchières, Côtes du Rhône Villages-Cairanne*
RHÔNE, FR   IE| B+   PV| WPL| $14   B+

Dom. Grand Nicolet, 2000 *Côtes du Rhône Villages-Rasteau*
RHÔNE, FR   IE| B+   PV| WPL| $12   B+

Dom. Grand Romane, 2000 *Gigondas*
RHÔNE, FR   IE| A-   PV| WPL| $18   A-

Grand Veneur, 2000 *Les Champauvins, Côtes du Rhône*
RHÔNE, FR   IE| B+   PV| WPL| $14   B+

Ch. Grande Cassagne, 2001 *G.S. la Civette, Costières de Nimes*
LANGUEDOC, FR   IE| B+   PV| 00 B+   WPL| B $10   B+

Ch. Grande Cassagne, 2001 *S. les Rameaux, Costières de Nimes*
LANGUEDOC, FR   IE| B+   PV| 99 B+   WPL| $13   B+

Dom. du Grapillon d'Or, 2000 *Gigondas*
RHÔNE, FR   IE| A   PV| 99 A+   WPL| S $30   A

E. Guigal, 1999 *Châteauneuf-du-Pape*
RHÔNE, FR   IE| A+   PV| WPL| S $30   A+

Haut-Carles, 2000 *Fronsac*
BORDEAUX, FR   IE| A   PV| WPL| $25   A

OTHER RED (CONTINUED)

J.C. & Boris Leclercq, 1998 *Cabernet/Merlot, Vin de Pays, d'Oc les Portes de St.-Ros*
LANGUEDOC, FR   IE| A-   PV| WPL| $15 A-

Dom. R. & M. Labbe, 2001 *Abymes*
SAVOIE, FR   IE| B+   PV| WPL| B $9   B+

Dom. Lacroix-Vanel, 2001 *Clos Fine Amor, Coteaux du Languedoc*
LANGUEDOC, FR   IE| B+   PV| WPL| $12 B+

Dom. Lacroix-Vanel, 2000 *Clos Melanie, Coteaux du Languedoc*
LANGUEDOC, FR   IE| A-   PV| WPL| $17 A-

Ch. Lagrezette, 1998
CAHORS, FR   IE| A-   PV| WPL| $20 A-

Dom. des Lambertins, 2000 *Côtes du Rhône-Vacqueyras*
RHÔNE, FR   IE| A-   PV| WPL| $12 A-

Patrick Lesec, 2000 *Minervois Tonneaux*
LANGUEDOC, FR   IE| B+   PV| WPL| $15 B+

Domaine de l'Harmas, 2000 *Grenache-Syrah-Mourvedre, Côtes du Rhône*
RHÔNE, FR   IE| B+   PV| WPL| $11 B+

Dom. de la Lyre, 2000 *Controlee, Côtes du Rhône*
RHÔNE, FR   IE| B+   PV| WPL| B $10 B+

Ch. Massamier la Mignarde, 1999 *Domus Maximus, La Livinière, Minervois*
LANGUEDOC, FR   IE| A   PV| WPL| $25 A

Ch. de Mauvanne, 1999 *Cru Classé Cuvée, Côtes de Provence*
LANGUEDOC, FR   IE| A-   PV| WPL| $19 A-

Dom. de Mourchon, 1998 *Seguret Tradition, Côtes du Rhône Villages*
RHÔNE, FR   IE| B+   PV| WPL| $13 B+

Dom. Navarre, 1999 *Saint-Chinian*
LANGUEDOC, FR   IE| A-   PV| WPL| $20 A-

Maison Nicolas, 2000 *Languedoc/Roussillon, Consensus, Coteaux du Languedoc*
LANGUEDOC, FR   IE| A   PV| WPL| $15 A

Caves des Papes, 2000 *Oratorio, Gigondas*
RHÔNE, FR   IE| A-   PV| WPL| $23 A-

Perrin, 2000 *Côtes du Rhône-Vacqueyras*
RHÔNE, FR   IE| A-   PV| WPL| $21 A-

Perrin, 1999 *Côtes du Rhône-Vacqueyras*
RHÔNE, FR   IE| A-   PV| 00 A-   WPL| $19 A-

Ch. Pesquié, 1999 *Quintessence, Côtes du Ventoux*
RHÔNE, FR   IE| B+   PV| WPL| $15 B+

Ch. Peyros, 1999 *Madiran*
PROVENCE, FR   IE| B+   PV| WPL| $14 B+

Ch. Puygueraud, 2000 *Côtes de Francs*
BORDEAUX, FR   IE| A-   PV| WPL| $15 A-

Jean-Maurice Raffault, 2001 *Chinon les Galluches, Chinon*
LOIRE, FR   IE| B+   PV| WPL| $14 B+

Dom. Rimbert, 2001 *Le Chant de Marjolaine, Vin de Pays d'Oc*
LANGUEDOC, FR   IE| B+   PV| 99 B+   WPL| $13   B+

Dom. Rocher, 2000 *Côtes du Rhône Villages-Cairanne*
RHÔNE, FR   IE| A   PV| 99 B+   WPL| $12   A

Ch. Romanin, 1998 *Les Baux*
PROVENCE, FR   IE| A-   PV| WPL| $25   A-

Ch. Saint-Martin de la Garrigue, 2000 *Bronzinelle*
LANGUEDOC, FR   IE| B+   PV| 99 A+   WPL| $15   B+

Ch. Saint-Martin de la Garrigue, 2000 *Cuvée Réservée, Coteaux de Bessilles*
LANGUEDOC, FR   IE| A   PV| WPL| B $10   A

Ch. Saint-Martin de la Garrigue, 2000 *Cuvée Tradition, Coteaux du Languedoc*
LANGUEDOC, FR   IE| A-   PV| WPL| B $9   A-

Dom. le Sang des Cailloux, 2000 *Cuvée Azaliaïs, Côtes du Rhône-Vacqueyras*
RHÔNE, FR   IE| A+   PV| WPL| $23   A+

Dom. de la Sauveuse, 1999 *Côtes de Provence*
PROVENCE, FR   IE| B+   PV| WPL| $13   B+

Ch. des Ségriès, 2001 *Côtes du Rhône*
RHÔNE, FR   IE| B+   PV| WPL| B $8   B+

Ch. des Ségriès, 2001 *Clos de l'Hermitage, Côtes du Rhône*
RHÔNE, FR   IE| A   PV| WPL| $15   A

Ch. des Ségriès, 2001 *Cuvée Réservée, Lirac*
RHÔNE, FR   IE| B+   PV| 99 B+   WPL| B $9   B+

Ch. Signac, 2000 *Cuvée Terra Amata, Côtes du Rhône Villages-Chusclan*
FR   IE| A-   PV| WPL| $22   A-

Ch. Signac, 2000 *Village Chuscian, Côtes du Rhône*
RHÔNE, FR   IE| B+   PV| WPL| $15   B+

Dom. Tempier, 2000 *Appellation Bandol controlee, Bandol*
PROVENCE, FR   IE| A   PV| WPL| S $27   A

Dom. de la Tour du Bon, 1999 *Bandol*
PROVENCE, FR   IE| A+   PV| WPL| $24   A+

Ch. les Trois Croix, 2000 *Fronsac*
BORDEAUX, FR   IE| A-   PV| WPL| $14   A-

Dom. du Tunnel, 2000 *Cuvée Prestige, Cornas*
RHÔNE, FR   IE| A   PV| WPL| S $30   A

Raymond Usseglio, 2000 *Châteauneuf-du-Pape*
RHÔNE, FR   IE| A   PV| WPL| S $30   A

Cave de Vacqueyras, 2001 *Chateau des Hautes Ribes, Vacqueyras*
RHÔNE, FR   IE| B+   PV| WPL| $12   B+

Cave de Vacqueyras, 2001 *Domaine Mas du Bouquet, Vacqueyras*
RHÔNE, FR   IE| B+   PV| WPL| $12   B+

Ch. Valcombe, 2000 *Cuvée Prestige, Costières de Nimes*
LANGUEDOC, FR   IE| A, B   PV| WPL| $12   B+

Le Vieux Donjon, 2000 *Châteauneuf-du-Pape*
RHÔNE, FR   IE| A+, A   PV| 99 A-   WPL| S,BBC $30   A+

FRANCE

Les Vignerons de Villeveyrac, 2000 *Moulin de Gassac Albaran, Vieilles Vignes, Vin de Pays de l'Herault*

LANGUEDOC, FR	IE| A-	PV|	WPL|	$11 A-

Les Vignerons de Villeveyrac, 2000 *Moulin de Gassac Elise, Vieilles Vignes, Vin de Pays de l'Herault*

LANGUEDOC, FR	IE| B+	PV|	WPL|	$11 B+

Vignobles, 2000 *Jean Royer Cuvèe Prestige*

RHÔNE, FR	IE| A-	PV|	WPL|	$23 A-

WHITES

CHARDONNAY

Jean-Marc Brocard, 2000 *Côte de Jouan*

CHABLIS, FR	IE| A	PV| 99 A-	WPL|	$25 A

Dom. Jean Collet, 2000 *Montée de Tonnerre*

CHABLIS, FR	IE| A	PV|	WPL| S	$29 A

Benoit Ente, 1999 *Puligny-Montrachet*

BURGUNDY, FR	IE| A-	PV|	WPL| S	$30 A-

Dom. Jean-Pierre Grossot, 2000 *Mont de Milieu*

CHABLIS, FR	IE| A	PV|	WPL| S	$30 A

Dom. Jean-Pierre Grossot, 2000 *Vaucoupins*

CHABLIS, FR	IE| A	PV|	WPL|	$25 A

Daniel Junot, 2001

BURGUNDY, FR	IE| B+	PV|	WPL|	$11 B+

Dom. Hubert Lamy, 2000 *Les Frionnes, Saint-Aubin*

BURGUNDY, FR	IE| A	PV|	WPL| S	$28 A

Le Noble, 2001 *Vin de Pays*

SOUTH, FR	IE| B+	PV|	WPL| B	$7 B+

Dom. Alain Normand, 2000 *La Roche Vineuse, Mâcon*

BURGUNDY, FR	IE| B+	PV|	WPL|	$13 B+

Verget, 2000 *Cuvèe des 10 Ans*

CHABLIS, FR	IE| A	PV|	WPL| S	$30 A

CHENIN BLANC

Dom. Des Baumard, 2000 *Clos de Papillon, Savennieres*

LOIRE, FR	IE| A-	PV|	WPL|	$23 A-

Benoit Gautier, 2001 *Vouvray*

LOIRE, FR	IE| A-	PV|	WPL|	$11 A-

S. A. Huët, 2000 *Demi Sec, Clos du Bourg, Vouvray*

LOIRE, FR	IE| A	PV|	WPL|	$20 A

S. A. Huët, 2000 *Sec, Clos du Bourg, Vouvray*

LOIRE, FR	IE| A-	PV|	WPL|	$20 A-

J.-C. Pichot, 2002 *Vouvray, Dom. Le Peu de la Moriette*

LOIRE, FR	IE| A-	PV|	WPL|	$11 A-

Pierre & Yves Soulez, 1999 *Cuvée d'Avant, Ch. de Chamboureau, Savennières-Roche aux Moines Doux*

LOIRE, FR	IE| A+	PV|	WPL| S	$29 A+

Ch. Villeneuve, 2001 *Samur*
LOIRE, FR   IE| B+   PV| WPL| $11   B+

GEWÜRZTRAMINER

Pierre Sparr, 2001 *Réserve*
ALSACE, FR   IE| A+, B+   PV| WPL| BBC $15   A

Pierre Sparr, 2001
ALSACE, FR   IE| B+, B+   PV| WPL| $13   B+

PINOT GRIS/GRIGIO

J. B. Adam, 2001 *Réserve*
ALSACE, FR   IE| B+   PV| WPL| $13   B+

Albert Boxler, 2000 *Tokay Pinot Gris*
ALSACE, FR   IE| A-   PV| WPL| $23   A-

Dom. Schlumberger, 1999 *Les Princes Abbés*
ALSACE, FR   IE| A   PV| WPL| $20   A

Pierre Sparr, 2001
ALSACE, FR   IE| B+   PV| WPL| $13   B+

Vieil Armand, 2000 *Tokay, Grand Cru Ollviller*
ALSACE, FR   IE| A   PV| WPL| $22   A

RIESLING

J. B. Adam, 2001 *Cuvée Jean-Baptiste, Kaefferkopf*
ALSACE, FR   IE| A   PV| WPL| $20   A

Dopff & Irion, 2001 *Dom. de Ch. de Riquewihr, Les Murailles*
ALSACE, FR   IE| A-   PV| WPL| $19   A-

Dom. Schlumberger, 1998 *Les Princes Abbés*
ALSACE, FR   IE| A-, B+   PV| WPL| BBC $16   A-

André Schneider & Fils, 1998
ALSACE, FR   IE| A+   PV| WPL| $12   A+

SAUVIGNON/FUMÉ BLANC

Henri Bourgeois, 2001 *La Porte du Caillou, Sancerre*
LOIRE, FR   IE| A-   PV| WPL| $18   A-

Henri Bourgeois, 2000 *Haute Victoire, Quincy*
LOIRE, FR   IE| B+   PV| WPL| B $10   B+

Didier Dagueneau, 2000 *En Chailloux, Pouilly Fumé*
LOIRE, FR   IE| A   PV| WPL| S $26   A

Pascal Jolivet, 2001 *Ch. du Nozay, Sancerre*
LOIRE, FR   IE| A-   PV| WPL| $23   A-

Pascal Jolivet, 2000 *Les Caillottes, Sancerre*
LOIRE, FR   IE| A-, B, A-   PV| WPL| $22   B+

Philippe Portier, 2000 *Quincy*
LOIRE, FR   IE| B+   PV| WPL| $14   B+

Pascal & Nicolas Reverdy, 2000 *Vieilles Vignes, Sancerre*
LOIRE, FR   IE| A-   PV| WPL| $24   A-

FRANCE

Tour St. Martin, 2000 *Menetou Salon-Morogues*
LOIRE, FR   IE| B+   PV| WPL| $15 B+

VIOGNIER

Ch. de Campuget, 2001 *Vin de Pays du Gard*
LANGUEDOC, FR   IE| B+   PV| WPL| $11 B+

Dom. Des Cantarelles, 2001 *Vin de Pays du Gard*
LANGUEDOC, FR   IE| A-   PV| 00 A-   WPL| $13 A-

OTHER WHITE

Pierre Boniface, 2001 *Apremont*
SAVOIE, FR   IE| B+   PV| WPL| B $9 B+

Dom. du Closel, 2001 *Les Caillardieres*
LOIRE, FR   IE| B+   PV| WPL| $16 B+

Dom. Gardies, 2001 *Muscat Sec, Vin de Pays de Côtes Catalanes*
ROUSSILLON, FR   IE| B+   PV| WPL| $12 B+

Grange de Rouquettes, 2001 *Le Pelican, Vin de Pays d'Oc*
LANGUEDOC, FR   IE| B+   PV| WPL| $15 B+

Grange de Rouquettes, 2001 *Marsanne-Viognier, Vin de Pays d'Oc*
LANGUEDOC, FR   IE| B+   PV| WPL| $12 B+

Jacques Guindon, 2001 *Muscadet des Coteaux du Loire*
LOIRE, FR   IE| B+   PV| WPL| B $9 B+

Dom. de l' Hortus, 2001 *Cuvée Classique, La Bergerie de l'Hortus, Vin de Pays du Val de Montferrand*
LANGUEDOC, FR   IE| B+   PV| WPL| $12 B+

De Ladoucette, 2000 *Pouiilly-Fume*
LOIRE, FR   IE| A-   PV| WPL| S $30 A-

Mas Carlot, 2001 *Marsanne-Roussanne, Cuvée Tradition, Vin de Pays d'Oc*
LANGUEDOC, FR   IE| B+   PV| WPL| B $8 B+

Mas de Bressades, 2001 *Roussanne-Viognier, Vin de Pays du Gard*
LANGUEDOC, FR   IE| B+   PV| WPL| $14 B+

Dom. de la Pépière, 2001 *Sur Lie, Cuvée Vieilles Vignes, Clos des Briords, Muscadet de Sèvre et Maine*
LOIRE, FR   IE| B+   PV| WPL| $12 B+

Francois Pinon, 2001 *Cuvée Tradition*
LOIRE, FR   IE| B+   PV| WPL| $12 B+

Dom. de Pouy, 2001 *Vin de Pays des Côtes de Gascogne*
SOUTHWEST, FR   IE| B+   PV| 99 B+, 00 B+ WPL| B $7 B+

Dom. de la Quilla, 2000 *Sur Lie, Muscadet de Sèvre et Maine*
LOIRE, FR   IE| B+   PV| WPL| B $10 B+

Cave de Tain l'Hermitage, 2001 *White Nobles Rives, Crozes-Hermitage*
RHÔNE, FR   IE| B+   PV| WPL| $12 B+

Chat. la Touche, 2000 *Muscadet Sur Lie Cuvée Choisie*
LOIRE, FR   IE| A-   PV| WPL| $15 A-

George Vernay, 2001 *Les Terrasses de L'Empire*
CONDRIEU, FR   IE| A+   PV| WPL| S $29 A+

ROSÉ

Ch. d' Aquéria, 2001 *Tavel*
RHÔNE, FR　　　IE| B+　　　　PV|　　　　　　WPL|　　　　$15　B+

Bargemone, 2001 *Coteaux d'Aix en Provence*
PROVENCE, FR　　IE| B+　　　　PV|　　　　　　WPL| B　　　$10　B+

Mas de Bressades, 2001 *Costières de Nimes*
LANGUEDOC, FR　　IE| B+　　　　PV|　　　　　　WPL| B　　　$10　B+

Dom. de la Mordoree, 2001 *Tavel*
RHÔNE, FR　　　IE| A-　　　PV| 99 B+　　WPL| B　　　$10　A-

Dom. de la Mordoree, 2001 *Côtes du Rhône*
RHÔNE, FR　　　IE| B+　　　　PV|　　　　　　WPL| B　　　$10　B+

SPARKLING

Bouvet, NV *Signature Brut, Saumur*
LOIRE, FR　　　IE| B+　　　　PV|　　　　　　WPL|　　　　$13　B+

de Bruyne, *Cuvée Absolue NV, à-Sezanne*
FR　　　　　　IE| A+　　　　PV|　　　　　　WPL| S　　　$27　A+

Cuvée Cle'Mente, 2000 *Brut, Blancs de Blanc, Chardonnay*
FR　　　　　　IE| A-　　　　PV|　　　　　　WPL| B　　　　$9　A-

Duval-Leroy, NV *Brut*
CHAMPAGNE, FR　IE| A　　　　PV|　　　　　　WPL| S　　　$28　A

Nicolas Feuillatte, NV *Brut*
CHAMPAGNE, FR　IE| B+　　　　PV|　　　　　　WPL| W　　　$25　B+

Paul Goerg, NV *Brut Rose Champagne*
CHAMPAGNE, FR　IE| B+　　　　PV|　　　　　　WPL| S　　　$29　B+

Piper Heidsieck , NV *Brut*
CHAMPAGNE, FR　IE| A　　　　PV|　　　　　　WPL| W,S　$30　A

Raymond Henriot, NV *Brut*
CHAMPAGNE, FR　IE| A+　　　　PV|　　　　　　WPL|　　　　$21　A+

Frederic Lornet, NV *Cremant de Jura Rosa*
FR　　　　　　IE| B+　　　　PV|　　　　　　WPL| B　　　$10　B+

Pol Roger, NV *Brut*
CHAMPAGNE, FR　IE| A-　　　　PV|　　　　　　WPL| S　　　$30　A-

SWEET

OTHER SWEET

Dom. Gardies, 2000 *MuscatMuscat di Rivesaltes*
ROUSSILLON, FR　IE| B+　　　　PV|　　　　　　WPL|　　　　$14　B+

Régis Minet, 2001 *Pouilly-Fumé, Vieilles Vignes*
LOIRE, FR　　　IE| A-　　　　PV|　　　　　　WPL|　　　　$17　A-

Éric Texier, 1999 *Nôble Rot Botrytis*
FR　　　　　　IE| A-　　　　PV|　　　　　　WPL| S　　　$30　A-

Pierre-Yves Tijou, 2001 *Ch. Soucherie, Coteaux du Layon-Chaume*
LOIRE, FR　　　IE| B+　　　　PV|　　　　　　WPL|　　　　$16　B+

COMPREHENSIVE BUYING GUIDES TO TOP RATED WINES

GERMANY

WHITES

RIESLING

Dr. von Bassermann-Jordan, 2001 *Spätlese trocken, Forster Ungeheuer*
PFALZ, GER   IE| A   PV| WPL| $22   A

Dr. Pauly Bergweiler, 20001 *Kabinett, Graacher Himmelreich*
MOSEL-SAAR-RUWER, GER   IE| B+   PV| WPL| $14   B+

Dr. Pauly Bergweiler, 2001 *Auslese, Wehlener Sonnenuhr*
MOSEL-SAAR-RUWER, GER   IE| A-   PV| WPL| S $26   A-

Dr. Pauly Bergweiler, 2001 *Kabinett, Bernkasteler Badstube*
MOSEL-SAAR-RUWER, GER   IE| A-   PV| WPL| $14   A-

Dr. Pauly Bergweiler, 2001 *Kabinett, Bernkasteler alte Badstube am Doctorberg*
MOSEL-SAAR-RUWER, GER   IE| A+   PV| WPL| $16   A+

Dr. Pauly Bergweiler, 2001 *Noble House Riesling QbA*
MOSEL-SAAR-RUWER, GER   IE| B+   PV| WPL| B $8   B+

Ch. W. Bernard, 2001 *Kabinett, Hackenheimer Kirchberg*
RHEINHESSEN, GER   IE| A-   PV| WPL| $16   A-

Georg Breuer, 2001 *Terra Montosa QbA*
MOSEL-SAAR-RUWER, GER   IE| A-   PV| WPL| $20   A-

Dr. Bürklin-Wolf, 2001 *Bürklin Estate QbA*
MOSEL-SAAR-RUWER, GER   IE| A-   PV| WPL| $16   A-

A. Christmann, 2001 *Auslese, Ruppertsberger Reiterpfad*
GER   IE| A+   PV| WPL| S $30   A+

Jon. Jos. Christoffel, 2001 *Kabinett, Erdener Treppchen*
MOSEL-SAAR-RUWER, GER   IE| A   PV| WPL| $23   A

Crusius, 2001 *Kabinett, Traiser Rotelfels*
NAHE, GER   IE| A   PV| WPL| $22   A

Emrich-Schönleber, 2001 *Kabinett, Monzinger Frülingsplätzchen*
NAHE, GER   IE| A+   PV| WPL| $16   A+

Emrich-Schönleber, 2001 *Kabinett Halbtrocken, Monzinger Halenberg*
NAHE, GER   IE| A-   PV| WPL| $16   A-

Karl Erbes, 2001 *Spätlese, Urziger Würzgarten*
MOSEL-SAAR-RUWER, GER   IE| B+   PV| WPL| $14   B+

Robert Eymael (Mönchhof), 2001 *QbA*
MOSEL-SAAR-RUWER, GER   IE| A-   PV| WPL| $14   A-

Friedrich-Wilhelm-Gymnasium, 2001 *Spätlese, Graacher Himmelreich*
MOSEL-SAAR-RUWER, GER   IE| A   PV| WPL| $18   A

Carl Graff, 2001 *Auslese, Erdener Prälat*
MOSEL-SAAR-RUWER, GER   IE| B+   PV| WPL| $14   B+

Grans-Fassian, 2001 *Kabinett, Trittenheirmer*
MOSEL-SAAR-RUWER, GER   IE| A-, A   PV| WPL| BBC $17   A

Johann Haart, 2001 *Spätlese, Piesporter Goldtröpfchen*
MOSEL-SAAR-RUWER, GER   IE| A   PV| WPL| $20 A

Helmut Hexamer, 2001 *Kabinett, Meddersheimer Rheingrafenberg*
NAHE, GER   IE| B+   PV| WPL| $16 B+

Helmut Hexamer, 2001 *Spätlese, Meddersheimer Rheingrafenberg*
NAHE, GER   IE| A-, A- PV| WPL| BBC $19 A-

Jakoby-Mathy, 2001 *Riesling Kabinett, Kinheimer Rosenberg*
MOSEL-SAAR-RUWER, GER   IE| A-   PV| WPL| $13 A-

Schloss Johannisberger, 2001 *QbA*
RHEINGAU, GER   IE| A-   PV| 00 A-   WPL| $18 A-

Schloss Johannisberger, 2001 *Spätlese*
RHEINGAU, GER   IE| A+   PV| WPL| S $28 A+

Johannishof, 2001 *Spätlese, Rudesheimer Berg Rottland*
RHEINGAU, GER   IE| A   PV| WPL| $22 A

Karlsmühle, 2001 *Kabinett, Kaseler Nies'chen*
MOSEL-SAAR-RUWER, GER   IE| A-   PV| WPL| $20 A-

Heribert Kerpen, 2001 *Kabinett, Wehlener Sonnenuhr*
MOSEL-SAAR-RUWER, GER   IE| A-   PV| WPL| $19 A-

Reichsgraf von Kesselstatt, 2001 *Spätlese, Piesporter Goldtröpfchen*
MOSEL-SAAR-RUWER, GER   IE| A-   PV| WPL| $24 A-

Reichsgraf von Kesselstatt, 2001 *Spätlese, Scharzhofberger*
MOSEL-SAAR-RUWER, GER   IE| A-   PV| WPL| $25 A-

Kirsten, 1998 *Riesling Brut*
MOSEL, GER   IE| B+   PV| WPL| $16 B+

Staatsweingüter Kloster Eberbach, 2001 *Kabinett, Steinberger*
RHEINGAU, GER   IE| A   PV| WPL| $18 A

Staatsweingüter Kloster Eberbach, 2001 *Kabinett, Erbacher Marcobrunn*
RHEINGAU, GER   IE| A   PV| WPL| $19 A

Baron zu Knyphäusen, 2001 *Spätlese, Erbacher Steinmorgen*
RHEINGAU, GER   IE| A   PV| WPL| $22 A

Krüger-Rumpf, 2001 *Kabinett, Münsterer Pittersberg*
NAHE, GER   IE| A   PV| 99 A-   WPL| $17 A

Lingenfelder, 2001 *QbA Bird Label*
PFALZ, GER   IE| A-   PV| WPL| $13 A-

Carl Loewen, 2001 *Spätlese, Thörnicher Ritsch*
MOSEL-SAAR-RUWER, GER   IE| A-   PV| WPL| $20 A-

Dr. Loosen, 2001 *Kabinett, Erdener Treppchen*
MOSEL-SAAR-RUWER, GER   IE| A-   PV| WPL| $18 A-

Dr. Loosen, 2001 *Riesling Kabinett, Wehlener Sonnenuhr*
MOSEL-SAAR-RUWER, GER   IE| A+   PV| WPL| $18 A+

Dr. Loosen, 2001 *Riesling Spätlese, Graacher Himmelreich*
MOSEL-SAAR-RUWER, GER   IE| A+   PV| WPL| $25 A+

Dr. Loosen, 2001 *Riesling Kabinett, Bernkasteler Lay*
MOSEL-SAAR-RUWER, GER   IE| A+, A- PV| WPL| BBC $17 A

Dr. Loosen, 2001 *Spätlese, Wehlener Sonnenuhr*
MOSEL-SAAR-RUWER, GER   IE| A   PV| WPL| $25 A

RIESLING (CONTINUED)

Dr. Loosen, 2001 *Spätlese, Ürziger Würzgarten*
MOSEL-SAAR-RUWER, GER   IE| A-   PV| WPL| $25   A-

Dr. Loosen, 2001 *Spätlese, Erdener Treppchen*
MOSEL-SAAR-RUWER, GER   IE| A-   PV| WPL| $25   A-

Helmut Mathern, 2001 *Kabinett, Niederhäuser Felsensteyer*
NAHE, GER   IE| WPL| $18   A

Alfred Merkelbach, 2001 *Spätlese, Ürziger Würzgarten Fuder 11*
MOSEL-SAAR-RUWER, GER   IE| A-   PV| $17   A-

Meulenhof, 2001 *Auslese, Wehlener Sonnenuhr*
MOSEL-SAAR-RUWER, GER   IE| A+   PV| WPL| $24   A+

Meulenhof, 2001 *Kabinett, Wehlener Sonnenuhr*
MOSEL-SAAR-RUWER, GER   IE| A-   PV| 99 B+   WPL| $16   A-

Meulenhof, 2001 *Riesling Kabinett, Erdener Treppchen*
MOSEL-SAAR-RUWER, GER   IE| A   PV| WPL| $16   A

Schumann Nägler, 2001 *Kabinett, Johannisberger Erntebringer*
RHEINGAU, GER   IE| A   PV| WPL| $15   A

Peter Nicolay, 2001 *Kabinett, Berkasteler Badstube*
MOSEL-SAAR-RUWER, GER   IE| B+   PV| WPL| $15   B+

Peter Nicolay, 2001 *Spätlese, Urziger Goldwingert*
MOSEL-SAAR-RUWER, GER   IE| A-   PV| WPL| S $26   A

Peter Nicolay, 2001 *Spätlese, Bernkasteler alte Badstube am Doctorberg*
MOSEL-SAAR-RUWER, GER   IE| A-   PV| 00 B+   WPL| S $28   A-

Von Othegraven, 2001 *Maria v. O. Riesling QbA*
MOSEL-SAAR-RUWER, GER   IE| A-   PV| WPL| $15   A-

Von Othegraven, 2001 *Ockfen Bockstein*
MOSEL-SAAR-RUWER, GER   IE| A-   PV| WPL| $24   A-

Von Othegraven, 2001 *QbA Riesling, Kanzemer Althenberg*
MOSEL-SAAR-RUWER, GER   IE| A   PV| WPL| S $27   A

Pazen, 2001 *Kabinett, Zeltinger Himmelreich*
MOSEL-SAAR-RUWER, GER   IE| A   PV| WPL| $14   A

Jon. Jos. Prüm, 2001 *Kabinett, Wehlener Sonnenuhr*
MOSEL-SAAR-RUWER, GER   IE| A-   PV| WPL| $25   A-

Balthasar Ress, 2001 *Kabinett, Hattenheimer Schützenhaus*
RHEINGAU, GER   IE| B+   PV| WPL| $12   B+

Balthasar Ress, 2001 *Kabinett, Schloss Reichartshausen*
RHEINGAU, GER   IE| B+   PV| WPL| $14   B+

Schloss Saarstein, 2001 *QbA, Trocken*
MOSEL-SAAR-RUWER, GER   IE| B+   PV| WPL| $11   B+

Prinz zu Salm-Dalberg'sches, 2001 *Kabinett, Schloss Wallhausen*
NAHE, GER   IE| B+   PV| WPL| $15   B+

Willi Schaefer, 2001 *Kabinett, Wehlener Sonnenuhr*
MOSEL-SAAR-RUWER, GER   IE| A-   PV| WPL| $20   A-

Carl Schmitt-Wagner, 2001 *Auslese, Longuicher Maximiner Herrenberg*
MOSEL-SAAR-RUWER, GER   IE| A+, A- PV| WPL| S,BBC $26   A

Schloss Schönborn, 2001 *Kabinett,*
RHEINGAU, GER IE| B+ PV| WPL| B $10 B+

Schloss Schönborn, 2001 *Kabinett, Hattenheimer Pfaffenberg*
RHEINGAU, GER IE| A- PV| WPL| $12 A-

Schloss Schönborn, 2001 *Kabinett, Erbacher Marcobrunn*
RHEINGAU, GER IE| A- PV| WPL| $14 A-

Schloss Schönborn, 2001 *Spätlese, Hattenheimer Pfaffenberg*
RHEINGAU, GER IE| A PV| WPL| $17 A

Schloss Schönborn, 2001 *Spätlese, Erbacher Marcobrunn*
RHEINGAU, GER IE| A PV| 00 A- WPL| $23 A

Schloss Schönborn, 2001 *Spätlese, Domanenweingut Hattenheimer Pfaffenberg*
RHEINGAU, GER IE| A- PV| WPL| S $28 A-

Selbach-Oster, 2001 *Kabinett, Bernkasteler Badstube*
MOSEL-SAAR-RUWER, GER IE| A- PV| WPL| $19 A-

Selbach-Oster, 2001 *Kabinett, Zeltinger Schlossberg*
MOSEL-SAAR-RUWER, GER IE| A PV| WPL| S $27 A

Selbach-Oster, 1999 *Auslese, Zeltinger Sonnenuhr*
MOSEL-SAAR-RUWER, GER IE| A+ PV| WPL| $17 A+

St. Urbans-Hof, 2001 *QbA*
MOSEL-SAAR-RUWER, GER IE| A- PV| WPL| B $10 A-

J. & H. A. Strub, 2001 *Spätlese, Niersteiner Paterberg Three Star*
RHEINHESSEN, GER IE| A PV| WPL| S $27 A

Tesch, 2001 *Auslese, Langenlonsheimer Löhrer Berg*
NAHE, GER IE| A- PV| WPL| S $30 A-

Tesch, 2001 *Kabinett, Langenlonsheimer Löhrer Berg*
NAHE, GER IE| B+ PV| WPL| $15 B+

Dr. H. Thanisch-Erben Müller-Burggraef, 2001 *Kabinett, Wehlener Sonnenuhr*
MOSEL-SAAR-RUWER, GER IE| B+ PV| WPL| $15 B+

Dr. H. Thanisch-Erben Müller-Burggraef, 2001 *Kabinett, Berncasteler Doctor*
MOSEL-SAAR-RUWER, GER IE| A- PV| WPL| S $27 A-

P. J. Valckenberg, 2001 *QbA, Trocken*
RHEINHESSEN, GER IE| B+ PV| WPL| B $10 B+

Euguen Wehrheim, 2001 *Spätlese, Niersteiner Orbel*
RHEINHESSEN, GER IE| B+ PV| WPL| $15 B+

Robert Weil, 2001 *Kabinett,*
RHEINGAU, GER IE| A- PV| WPL| $25 A-

Weingut Eilenz, 2001 *Kabinett, Ayler Kupp Riesling*
MOSEL-SAAR-RUWER, GER IE| B+ PV| WPL| $12 B+

Weingut Johannishof, 2001 *Charta QbA*
RHEINGAU, GER IE| A- PV| WPL| $14 A-

Weingut Johannishof, 2001 *Kabinett, Johannisberger Vogelsang*
RHEINGAU, GER IE| A- PV| WPL| $11 A-

Weingut Johannishof, 2001 *Kabinett, Johannisberger Goldatzel*
RHEINGAU, GER IE| B+ PV| WPL| $11 B+

RIESLING (CONTINUED)

Weingut Karl Erbes, 2001 *Kabinett, Urziger Wurzgarten*
MOSEL-SAAR-RUWER, GER IE| B+ PV| WPL| $12 B+

Weingut Wwe. Dr. Thanisch, 2001 *Kabinett, Bercasteler Doctor*
MOSEL-SAAR-RUWER, GER IE| A- PV| WPL| S $27 A-

J.L. Wolf, 2001 *Auslese, Wachenheimer Gerümpel*
GER IE| A+ PV| WPL| S $30 A+

J.L. Wolf, 2001 *Qualitätswein Trocken, Forster Pechstein*
PFALZ, GER IE| A- PV| WPL| $14 A-

J.L. Wolf, 2001 *Spätlese Trocken, Wachenheimer Gerümpel*
PFALZ, GER IE| A PV| WPL| $18 A

J.L. Wolf, 2001 *Spätlese Trocken, Ruppertsberger Hoheburg*
PFALZ, GER IE| A+ PV| WPL| S $27 A+

OTHER WHITE

Paul Blanck, 2001 *Pinot Blanc*
ALSACE, GER IE| A- PV| WPL| $11 A-

**"DRINKING GOOD WINE WITH GOOD FOOD
IN GOOD COMPANY IS ONE OF LIFE'S
MOST CIVILIZED PLEASURES."**

Michael Broadbent

COMPREHENSIVE BUYING GUIDES TO TOP RATED WINES

ITALY

REDS

BARBERA

La Ghersa, 1999 *Camparo*
ASTI SUPERIORE, IT   IE| B+   PV| WPL| $14   B+

Neirano, 1998 *Le Croci, Barbara Asti d'Superiore*
PIEDMONT, IT   IE| A   PV| WPL| S $30   A

CHIANTI

Banfi, 1998 *Classico, Chianti Classico*
TUSCANY, IT   IE| B+   PV| WPL| $17   B+

Le Corti, 2000 *Chianti Classico*
TUSCANY, IT   IE| B+   PV| 99 B+   WPL| $14   B+

Castello di Monsanto, 1999 *Riserva, Chianti Classico*
TUSCANY, IT   IE| A-   PV| WPL| $23   A-

Castello Vicchiomaggio, 1998 *La Prima Riserva, Chianti Classico*
TUSCANY, IT   IE| A   PV| WPL| $25   A

DOLCETTO

Francesco Boschis, 1998 *Vigna dei Prey, Dogliani*
PIEDMONT, IT   IE| A, A-   PV| WPL| BBC $17   A-

Luigi Einaudi, 2000 *Vigna Tecc, Dogliani*
PIEDMONT, IT   IE| A-   PV| WPL| $21   A-

Fratelli Pecchenino, 2000 *Siri d'Jermu, Dogliani*
PIEDMONT, IT   IE| A-, A   PV| 99 A-   WPL| S,BBC $29   A

MERLOT

Bolla, 2000 *Colforte*
VENETO, IT   IE| B+   PV| WPL| $15   B+

SANGIOVESE

Boscarelli, 1999 *Vino Nobile, Montepulciano*
TUSCANY, IT   IE| A-   PV| WPL| S $27   A-

Castello di Brolio, 1999 *Chianti Classico*
TUSCANY, IT   IE| B+   PV| WPL| $16   B+

Capezzana, 1999 *Carmignano*
TUSCANY, IT   IE| A   PV| WPL| $21   A

Capezzana, 1999 *Conte Contini Bonacossi, Carmignano*
TUSCANY, IT   IE| A-, A-   PV| WPL| BBC $20   A-

Carpineto, 1998 *Riserva, Chianti Classico*
TUSCANY, IT   IE| A-, A-   PV| WPL| W,BBC $22   A-

SANGIOVESE (CONTINUED)

Casa Emma, 1999 *Riserva, Chianti Classico*
TUSCANY, IT   IE| A-   PV| WPL| $25   A-

Conti Contini, 2001 *Bonacossi, Capezzana Barco Reale, Carmignano*
TUSCANY, IT   IE| A   PV| WPL| $15   A

Le Corti, 2000 *Don Tommaso, Chianti Classico*
TUSCANY, IT   IE| A-   PV| 99 B+   WPL| S $29   A-

Dei, 1999 *Vino Nobile, Montepulciano*
TUSCANY, IT   IE| A   PV| WPL| $24   A

Frescobaldi, 1998 *Nipozzano Riserva, Chianti Classico*
TUSCANY, IT   IE| B+   PV| WPL| $15   B+

Castello di Gabbiano, 1999 *Riserva, Chianti Classico*
TUSCANY, IT   IE| A-   PV| WPL| $17   A-

La Massa, 2000 *Chianti Classico*
TUSCANY, IT   IE| A-   PV| 99 A+   WPL| $23   A-

Poggio Bertaio, 2000 *Cimbolo*
UMBRIA, IT   IE| A-   PV| WPL| $20   A-

Trenuta di Riseccoli, 1999 *Chianti Classico*
TUSCANY, IT   IE| B+   PV| WPL| $12   B+

Rocca di Fabbri, 2000 *Satiro, Colli Martani*
UMBRIA, IT   IE| B+   PV| WPL| $12   B+

Santa Anastasia, 1999 *Passomaggio*
SICILY, IT   IE| B+, A-   PV| WPL| W $14   A-

Selvapiana, 1999 *Bucerchiale Reserva, Chianti Rufina*
TUSCANY, IT   IE| A   PV| WPL| S $30   A

Castello Vicchiomaggio, 1998 *Petri Riserva, Chianti Classico*
TUSCANY, IT   IE| A-   PV| WPL| $24   A-

Villa Cafaggio, 1999 *Riserva, Chianti Classico*
TUSCANY, IT   IE| A-   PV| WPL| S $30   A-

Castello di Volpaia, 2000 *Classico, Chianti Classico*
TUSCANY, IT   IE| B+   PV| WPL| $17   B+

ZINFANDEL

Amano, 2000 *Primitivo*
PUGLIA, IT   IE| B+   PV| WPL| B $10   B+

OTHER RED

Antonelli, 1999 *Rosso, Montefalco*
UMBRIA, IT   IE| B+   PV| WPL| $14   B+

Beni di Batasiolo, 2001 *Barolo*
BARBARA D'ALBA, IT   IE| B+   PV| WPL| $18   B+

Beni di Batasiolo, 1998 *Barolo*
LA MORRA, IT   IE| A-   PV| WPL| W,S $30   A-

Arnaldo Caprai, 2000 *Rosso, Montefalco*
UMBRIA, IT   IE| A   PV| WPL| $22   A

Arnaldo Caprai, 2000 *Poggio Belvedere*
UMBRIA, IT   IE| B+   PV| WPL| $14   B+

Casanova di Neri, 2000 *Rosso, Montalcino*
TUSCANY, IT   IE| A-   PV| WPL| $23   A-

Leone de Castris, 1999 *Primitivo di Manduria Santera*
IT   IE| B+   PV| WPL| $15   B+

Leone de Castris, 1999 *Salice Salentino Riserva*
IT   IE| B+   PV| WPL| $13   B+

Michele Chiarlo, 1998 *Barolo*
PIEDMONT, IT   IE| A-   PV| WPL| S $30   A-

Podere Colla, 1998 *Langhe Rosso Bricco*
PIEDMONT, IT   IE| A   PV| WPL| S $28   A

Colpetrone, 1999 *Rosso di Montefalco*
UMBRIA, IT   IE| A   PV| WPL| $14   A

Di Majo Norante, 1998 *Terra degli Osci, Ramitello*
MOLISE, IT   IE| B+   PV| WPL| W $12   B+

Falesco, 2001 *Vitiano*
UMBRIA, IT   IE| B+   PV| 00 A-   WPL| B $10   B+

Remo Farina, 2000 *Valpolicella Classico Superiore, Ripasso*
VENETO, IT   IE| A-   PV| 99 B+   WPL| $19   A-

Fassati, 1999 *Vino Nobile di Montepulciano Pasiteo*
TUSCANY, IT   IE| B+   PV| WPL| $17   B+

Fontanavecchia, 2000 *Aglianico del Taburno*
CAMPANIA, IT   IE| B+   PV| WPL| $15   B+

Giribaldi, 1999 *Barbaresco*
PIEDMONT, IT   IE| A   PV| WPL| S $28   A

Feudo Monaci, 2000 *Salice Salentino Rosso*
IT   IE| B+   PV| WPL| B $9   B+

Moroder, 1998 *Rosso Conero Dorico Riserva*
MARCHES, IT   IE| A-   PV| WPL| $25   A-

Nino Negri, 1998 *Valtellina Superiore, Inferno Mazér*
LOMBARDY, IT   IE| A-   PV| WPL| $17   A-

Fattoria Nicodemi, 2000 *Montepulciano*
ABRUZZI, IT   IE| B+   PV| WPL| $16   B+

Nociano, 1998 *Rosso IGT*
UMBRIA, IT   IE| A-   PV| WPL| B $9   A-

Fattoria le Pupille, 2001 *Maremma Toscana*
TUSCANY, IT   IE| B+   PV| 99 A-   WPL| $12   B+

Rainoldi, 1998 *Valtellina Superiore, Il Crespino*
LOMBARDY, IT   IE| A-   PV| WPL| S $30   A-

Rainoldi, 1998 *Valtellina Superiore, Prugnolo*
LOMBARDY, IT   IE| A-   PV| WPL| $17   A-

Rocca di Fabbri, 2000 *Montefalco*
UMBRIA, IT   IE| A-   PV| WPL| $20   A-

Rocche dei Manzoni, 1997 *Bricco, Vino da Tavola*
PIEDMONT, IT   IE| A, A-   PV| WPL| S,BBC $30   A

OTHER RED (CONTINUED)

Scacciadiavoli, 2000 *Rosso, Montefalco*
UMBRIA, IT IE| B+ PV| WPL| $12 B+

Seghesio, 1999 *Bouquet*
PIEDMONT, IT IE| A PV| WPL| $18 A

Tasca d'Almerita, 1999 *Cabernet/Nero d'Avola Cygnus*
SICILY, IT IE| A- PV| WPL| $21 A-

Terrabianca, 1999 *Piano del Cipresso*
TUSCANO, IT IE| A- PV| WPL| $22 A-

Tommasi, 1998 *Valpolicella Ripasso Classico Superiore*
VENETO, IT IE| A- PV| WPL| $20 A-

Tormaresca, 2000 *Red Table Wine*
APULIA, IT IE| B+ PV| WPL| $11 B+

Val delle Rose, 1999 *Morellino di Scansano*
TUSCANY, IT IE| B+ PV| WPL| $14 B+

Valle dell'Acate, 2001 *Nero d'Avola, Poggio Bidini*
SICILY, IT IE| B+ PV| WPL| B $9 B+

WHITES

CHARDONNAY

Vie di Romans, 2000 *Isonzo*
FRIULI, IT IE| A- PV| WPL| S $28 A-

PINOT GRIS/GRIGIO

Castello Banfi, 2001 *Pinot Grigio, San Angelo*
TUSCANY, IT IE| B+ PV| WPL| $15 B+

Ca' Montini, 2001 *Trentino*
TRENTINO-ALTO ADIGE, ITIE| A- PV| WPL| $15 A-

Marco Felluga, 2001 *Collio*
FRIULI, IT IE| B+ PV| WPL| W $15 B+

Lis Neris, 2000
FRIULI, IT IE| A- PV| WPL| S $28 A-

Vie di Romans, 2000 *Dessimis, Isonzo*
FRIULI, IT IE| A- PV| WPL| S $28 A-

SAUVIGNON/FUMÉ BLANC

Fattoria Il Palagio, 2001 *Sauvignon*
TOSCANA, IT IE| B+ PV| WPL| $12 B+

OTHER WHITE

Antinori, 2001 *Vermentino, Guado al Tasso, Bolgheri*
TUSCANY, IT IE| A, B+ PV| WPL| BBC $18 A-

Livio Felluga, 2001 *del Friuli Tocai Friulano, Colli Orientali*
FRIULI, IT IE| A- PV| WPL| $24 A-

Marco Felluga, 2001 *Molamatta, Pinot Bianco/Ribolla Gialla/Tocai Friulano, Collio*
FRIULI, IT   IE| B+   PV| WPL| $15 B+

Marco Felluga, 2001 *Tocai Friulano, Colli*
FRIULI, IT   IE| B+   PV| WPL| $14 B+

Feudi di San Gregorio, 2001 *Falanghina Sannio*
CAMPANIA, IT   IE| A-   PV| 99 B+, 00 B+ WPL| W $14 A-

Feudi di San Gregorio, 2001 *Greco di Tufo, Tufo*
CAMPANIA, IT   IE| A-   PV| WPL| W $18 A-

Maculan, 2001 *Pinot & Toi*
VENETO, IT   IE| B+   PV| WPL| $11 B+

Masi, 2001 *Bianco Garganega/Sauvignon, Veneto Serego Alighieri Possessioni*
VENETO, IT   IE| B+   PV| WPL| $12 B+

Cantina dei Monaci, 2001 *Greco*
CAMPANIA, IT   IE| A   PV| WPL| $14 A

Tasca d'Almerita, 2000 *Inzolia/Sauvignon Blanc, Nozze d'Oro*
SICILY, IT   IE| A-   PV| WPL| $23 A-

Teruzzi & Puthod, 2001 *Terre di Tufi*
TUSCANY, IT   IE| B+   PV| WPL| W $20 B+

ROSÉ

Tasca d'Almerita, 2001 *Nerrello Mascalese/Nero d'Avola, Rosé di Regaleali*
SICILY, IT   IE| A-   PV| WPL| $11 A-

SPARKLING

Astoria, NV *Extra Dry, Prosecco di Valdobbiandene*
IT   IE| A-   PV| WPL| B $9 A-

Astoria, NV *Prosecco di Conegliano*
IT   IE| B+   PV| WPL| $13 B+

Bellenda, 2000 *Prosecco, Brut, Conegliano-Valdobiaddene*
VENETO, IT   IE| A-   PV| WPL| $12 A-

Bisol, NV *Crede, Prosecco di Valdobbiadene*
IT   IE| A-   PV| WPL| $12 A-

Canella, NV *Prosecco, Extra Dry, Prosecco di Conegliano*
IT   IE| A-   PV| WPL| $11 A-

Carpene Malvolti, NV *ProseccoProsecco di Conegliano*
IT   IE| B+   PV| WPL| $12 B+

Collalbrigo, NV *Prosecco, Brut, Conegliano*
VENETO, IT   IE| B+   PV| WPL| $12 B+

Giribaldi, NV *Selezioni Rodellesi Dolce Brachetto*
PIEDMONT, IT   IE| B+   PV| WPL| $15 B+

Masottina, NV *ProseccoProsecco di Conegliano Valdobbiadene*
IT   IE| B+   PV| WPL| $14 B+

Mionetto, NV *Brut, Prosecco*
VENETO, IT   IE| B+   PV| WPL| B $10 B+

Mionetto, NV *Sergio Extra Dry, Prosecco di Valdobbiandene*
VENETO, IT   IE| A   PV| WPL| $16   A

Mionetto, NV *Spumante Brut, Prosecco*
VENETO, IT   IE| B+   PV| WPL| $11   B+

Rebuli, NV *Prosecco, Brut, Cuvèe d'Oro, Conegliano-Valdobiaddene*
VENETO, IT   IE| B+   PV| WPL| $11   B+

Riondo, NV *ProseccoConegliano-Valdobiaddene*
VENETO, IT   IE| A-   PV| WPL| B $9   A-

Santero, NV *Prosecco, Brut*
VENETO, IT   IE| B+   PV| WPL| B $9   B+

Villa Sandi, NV *Cuvée, Prosecco di Valdobbiadene*
IT   IE| B+   PV| WPL| $15   B+

Zardetto, NV *Prosecco, Brut*
VENETO, IT   IE| B+, B, B+   PV| WPL| $11   B+

SWEET

OTHER SWEET

Tenuta di Capezzana, 1996 *Vin Santo di Carmignano, Reserva, Carmignano*
TUSCANY, IT   IE| A   PV| WPL| S $27   A

**"WINE... OFFERS A GREATER RANGE FOR ENJOYMENT
AND APPRECIATION THAN POSSIBLY ANY OTHER PURELY
SENSORY THING WHICH MAY BE PURCHASED."
ATTRIBUTED TO:**

Ernest Hemingway

COMPREHENSIVE BUYING GUIDES TO TOP RATED WINES

NEW ZEALAND

REDS

MERLOT

Mills Reef, 2000 *Elspeth Syrah, Mere Road Vineyard*
HAWKES BAY, NZ   IE| A   PV| WPL| S $30   A

PINOT NOIR

Gibbston Valley, 2001
CENTRAL OTAGO, NZ   IE| A-   PV| WPL| S $30   A-

Mountford, 2001
WAIPARA VALLEY, NZ   IE| A-   PV| WPL| S $30   A-

Nautilus, 2001
MARLBOROUGH, NZ   IE| A-   PV| WPL| $20   A-

Pencarrow, 2001 *Palliser Estate*
MARTINBOROUGH, NZ   IE| A-   PV| WPL| $20   A-

SYRAH/SHIRAZ

Mills Reef, 2000 *Elspeth Syrah, Mere Road Vineyard*
HAWKES BAY, NZ   IE| A+, A   PV| 99 A-   WPL| S,BBC $30   A+

OTHER RED

Okahu, 2000 *Ninety Mile*
NZ   IE| A-   PV| WPL| $17   A-

WHITES

CHARDONNAY

Cellars of Canterbury, 2000 *Momona*
MARLBOROUGH, NZ   IE| A-   PV| WPL| W $13   A-

Kumeu River, 2000 *Kumeu River*
AUCKLAND, NZ   IE| A+   PV| 99 A-   WPL| $22   A+

Linden, 2000 *Hawkes Bay, Esk Valley*
HAWKES BAY, NZ   IE| B+   PV| WPL| B $10   B+

Muddy Water, 2000
WAIPARA VALLEY, NZ   IE| A-   PV| WPL| $20   A-

Nga Waka, 2000
MARTINBOROUGH, NZ   IE| A+   PV| WPL| $25   A+

Okahu, 2000
NORTHLAND CHIFTON, NZ IE| A   PV| WPL| $17   A

Pegasus Bay, 2000
WAIPARA VALLEY, NZ   IE| A, B+   PV| 99 A   WPL| S,BBC $30   A-

NEW ZEALAND

Saint Clair, 2001
MARLBOROUGH, NZ   IE| A-, B   PV| WPL| $15 A-

Saint Clair, 2001 *Unoaked*
MARLBOROUGH, NZ   IE| B+   PV| WPL| $15 B+

Te Mata, 2000
HAWKES BAY, NZ   IE| B+   PV| WPL| $18 B+

GEWÜRZTRAMINER

Spy Valley, 2001
MARLBOROUGH, NZ   IE| B+, B+   PV| WPL| $12 B+

RIESLING

Giesen, 2001
CANTERBURY, NZ   IE| A-   PV| 00 B+   WPL| $13 A-

Martinborough, 2001
MARTINBOROUGH, NZ IE| A-   PV| 99 B+   WPL| $15 A-

Omaka Springs, 2002
MARLBOROUGH, NZ   IE| B+   PV| 00 A-   WPL| $14 B+

Saint Clair, 2001
MARLBOROUGH, NZ   IE| A-   PV| 99 B+   WPL| $13 A-

SAUVIGNON/FUMÉ BLANC

Allan Scott, 2002 *Vintage Select*
MARLBOROUGH, NZ   IE| A-   PV| WPL| $11 A-

Allan Scott, 2002
MARLBOROUGH, NZ   IE| B+   PV| WPL| W $11 B+

Allan Scott, 2001
MARLBOROUGH, NZ   IE| B+   PV| WPL| $15 B+

Babich, 2002
MARLBOROUGH, NZ   IE| B+   PV| WPL| W $12 B+

Brancott, 2001 *Reserve*
MARLBOROUGH, NZ   IE| A-, B   PV| WPL| BBC $18 B+

Cairnbrae, 2002 *The Stones*
MARLBOROUGH, NZ   IE| B+   PV| 00 B+, 01 B+   WPL| $14 B+

Caroline Bay, 2001
MARLBOROUGH, NZ   IE| A-   PV| 00 A-   WPL| $20 A-

Charles Wiffen, 2002
MARLBOROUGH, NZ   IE| A-   PV| WPL| $15 A-

Cloudy Bay, 2001
MARLBOROUGH, NZ   IE| A, A   PV| 99 A-, 00 A   WPL| W,BBC $24 A

Coopers Creek, 2001 *Reserve*
MARLBOROUGH, NZ   IE| B+   PV| 99 A-   WPL| $15 B+

Craggy Range, 2002 *Te Muna Road Vineyard, Martinborough*
MARLBOROUGH, NZ   IE| A-   PV| WPL| $19 A-

Craggy Range, 2001 *Old Renwick Vineyard*
MARLBOROUGH, NZ   IE| A-   PV| WPL| $17 A-

Drylands, 2001 *Winemaker's Reserve*
MARLBOROUGH, NZ   IE| A-   PV| WPL| $19   A-

Fairhall Downs, 2001
MARLBOROUGH, NZ   IE| A   PV| WPL| $18   A

Forefathers, 2002
MARLBOROUGH, NZ   IE| B+   PV| 00 B+   WPL| $14   B+

Framingham, 2001
MARLBOROUGH, NZ   IE| B+   PV| WPL| $14   B+

Goldwater, 2002 *Dog Point*
MARLBOROUGH, NZ   IE| A-   PV| 99 A-, 00 A-   WPL| S $30   A-

Highfield, 2002
MARLBOROUGH, NZ   IE| A   PV| WPL| $18   A

Highland, 2001
MARLBOROUGH, NZ   IE| A   PV| WPL| $17   A

Huia, 2002
MARLBOROUGH, NZ   IE| A   PV| 01 B+   WPL| $16   A

Isabel, 2001
MARLBOROUGH, NZ   IE| A, A   PV| WPL| BBC $18   A

Kim Crawford, 2002
MARLBOROUGH, NZ   IE| A-   PV| WPL| $18   A-

LeGrys, 2001
MARLBOROUGH, NZ   IE| A-   PV| 00 A-   WPL| $15   A-

Matariki, 2001
HAWKES BAY, NZ   IE| A   PV| 99 A-   WPL| $15   A

Matua Valley, 2002
MARLBOROUGH, NZ   IE| A-, B+   PV| WPL| BBC $13   A-

Mills Reef, 2001 *Reserve*
HAWKES BAY, NZ   IE| B+   PV| WPL| $15   B+

Mount Riley, 2001
MARLBOROUGH, NZ   IE| A-, B+   PV| WPL| $15   A-

Mt. Difficulty, 2001
CENTRAL OTAGO, NZ   IE| A+   PV| 00 B+   WPL| $16   A+

Mud House, 2001
MARLBOROUGH, NZ   IE| A-   PV| 00 A-   WPL| $15   A-

Nautilus, 2002
MARLBOROUGH, NZ   IE| A-, B   PV| WPL| $17   B+

Nobilo, 2002 *Icon Series*
MARLBOROUGH, NZ   IE| A   PV| 01:A-   WPL| $19   A

Nobilo, 2001 *Icon Series*
MARLBOROUGH, NZ   IE| A-   PV| WPL| $19   A-

Omaka Springs, 2002
MARLBOROUGH, NZ   IE| A-   PV| 00 B+   WPL| W $17   A-

Palliser, 2001
MARLBOROUGH, NZ   IE| A-, B, A   PV| WPL| $18   A-

Red Hill, 2002
MARLBOROUGH, NZ   IE| B+   PV| WPL| $11   B+

NEW ZEALAND

SAUVIGNON/FUMÉ BLANC (CONTINUED)

Saint Clair, 2001 *Reserve, Wairau Valley*
MARLBOROUGH, NZ   IE| A   PV| WPL| $18 A

Saint Clair, 2001
MARLBOROUGH, NZ   IE| A   PV| 00 B+   WPL| $14 A

Selaks, 2001 *Premium Selection*
MARLBOROUGH, NZ   IE| B+   PV| WPL| $14 B+

Selaks, 2001
MARLBOROUGH, NZ   IE| A   PV| 99 B+, 00 B+ WPL| $14 A

Seresin, 2001
MARLBOROUGH, NZ   IE| A   PV| WPL| $20 A

Shepherds Ridge, 2001
MARLBOROUGH, NZ   IE| A-   PV| 99 A-   WPL| $15 A-

Sherwood Estates, 2001
MARLBOROUGH, NZ   IE| B+   PV| WPL| $11 B+

Shingle Peak, 2001
MARLBOROUGH, NZ   IE| A-   PV| 99 B+   WPL| $12 A-

Spy Valley, 2001
MARLBOROUGH, NZ   IE| B+   PV| WPL| $13 B+

Te Kairanga, 2001
MARLBOROUGH, NZ   IE| A+   PV| 99 A   WPL| $14 A+

Terrace Road, 2001
MARLBOROUGH, NZ   IE| A   PV| WPL| $17 A

Villa Maria, 2002 *Cellar Selection*
MARLBOROUGH, NZ   IE| A-   PV| 00 A-   WPL| $22 A-

Villa Maria, 2001 *Private Bin, Dillons Point*
MARLBOROUGH, NZ   IE| A-   PV| WPL| $15 A-

Villa Maria, 2001 *Reserve, Clifford Bay, Awatere Valley*
MARLBOROUGH, NZ   IE| A+   PV| WPL| S $29 A+

Wairau River, 2000 *Reserve*
MARLBOROUGH, NZ   IE| A-, A-, B+   PV| WPL| BBC $16 A-

Whitehaven, 2001
MARLBOROUGH, NZ   IE| A-   PV| WPL| $16 A-

SWEET

OTHER SWEET

Konrad & Conrad, 2001 *Riesling, Late Harvest, Noble*
MARLBOROUGH, NZ   IE| A   PV| WPL| $20 A

Selaks, 2001 *Ice Wine*
MARLBOROUGH, NZ   IE| A-   PV| WPL| $15 A-

COMPREHENSIVE BUYING GUIDES TO TOP RATED WINES

PORTUGAL

REDS

PINOT NOIR

Luis Pato, 2000 *Quinta do Ribeirinho Primeira Escolha*
BEIRAS, POR   IE| A-   PV| WPL| S $29 A-

SYRAH/SHIRAZ

Herdade de Esporão, 2000
ALENTEJO, POR   IE| B+   PV| WPL| $11 B+

J. Portugal Ramos, 2001
ALENTEJO, POR   IE| A-   PV| WPL| $18 A-

OTHER RED

Caves Aliança, 1999 *Aliança Particular, Palmela*
TERRAS DO SADO, POR IE| B+   PV| WPL| $15 B+

Caves Aliança, 1999 *Galeria Tinta Roriz*
DOURO, POR   IE| A-   PV| WPL| B $9 A-

Caves Aliança, 1998 *Foral Grande Escolha*
DOURO, POR   IE| B+   PV| WPL| $13 B+

Caves Aliança, 1997 *Quinta da Terrugem*
ALENTEJO, POR   IE| A-   PV| WPL| $20 A-

Campo Ardosa, 2000 *Carvalhosa*
DOURO, POR   IE| A+   PV| WPL| S $28 A+

Casa de Santar, 1999 *Reserva*
DÃO, POR   IE| A-   PV| WPL| $15 A-

Quinto do Casal Branco, 1999 *Castelao/Trincadeira, Falcoaria*
RIBATEJO, POR   IE| A-   PV| WPL| $15 A-

Dão Sul, 2000 *Quinta da Cabris Colheita Seleccionada*
DÃO, POR   IE| B+   PV| WPL| B $6 B+

Dão Sul, 2000 *Touriga Nacional, Quinta de Cabriz*
DÃO, POR   IE| A   PV| WPL| $19 A

Dão Sul, 1999 *Quinta de Cabriz Alfrocheiro Preto*
DÃO, POR   IE| A   PV| WPL| $16 A

DFJ, 2000 *Grand'Arte Alicante Bouschet*
ESTREMADURA, POR   IE| A   PV| WPL| $20 A

DFJ, 2000 *Tinta Miuda-Cabernet Sauvignon*
ESTREMADURA, POR   IE| A-   PV| WPL| B $9 A-

DFJ, 2000 *Tinta Roriz-Merlot*
ESTREMADURA, POR   IE| A   PV| WPL| B $10 A

DFJ, 2000 *Touriga Nacional, Grand'Arte*
ESTREMADURA, POR   IE| A   PV| WPL| S $30 A

PORTUGAL

OTHER RED (CONTINUED)

DFJ, 2000 *Touriga Nacional-Touriga Franca*
ESTREMADURA, POR IE| A- PV| WPL| $23 A-

José Maria da Fonseca, 2000 *Domini*
DOURO, POR IE| B+ PV| WPL| $15 B+

José Maria da Fonseca, 2000 *Domini Plus*
DOURO, POR IE| A+ PV| WPL| $25 A+

Herdade de Esporão, 2000 *Aragones*
ALENTEJO, POR IE| B+ PV| WPL| $14 B+

Herdade de Esporão, 2000 *Esporão Reserva*
ALENTEJO, POR IE| A PV| WPL| $15 A

Herdade de Esporão, 2000 *Touriga Nacional*
ALENTEJO, POR IE| A- PV| WPL| $15 A-

Luis Pato, 2000 *Vinha Barrosa Vina Velha*
BEIRAS, POR IE| A PV| WPL| S $29 A

Luis Pato, 2000 *Vinha Pan*
BEIRAS, POR IE| A- PV| WPL| $13 A-

Compania das Quintas, 1999 *Quinta do Cardo Touriga*
BEIRA INTERIOR, POR IE| B+ PV| WPL| $14 B+

J. Portugal Ramos, 2001 *Vila Santa*
ALENTEJO, POR IE| A- PV| 99 A- WPL| $20 A-

J. Portugal Ramos, 2000 *Marques de Borba Reserva*
ALENTEJO, POR IE| B+ PV| WPL| $12 B+

Quinta de Romera, 1999 *Fronteira Reserva*
DOURO, POR IE| B+ PV| WPL| $11 B+

Quinta dos Roques, 2001
DOURO, POR IE| A- PV| WPL| $18 A-

Quinta dos Roques, 2000 *Tinta Roriz*
DÃO, POR IE| A- PV| WPL| $22 A-

Quinta de Roriz, 2001 *Prazo de Roriz*
DOURO, POR IE| B+ PV| WPL| $13 B+

Quinta de Roriz, 2000 *Reserva*
DOURO, POR IE| A PV| WPL| S $29 A

Cooperativa Agricola de Santo, Isidro de Pegoes, 2000 *Cabernet/Touriga Nacional, Adega de Peg'es Colheita Seleccionada*
TERRAS DO SADO, POR IE| A- PV| WPL| $13 A-

Faldas da Serra, 2000 *Quintas das Maias Jaen*
DÃO, POR IE| A PV| WPL| $22 A

J. P. Vinhos, 1995 *J. P. Garrafeira, Palmela*
TERRAS DO SADO, POR IE| A PV| WPL| B $9 A

WHITES

ALBARIÑO

Adega de Monção, 2001 *Alvarinho*
VINHO VERDE, POR   IE| B+   PV| WPL| $11 B+

A. Esteves Ferreira, 2001 *Alvarinho, Soalheiro*
VINHO VERDE, POR   IE| A+   PV| 99 A   WPL| $14 A+

Quinta da Pedra, 2001 *Alvarinho*
VINHO VERDE, POR   IE| A+   PV| 99 A+   WPL| B $10 A+

Portal do Fidalgo, 2001 *Alvarinho*
VINHO VERDE, POR   IE| B+   PV| 99 A-, 00 A-   WPL| $15 B+

OTHER WHITE

Arca Nova, 2001
VINHO VERDE, POR   IE| B+   PV| 00 A   WPL| B $6 B+

Quinta da Aveleda, 2001 *Loureiro*
VINHO VERDE, POR   IE| B+   PV| WPL| B $8 B+

Quinta da Aveleda, 2001 *Trajadura*
VINHO VERDE, POR   IE| B+   PV| WPL| B $8 B+

Casa de Vila Verde, 2001
VINHO VERDE, POR   IE| B+   PV| WPL| B $7 B+

Casa de Vila Verde, 2001 *Senhorio d'Agras*
VINHO VERDE, POR   IE| A   PV| WPL| B $8 A

Casa do Valle, 2001
VINHO VERDE, POR   IE| B+   PV| WPL| B $6 B+

Ponte do Lima, 2001 *Loureiro, Encostas do Lima*
VINHO VERDE, POR   IE| B+   PV| WPL| B $6 B+

SWEET

PORT

Cálem, 1997 *LBV Port, Bottled 2002*
DOURO, POR   IE| A-   PV| WPL| $23 A-

Gould Campbell, 1996 *LBV Port, Bottled 2002*
DOURO, POR   IE| A   PV| WPL| $20 A

Quinta de Crasto, 1996 *LBV Port, Bottled 2000*
DOURO, POR   IE| A-   PV| WPL| $20 A-

Dow, 1996 *LBV Port, Bottled 2002*
DOURO, POR   IE| A-   PV| WPL| $20 A-

José Maria da Fonseca, 1996 *Late Bottled Vintage*
DOURO, POR   IE| A-, A   PV| WPL| BBC $21 A

Niepoort, 1998 *LBV Port, Bottled 2002*
DOURO, POR   IE| A-   PV| WPL| $22 A-

Niepoort, 1997 *LBV Port, Bottled 2001*
DOURO, POR   IE| A-   PV| WPL| $20 A-

PORTUGAL

PORT (CONTINUED)

Ramos-Pinto, NV *Urtiga*

| POR | IE| B+ | PV| | | WPL| | $16 | B+ |

Ramos-Pinto, 1996 *Late Bottle Vintage*

| POR | IE| B+ | PV| | | WPL| | $15 | B+ |

Ramos-Pinto, 1995 *LBV Port, Bottled 1999*

| DOURO, POR | IE| B+ | PV| | | WPL| | $15 | B+ |

Warre's, NV *Tawny, 10-Year-Old, Optima*

| DOURO, POR | IE| A | PV| | | WPL| | $25 | A |

Warre's, 1992 *Late-Bottled, Traditional, Bottled in 1996*

| DOURO, POR | IE| A-, A | PV| | WPL| BBC | $23 | A |

"ANYONE WHO TRIES TO MAKE YOU BELIEVE THAT HE KNOWS ALL ABOUT WINES IS OBVIOUSLY A FAKE."

Leon Adams

"THE COMMONSENSE BOOK OF WINE," 1962

COMPREHENSIVE BUYING GUIDES TO TOP RATED WINES

SOUTH AFRICA

REDS

CABERNET FRANC

Bellevue, 2001 *Umkhulu Titan*
STELLENBOSCH, SA   IE| A-   PV| WPL| $23 A-

Warwick, 2000 *Estate Reserve*
STELLENBOSCH, SA   IE| A   PV| WPL| S $29 A

CABERNET SAUVIGNON

Cathedral, 1999
COASTAL REGION, SA   IE| B+   PV| WPL| $15 B+

Dakensig, 2001 *Coastal*
SA   IE| B+   PV| WPL| $13 B+

Guardian Peak, 2001
STELLENBOSCH, SA   IE| B+   PV| WPL| B $10 B+

KWV, 2000
WESTERN CAPE, SA   IE| A-   PV| WPL| B $10 A-

Laborie, 2001
PAARL, SA   IE| B+   PV| WPL| $12 B+

Rust en Vrede, 1999
STELLENBOSCH, SA   IE| B+   PV| WPL| $20 B+

Thelema, 2000
STELLENBOSCH, SA   IE| A   PV| 99 A   WPL| S $30 A

Thelema, 1999
STELLENBOSCH, SA   IE| A   PV| WPL| S $30 A

MERLOT

Du Preez, 2000
GOUDINI VALLEY, SA   IE| B+   PV| WPL| $11 B+

KWV, 2001
WESTERN CAPE, SA   IE| B+   PV| WPL| B $10 B+

Porcupine Ridge, 2001
COASTAL REGION, SA   IE| B+   PV| WPL| $13 B+

Thelema, 1999
STELLENBOSCH, SA   IE| A-   PV| WPL| S $27 A-

SYRAH/SHIRAZ

Fairview, 2000
PAARL, SA   IE| A-   PV| WPL| S $28 A-

Guardian Peak, 2001
WESTERN CAPE, SA   IE| B+   PV| WPL| B $9 B+

SOUTH AFRICA

Two Oceans, 2001
WESTERN CAPE, SA   IE| B+   PV| WPL| B $7   B+

OTHER RED

Baobab, 2001 *Pinotage*
WESTERN CAPE, SA   IE| B+   PV| WPL| B $10   B+

Bellevue, 2001 *Cabernet/Pinotage Atticus*
STELLENBOSCH, SA   IE| B+   PV| WPL| $15   B+

Fairview, 2001 *Carignane, Pegleg*
PAARL, SA   IE| B+   PV| WPL| $25   B+

Fairview, 2001 *Pinotage*
PAARL, SA   IE| A   PV| 00 B+   WPL| $25   A

Kanonkop, 2000 *Pinotage*
STELLENBOSCH, SA   IE| A-   PV| 99 A-   WPL| S $28   A-

KWV, 2001 *Roodeberg*
WESTERN CAPE, SA   IE| B+   PV| WPL| $13   B+

Warwick, 2000 *Cabernet/Merlot/Pinotage Three Cape Ladies*
STELLENBOSCH, SA   IE| A+   PV| WPL| $23   A+

WHITES

CHARDONNAY

Buitenverwachting, 2001
CONSTANTIA, SA   IE| B+   PV| WPL| $15   B+

Cathedral, 2001
WESTERN CAPE, SA   IE| A-   PV| WPL| W $12   A-

De Wetshof, 2001 *Bon Vallon*
ROBERTSON, SA   IE| A-   PV| 00 B+   WPL| $14   A-

Morgenhof, 1999
STELLENBOSCH, SA   IE| A-   PV| WPL| $14   A-

Pine Crest, 2000
FRANSCHHOEK, SA   IE| B+   PV| WPL| $13   B+

Simonsig, 2000
STELLENBOSCH, SA   IE| B+, B, B, B+ PV| WPL| B $10   B+

CHENIN BLANC

Mulderbosch, 2002
STELLENBOSCH, SA   IE| B+   PV| WPL| $14   B+

SAUVIGNON/FUMÉ BLANC

Boschendal, 2002 *Grande Cuvée*
COASTAL REGION, SA   IE| B+   PV| 99 B+   WPL| $14   B+

Boschendal, 2002
COASTAL REGION, SA   IE| B+   PV| WPL| $12   B+

Brampton, 2002
COASTAL, SA   IE| B+   PV| WPL| B $10   B+

Clos Malverne, 2001
STELLENBOSCH, SA   IE| A, B, B+   PV| WPL| $15   B+

Du Preez, 2001
GOUDINI VALLEY, SA   IE| B+   PV| WPL| B $9   B+

Groot Constantia, 2001
CONSTANTIA, SA   IE| A+   PV| WPL| $15   A+

Kanu, 2002 *Limited Release*
STELLENBOSCH, SA   IE| B+   PV| WPL| $13   B+

Klein Constantia, 2001
CONSTANTIA, SA   IE| A+, B   PV| WPL| BBC $15   A-

Morgenhof Estate, 2002 *Simonsberg*
STELLENBOSCH, SA   IE| B+   PV| WPL| $12   B+

Thelema, 2002
STELLENBOSCH, SA   IE| B+   PV| WPL| $16   B+

OTHER WHITE

Fairview, 2001 *Semillon, Oom Pagel*
PAARL, SA   IE| B+   PV| WPL| $25   B+

"IF ALL BE TRUE THAT I DO THINK,
THERE ARE FIVE REASONS WE SHOULD DRINK;
GOOD WINE — A FRIEND — OR BEING DRY —
OR LEST WE SHOULD BE BY AND BY —
OR ANY OTHER REASON WHY."

Henry Aldrich

"FIVE REASONS FOR DRINKING," COLUMBIA
DICTIONARY OF QUOTATIONS, 1995

SOUTH AFRICA

COMPREHENSIVE BUYING GUIDES TO TOP RATED WINES

SPAIN

REDS

CABERNET SAUVIGNON

Covides, 1996 *Gran Castellflorit Reserva*
PENEDÈS, SP — IE| B+ — PV| — WPL| B — $10 B+

Lazzaro, 2000
MENDOZA, SP — IE| B+ — PV| — WPL| — $12 B+

Condesa de Leganza, 1998 *Crianza*
MANCHA, SP — IE| B+ — PV| — WPL| B — $9 B+

GRENACHE

Borja, 2001 *Borsao*
CAMPO DE BORJA, SP — IE| B+ — PV| 00 B+ — WPL| B — $6 B+

Borja, 2001 *Borsao, 3 Picos*
CAMPO DE BORJA, SP — IE| A- — PV| 00 A- — WPL| B — $10 A-

Castillo de Maluenda, 2001 *Viña Alarba*
CALATAYUD, SP — IE| B+ — PV| — WPL| B — $6 B+

Castillo de Maluenda, 2001 *Viña Alarba, Old Vines*
CALATAYUD, SP — IE| B+ — PV| — WPL| B — $6 B+

TEMPRANILLO

Marqués de Arienzo, 1998 *Crianza*
RIOJA, SP — IE| B+ — PV| — WPL| B — $10 B+

Marqués de Arienzo, 1994 *Gran Reserva*
RIOJA, SP — IE| A- — PV| — WPL| — $25 A-

Artadi, 1999 *Viñas de Gain*
RIOJA, SP — IE| A- — PV| — WPL| — $18 A-

Ramon Bibao, 1999 *Limited Edition Crianza*
RIOJA, SP — IE| B+ — PV| — WPL| — $13 B+

Ramon Bibao, 1999
RIOJA, SP — IE| B+ — PV| — WPL| B — $10 B+

Bodegas Bilbainas, 1996 *La Vicalanda de Viña Pomal, Reserva*
RIOJA, SP — IE| A-, B+ — PV| — WPL| BBC — $20 A-

Bodegas Breton, 1999 *Loriñon, Crianza*
RIOJA, SP — IE| B+ — PV| — WPL| — $11 B+

Marqués de Cáceres, 1994 *Reserva*
RIOJA, SP — IE| A, B+ — PV| — WPL| S,BBC — $26 A-

CVNE (CUNE), 1996 *Viña Real, Reserva*
RIOJA, SP — IE| A, A, B, B — PV| — WPL| S — $29 B+

Viña Izadi, 1999 *Crianza*
RIOJA, SP — IE| B+ — PV| — WPL| — $14 B+

Montegaredo, 1999 *Tinto*
RIBERA DEL DUERO, SP IE| B+   PV| WPL| $13 B+

Navarrsotillo, 1999 *Crianza Magister Bibendi*
RIOJA, SP   IE| B+   PV| WPL| $11 B+

Bodega Nekeas, 1999
SP   IE| B+   PV| WPL| B $10 B+

Marqués del Puerto, 1999 *Crianza*
RIOJA, SP   IE| B+   PV| WPL| $12 B+

Marqués de Riscal, 1995 *Gran Reserva*
RIOJA, SP   IE| B+   PV| WPL| $15 B+

Viña Salceda, 1998
RIOJA, SP   IE| A-   PV| WPL| $15 A-

Hnos. Sastre, 2000 *Viña Sastre*
RIBERA DEL DUERO, SP IE| B+   PV| WPL| $14 B+

Vallobera, 1999 *Crianza*
RIOJA, SP   IE| B+   PV| WPL| $15 B+

Campo Viejo, 1998 *Crianza*
RIOJA, SP   IE| A-   PV| WPL| B $10 A-

Paisajes y Viñedos, 1999 *Paisajes V Vinas Seleccionadas*
RIOJA, SP   IE| A-   PV| WPL| $23 A-

OTHER RED

Abadia Retuerta, 2001 *Rivola*
SARDON DE DUERO, SP IE| A-   PV| 99 A-   WPL| $12 A-

Marqués de Arienzo, 1998 *Crianza*
RIOJA, SP   IE| B+   PV| WPL| B $10 B+

Artadi, 2000 *Viñas de Gain*
RIOJA, SP   IE| A-   PV| 99 A-   WPL| $22 A-

Berberana, 1997 *Garnacha/Mazuelo/Tempranillo, Viña Alarde Reserva*
RIOJA, SP   IE| B+   PV| WPL| $18 B+

Campo Viejo, 1995 *Gran Reserva*
RIOJA, SP   IE| A-   PV| WPL| $25 A-

Casa de la Ermita, 2000 *Tinto*
JUMILLA, SP   IE| A-   PV| 99 A-   WPL| $12 A-

Casa de la Ermita, 2000
JUMILLA, SP   IE| B+   PV| WPL| $12 B+

Castaño, 2001 *Hecula*
YECLA, SP   IE| A   PV| 99 A-   WPL| B $9 A

Castaño, 2001 *Solanera*
YECLA, SP   IE| A+   PV| 99 A-, 00 A-   WPL| $12 A+

Castillo, 2001 *Mourvedre, Monastrell*
JUMILLA, SP   IE| B+   PV| 99 B+   WPL| B $9 B+

Condado de Haza, 2000
RIBERA DEL DUERO, SP IE| B+   PV| WPL| W $20 B+

Enate, 1999 *Crianza*
SOMONTANO, SP   IE| B+   PV| WPL| $12 B+

SPAIN

OTHER RED (CONTINUED)

Gran Cermeño, 1996 *Reserva*
TORO, SP   IE| A   PV| WPL| $19   A

Guelbenzu, 2000 *Azul*
RIBERA DEL QUEILES, SP IE| B+   PV| WPL| $13   B+

R. Lopez de Heredia , 1993 *Garnacha/Malvasia/Viura, Vina Tondonia*
RIOJA, SP   IE| A-   PV| WPL| $21   A-

Marqués de Monistrol, 2000 *Cabernet/Tempranillo*
PENEDÈS, SP   IE| B+   PV| WPL| B $7   B+

Marqués de Monistrol, 1999 *Masia Monistrol Single Vineyard Reserva Especial Cabernet/Merlot*
PENEDÈS, SP   IE| A-   PV| WPL| $20   A-

Marqués de Monistrol, 1998 *Reserva Privada*
PENEDÈS, SP   IE| B+   PV| WPL| W, B $10   B+

Bodegas Montecillo, 1998 *Crianza*
RIOJA, SP   IE| B+   PV| WPL| $12   B+

Bodegas Montecillo, 1997 *Reserva*
RIOJA, SP   IE| A-   PV| WPL| $17   A-

Ontañon, 1994 *Gran Reserva*
RIOJA, SP   IE| A   PV| WPL| S $30   A

Alvaro Palacios, 1999 *Les Terrasses*
PRIORAT, SP   IE| A-   PV| WPL| $25   A-

Castillo de Perelada, 2000 *Emporda Costa Brava Tinto Crianza*
SP   IE| B+   PV| WPL| B $10   B+

Viñas Pomal, 1996 *La Vicalanda Reserva*
RIOJA, SP   IE| A-   PV| WPL| $21   A-

Cims de Porrera, 2000 *Solanes, Denominacion de Orgen*
SP   IE| A-   PV| WPL| $24   A-

Castell del Remei, 2000 *Gotim Bru*
COSTERS DEL SEGRE, SP IE| A   PV| WPL| B $10   A

Remelluri, 2000
RIOJA, SP   IE| A   PV| WPL| $24   A

Rotllan Torra, 1997 *Garnacha-Carinena-Cabernet Sauvignon, Reserva*
PRIORAT, SP   IE| B+   PV| WPL| $15   B+

Finca Sobreno, 2000 *Crianza*
TORO, SP   IE| B+   PV| WPL| $12   B+

Vall Llach, 1999 *Embruix,*
PRIORAT, SP   IE| A   PV| WPL| $25   A

Venta Mazzaron, 2001
TORO, SP   IE| B+   PV| WPL| B $10   B+

WHITES

ALBARIÑO

Palacio de Fefinanes, 2001
RÍAS BAIXAS, SP　　IE| B+　　　　PV|　　　　　　　WPL|　　　　$15　B+

Pazo de Barrantes, 2001
RÍAS BAIXAS, SP　　IE| A-　　　　PV|　　　　　　　WPL|　　　　$15　A-

Pazo de Señorans, 2001
RÍAS BAIXAS, SP　　IE| A-　　　　PV| 99 A+, 00 A-　WPL|　　　　$15　A-

Pedro de Soutomaior, 2000
RÍAS BAIXAS, SP　　IE| B+　　　　PV| 99 A-　　　　WPL|　　　　$15　B+

OTHER WHITE

Martinsancho, 2001 *Verdejo*
RUEDA, SP　　　　IE| B+　　　　PV|　　　　　　　WPL| B　$10　B+

Marqués de Murrieta, 1997 *Ygay, Capellania*
RIOJA, SP　　　　IE| B+　　　　PV|　　　　　　　WPL|　　　　$15　B+

ROSÉ

Vega Sindoa (Nekeas), 2001
NAVARRA, SP　　　IE| B+, B+　　PV|　　　　　　　WPL| B　$6　B+

SPARKLING

Avinyo, NV *Cava, Brut*
SP　　　　　　IE| B+　　　　PV|　　　　　　　WPL|　　　　$13　B+

Cordorniu, NV *Cava, Brut, Pinot Noir*
SP　　　　　　IE| B+　　　　PV| ·　　　　　　WPL|　　　　$11　B+

Jaume Serra, NV *Cava, Extra Dry, Cristalino*
SP　　　　　　IE| B+　　　　PV|　　　　　　　WPL| B　$9　B+

Juvé y Camps, NV *Cava, Brut, Gran Juvé*
SP　　　　　　IE| A+　　　　PV|　　　　　　　WPL| S　$30　A+

Marqués de Monistrol, NV *Reserva Brut (Cava)*
SP　　　　　　IE| B+　　　　PV|　　　　　　　WPL| B　$9　B+

Parxet, NV *Cava, Pinot Noir, Cuvée Dessert*
SP　　　　　　IE| A　　　　　PV|　　　　　　　WPL|　　　　$17　A

Agusti Torello, 1999 *Cava, Brut Reserva*
SP　　　　　　IE| B+　　　　PV|　　　　　　　WPL|　　　　$12　B+

Agusti Torello, 1998 *Cava, Gran Reserva Extra Brut*
SP　　　　　　IE| B+　　　　PV|　　　　　　　WPL|　　　　$16　B+

SWEET

SHERRY

Antonio Barbadillo, NV *Cream, Eva*
JEREZ, SP　　　　IE| A-　　　　PV|　　　　　　　WPL|　　　　$12　A-

SPAIN

SHERRY (CONTINUED)

Antonio Barbadillo, NV *Oloroso, Full Dry*
JEREZ, SP   IE| B+   PV| WPL| W, B $9   B+

Antonio Barbadillo, NV *Oloroso, Seco Cuco*
JEREZ, SP   IE| A-   PV| WPL| S $30   A-

Antonio Barbadillo, NV *Pedro Ximénez, Extra Rich*
JEREZ, SP   IE| B+   PV| WPL| $15   B+

Hidalgo, NV *Cream, Napoléon*
JEREZ, SP   IE| B+   PV| WPL| $12   B+

Hildago, NV *Pedro Ximénez, Viejo*
JEREZ, SP   IE| A-   PV| WPL| $18   A-

Emilio Lustau, NV *East India Solera*
JEREZ, SP   IE| A-   PV| WPL| $18   A-

Toro Albalá, 1975 *Pedro Ximénez, Don Gran Reserva*
MONTILLA-MORILES, SP IE| A-   PV| WPL| S $28   A-

OTHER SWEET

Caves Aliance, 1999 *Single Estate, Quinta dos Quatro Ventos*
DOURO, SP   IE| A   PV| WPL| S $30   A

Antonio Barbadillo, NV *Moscatel, Laura*
JEREZ, SP   IE| A-   PV| WPL| $22   A-

Quinta do Crasto, 1998 *Reserva*
DOURO, SP   IE| A   PV| WPL| S $28   A

Quintas Juntas, 2000 *Reserva*
DOURO, SP   IE| A   PV| WPL| $20   A

Domingos Alves Sousa, 2001 *Quinta do Vale da Raposa*
DOURO, SP   IE| B+   PV| WPL| B $9   B+

**"AS FAR AS I AM CONCERNED, THERE ARE ONLY TWO
TYPES OF WINE, THOSE I LIKE AND THOSE I DON'T."**

**FROM "THE ESSENTIAL WINE BUFF,"
EDITED BY JENNIFER TAYLOR, 1996**

COMPREHENSIVE BUYING GUIDES TO TOP RATED WINES

OTHER COUNTRIES

ARGENTINA

CABERNET SAUVIGNON

Terra Rosa, 2000
MENDOZA, ARG — IE| B+ — PV| — WPL| B — $10 — B+

MALBEC

Broquel, 2000
MENDOZA, ARG — IE| B+ — PV| — WPL| — $15 — B+

Cavas del Valle, 2000
MENDOZA, ARG — IE| B+ — PV| — WPL| — $15 — B+

Davis Family, 2000 *Gusto Vita*
MENDOZA, ARG — IE| A- — PV| — WPL| S — $30 — A-

Felipe Rutini, 2000
TUPUNGATO, ARG — IE| A- — PV| — WPL| — $18 — A-

Susana Balbo, 2001 *Mendoza Crios*
MENDOZA, ARG — IE| B+ — PV| — WPL| — $15 — B+

Vinterra, 1999
LUJAN DE CUYO, ARG — IE| A- — PV| — WPL| — $15 — A-

SYRAH/SHIRAZ

Vinterra, 1999
MENDOZA, ARG — IE| A- — PV| — WPL| B — $10 — A-

CHARDONNAY

Anastasia, 2001
MENDOZA, ARG — IE| B+ — PV| — WPL| B — $10 — B+

Catena, 2001 *Agrelo Vineyards*
MENDOZA, ARG — IE| A- — PV| — WPL| — $20 — A-

SAUVIGNON/FUMÉ BLANC

Valentin Bianchi, 2002
MENDOZA, ARG — IE| B+ — PV| — WPL| — $12 — B+

AUSTRIA

OTHER RED

Nittnaus, 2000 *Blaufränkisch/Cabernet, Qualitätswein Trocken*
BURGENLAND, AUT — IE| A- — PV| — WPL| S — $28 — A-

RIESLING

Bründlmayer, 2001 *Steinmassel, Lagenlois*
KAMPTAL, AUT   IE| A, A+   PV| 99 A-, 00 A   WPL| BBC   **$25**   A

R. & A. Pfaffl, 2001 *Terrassen Sonnleiten Riesling*
WEINVIERTEL, AUT   IE| A+   PV| WPL| **$18**   A+

Prager, 1998 *Federspiel, Weissenkirchen Steinriegl*
WACHAU, AUT   IE| A-   PV| WPL| **$22**   A-

Weingut Salomon (Undhof), 2001 *Kremser Koegl*
KREMSTAL, AUT   IE| A-   PV| WPL| **$23**   A-

Weingut Salomon (Undhof), 2001 *Pfaffenberg*
KREMSTAL, AUT   IE| A   PV| WPL| **$18**   A

Sonnhof, 2001 *Qualitätswein Trocken, Zoebinger Heiligensteirn*
KAMPTAL, AUT   IE| A-, A-   PV| WPL| S,BBC   **$28**   A-

SAUVIGNON/FUMÉ BLANC

Alois Gross, 1999 *Sulz*
AUT   IE| A-   PV| WPL| S   **$30**   A-

Manfred Tement, 2001 *Grassnitzberg*
SUDSTEIERMARK, AUT   IE| A   PV| WPL| S   **$30**   A

Manfred Tement, 2001 *Zieregg*
SUDSTEIERMARK, AUT   IE| A   PV| WPL| **$25**   A

OTHER WHITE

Leopold & Silvane Sommer, 2001 *Grüner Veltliner*
NEUSIEDLERSEE, AUT   IE| A   PV| WPL| **$13**   A

R. & A. Pfaffl, 2001 *Grüner Veltliner, Trocken, Hundsleiten/Sandtal*
WEINVIERTEL, AUT   IE| A-   PV| WPL| **$18**   A-

R. & A. Pfaffl, 2001 *Grüner Veltliner, Goldjoch*
WEINVIERTEL, AUT   IE| A+   PV| WPL| **$18**   A+

R. & A. Pfaffl, 2000 *Grüner Veltliner, Hundsleiten/Sandtal*
WEINVIERTEL, AUT   IE| A   PV| WPL| **$18**   A

Jurtschitsch Sonnhof, 2001 *Grüner Veltliner, Schenkenbichl*
KAMPTAL, AUT   IE| A-   PV| WPL| **$25**   A-

CANADA

CABERNET FRANC

Colio, 1999 *Reserve, CEV, Lake Erie North Shore*
ONTARIO, CAN   IE| B+   PV| WPL| **$15**   B+

Hernder Estate, 1999 *Niagara Peninsula*
ONTARIO, CAN   IE| A   PV| WPL| **$11**   A

GAMAY

Sandhill, 2001 *Gamay Noir, Burrowing Owl Vineyard, Okanagan Valley*
BC, CAN   IE| B+   PV| WPL| **$11**   B+

Sandstone, 2000 *Reserve, Niagara Peninsula*
ONTARIO, CAN   IE| A   PV| 99 A   WPL| $19   A

MERLOT

Lakeview, 1999 *Reserve, Niagara Peninsula*
ONTARIO, CAN   IE| A   PV| WPL| $23   A

Stoney Ridge, 1999 *Reserve, Niagara Peninsula*
ONTARIO, CAN   IE| B+   PV| WPL| $14   B+

Sumac Ridge, 1999 *Black Sage Vineyard, Okanagan Valley*
BC, CAN   IE| A   PV| WPL| $11   A

OTHER RED

Inniskillin Okanagan, 1999 *Meritage, Reserve, Niagara Peninsula*
ONTARIO, CAN   IE| A-   PV| WPL| $13   A-

Jackson-Triggs, 1999 *Meritage Grand Reserve, Niagara Peninsula*
ONTARIO, CAN   IE| A-   PV| WPL| $17   A-

Maleta, 1999 *Meritage, Niagara Peninsula*
ONTARIO, CAN   IE| A   PV| WPL| $19   A

CHARDONNAY

Sandhill, 2001 *Burrowing Owl Vineyard, Okanagan Valley*
BC, CAN   IE| B+   PV| WPL| $11   B+

RIESLING

Sandstone, 2000 *Select Late Harvest, Niagara Peninsula*
ONTARIO, CAN   IE| A+   PV| WPL| $14   A+

OTHER WHITE

Sandhill, 2001 *Semillon, Burrowing Owl Vineyard, Okanagan Valley*
BC, CAN   IE| B+   PV| WPL| $14   B+

ROSÉ

Peninsula Ridge, 2000 *Cabernet Franc, Niagara Peninsula*
ONTARIO, CAN   IE| B+   PV| WPL| B $8   B+

Vineland, 2000 *Niagara Peninsula*
ONTARIO, CAN   IE| B+   PV| WPL| B $9   B+

GREECE

MERLOT

Boutari, 2000 *Merlot-Xinomavro, Imathia*
GRC   IE| B+   PV| 99 B+   WPL| $11   B+

Ktima Kyr-Yianni, 1999 *Imathia Yiannakohori*
NÁOUSSA, GRC   IE| A   PV| WPL| S $28   A

SYRAH/SHIRAZ

Ktima Kyr-Yianni, 1999 *Imathia Yiannakohori*
GRC   IE| A-   PV| WPL| S $28   A-

OTHER RED

Boutari, 2000 *Goumenissa*
GRC   IE| B+   PV| WPL| $11   B+

Boutari, 1997 *Grand Reserve*
NÁOUSSA, GRC   IE| A-   PV| WPL| $15   A-

Gaia, 2000 *Agiorghitiko*
NEMEA, GRC   IE| A-   PV| WPL| $20   A-

Ionian, 1998 *Agiorghitiko, Veros Moriatikos*
PELOPONNESE, GRC   IE| B+   PV| WPL| B $10   B+

Ktima Kyr-Yianni, 1998 *Imathia Yiannakohori*
GRC   IE| A   PV| WPL| $19   A

Ktima Kyr-Yianni, 1997 *Xinomavro, Ramnista*
NÁOUSSA, GRC   IE| A+   PV| WPL| $15   A+

Dom. Mercouri, 1999 *Refosco*
GRC   IE| B+   PV| WPL| $15   B+

Skouras, 1998 *Megas Oenos*
PELOPONNESE, GRC   IE| A   PV| WPL| $19   A

Tsantali, 1997 *Rapsani Reserve, Epilegmonos*
GRC   IE| A-   PV| WPL| $18   A-

Dom. Tselepos, 2000 *Agiorghitiko*
NEMEA, GRC   IE| A-   PV| WPL| $15   A-

OTHER WHITE

Boutari, 2001 *Kallisti*
ANTORINI, GRC   IE| B+   PV| 99 A, 00 A   WPL| $15   B+

Boutari, 2001 *Moschofilero*
ARCADIA, GRC   IE| B+   PV| WPL| $12   B+

Boutari, 2000
NEMEA, GRC   IE| B+   PV| WPL| B $10   B+

Boutari, 2000 *Kallisti*
SANTORINI, GRC   IE| A   PV| 99 A   WPL| $17   A

Dom. Gerovassiliou, 2001 *White*
THESSALONIKI, GRC   IE| A-   PV| WPL| $13   A-

Kourtaki, 2000 *Assyrtiko*
SANTORINI, GRC   IE| B+   PV| WPL| $11   B+

Samos, 2000 *Grand Cru Vin Doux Naturel*
SAMOS, GRC   IE| B+   PV| WPL| B $10   B+

Vegoritis, 2000 *Florina Samaropetra*
GRC   IE| B+   PV| WPL| $13   B+

ROSÉ

Gaia, 2001 *14-18th*
PELOPONNESE, GRC   IE| B+   PV| WPL| B $8   B+

OTHER SWEET

Samos, 2000 *Muscat, Grand Cru*
GRC   IE| A-   PV| WPL| $20   A-

GLOSSARY OF WINE TERMS

———— ✎ ————

*T*his glossary of wine terms covers basic wine types, growing regions, and technical and tasting terms, providing you with the essential information you'll need to decipher wine labels and tasting notes, or easily translate from "wine-ese" if you find yourself questioning the intent or meaning of a particular wine writer or critic.

Though Wine PocketList guides don't focus on the descriptors most wine writers use to communicate their experience with a particular bottle of wine, it is helpful to understand the basic "verbal building blocks" used to articulate the highly personal experience of enjoying wine.

A

ACETIC ACID All wines contain acetic acid or vinegar, normally the amount is quite small, somewhere between .03 percent–.06 percent, and not noticeable to taste or smell. Once wines reach .07 percent to just under .10 percent, a sweet, sour vinegary smell and taste becomes noticeable. At low levels, acetic acid can enhance the flavor of a wine, while at higher levels—over 0.1 percent—this flavor can dominate and flaw the wine.

ACID An essential component of wine, that preserves it, enlivens, shapes its flavors, and helps prolong its aftertaste. There are four major kinds of acids—tartaric, malic, lactic, citric—found in wine. Acid contributes to the crispness and longevity of a wine, particularly white wine. Acid is identifiable by the crisp, sharp character it imparts to a wine.

ACIDIC A term used to describe wines whose total acid is so high that they taste tart or sour and have a sharp edge on the palate.

AERATION The process of letting a wine 'breathe' in the open air or the swirling of wine in a glass. It's a cause for debate whether aerating bottled wines, usually reds, improves their quality, as aeration can soften young, tannic wines, but fatigue older ones.

AFTERTASTE The taste or flavors that linger in the mouth after tasting or swallowing wine. Also known as a wine's finish, the aftertaste or finish is one of the most important factors in judging a wine's character or quality. Some say great wines have rich, long, complex aftertastes. Aftertastes may also be harsh, hot, soft, lingering, short, smooth, tannic or non existent.

ALBARIÑO *(Ahl-ba-REE-n'yo)* Albariño is a premium white wine grape grown in the Galicia region of Spain. The skin is so thick, that only a small amount of juice can be squeezed from it. The results are often creamy citrus and peachy. Albariños are crisp, refreshing and light bodied.

ALCOHOL This integral component of wine is a natural by-product of fermentation, and one of the mainstays of perceived flavor. Most wines range from 7 percent to 14 percent alcohol by volume.

ALEATICO *(ah lay AH tee co)* A red member of the Muscat family of grapes and a popular variety in Italy, where it produces an array of table and dessert wines, also found in California

ALICANTE BOUSCHET *(ah lee KAHNT boo SHAY)* A unique grape variety that was developed in France in the late 1880s by Henri Bouschet. It is unique in that it is the only red grape variety that actually possesses red flesh. All other red grape varieties get their color from their skins, not their juice. Also found in California's Central Valley.

ALIGOTE *(Ah lee go TAY)* Burgundian white-wine grape. Usually a medium-bodied, crisp, dry wine with spicy character.

ALSACE *(Al ZAHSS)* Northeastern province of France, bordering the Rhine, known for its rich dry white wines made from grapes of German heritage, primarily Riesling and Gewürztraminer. The wines are light to full bodied with great varietal character. Alsace has nearly 100 picturesque villages and also produces wonderful late harvest sweet wines.

AMARONE *(Ah ma ROE nay)* A powerful, hearty dry red wine from Italy's Veneto region, made from a blend of partially dried red grapes.

AMERICAN OAK Used primarily for aging Cabernet, Merlot and Zinfandel, this alternative to French Oak is becoming increasingly popular for making wine aging barrels. Marked by distinct vanilla, dill and cedar notes. Used occasionally for Pinot Noir and Chardonnay.

AMERICAN VITICULTURAL AREA (AVA) In the USA, a delimited, geographical grape-growing area that has officially been given appellation status by the Bureau of Alcohol, Tobacco and Firearms. The Napa Valley and the Sonoma Valley are two examples.

AMONTILLADO *(Ah mon tee YAH doe)* A dry, rather full-bodied style of Sherry from Spain, aged in barrels, made famous by Edgar Allan Poe.

APERITIF A French word that describes an alcoholic beverage served before dinner to stimulate the appetite. Traditional French examples include kir, Lillet and both sweet and dry vermouth.

APPELLATION Defines the area where a wine's grapes were grown.

APPELLATION D'ORIGINE CONTROLEE (AOC) The French system of appellations, originated in 1935, is considered the wine world's prototype for legally defined and regulated wine regions. In this system a wine must follow rules describing the area the grapes are grown in, varieties used, ripeness, alcoholic strength, vineyard yields and methods used in growing the grapes and making the wine.

APPLEY Refers to an apple related wine aroma. Some Chardonnays are associated with a full, fruity, clean smell described as "ripe apples." "Fresh apples" is similarly used for some types of Riesling. However, "green apple" is almost always used for wines made from barely ripe or under-ripe grapes, and "stale apples" applies almost exclusively to flawed wine exhibiting first stage oxidation.

ARNEIS *(ahr-NAYZ)* A white wine grape grown in the Piedmont area of Italy. Can produce excellent wines with perfumy characteristics of apple, pear and hints of licorice. In Italian means "little difficult wine."

AROMA Usually refers to the particular scent of the grape in the wine. Commonly means the wine's total smell, including changes that occurred from oak aging or in the bottle.

AROMATIC Refers to the distinctive spicy character of certain grape varieties Gewürztraminer, Muscat.

ASCESCENCE Term used to mark the presence of acetic acid and ethyl acetate. Can be detected by sweet and sour, sometimes vinegary smell and taste together with a sharp feeling in the mouth.

ASTI SPUMANTE A semidry sparkling wine produced from the Moscato di Canelli grape in the village of Asti, in the Piedmont region of Italy.

ASTRINGENT Descriptive of a rough, harsh, puckery taste and feel in the mouth, usually from tannin or high acidity that red wines, and a few whites have. When the harshness stands out the wine is considered astringent.

AUSLESE *(OWZ lay zeh)* Designated quality level for a German white wine made from very ripe grape bunches picked out for their sweetness. The word Auslese means 'selection'.

AUSTERE Usually used to describe relatively hard, high acid wines that lack depth and roundness. Often said of young wines that may soften a bit with age. Term sometimes applied to wines made from noble grape varieties grown in cool climates or harvested too early in the season.

AWKWARD Describes a wine with poor structure—one that is out of balance.

B

BACCHUS The Roman name for Dionysus, the Greek god of wine.

BACKBONE Used to describe red wines that are big, full bodied, well structured and balanced by a desirable level of acidity.

BACKWARD Used to describe a wine that retains youthful characteristics despite considerable aging. A wine that should be more developed than it is for its age.

BAKED A perceptible roasted quality in grapes grown in hot climates.

BALANCE A wine has balance when its elements are harmonious and no single element dominates. Acid balances sweetness; fruit balances against oak and tannin; alcohol balances against acidity and flavor.

BALTHAZAR An oversized bottle which can hold the equivalent of 12 to 16 standard sized bottles.

BANDOL *(bahn DOLE)* Wine region in southwestern France. Gaining increasing attention for its rustic reds, particularly those of Domaine Tempier.

BANYULS *(bah NYOOL)* A French dessert wine made from late harvest Grenache grapes, which by law must contain 15 percent alcohol. Banyuls is a small village with steep hillside vineyards, above the Mediterranean in the southern Roussillon.

BARBARESCO An excellent and respected red table wine made from the Nebbiolo grape in the Piedmont of Northwestern Italy.

BARBERA A noble red grape used to make hearty red wines in the Piedmont of Northwestern Italy and also in California. Produces dark, fruity, astringent wines and may also be made into sparkling and semi-sweet wines.

BARDOLINO A light, simple red wine from the Veneto in Northeastern Italy, blended from several grapes and sometimes lightly sparkling. The wine is garnet colored, dry and can be slightly bitter.

BAROLO One of the most highly regarded Italian reds. Outstanding, full bodied and complex Nebbiolo-based red wine from the Piedmont of Northwestern Italy. The wine is dark, high in tannin and alcohol and can improve with decades of aging.

BARREL FERMENTED Refers to wine that has been fermented in casks, usually 55-gallon oak barrels, rather than larger tanks. It is the belief of some advocates that barrel fermentation contributes greater harmony between the oak and the wine, increases body and adds complexity, texture and flavor to certain wine types. Used mainly for whites.

BARRIQUE The French name for a 225 liter Bordeaux style barrel.

BARSAC *(bar SAHK)* Sub region of Sauternes in Bordeaux, making generally less expensive, Sauterne-like sweet wines.

BEAUJOLAIS *(Boe zho LAY)* Typically light, fresh fruity red wines from the area of the same name, immediately south of Burgundy in France.

BEAUMES-DE-VENISE *(BOME du veh NEES)* A region in the Southern Rhône of France best known for its delicious white dessert wine made from Muscat grapes.

BEAUNE *(bone)* Small city in Burgundy, at the center of its wine region.

BEERENAUSLESE *(BEHR en OWZ lay zeh)* Quality rating for very sweet, rich, golden German dessert wines, made mostly from overripe Riesling grapes. A German word meaning 'selected berry picking'.

BEREICH *(beh REYK)* The word for a German wine region—usually a rather broad area including a number of neighboring villages and vineyards.

BERRYLIKE Like the ripe, sweet, fruity quality of raspberries, blackberries, cranberries and cherries. The aroma and taste of red wines, usually Zinfandel, are often partly described with this term.

BIG Overall flavor of a wine, red or white, that has full, rich flavors. Generally has a positive ring to it, but can imply some clumsiness, the opposite of elegance. 'Big' reds are often tannic. 'Big' whites are generally high in alcohol and glycerin.

BITE A marked degree of acidity or tannin. An acid 'grip' in the finish which should be like a zestful tang and is favorable only in red full-bodied wine.

BITTER One of the four basic tastes along with salty, sour, and sweet. Can signify the fruit of immature vines or excessive tannin. If the bitter component dominates in the aroma or taste of a wine, it is considered a fault. In sweet wines a hint of bitterness enhances and complements the other flavors, creating an overall taste balance.

BLACK CURRANT The predominant aroma in Cabernet grapes.

BLANC DE BLANCS 'White of whites', meaning a white wine made of white grapes, such as Champagne made of Chardonnay.

BLANC DE NOIRS 'White of blacks' a white or blush wine made of dark (red or black) grapes, where the juice is squeezed from the grapes and fermented without skin contact.

BLENDING A winemaker's task, taking wines from different lots or barrels and blending them together for bottling. Traditional and regional laws and regulations dictate what particular grape varieties may be blended together to produce a specific wine. It is the winemaker's decision on the percentages of each to use, with vintage often playing a crucial role in this equation.

BLUNT Strong in flavor, often alcoholic and contrarily lacking in aromatic interest and fine development on the palate.

BLUSH A term for rosé, and any wine that is pink in color.

BOAL (or **BUAL**) One of the top grape varieties grown on the island of Madeira, that produces a medium-sweet wine.

BODY The mouth feel: the weight of the wine in the mouth and on the palate. Commonly referred to as full-, medium- or light-bodied.

BORDEAUX *(bore DOH)* Major wine region of Southwestern France, located along the Gironde, Garonne, and Dordogne rivers that produces some of the world's most famous and long-lived wines, made from Cabernet Sauvignon blended with Merlot, Cabernet Franc and other minor grapes. Advocates say that Bordeaux from specific delimited sub-regions, from Medoc and Haut-Medoc down to specific villages like Pauillac and Margaux, are considered most desirable. Wines from the 'right bank' of the river, St. Emillion and Pomerol, often contain higher proportions of Merlot.

BOTRYTIS The 'noble rot' —a beneficial mold that may appear on late-harvested grapes, causing them to shrink and dry so the natural sugars become highly concentrated, and honey charactered.

BOUQUET The perfume of fermented wine, often the first indicator of a wine's quality during a testing. Most appropriate for mature wines that have developed complex flavors beyond basic young fruit and oak aromas.

BOURGOGNE *(Boor GON yeh)* French for 'Burgundy'.

BRAWNY Used mainly to describe young red wines and wines that are hard, intense, tannic and have raw woody flavors.

BREATHE/BREATHING The act of allowing a wine to mix with the air, for example when wine is poured into another container, such as a decanter or wineglass. Breathing is thought to be beneficial for many red wines and also for some young, white wines.

BREED Term reserved for wines of high quality, from the best grape varieties, often referred to as 'noble grapes'. Wines with elegance and finesse.

BRIARY Describes a young wine having an earthy, prickly taste best described as peppery often with as stemmy wild berry character.

BRIGHT Used to describe fresh, zesty, lively young wines with vivid, focused flavors.

BRILLIANT Wines with very clear appearance and no visible suspended or particulate matter. Not always thought to be positive as it can indicate some loss of flavor in highly filtered wines.

BRIX Measurement system for sugar content of grapes and wine, indicating the degree of the grapes' ripeness (meaning sugar level) at harvest. Most table-wine grapes are harvested at between 21 and 25 Brix. To get an alcohol conversion level, multiply the stated Brix by .55.

BROWNING Denotes aging in a wine. Describes a wine's color , and is a sign that a wine is mature and may be faded. A wine of good character and depth can still be most enjoyable even with a significant 'brown' tint. Wines 20 to 30 years old may have a brownish edge yet still be pleasurable.

BRUNELLO DI MONTALCINO The Brunello grape, grown in the town of Montalcino in southern Tuscany in Italy, produces excellent, full-bodied, rich, powerful, red wines.

BRUT A French term meaning 'raw' used to designate a dry finish Champagne or sparkling wine. Can be the driest wine made by a producer.

BURGUNDY Region of France that is 160 miles southeast of Paris, between Dijon and Lyons. The noble grapes grown here, Chardonnay and Pinot Noir, produce elegant wines with extreme finesse and subtle earthy characteristics.

BURNT Describes a wine that has an overdone, smoky, toasty or singed edge. Also used to describe overripe grapes.

BUTTERY A smell and taste sensation found in white wines, particularly oak-aged Chardonnay. Indicates a smell of melted butter. Can also be reference to texture and mouth-feel, as in a rich 'buttery' Chardonnay.

CABERNET FRANC *(CAB-air-NAY FRAHNK)* French red wine grape used in a Bordeaux blend. The Cabernet Franc grown in California and the Loire Valley produce a spicy wine with medium body. Increasingly trendy as a varietal, in which blueberry aromas are characteristic.

CABERNET SAUVIGNON *(CAB-air-NAY SO-vee-n'YAWn)* One of the noblest of the red wine grape varieties, used in Bordeaux, and successfully grown in many countries. Cabernet Sauvignon is often referred to as the king of red wines.

CAHORS *(ca ORE)* Wine region in Southwestern France, close to Bordeaux and well known for inky-dark red wines made from the Malbec grape.

CANDYLIKE In wines made for early consumption this term is used to describe the perfumed fresh fruit aromas and flavors of the grape.

CAPSULE Refers to the metal or sometimes plastic protective sheath over the cork and neck of a wine bottle. A capsule protects the cork from drying out and letting air into the bottle.

CARAMEL Refers to a burnt-sugar smell and taste.

CARBONIC MACERATION Fermentation for light red wines, especially Beaujolais, that takes place inside the skins of whole, uncrushed grapes in the absence of air, in a carbon dioxide atmosphere.

CARIGNAN *(Cah ree n'YAWN)* Increasing popular red grape from Southern France with a sometimes peppery character like Syrah.

CAVA Spanish sparkling wine produced by the traditional French méthode champenoise, of bottle fermenting champagne. The word cava originated in Catalonia and means 'cellar'.

CEDAR/CEDARY Refers to an element of cedar wood in the bouquet of Cabernet Sauvignon that has been aged in either American or French oak. Can also be present in Cabernet blends that are aged in the same way.

CELLARED BY Means the wine was not produced at the winery where it was bottled.

CÉPAGE *(say PAHJ)* A variety of grape.

CHABLIS *(shah BLEE)* Excellent dry, full-flavored, white wine made from Chardonnay grapes in the region of the same name in northern Burgundy.

CHAMBOURCIN *(sham boor SAN)* A pleasing red French-American hybrid wine grape, widely used for in the Eastern USA in the production of table wines.

CHAMPAGNE Sparkling wine made in the region of the same name, just 70 some miles northeast of Paris, using a traditional process in which the wines are bottle fermented, and made only from Chardonnay, Pinot Noir and/or Pinot Meunier grapes.

CHANCELLOR A French hybrid grape used to produce hearty red wines mostly in the Canada and the Eastern USA.

CHAPTALIZATION The process of adding sugar to the fermenting wine to raise the final alcohol level. A process that can give wine a candied nose. Because the sugar is converted to alcohol, it does not add sweetness to the finished wine. Forbidden in some regions.

CHARACTER A wine's distinctive personality that stems from a combination of a region's wine-making traditions, soils, and grape varieties.

CHARBONO An Italian style red grape used mostly in California to produce robust, richly flavored red wines.

CHARDONNAY One of the world's best known and noble white grape varieties that produces possibly the most popular medium to full-bodied white wines. Varies widely in style from crisp lemon-lime-mineral flavors of classic Chablis to rich, oaky, buttery wines popularized by California wineries. Apple and green apple aromas are classic, although tropical fruit, pineapple, vanilla and spice often show up in US and Australian Chardonnays that have been aged in oak barrels.

CHARMAT The process of mass producing, generally inexpensive, sparkling wines in large stainless steel tanks, and then bottling under pressure.

CHASSELAS White wine grape variety most common in dry Swiss white wines.

CHATEAUNEUF-DU-PAPE *(shah toe neuf du PAHP)* A favored, complex, dry red wine produced in the Rhône region of Southern France, made from a blend of up to 13 specific grape varieties. It boasts a history reaching back to the 14th century sojourn of the Catholic Popes in nearby Avignon.

CHENIN BLANC A versatile, noble, French white wine grape used to make the famous dry, slightly sweet whites of the Loire Valley. Can be found in California and other regions too, and is somewhat variable, although pleasant honey overtones along with cantaloupe and honeydew melon flavors and light muskiness are common.

CHEWY Rich, full-bodied wines with unusual thickness of texture or tannins that one almost "chews" before swallowing.

CHIANTI The fruity, classic, dry red wine from Tuscany, made from Sangiovese and other grape varieties in North Central Italy.

CHIANTI CLASSICO The particular delimited region within the Firenze and Siena provinces. This Chianti follows stringent rules and sports a pink DOCG label around its neck with the symbol of a black rooster.

CINSAUT (or **CINSAULT**) *(san SO)* A dark red French wine grape, most common in Languedoc.

CITRIC/CITRUSY The smell of lemon, grapefruit or lime in the bouquet and as an aftertaste, most common in white wines made from grapes grown in cooler regions of California, Canada and other regions.

CLARET An old British term for red Bordeaux, sometimes used by wineries to describe a wine.

CLONE A group of vines derived by propagation from a single mother vine, or source. Clones are selected for the unique qualities of the grapes and wines they yield, such as flavor, productivity and adaptability to growing conditions.

CLOS *(CLOH)* An old term often used in French wine names that means a walled vineyard. Used by some California producers.

CLOSED Young, undeveloped wines that do not readily reveal their character, that are shy in aroma or flavor. Can be expected to develop with age.

CLOUDY Opposite of clear or brilliant. Characteristic of old wines with sediment, but it can be a warning signal of protein instability, yeast spoilage or re-fermentation in the bottle in younger wines. Sometimes also results from sediment being stirred up during transportation.

CLOYING Refers to ultra-sweet or sugary wines that lack the balance provided by acid, alcohol, bitterness or intense flavor. Can sit heavily on the palate not unlike honey.

COARSE Usually refers to harsh or clumsy flavor and texture, such as excessive tannin or oak. Also used to describe harsh bubbles in sparkling wines.

COLLIOURE A dry red wine produced in Bayuls in southwestern France.

COMPLETE Refers to a mature wine that provides good follow-through on the palate, a satisfying mouth-feel and firm aftertaste.

COMPLEX Wines that possess the elusive qualities where many layers of flavor seem to unfurl and change over time in the glass and mouth. A balance that combines all flavor and taste components in perfect harmony. A complex wine is a combination of richness, depth, flavor intensity, focus, balance, harmony and finesse.

CONCORD A native American grape—*vitis labrusca*—used in making traditional country style red wines with the aroma of grape jelly and a flavor that tasters sometimes refer to as 'foxy'.

CONSTANTIA A legendary sweet wine produced in South Africa, said to have been a favorite of Napoleon.

CORK Traditional bottle stopper produced from the bark of cork trees

CORBIERES *(cor BYAIR)* A Languedoc region where desirable red wines are made based on Syrah, Carignane and other varietals.

CORKED Describes a bottle of wine that is "off" due to air spoilage, a tainted cork or improper cellaring.

CORNAS *(kor NAHS)* Wine region in northern Rhône that produces a fine, ageworthy wine from Syrah.

Cortese White wine grape grown in the Piedmont and Lombardy regions of Italy, that produces a light-bodied, crisp, well balanced wine. Best known for the wine called Gavi.

Cosecha Spanish word for 'vintage'.

Cote Rotie *(KOTE ro TEE)* Superb, age-worthy red wine produced in the northern Rhône which is primarily Syrah based and named for the 'roasted slopes' on which the vineyards grow.

Coteaux du Languedoc *(cote OH du lahng DOK)* Appellation in Southern France and a popular, fine dry red wine produced with various blends, combinations or individually using Grenache, Syrah, Cinsault and others.

Cotes-du-Rhône *(kote due RONE)* General term for Rhône Valley appellation and the red or white wines produced there.

Creamy A 'silk like' texture - taste component - some wines have in the mouth. Can refer to the texture of champagne, or the vanillin smell that new oak imparts to wine. Creamy is in contrast to crisp.

Crianza Spanish term for 'aged in oak'.

Crisp A fresh, almost green apple like, brisk character, usually with lively acidity, and usually referring to white wines.

Cru Classe French legalese meaning 'classed growth', referring to a vineyard historically identified as being of exceptional quality.

Cuvee The blend of different grapes that make up a specific wine. A French term for 'vat'

D

DOC (Denominazione de Origene Controllata) The regulatory wine system, set up in Italy in 1963. Set up to protect the quality of the wines by specifying geographical limits, grape varieties, alcohol levels, top yields per acre, and aging requirements for particular wines.

DOCG (Denominazione di origine Controllata e Garantita) Represents the highest level of quality among Italian wines, and is basically the next step above DOC in Italy's regulatory wine system.

Decant To pour aged bottled wine carefully into a larger vessel, often a glass decanter, for the purpose of leaving any accumulated sediment behind. Decanting also lets a wine breathe, and almost always pertains to red wine.

Delicate Used to describe light- to medium-weight wines with pleasant mild flavor and fragrance. A desirable quality in wines such as Pinot Noir or Riesling. Sometimes pertains to well made wines produced from so called 'lesser grape' varieties.

Demi-Sec Meaning "half-dry" usually pertaining to Champagne and relating to sweetness. Demi-sec sparkling wines are usually slightly sweet to medium sweet, so half dry, half sweet.

Dense Considered a favorable quality in young wines this describes a wine that has concentrated aromas on the nose and palate.

Depth Describes complexity in a wine that fills the mouth with subtly changing flavors subtle layers of flavor that go 'deep'.

DESSERT WINE (1) A Sherry or other fortified wine. (2) Sweet wine customarily drunk with dessert or by themselves 'as' dessert, usually in small amounts or single portions. Many so-called dessert wines can also serve as an aperitif.

DEVELOPED A mature wine that displays flavors that emerge after aging for a period of time in the bottle.

DIRECT Wines that reveal their entire personality immediately.

DISGORGEMENT/DISGORGED A step in the traditional process of sparkling wine or champagne production of removing frozen sediment from the neck of the bottle after secondary fermentation.

DOLCETTO Pleasing red grape variety of the Piedmont region of northern Italy, that produces a light, fruity wine. Dolcetto literally means 'little sweet one', and likely stems from a quality of the grapes rather than the wine that is not sweet. Some production in California as well.

DOMAINE French term meaning 'estate'. In Burgundy a domaine may incorporate numerous separate vineyards.

DOSAGE The process of adding sweetened wine to champagne just prior to closure.

DRY Description of a wine produced specifically to possess little or no sweetness, whereby the sugars have been almost totally fermented. Commonly defined as containing less than about 0.5 percent residual sugar.

DRYING OUT The fading of the fruit in mature red wines. Acid, tannin and oak begin to predominate over fruit flavors and at this stage the wine will not improve.

E

EARTHY At its best, a pleasant, clean quality that adds complexity to aroma and flavors and hints of rich soil. A certain earthiness can be favorable; too much can cross over to the more unfavorable barnyardy aspects of a wine.

EISWEIN *(EYZ vine)* Just like it sounds in English 'ice wine', the German term also refers to a rare sweet wine made from late-harvested grapes that have frozen on the vine. British Columbia and Ontario also produce delightful ice wines.

ELEGANT Used to describe well-balanced wines of distinguished quality and grace.

ENOLOGY The science and study of wine and winemaking. Also spelled oenology.

EN TIRAGE *(ahn tee RAHJ)* A French term for the period of time a sparkling wine has rested in the bottle in contact with the yeast sediment from the secondary fermentation.

ERZEUGERABFULLUNG *(EHR tzoyg ehr AB full ung)* 'Estate bottled' under German wine regulations.

ESSENCE (1) Aroma 'kits' containing vials of various flavor essences—designed to 'pull' specific bouquet and taste qualities from the wine. (2) Sometimes used to describe a sweet, late-harvest red wine.

ETHYL ACETATE A substance that contributes the sweet, vinegary smell that often accompanies acetic acid.

Extra Dry A term not to be taken literally that appears on Champagne or other sparkling wine labels to indicate not-quite-dry; not as dry as Brut.

Extract/Extracted Commonly refers to the coloring imparted to wine during the fermentation process by the grape skins used. Usually a positive quality, although high extract wine can also be highly tannic. Can also refer to the richness and depth of concentration of fruit flavor in a wine.

Eucalyptus A term sometimes used to describe the characteristic in the bouquet of Cabernet Sauvignon grown in warm climates.

F

Fading Describes a wine that is losing its color, fruitiness or flavor, most often as a result of age.

Fat Full-bodied, bold, ripe, rich, flavor laden, high alcohol wines that are low in acidity and give a fleshy impression on the palate.

Faugeres *(fo JHAIR)* Refers to a Languedoc region and the wines produced there.

Fendant *(fohn DOHN)* A dry Swiss white wine produced from the Chasselas grape.

Fermentation The primary chemical process in winemaking by which yeast converts sugar into alcohol and carbon dioxide thus turning grape juice into wine.

Field Blend Refers to the single wine produced when a vineyard is planted with several different varieties and the grapes are harvested together.

Filtering The process of removing particles from wine after fermentation.

Finesse The distinctive balance and elegance, subtlety and delicacy of a wine.

Fining A technique for clarifying wine using agents such as a powdered clay called bentonite, gelatin or egg whites, which bind with sediment particles and cause them to settle to the bottom, where they can be easily removed.

Finish One of the keys to judging a wine's quality is finish, also called aftertaste; the way flavors and textures linger or fail to linger on the palate after a wine is swallowed. As in "This wine has a silky finish." Great wines are said to have rich, long, complex finishes.

Fino A light-bodied dry Sherry that is light in color, commonly served cold as an aperitif.

Firm Distinctive tightly knit flavor, often used when referring to a young wine.

Flabby A soft, feeble wine that falls apart on the palate, lacking the definition acidity gives.

Flat A wine without liveliness, lacking in flavor due to low acidity. Can also sometimes refer to a sparkling wine that has lost its bubbles.

Fleshy Soft and smooth in both body and texture due to limited tannin.

FLORAL/FLOWERY Almost always pertains to white wines having a characteristic aroma of fresh flowers, as do Mosel and Rheingau Riesling.

FORTIFIED Refers to a wine whose alcohol content has been increased by the addition of brandy or neutral spirits.

FORWARD Wines that give you the immediate impression of fruitiness, often pertaining to a wine having reached its peak prematurely.

FRAGRANT A fragrant wine is aromatic and flowery.

FRASCATI A fruity, golden white wine produced from the hilly vineyards close to Rome that can range from dry to sweet.

FREE-RUN JUICE A term used for the juice that escapes after the grape skins are crushed or squeezed prior to fermentation.

FRENCH COLOMBARD Used primarily in California's Central Valley, this productive white wine grape makes an inexpensive jug wine.

FRENCH OAK The traditional wood for wine barrels, which supplies vanilla, cedar and sometimes butterscotch flavors, and used in the production of both red and white wines.

FRESH Quality found mostly in young white wines from an acidity which suggests a clean, liveliness on the palate.

FRIZZANTE A lightly sparkling Italian wine.

FRUITY A wine whose character has developed from fully ripened grapes, which pleasingly offers fruit-like tastes and aromas.

FULL-BODIED Full proportion of flavor and alcohol; feels weighty on the tongue.

FUMÉ BLANC Same as Sauvignon Blanc, the two names are used interchangeably.

G

GAMAY Red grape of Beaujolais that is best known for producing fruity, light to medium-bodied wines, that are low in alcohol and very refreshing. Gamay is also grown successfully in California, and the Loire Valley of France. Generally speaking these wines are best consumed young.

GARNACHA Spanish term for the Grenache red wine grape.

GATTINARA A powerful, long-lived red wine made from Nebbiolo blended with other grapes, in northwestern Italy's Piedmont region.

GEWÜRZTRAMINER A perfumed, pungent, spicy and flamboyant white grape best-known in Alsace, France that produces semisweet to dry wines. Also grown in California, Oregon, Washington, New York, Germany, Eastern Europe, Australia, and New Zealand.

GLYCEROL An alcohol formed during fermentation said to add sweetness and roundness to a wine.

GRACEFUL Describes a wine that is pleasingly harmonious in very subtle ways.

GRAPEY A distinct impression of the flavors and aromas associated with fresh table grapes.

GRAPPA An Italian spirit, dry and high in alcohol, that it is typically consumed after dinner.

GRASSY Refers to the pleasant, herbaceous aromas and flavors reminiscent of newly cut spring grasses, that specifically describe the overall character of Sauvignon Blanc. British or European tasters sometimes use the word 'gooseberry' to describe this flavor.

GRAVES *(GRAHV)* A region inside the larger Bordeaux region of France, named for its gravelly soil, and known mostly for red wines as well as Bordeaux's classic dry, whites.

GREEN A wine made from and tasting of unripe grapes, with a tartness on the tongue.

GRENACHE *(greh NAHSH)* Red wine grape variety widely planted in Southern France, typically producing hearty, peppery wines, with strawberry and red berry overtones.

GRIP A pleasing firmness of texture, and structure, usually from tannin, which helps give definition to wines such as Cabernet and Port.

GROSSLAGE *(GROS lahg eh)* A legal German wine designation meaning 'large vineyard', used for a group of individual vineyards whose fruit may be assembled into a wine sold under the Glosslage name.

GRÜNER VEITLINER *(GROEN ehr FITE line ehr)* A distinctive white grape variety widely planted in Austria that produces light, but crisp, racy dry white wines.

H

HALBTROCKEN *(HALB trok en)* Refers to the German term 'half dry', characteristic of wines intentionally made with less than the typical amount of residual sugar.

HARD High acidity or tannin content that creates a mouth puckering effect. Often descriptive of young red wines suitable for aging.

HARMONIOUS All elements: the fruit, acid, and tannin, in perfect balance.

HARSH Very astringent wines, usually with a high alcohol component and excessive tannin, often display this rough, rustic taste characteristic.

HAUT-MEDOC *(OH meh dok)* Major sub-region within the infamous Medoc region of Bordeaux, that produces many great red wines.

HAZY Used to describe a wine that has small amounts of visible particles when viewed against the light. A good quality if a wine is unrefined and unfiltered.

HEARTY Most often used to describe the full, warm, sometimes rustic qualities found in red wines with high alcohol component.

HEADY Descriptive of full-bodied, high alcohol wines.

HERBACEOUS Wines having green, grassy, herblike taste and aroma. Usually associated with the grape variety, such as Sauvignon Blanc, Semillon and Merlot, not the climate or soil.

HERMITAGE *(air mee TAHJ)* Considered one of the best wines produced in the Rhône, usually red and made from Syrah grapes. It is told that a white was also produced by a Crusader who returned from the Holy Land coveting Syrah vine stock and declaring that he would war no more. Instead, it was time to plant a vineyard and his would be an 'hermitage'.

HONEST Simple, straightforward, typical of its kind, but nothing more.

HONEYED A term usually used to describe the cohesive sweetness of late-harvest Riesling or mature Sauternes.

HOT Term used for high alcohol, sometimes unbalanced wines that tend to burn with "heat" on the finish, giving a prickly, sensation of heat on the palate. Can be acceptable in Port-style wines only.

I

IMPERIAL An oversized bottle, usually holding 4 to 6 liters.

INKY Refers to the slightly metallic flavors that can be present in some red wines.

INTRICATE A term used to describe a wine with underlying complexities of bouquet and flavor.

J

JAMMY Usually refers to a natural berrylike taste of a certain grape variety, and most often describes wines such as California Zinfandel made from Amador County grapes.

JURANCON Tasty, dry, aromatic wine produced in southwestern France in the Pyrenees region.

JEROBOAM An oversized bottle holding the equivalent of four to six regular sized bottles.

K

KABINETT *(KAB in ett)* The term used for light, un-sweet (low alcohol) German wines.

KIR A popular apéritif that originated in France, in the Burgundy region, whereby a spoonful of creme de cassis (currant) is added to a glass of dry white wine.

KIR ROYALE The same as above, using champagne instead of white wine.

KOSHER WINE In the Jewish traditional manner, wine that is produced under strict rabbinical supervision with requirements that can differ from country to country.

L

LAMBRUSCO A fizzy red, amber or white, dry to sweet wine produced primarily in the Emilia Romagna region of Italy.

LANGUEDOC *(lang DOK)* A wine producing region in Southern France, gaining in popularity with its production of varied wines of interest.

LATE HARVEST Refers to wines made from grapes picked later than normal, with high sugar levels, and usually affected with noble rot or botrytis, thus producing lush, high sugar content, dessert-style wines. Popular with Riesling and Gewürztraminer, among others.

LEAFY Describes somewhat herbaceous, green overtones reminiscent of leaves. Can add to the complexity of a wine if present only in negligible amounts.

LEAN Not necessarily a bad quality, but indicates the presence of more body would be favorable; describes austere wines with evident acidity.

LEES Derived from a French term that means 'lies' and referring to the sediment remaining in a barrel or tank after fermentation and generally composed of dead yeast cells and small grape particles.

LEGS Term used to describe the droplet trails left on the side of the glass after swirling. The thicker the legs and the more slow-moving they are, the higher the alcohol content.

LEMONY Usually descriptive of a slightly acidic white wine that reminds one of the flavor of fresh lemons.

LENGTH The amount of time the flavor and aroma of a wine stay on the palate after swallowing., the longer the better the wine.

LIGHT Can refer to wines light in alcohol or wines light in texture, weight, body how the wine feels in the mouth.

LIMOUSIN *(lee moo ZAn)* A forested area, province, of France near the town of Limoges which is the major source of French Oak for wine barrels.

LINGERING Used to describe the persistence of the flavor of a wine on the palate after tasting.

LIVELY Crisp, fresh and fruity wines with vitality and the presence of acidity.

LOIRE *(lwahr)* Famous wine region in northeastern France, known for a goodly variety of fine wines as well as its scenic beauty, and through which runs the country's longest river of the same name.

LUSH/LUSCIOUS Soft tasting, rich, opulent, and smooth; most often said of wines high in residual sugar, also sometimes refers to intensely fruity wines.

M

MACERATION During fermentation, the process of the steeping of the grape skins and solids in the wine, where alcohol acts as a solvent to extract color, tannin and aroma from the skins.

MACON *(ma-KOHn)* A large region of Burgundy that is known for good, modest table wines.

MADEIRA Portuguese island in the Atlantic, about 400 miles off the coast of Morocco that produces a fortified wine of the same name.

MADERIZED Usually pertaining to white wines that have oxidized, and describing the brownish color and slightly sweet, somewhat caramelized and often nutty character found in mature dessert-style wines.

MADIRAN A small but well known appellation in the Languedoc region of France that produces robust red wines.

MAGNUM An oversize bottle that holds 1.5 liters, twice the size of a regular 750 ml bottle.

MALBEC Used in France for blending in many Bordeaux wines, where its intense color and extracts add to the wine's body. Also used as primary grape in the inky red wines of the Cahors region of France, in some Argentine and California reds. Malbecs can be fairly deep in color with dark berry flavors and a fair amount of tannin.

MALIC Used to describe the green apple-like flavor found in young grapes which diminishes as they ripen and mature.

MALOLACTIC FERMENTATION A secondary fermentation occurring in most bottled wines, this process converts the naturally occurring malic acid into softer lactic acid plus carbon dioxide gas, thus reducing the wine's total acidity. Adds complexity to whites such as Chardonnay and softens reds such as Cabernet and Merlot.

MALVASIA One of the most ancient of Italy's white-wine grape varieties and said by some to be a member of the Muscat family.. Often blended with other grapes, including the traditional Chianti; also seen as a 100 percent varietal. As finished wines, Malvasias vary widely in style and color, from crisp, bone-dry whites to rich, unctuous dessert wines.

MANZANILLA Dry style Sherry, similar to Fino, made in a seaside town where it is said a saltwater tang from the air is perceptible in the wine.

MARC A distilled spirit made in all parts of the world from pomace, and is generally consumed after dinner. (Similar to Italy's grappa.)

MARECHAL FOCH A French hybrid grape used to make red wines, mostly in the Eastern United States.

MARGAUX *(mar GOE)* One of the most well known sub regions of the Medoc region of Bordeaux, France.

MARSANNE *(mahr SAN)* Excellent white-wine grape from the Rhône Valley of France, that produces medium-body to rich wines, and now enjoying some successful plantings in California regions.

MASTER OF WINE A title bestowed by the Institute of Masters of Wine which was founded in 1953 in England. An exclusive organization requiring a rigorous three-day exam, part of which includes blind-tasting about 36 wines with the aim of correctly identifying them. A person with this title may put the abbreviation M.W. after his or her name.

MATARO Spanish name for Mourvedre.

MATCHSTICK Descriptive of the odor of sulphur dioxide gas, not unlike the smell of burnt matches and found, very occasionally, in negligible amounts trapped in bottled white wine. With careful decanting can be dissipated.

MATURE Fully developed, ready to drink.

MEAD A wine common in medieval Britain and Europe, made by fermenting honey and water.

MELLOW Soft, smooth without harshness.

MERITAGE An invented term used by California wineries for Bordeaux-style red and white blended wines. Combines "merit" with "heritage."

MERLOT Often a key component of Bordeaux blends, and successfully grown in California and Washington as a varietal of its own accord. Runs the gamut from mellow to full bodied, typically with plummy, black cherry and herbal flavors.

METHODE CHAMPENOISE French term for the costly, labor intensive method to make champagne, whereby wine undergoes a secondary fermentation inside the bottle, creating bubbles. The monk Dom Pérignon is credited with inventing this method.

METHUSELAH An extra-large bottle holding 6 liters; the equivalent of eight standard bottles.

MICROCLIMATE Refers to the climate within a small, defined area, possibly different from the area directly surrounding this area, that can dramatically affect the character of the wine produced there.

MID-PALATE When you take a sip of good wine there is often a sequence of flavor and texture impressions, of which the mid-palate is the impression registered as you hold the wine in your mouth for a moment but before you swallow.

MINERVOIS *(mee nehr VWAH)* In the Languedoc wine region which produces fairly inexpensive, fruity red wines.

MINTY Sometimes refers to an aroma from certain Cabernet Sauvignon wines grown in warm climates.

MISE EN BOUTEILLE French term which literally means 'put in bottle'.

MISE EN BOUTEILLE AU CHATEAU French term, meaning 'estate bottled'; with some legal significance and referring to a wine produced and bottled at the property where the grapes are grown.

MONOPOLE A label used on some French wines to indicate sole ownership, or monopoly, of the wine's name, with no bearing on the wine's quality.

MONTEPULCIANO 1) Red grape from the Abruzzi region of Italy used to produce medium to full-body wines with good structure and color, such as Montepulciano d'Abruzzo. It is also the official grape used in Rosso Cónero and Rosso Piceno. 2) The town in Tuscany where Vino Nobile di Montepulciano is made from Sangiovese grapes.

MOSCATO The Italian word for Muscat, referring to the family of white wine grapes used to produce still and sparkling, medium sweet to sweet wines.

MOSEL/MOSELLE The scenic river valley in Germany, a tributary of the Rhine and the source of some of the best German white wines produced from Riesling grapes.

MOURVEDRE *(moor VEH druh)* A late-ripening red grape variety widely planted in southern France, Spain and increasingly California that is rich in color and extract producing dark, fruity wines that are sometimes said to have earthy bouquets, likened to tree bark.

MULLED WINE Any red wine, served hot, that has been mixed with any combination of sugar, fresh orange or lemon, even fresh apple, spices, usually including cinnamon, cloves, and nutmeg.

MÜLLER-THURGAU *(MUELL ehr TUR gow)* Modern grape variety that is a mainstay of England's small vineyard industry. Widely planted in Germany and common in Oregon, used to produce a straightforward, lighter wine than Riesling.

MURKY Mainly a fault in red wines that are lacking brightness; somewhat swampy.

MUSCADET A light, dry, French white wine made from grapes of the same name, sometimes said to have a slightly musky, cantaloupe quality and typically served with seafood.

MUSCAT Ancient, aromatic white wine grape with a very extended family—said by some to be the ancestor of most other vitis vinifera grapes—which produces fruity, softly perfumed wines, some fine Italian sparkling wines and some enticing dessert wines from Austria and other parts of the world.

MUST Mixture of grapes—grape juice, skins and pulp—that is fermented into wine.

MUSTY Having a stale, moldy or mildewy smell. The result of a wine being made from moldy grapes, stored in improperly cleaned tanks and barrels, or contaminated by a poor cork.

N

NEBBIOLO Noble red grape variety of northwestern Italy's Piedmont region used to produce the great ageworthy Barolo and Barbaresco wines. Often tannic by nature with good complexity; typical descriptives for aroma and taste include violets and intense dark fruit.

NEBUCHADNEZZAR A huge wine bottle holding 15 liters; the equivalent of about 20 standard bottles.

NEGOCIANT A French term used to describe wine merchants who may buy grapes and vinify them, or buy wines and combine them to bottle and sell under their own label. Most common in Burgundy.

NOBLE While many grape varieties are used to produce wines, only a few have distinguished themselves as being particularly suited for the production of fine wine. These 'noble grape varieties' must still be matched with the right micro-climate and winemaking techniques in order to live up to their potential.

NOBLE ROT Also called Botrytis Cinerea—a beneficial kind of mold that may appear on late-harvested grapes, causing them to shrink and dry so the natural sugars become highly concentrated, and honey charactered.

NONVINTAGE Wines produced with a blend of more than one vintage, often occurring with Champagnes and sparkling wines, as well as Ports and Sherries.

NOSE The character of a wine as determined by smell; the aroma or bouquet.

NOUVEAU French term meaning 'new', indicates a style of light, fruity, young, immediately drinkable wine, and most often applies to Beaujolais.

NUTTY Nutlike bouquet that develops in some wines especially barrel-fermented Chardonnays or Sherries.

O

OAKY Describes the aroma or taste quality imparted to a wine by the oak barrels or casks in which it is aged, and in a positive way can be characterized by toasty, vanilla, cedary, dill, coconut, sandalwood. Can also refer to less desirable qualities, when out of balance with the other characteristics of the wine.

OENOLOGY The science and study of wine and winemaking. Also spelled enology.

OFF-DRY Not quite a dry wine; refers to a very slightly sweet wine where the residual sugar is only faintly perceptible.

OLOROSO Spanish term meaning 'fragrant', and one of the two broad categories of Sherry, that are typically dark and full bodied.

OPTIMA German grape variety used primarily in a blend but can sometimes be found as a varietal.

ORVIETO The name of an ancient town in Umbria, Italy that produces a dry white wine.

OVERRIPE Grapes that have been left on the vine to dry in the sun to develop a desirable raisiny character or just a more concentrated sugar needed for making certain styles of Zinfandel and some specialty wines.

OXIDIZED Wine that has been overexposed to air and taken on a brownish color and a flat, stale or sherry-like aroma and flavor.

P

PASSITO An Italian wine-making process whereby harvested grapes are dried before being pressed to concentrate the sugars prior to fermentation.

PAUILLAC *(paw ee YAHK)* Name of a village in the Haut-Medoc area of the world famous Bordeaux region in France.

PEAK Being a very subjective issue of when the taste of a wine is at its best.

PENEDES A Spanish wine district near Barcelona with a good reputation, home to the Torres winery.

PEREQUITA A red-wine grape grown in southern Portugal that produces, hearty, medium-bodied, robust reds.

PERFUMED Distinct quality referring to the usually sweet and floral aromas of some white wines.

PETITE SIRAH A red grape variety, most widely grown in California, not to be confused with the true Syrah of the Rhône Valley of France.

PETIT VERDOT *(peu TEE vehr DOH)* Red wine grape variety most often grown in Bordeaux and used for blending with Cabernet Sauvignon.

PH A measure of the intensity of acid a wine contains; the lower the pH the more acidic the wine.

PHYLLOXERA Tiny aphids or root lice that attack Vitis vinifera roots and can devastate entire vineyards.

PIEDMONT Wine region of northwestern Italy that produces some of the world's best red wines. Literally means the 'foot of the mountains'.

PINOT BLANC White wine grape variety usually producing a favorable dry, medium-body white wine not unlike Chardonnay, that can be drunk young.

PINTO GRIS/PINTO GRIGIO French and Italian names respectively for the same white grape, known to produce flavorful, dry, crisp white wines, sometimes with a light musky overtone well-suited to accompany seafood and fish.

PINOT MEUNIER Red wine grapes originating from the Champagne region of France and used for blending with Pinot Noir and Chardonnay to add a certain fruitiness to champagne. Recently the Pinot Meunier varietal is being grown and marketed in Oregon.

PINOT NOIR Highly regarded, noble red grape variety originally from Burgundy, proven to produce some of the best velvety, voluptuous red wines to be had. Extremely popular with vineyards in California, Oregon and Washington.

PINOTAGE A red grape that is a cross between Pinot Noir and Cinsaut, grown commercially only in South Africa, where it is fermented at higher temperatures and matured in new oak for finesse and elegant berry flavors.

PLONK A British term for simple, usually inexpensive, 'ordinary' wine.

POMACE The residue from the grapes used to make a wine - the skins, seeds, pulp, and stems left in the fermenting vat or cask after wine making, and one of the necessary ingredients used in the distillation of French marc and Italian grappa.

POMEROL *(poh mehr OL)* French village on the right bank of the Dordogne, where some noteworthy Merlot-based red wines are produced.

PRIMARY FRUIT The recognizable fruity overtones of a young wine where distinct berry or cherry influences are present. Wines can lose primary fruit as they age, picking up other qualities that come with the maturation process.

PRIORATO Wine region of northeastern Spain, near Barcelona that produces hearty, dark red wines.

PRIVATE RESERVE Denotes quality and along with 'Reserve', once stood for the best wines a winery produced. However, many wineries have diluted the true quality seal behind this term by using similar tags such as Proprietor's Reserve for rather ordinary wines.

PRODUCED AND BOTTLED BY On the label indicates that the winery crushed, fermented and bottled at least 75 percent of the wine in the bottle.

PROVENCE Wine region of southeastern France, boasting an enviable Mediterranean climate, and well known for dry rosé and fruity red wines.

PRUNEY The flavor of overripe, sun-dried grapes that can add an unfavorable pungency to wines; not unlike the taste of dried prunes. Can add complexity in the right small doses.

PUCKERY Describes the mouth's reaction to highly tannic and very dry wines.

PUNGENT Describes a powerful, assertive aroma linked to high levels of active acidity.

Q

QBA (QUALITÄTSWEIN BESTIMMTER ANBAUGEBIETE) *(KWAL ih taytz vine BESH tim tehr AHN bow geh bee teh)* The German wine law enacted in 1971, that guarantees the consumer a particular level of quality.

R

RACKING Traditional method of wine clarification whereby wine is moved by hose from one container to another leaving behind the unwanted sediment.

RACY A good quality, light wine with a lively acidic quality.

RAW Undeveloped, young wines, that are often high in alcohol, acidity and quite tannic.

RECIOTO A typically sweet wine from the Veneto region of northeastern Italy, made from very ripe grapes.

REFINED Most often refers to well-balanced red wines.

REHOBOAM An oversized bottle, holding 4.5 liters or the equivalent of about six regular sized bottles.

REMUAGE A process used in the making of Champagne whereby the sediment is removed after secondary fermentation in bottle.

RESERVA A Spanish term relating to the regulatory specifications of the length of time wines are aged before being sold; for red wines, at least three years, including at leastone year in wooden barrels.

RESIDUAL SUGAR The unfermented grape sugar in a finished bottled wine; usually measured by percentage, by weight or volume.

RHEINGAU A German wine region along the Rhine River, highly regarded due to the very nature of the steep vineyards, most of which face due south.

RHÔNE Historic wine region in France, south of Lyons, best known for the production of hearty red wines, with a history dating to the 14th century.

RICH Enticing body, flavor and bouquet; full on the palate.

RIESLING *(REEZ ling)* One of the world's finest grape varieties, this classic, noble German white grape produces many great flavorful, wide ranging, crisp wines.

RIOJA Wine region of northern Spain that produces some of the country's best red wines, as well as some whites and rosés.

RIPASSO A unique Italian wine-making process in which the wine made during the current vintage is saved, put atop the pressed grapeskins and other particulate residue in the vats just used and allowed to ferment further, thereby acquiring additional flavor and body.

ROBUST Descriptive of a full-bodied, intense, vigorous, heady wine.

ROSÉ A pale pink wine, ranging from dry to sweet and traditionally made by removing the skins from red grapes early in the fermentation process, before they have the time to impart too much color. Less traditionally, some labels carry rosés that have been made by the blending of red and white wines.

ROUGH Not pleasing in texture or flavor; harsh, possibly biting.

ROUND Describes flavors that are smooth, with a sensation of completeness, balance; well developed without any rough edges.

ROUSANNE White grape grown in the northern Rhône Valley of France, most often used for blending with the white wine grape Marsanne.

RUSTIC Used to describe wines either made in old-fashioned or centuries old, traditional techniques and processes or tasting as if they had been.

S

SAINT-CHINIAN *(sahn shee nee AHn)* Wine region of the Languedoc area of southern France, that is gaining in popularity as its wines attract notice.

SAINT-EMILLION *(sahn tem ee ON)* Wine region of the Bordeaux area of France, on the right bank of the Dordogne, best known for its red wines often made with Merlot.

SAINT-ESTEPHE *(sahn tes TEHF)* An area of northern Haut-Medoc in the Bordeaux region.

SALMANAZAR An over-sized bottle holding nine liters, the equivalent of about 12 regular bottles.

SANGIOVESE The all important red-wine grape of Tuscany in central Italy, and the key to producing Chianti. Known to produce a range of styles from fresh, light, young wines to hearty, full-bodied reds that can age well. Literally translated 'blood of love'.

SAUTERNES Renown French sweet wine from the Bordeaux region made from a blend of mostly late-harvested Sauvignon Blanc and Semillon grapes that have been infected by botrytis (noble rot).

SAUVIGNON BLANC Noble, white grape variety grown in the Loire and Bordeaux regions of France, with plantings now in other regions including the United States, New Zealand and Australia. Usually blended with Semillon grapes, it varies in style, but generally produces soft, assertive, herbaceous, sometimes complex wines.

SAVENNIERES *(sah ven NYAIR)* A small region in the Loire area of France that produces top quality Chenin Blanc.

SCHAUMWEIN *(SHOWM vine)* German term referring to a 'sparkling wine'.

SCHEUREBE *(SHOY reh beh)* Newer variety grape from the Rhine region of Germany, made from a cross of Riesling and Sylvaner, that is generally used to produce sweet, late harvest wines.

SEDIMENT In red wines, the deposit or residue that can accumulate in the bottle during the aging process. Not considered a negative quality, and can be separated from a well aged wine by decanting.

SEKT *(ZEKT)* German term for sparkling wine that is usually produced using the charmat process.

SEMILLON White wine grape, native to the Bordeaux region of France, but now widely grown in many of the world's wine regions; most often used in a blend with Sauvignon Blanc grapes to produce a pleasant, somewhat dry, medium-bodied wine.

SEYVAL BLANC Hybrid grape of French origin that is widely used in the US, generally producing oak-aged dry whites.

SHARP A predominant acidity presence.

SHERRY Spanish style fortified wine from the Jerez de la Frontera region, most commonly using the Palomino grape. Sherries can range from sweet to dry, served either at room temperature or chilled.

SHORT A wine with very little aftertaste or finish.

SILKY Soft, flowing texture and finish.

SIMPLE Wine with straightforward character.

SHIRAZ A term used mostly in Australia or South Africa; same as Syrah.

SINEWY Usually referring to a wine with not much fruitiness, but a good balance of alcohol and acidity.

SMOKY (1) Simply refers to the aroma or taste imparted, such as anything 'smoked' might impart. (2) Flavor and aromatic quality associated with wines that have been oak-aged, as with certain Chardonnays, Rhône reds and so on.

Soft Refers to wines with low acidity and or tannins creating a mellow quality on the palate. Can also refer to low alcohol content.

Solid Firm textured, well structured.

Sommelier A wine steward in a restaurant.

Sour Refers to a wine with sharp acidity.

Spanna Local name for the Nebbiolo grape and the red wine produced from it in the northern Piedmont region of Italy.

Sparkling Wine with bubbles, either naturally occurring or created by injecting carbon dioxide gas.

Spatburgunder *(SHPAHT burg und ehr)* A German term for Pinot Noir.

Spatlese *(SHPAHT lay zeh)* German term meaning 'late harvest, late picked' and referring to white wines made with sweeter, late-harvested grapes.

Spicy Usually a complex, red or white wine imparting the soft nuances pepper, cloves, cinnamon, mint or other spices.

Split A six ounce, or quarter bottle of champagne, most frequently found in hotels, airplanes, ships or trains.

Spritzig *(SHPRITZ ik)* German term for a lightly sparkling wine.

Spritzy Very slight sensation of carbonation, most common in very young wines and can be considered a minor flaw.

Spumante Italian term meaning 'foaming' and referring to sparkling wines.

Stale Wines that are lifeless, having lost their fresh, lively qualities.

Steely Firm, taut, acidic.

Stony Term used to describe a clean, earthy characteristic in young white wines; flinty.

Strong Robust.

Structure Referring to how a wine is built, the flavor plan—the interaction and final composition of all elements, such as acid, tannin, alcohol, fruitiness, body. Usually used with another descriptor as in 'firm structure'.

Stylish Bold, lively character.

Subtle A positive characteristic usually referring to a delicate wine that offers up nuances of flavor and aroma.

Supple A positive characteristic that usually refers to red wines that are smooth, soft textured and rounded on the palate.

Sur Lie French term meaning 'on the lees' and referring to the technique/method of storing wine, prior to bottling, in the yeast sediment and grape particles (lees) from the fermentation, producing a more complex wine.

Sweet Refers to the presence of residual sugar, occurring when all of the grape sugar is not completely converted to alcohol.

Sylvaner German grape, generally of lesser quality than Riesling and usually planted as a blending grape.

SYRAH Classic red wine grape grown in the Rhône Valley of France, producing love-lived, spicy, aromatic wines. Grown increasingly in other wine regions.

T

TAFELWEIN *(TAHF ehl vine)* German term meaning 'table wine'.

TANKY Stale; usually refers to wines that display a somewhat dull, dank character, often from being aged too long in tanks.

TANNIC Usually refers to a wine whose tannins overpower the fruit and other components. Will mellow with aging.

TANNIN A naturally occurring substance found in grape skins, seeds and stems or sometimes from oak barrels, that gives wine its astringency. Most prominent in red wines where it creates a dry, puckering mouth-feel. Tannin acts as a natural preservative that helps wine age and develop, and in the right proportion contributes to the balance of a wine. Considered a fault if present in excess.

TART Acidic; sharp tasting.

TARTARIC ACID The prominent natural acid in wine. Also an additive.

TARTRATES Harmless crystals that often form on a cork, or in a bottle or cask, that are composed of potassium bitartrate from the tartaric acid naturally present in wine.

TEMPRANILLO Spanish, good quality red-wine grape that produces wines that are hearty and robust.

TERROIR *(tehr WAHr)* French term literally meaning 'soil' or 'earth', generally referring to all the physical/environmental characteristics in and around a particular vineyard site that are imparted into a wine such as climate, soil, geographical location etc.

THIEF Syringe-like instrument used for sampling wine from a cask, tank or barrel.

THICK Dense, heavy texture.

THIN Lacks body, depth and therefore flavor.

TIGHT Generally refers to the body and structure of young wines.

TIRAGE A term used in the production of Champagne or sparkling wine referring to the first bottling step in the process.

TINNY Somewhat of a metallic aftertaste.

TINTO Spanish term for red wine.

TIRED Past its peak; feeble.

TOASTY Aroma and flavor imparted by oak barrel aging; similarly 'caramel' and 'toffee' are used as descriptors of the same.

TOCAI FRIULANO White wine grape grown in the Friuli region, in the northeastern tip of Italy that produces uniquely floral, aromatic white wines.

TOKAJ/TOKAY *(toh KAY)* Renown grape used primarily for dessert wines in Hungary.

TOUGH Astringent; tannic.

TROCKENBEERENAUSLESE *(TROK en BEHR ehn OWZ lay zeh)* Top quality, costly German sweet, dessert wine.

TRONCAIS *(trohn KAY)* Name of a type of French oak and the region where it comes from.

TREBBIANO Italian white-wine grape. In France called Ugni Blanc.

TROCKEN *(TROK en)* German label term meaning 'dry'.

TUSCANY Renown wine region of Central Italy.

U

UGNI BLANC *(oo NYEE BLAHN)* White-wine grape grown in France generally producing crisp, fruity white wines. In Italy called Trebbiano.

ULLAGE The empty space in a wine bottle between the bottom of the cork and the surface of the wine. If the ullage is too big that is usually an indication of oxidation problems.

V

VALPOLICELLA Semi-dry, light-bodied Italian red wine produced in Veneto.

VALTELLINA Wine region in the Lombardy area of northern Italy that produces top quality red wines.

VANILLA A scent imparted by aging in oak, generally new oak.

VARIETAL A wine produced and named primarily from a single grape variety.

VEGETAL Aroma or taste that similar to that of leafy greens, of plants, of vegetables; a somewhat grassy character.

VELVETY Rich, silky smooth texture.

VENDANGE French term for 'vintage'.

VENDIMIA Spanish term for 'vintage'.

VENETO One of Italy's foremost wine regions, both in terms of quality and quantity of wine produced. In Northeastern Italy, encompassing both Venice and Verona.

VERDICCHIO Italian white-wine grape from Central Italy, generally producing a light-bodied, somewhat crisp white wine.

VERMOUTH A renown fortified wine, white or red, that has been flavored with the addition of aromatic herbs or spices and is most often used as a aperitif or in the mixing of cocktails.

VERNACCIA Historic Italian white-wine grape generally producing a crisp, dry white wine.

VIDAL BLANC French hybrid white-wine grape used commonly in the USA.

VIGNERON French term for 'winemaker' or 'winegrower'.

VIGNOBLE French term meaning 'wine growing area'.

VIGNOLES French hybrid white-wine grape, often used in the Eastern USA.

VIGOROUS Assertive flavor, strong bodied wine.

VIN French word for 'wine'.

VINA Spanish word for 'vineyard'.

VIN DE PAILLE *(vehn de PIE)* Literally, "wine of straw." A sweet wine traditionally produced from grapes that have been dried on straw mats.

VIN DE PAYS A French term meaning 'wine of the country' or region. Generally used for categorization.

VIN DOUX NATUREL *(vehn DOO na tue REHL)* Sweet French wine that has been fortified by the addition of brandy.

VINHO VERDE A specific Portuguese wine best when young; literally means 'green wine'.

VINICULTURE The study and science of grape production for the purpose of making wine.

VINOUS Tasting descriptive for 'wine-like', 'winey' qualities; the aroma and taste common to all wines.

VINTAGE Indicates the season; the year the grapes were grown and the wine was made.

VIOGNIER *(vee oh NYAY)* French white-wine grape variety most common in the Rhône Valley of France and California. These aromatic wines are best consumed young and vary in character.

VITICULTURE The science, cultivation and study of grape growing.

VITIS VINIFERA The classic, primary grape species used to produce nearly all of the world's best wines.

VOLATILE/VOLATILE ACIDITY Powerful, aggressive aroma denoting excessive acidity.

W

WATERY Lacking in flavor; thin.

WEEDY Grassy.

WEIGHTY Strong, full-bodied.

WEIN *(VINE)* German word for 'wine'.

WOODY Tasting term for too much of a oaky presence, usually caused by too lengthy an aging process in the barrel or cask.

Y

YEASTY The bready smell of yeast, most common in Champagne and pleasing if not excessive.

Z

ZINFANDEL Versatile, red wine grape variety most common in California, producing a wide range of wine styles.

ACKNOWLEDGEMENTS

*A*ny work this complex requires the dedicated support and commitment of many individuals. Without the generous help and advice of many friends, family members, wine makers, wine collectors and wine lovers, I could not have attempted it. I'd specifically like to acknowledge the following people:

A special thank you to my wife, Cameron. First, for finding the *Quarterly Pocket List of Wine* and sampling with me the many wines we enjoyed over the years as a result, then encouraging me to take the helm of the new Wine PocketList. For overseeing the tremendous research effort not just for the wines in this book, but for the online Wine PocketList as well. And most of all, for continuing to encourage and support me as we pursue new interests, new ventures and new ideas, no matter how busy we both are.

Denise della Santina, who orchestrated and managed the team effort required to produce the website and this book. She edited, wrote, suggested and drove until it was done right; every page bears her imprint. Her intelligence, wit, determination, and commitment to this project were instrumental in the production of this book. I could not have done it without her.

Judi Stowell of Valley Vineyards (www.valleyvineyards.com) in the heart of Canadian wine country. Her penchant for research and eye for detail is responsible for creating the Wine Lover's Glossary.

And finally, John Vankat, founder of the *Quarterly Pocket List of Wine*, whose original vision and love for wine are primarily responsible for my current passion for good wine. John's graciousness, insights and intelligence were instrumental in guiding us through the process of launching the Wine PocketList. I'd also like to thank John's wife, Betty Huffman, who treated me like one of the family as we spent meal after meal enjoying great wine, great food, great conversation, and instant friendship.

A REQUEST

Although great care has been take in the preparation of this book, it is our first one. Any corrections, suggestions, ideas or input for next year's version would be greatly appreciated. Please, send me your comments and insights:

BY EMAIL:	michael@winepocketlist.com
BY POST:	Michael Hinshaw
	The Wine PocketList
	Post Office Box 2867
	San Rafael, California 94912
BY FAX:	1.866.522.2652